Zenescope Entertainment Presents:

Grimm Fairy Tales™

VOLUME **TWO**

ARCANE ACRE

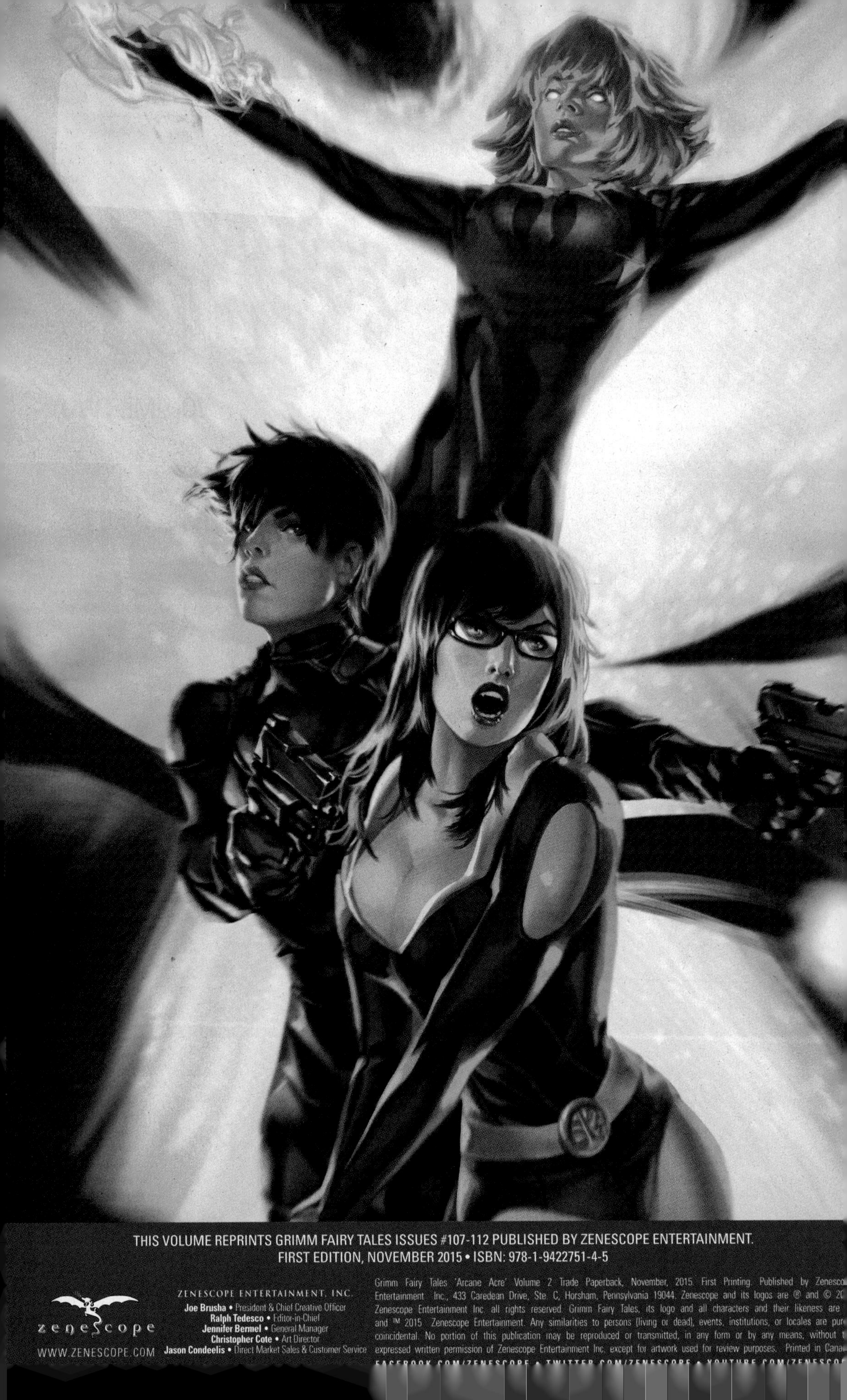

THIS VOLUME REPRINTS GRIMM FAIRY TALES ISSUES #107-112 PUBLISHED BY ZENESCOPE ENTERTAINMENT.
FIRST EDITION, NOVEMBER 2015 • ISBN: 978-1-9422751-4-5

zenescope
WWW.ZENESCOPE.COM

ZENESCOPE ENTERTAINMENT, INC.
Joe Brusha • President & Chief Creative Officer
Ralph Tedesco • Editor-in-Chief
Jennifer Bermel • General Manager
Christopher Cote • Art Director
Jason Condeelis • Direct Market Sales & Customer Service

ARCANE ACRE

GRIMM FAIRY TALES CREATED BY	STORY	ART DIRECTION & TRADE DESIGN	EDITOR
JOE BRUSHA RALPH TEDESCO	JOE BRUSHA RALPH TEDESCO PAT SHAND	CHRISTOPHER COTE	NICOLE GLADE

AFTER RE-BALANCING EARTH AND THE FOUR REALMS FROM AN AGE OF DARKNESS...

SELA MATHERS REUNITES WITH HER ESTRANGED DAUGHTER, SKYE.

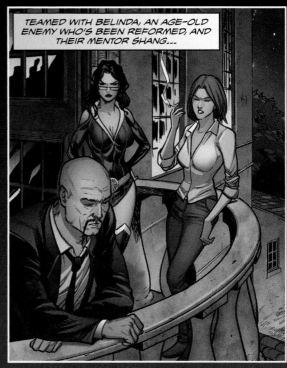

TEAMED WITH BELINDA, AN AGE-OLD ENEMY WHO'S BEEN REFORMED, AND THEIR MENTOR SHANG...

THEY SET OUT TO HELP HIGHBORN TEENS HONE THEIR UNIQUE ABILITIES WITH THE HOPE THEY TOO WILL FIGHT AGAINST THE EVIL FORCES THAT THREATEN EARTH.

THE CAST

FACULTY

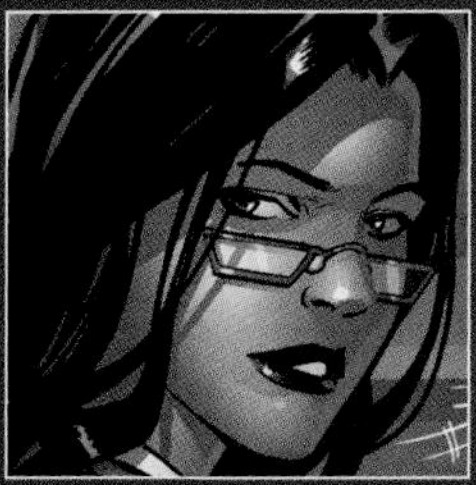

Sela

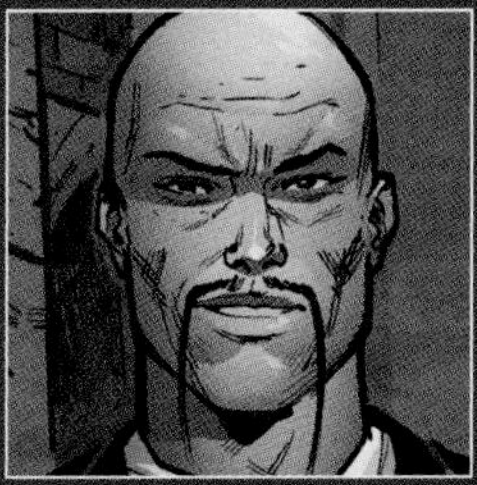

Shang

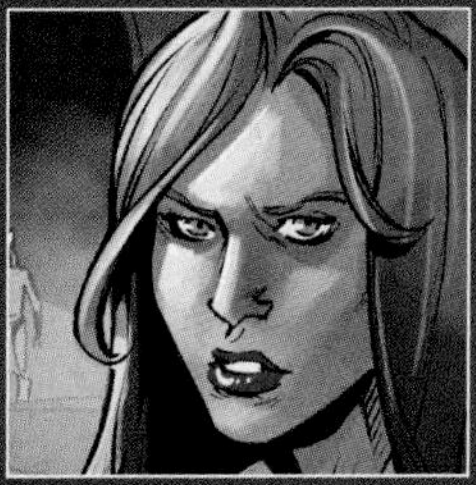

Belinda

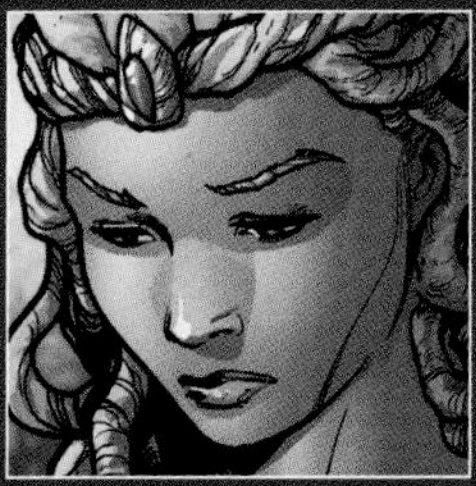

Druanna

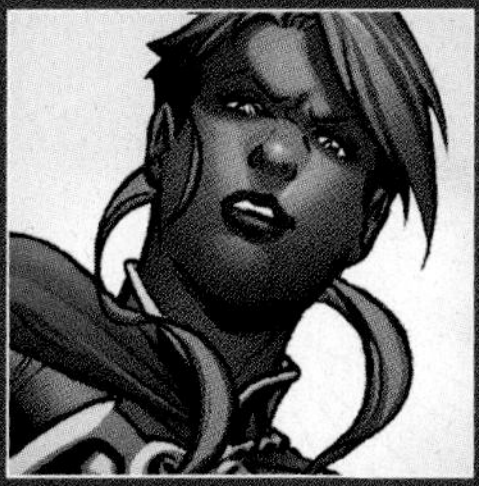

Adraste

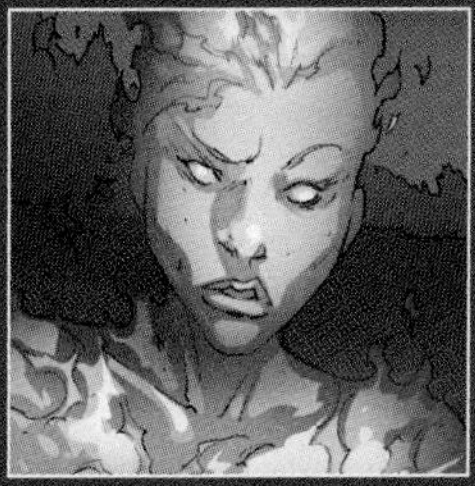

Kiera

STUDENTS

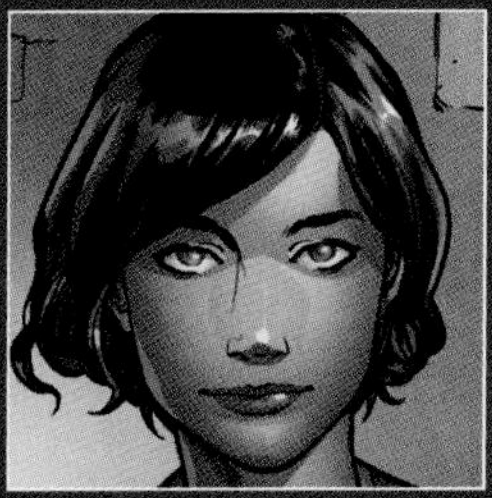

Skye

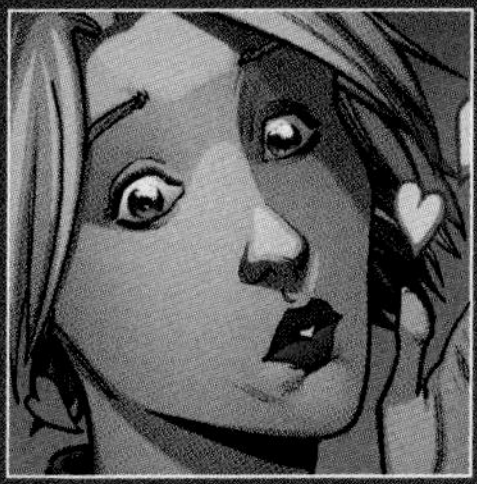

Violet

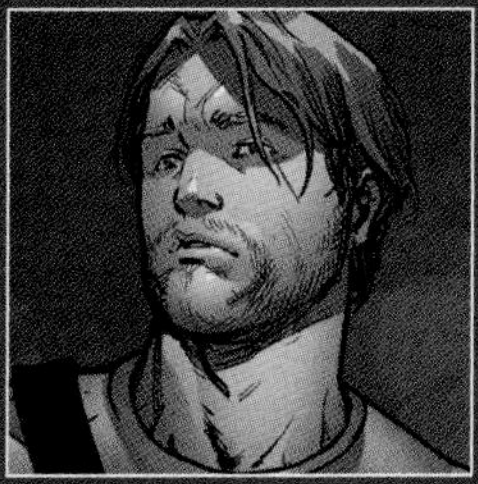

Wulf

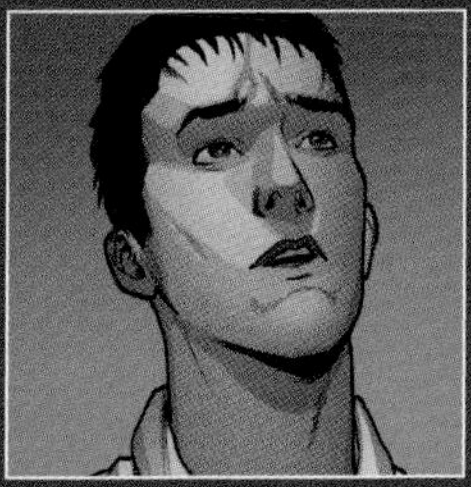

Ali

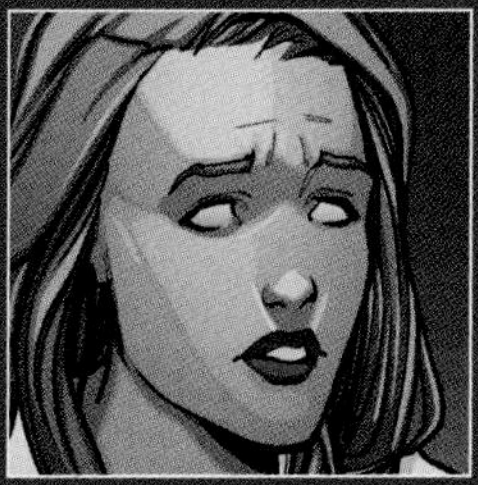

Hailey

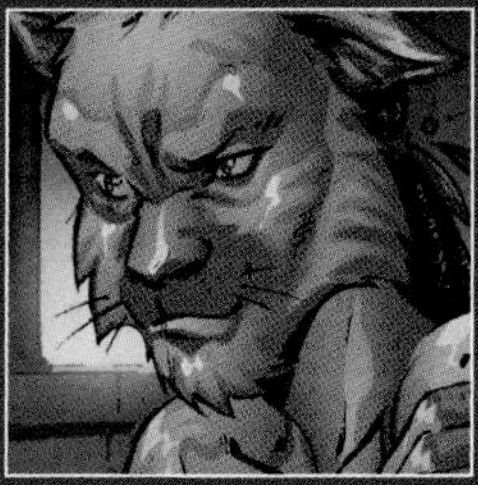

Wiglaf

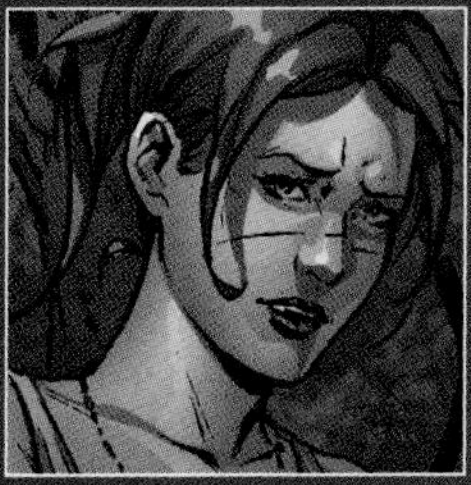

Natalie

VILLAINS

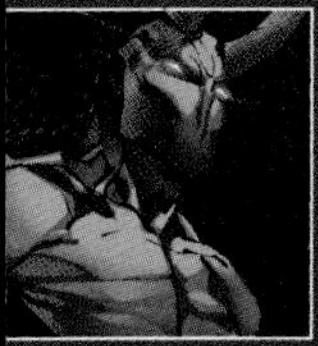

The Dark One

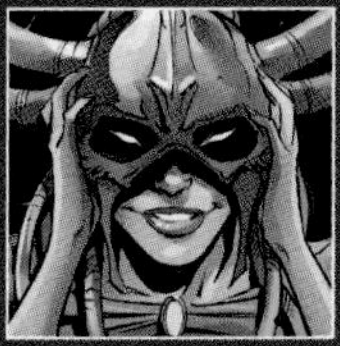

Maka

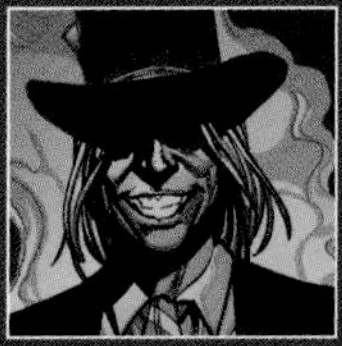

The Mad Hatter

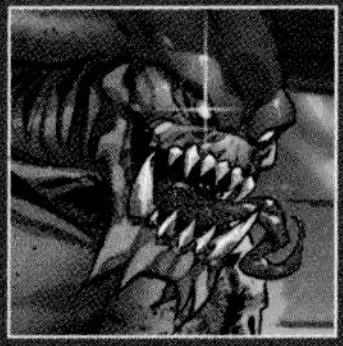

Grendel

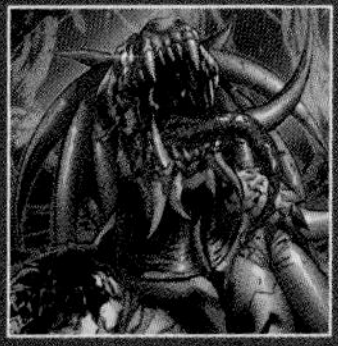

All-Modor

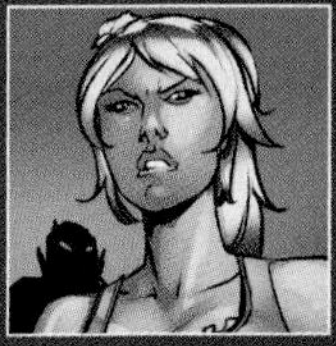

Cindy

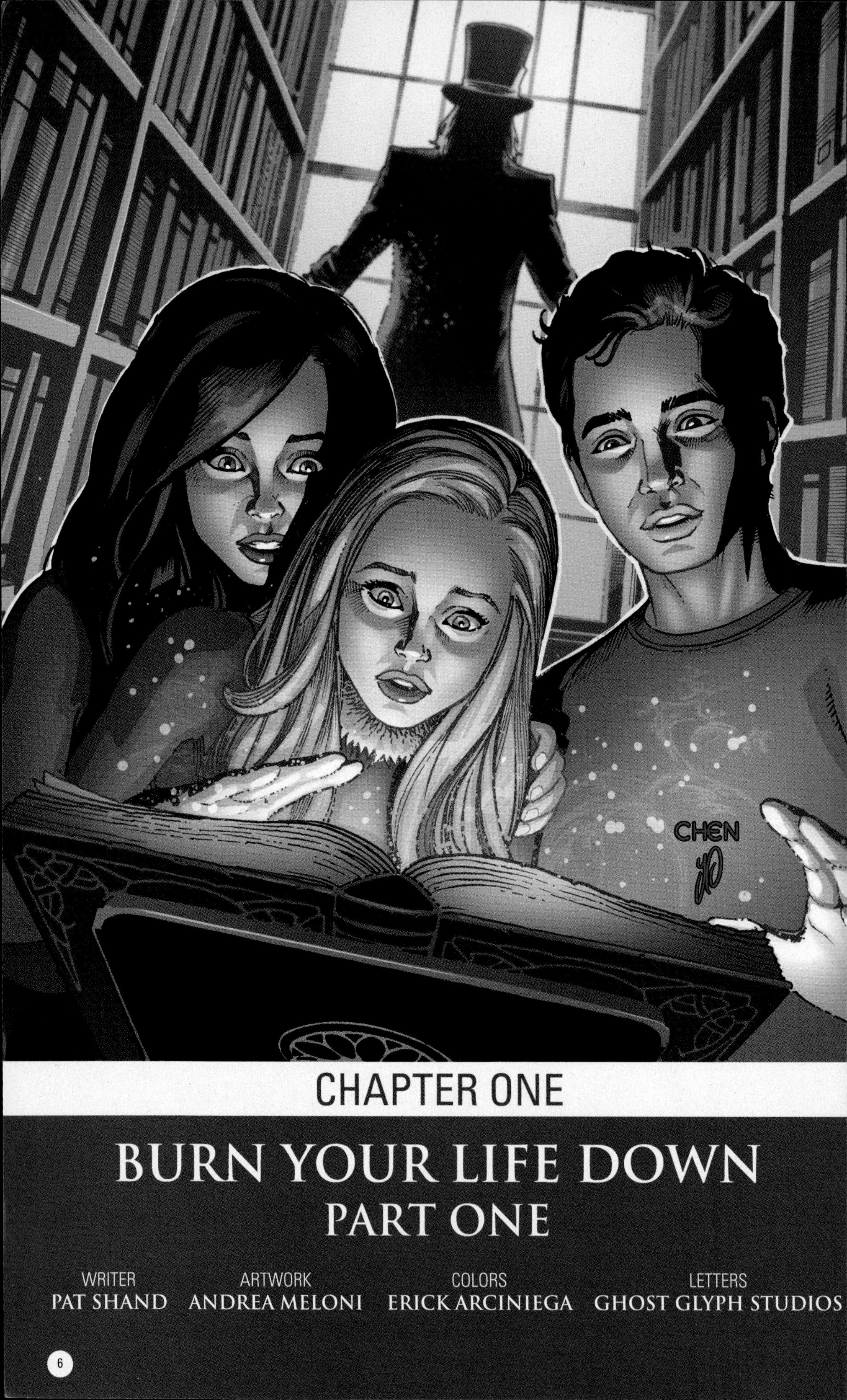
CHEN

CHAPTER ONE

BURN YOUR LIFE DOWN
PART ONE

WRITER
PAT SHAND

ARTWORK
ANDREA MELONI

COLORS
ERICK ARCINIEGA

LETTERS
GHOST GLYPH STUDIOS

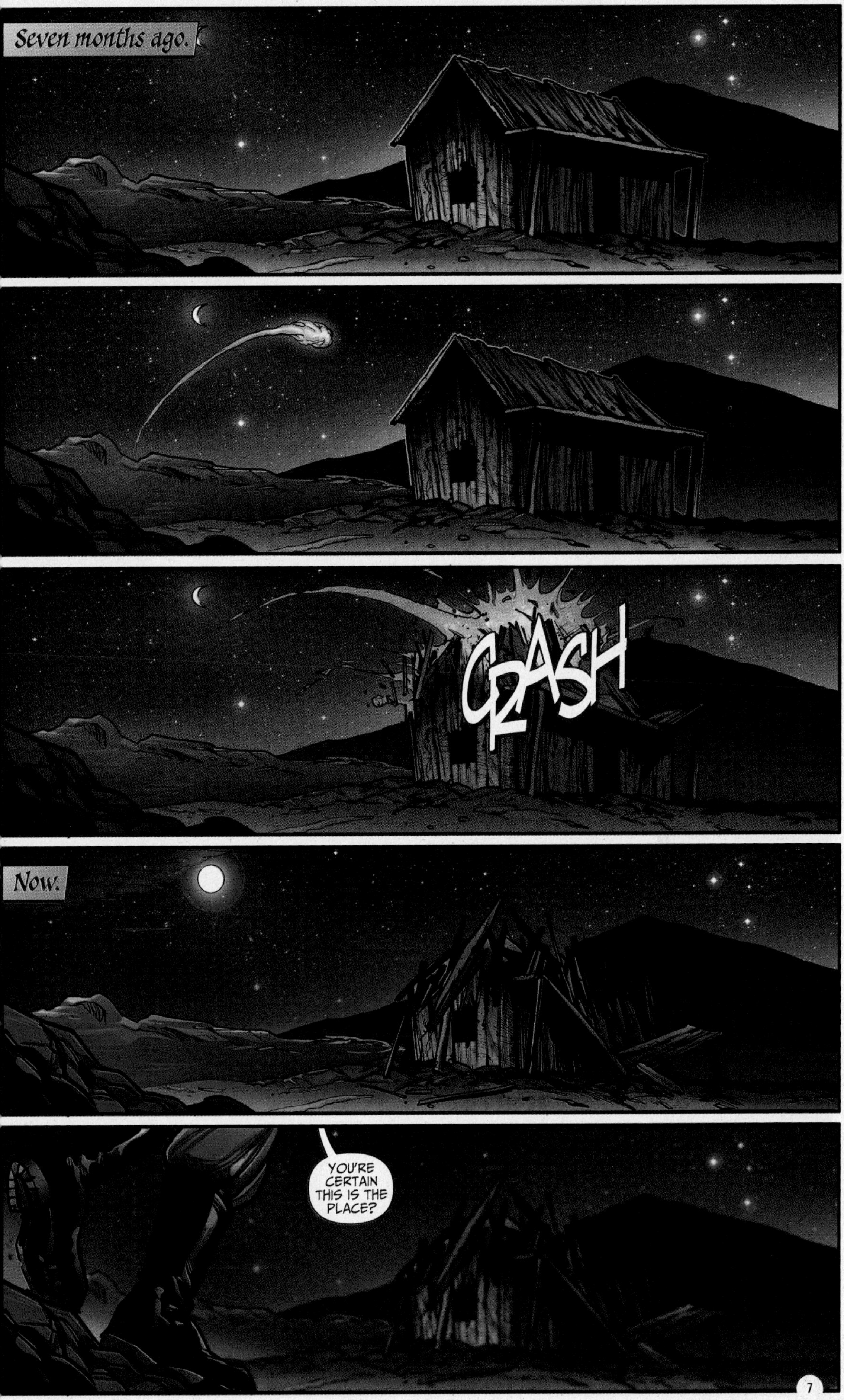
Seven months ago.
CRASH
Now.
YOU'RE CERTAIN THIS IS THE PLACE?

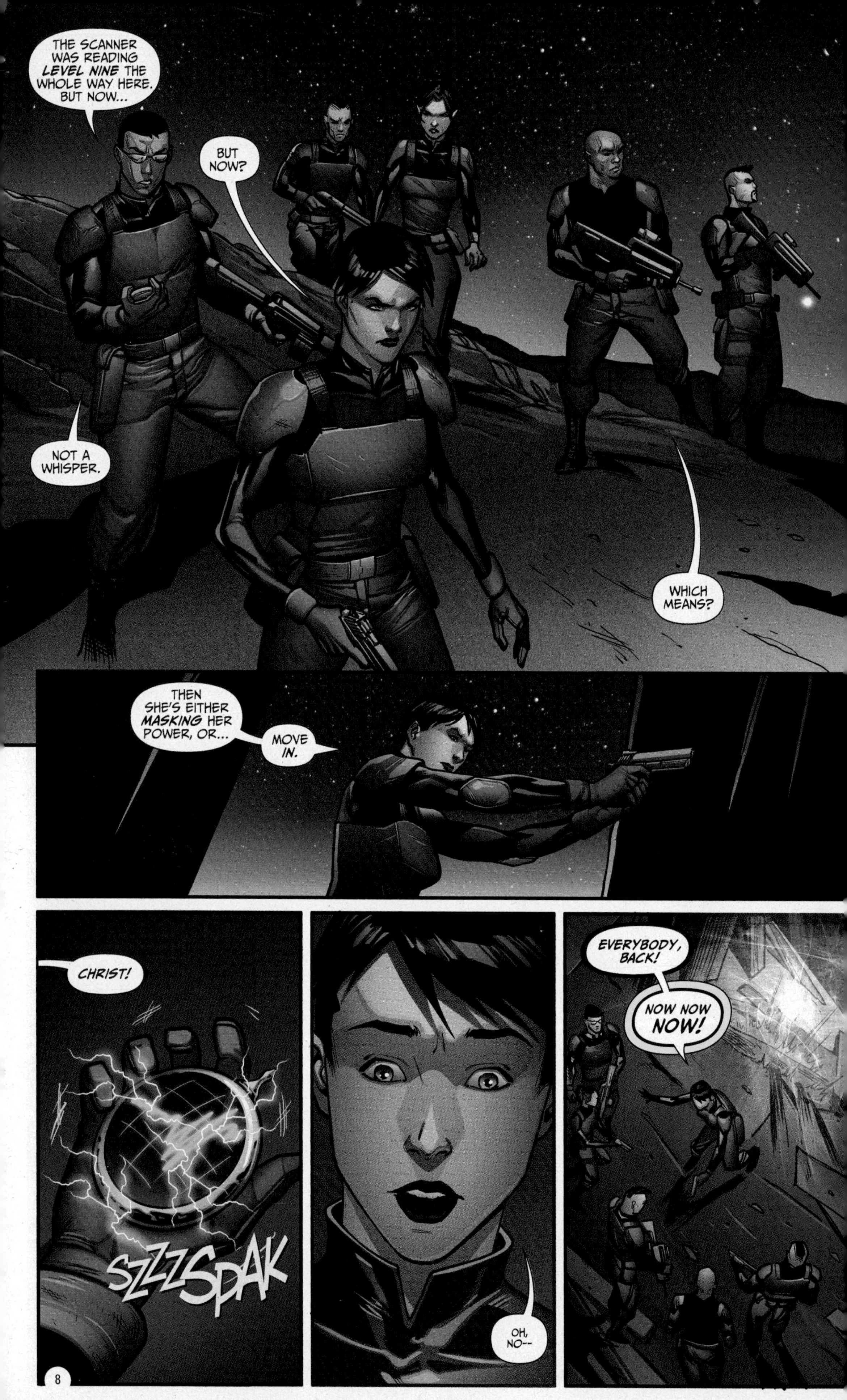
THE SCANNER WAS READING LEVEL NINE THE WHOLE WAY HERE. BUT NOW...
BUT NOW?
NOT A WHISPER.
WHICH MEANS?
THEN SHE'S EITHER MASKING HER POWER, OR...
MOVE IN.
CHRIST!
SZZZSPAK
OH, NO--
EVERYBODY, BACK!
NOW NOW NOW!

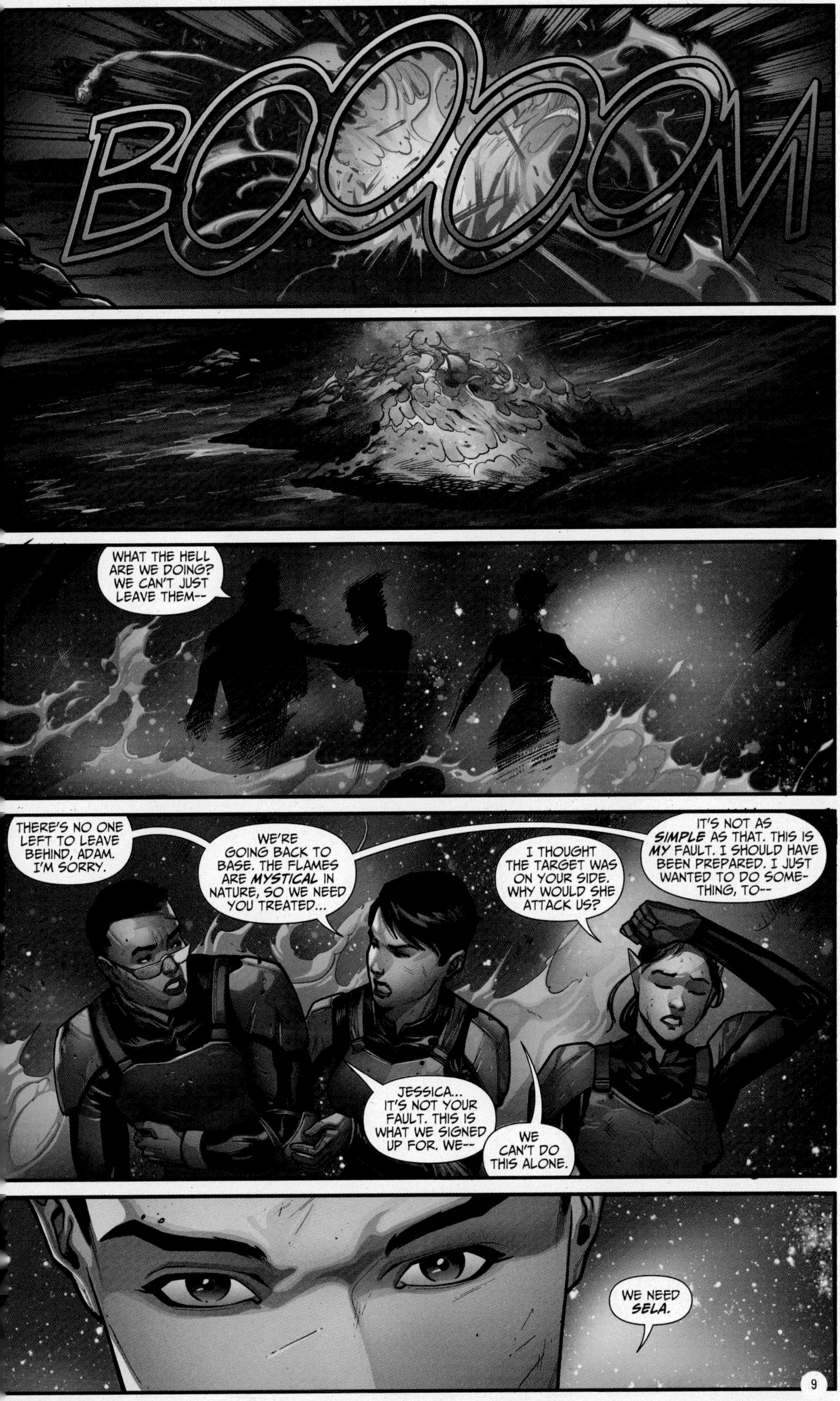
BOOOOOM
WHAT THE HELL ARE WE DOING? WE CAN'T JUST LEAVE THEM--
THERE'S NO ONE LEFT TO LEAVE BEHIND, ADAM. I'M SORRY.
WE'RE GOING BACK TO BASE. THE FLAMES ARE *MYSTICAL* IN NATURE, SO WE NEED YOU TREATED...
I THOUGHT THE TARGET WAS ON YOUR SIDE. WHY WOULD SHE ATTACK US?
IT'S NOT AS *SIMPLE* AS THAT. THIS IS *MY* FAULT. I SHOULD HAVE BEEN PREPARED. I JUST WANTED TO DO SOMETHING, TO--
JESSICA... IT'S NOT YOUR FAULT. THIS IS WHAT WE SIGNED UP FOR. WE--
WE CAN'T DO THIS ALONE.
WE NEED *SELA.*

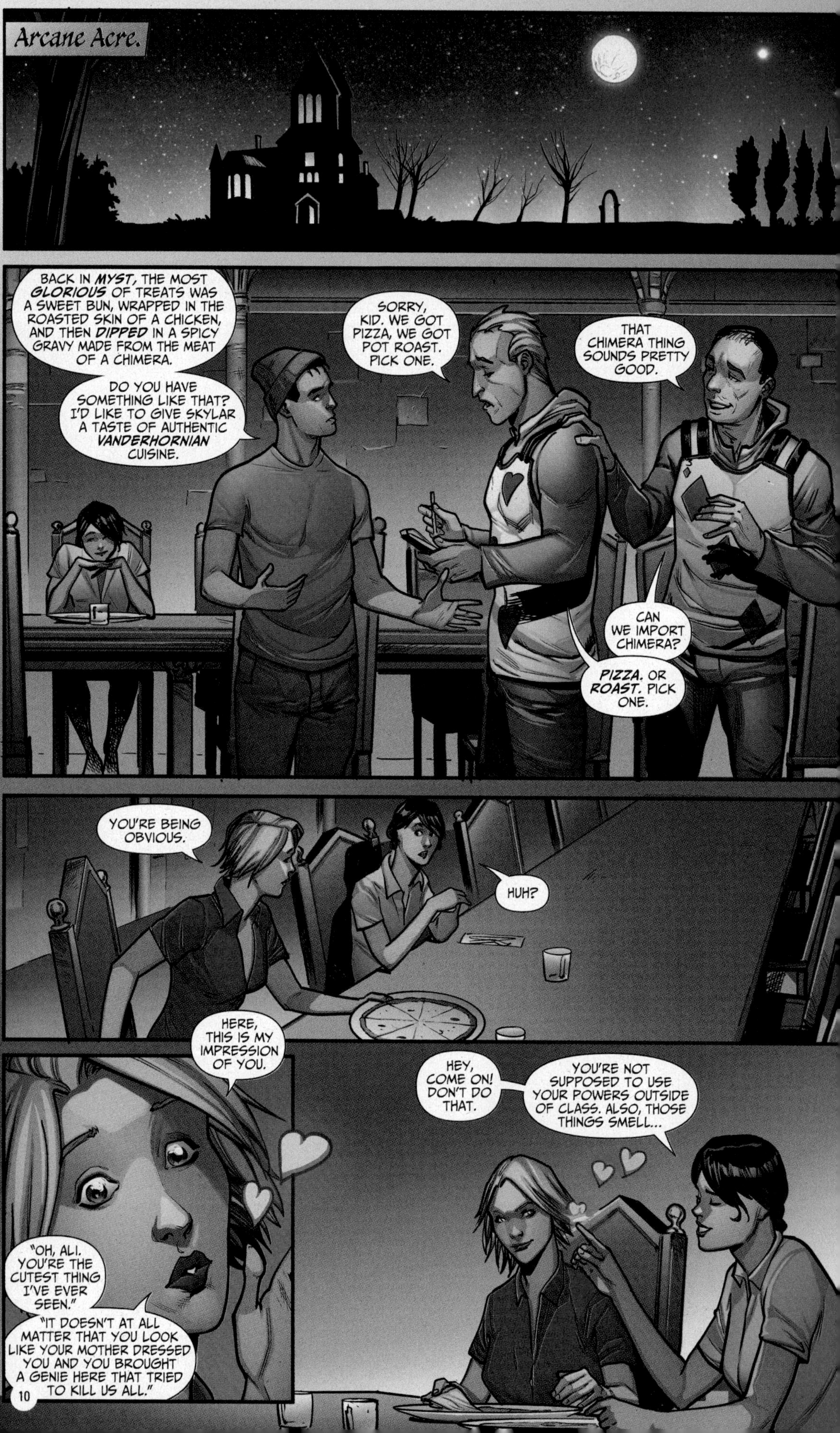

Arcane Acre.
BACK IN MYST, THE MOST GLORIOUS OF TREATS WAS A SWEET BUN, WRAPPED IN THE ROASTED SKIN OF A CHICKEN, AND THEN DIPPED IN A SPICY GRAVY MADE FROM THE MEAT OF A CHIMERA.
DO YOU HAVE SOMETHING LIKE THAT? I'D LIKE TO GIVE SKYLAR A TASTE OF AUTHENTIC VANDERHORNIAN CUISINE.
SORRY, KID. WE GOT PIZZA, WE GOT POT ROAST. PICK ONE.
THAT CHIMERA THING SOUNDS PRETTY GOOD.
CAN WE IMPORT CHIMERA?
PIZZA. OR ROAST. PICK ONE.
YOU'RE BEING OBVIOUS.
HUH?
HERE, THIS IS MY IMPRESSION OF YOU.
"OH, ALI. YOU'RE THE CUTEST THING I'VE EVER SEEN."
"IT DOESN'T AT ALL MATTER THAT YOU LOOK LIKE YOUR MOTHER DRESSED YOU AND YOU BROUGHT A GENIE HERE THAT TRIED TO KILL US ALL."
HEY, COME ON! DON'T DO THAT.
YOU'RE NOT SUPPOSED TO USE YOUR POWERS OUTSIDE OF CLASS. ALSO, THOSE THINGS SMELL...

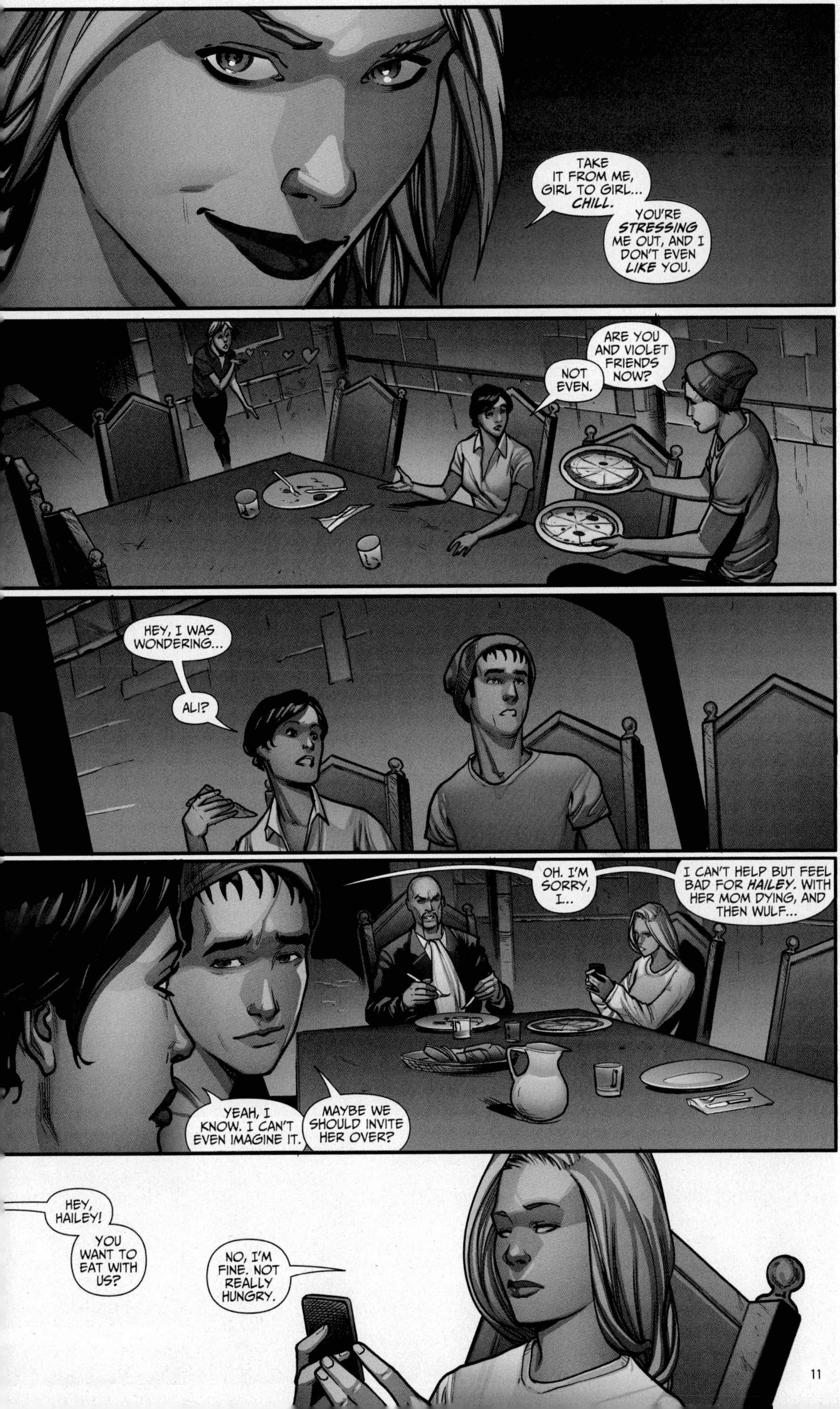
TAKE IT FROM ME, GIRL TO GIRL... CHILL.
YOU'RE STRESSING ME OUT, AND I DON'T EVEN LIKE YOU.
ARE YOU AND VIOLET FRIENDS NOW?
NOT EVEN.
HEY, I WAS WONDERING...
ALI?
OH. I'M SORRY, I...
I CAN'T HELP BUT FEEL BAD FOR HAILEY. WITH HER MOM DYING, AND THEN WULF...
YEAH, I KNOW. I CAN'T EVEN IMAGINE IT.
MAYBE WE SHOULD INVITE HER OVER?
HEY, HAILEY!
YOU WANT TO EAT WITH US?
NO, I'M FINE. NOT REALLY HUNGRY.

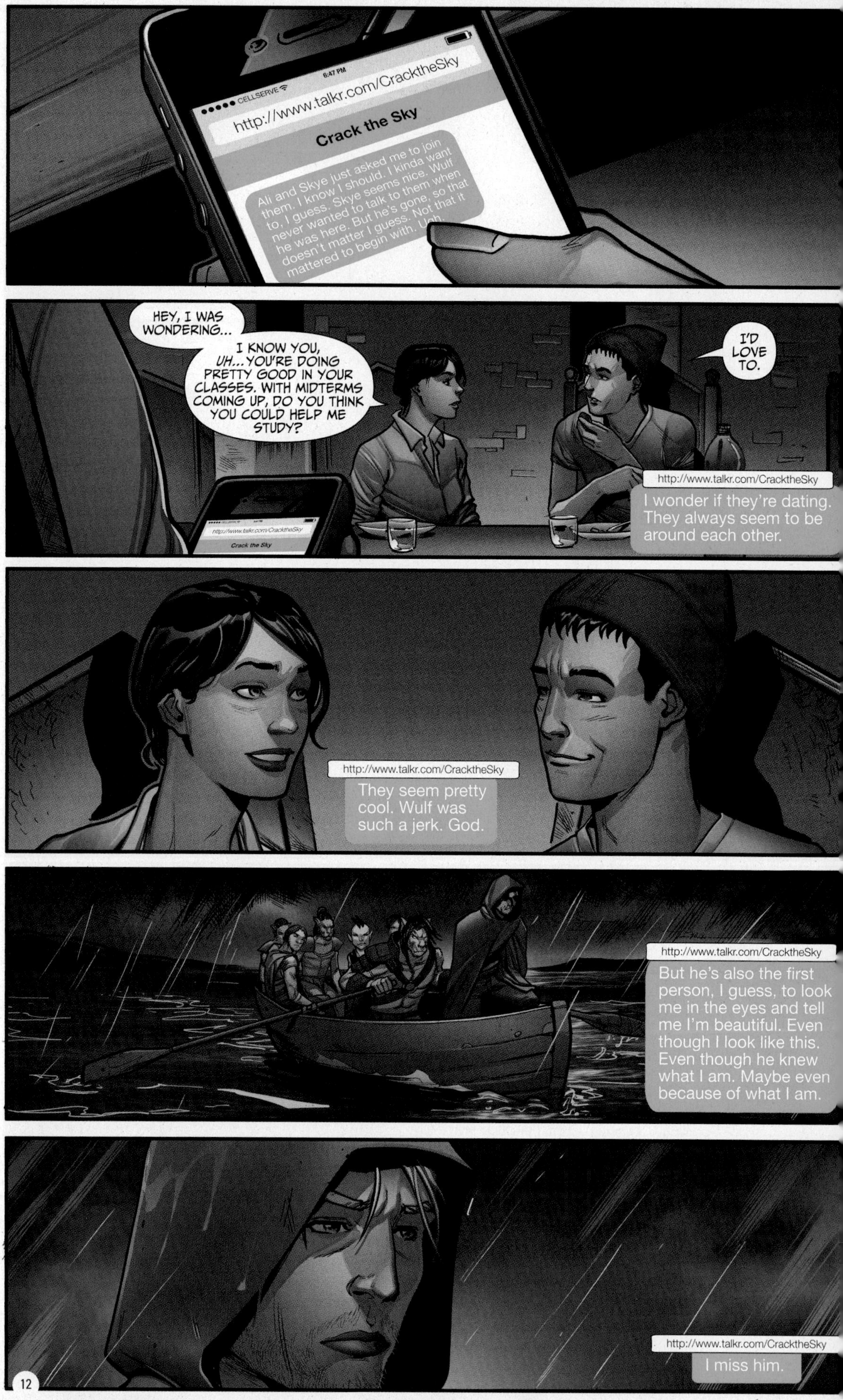

●●●●● CELLSERVE
6:47 PM
http://www.talkr.com/CracktheSky
Crack the Sky
Ali and Skye just asked me to join them. I know I should. I kinda want to, I guess. Skye seems nice. Wulf never wanted to talk to them when he was here. But he's gone, so that doesn't matter I guess. Not that it mattered to begin with. Ugh.
HEY, I WAS WONDERING...
I KNOW YOU, UH...YOU'RE DOING PRETTY GOOD IN YOUR CLASSES. WITH MIDTERMS COMING UP, DO YOU THINK YOU COULD HELP ME STUDY?
I'D LOVE TO.
http://www.talkr.com/CracktheSky
I wonder if they're dating. They always seem to be around each other.
http://www.talkr.com/CracktheSky
They seem pretty cool. Wulf was such a jerk. God.
http://www.talkr.com/CracktheSky
But he's also the first person, I guess, to look me in the eyes and tell me I'm beautiful. Even though I look like this. Even though he knew what I am. Maybe even because of what I am.
http://www.talkr.com/CracktheSky
I miss him.

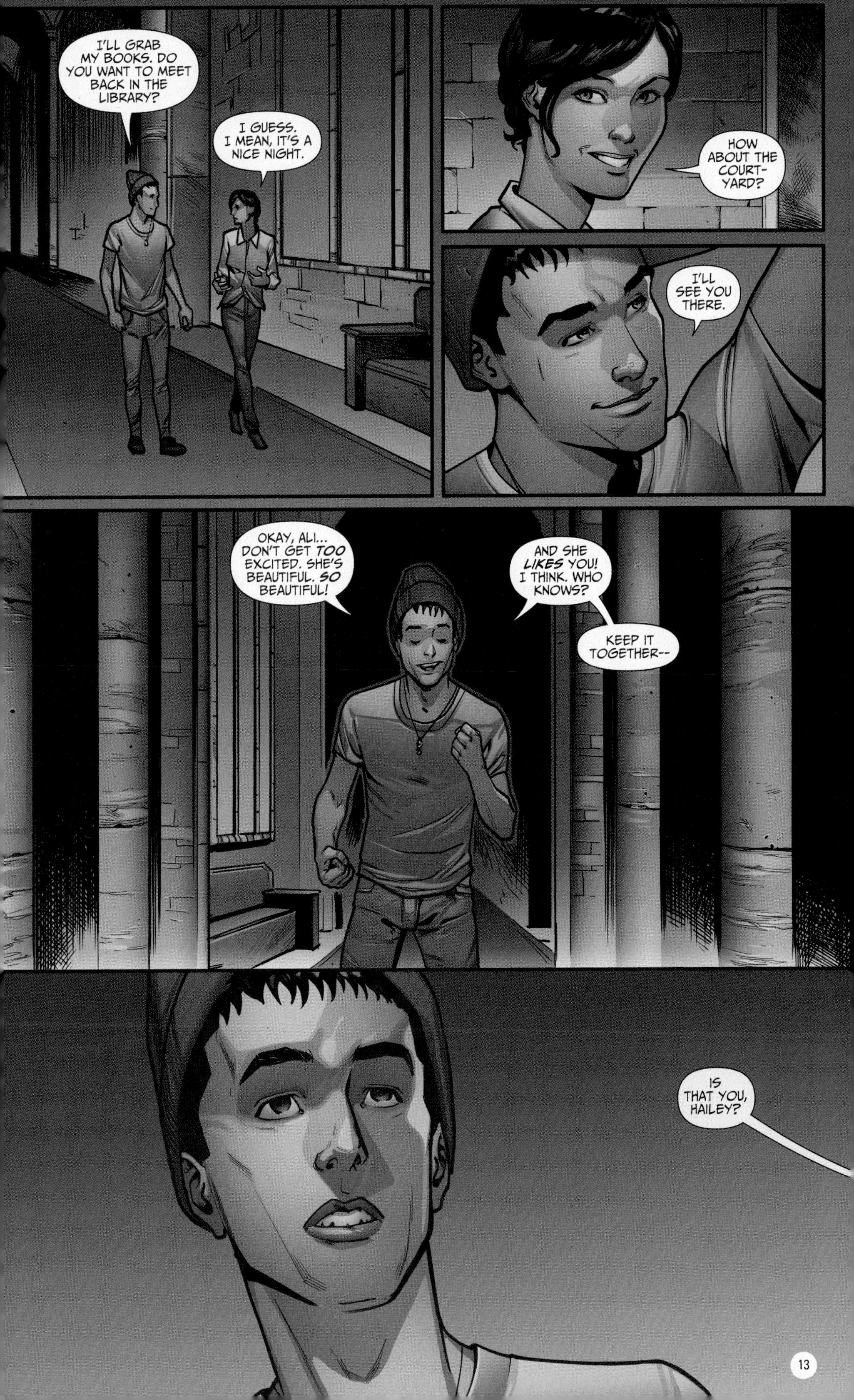
I'LL GRAB MY BOOKS. DO YOU WANT TO MEET BACK IN THE LIBRARY?
I GUESS. I MEAN, IT'S A NICE NIGHT.
HOW ABOUT THE COURT-YARD?
I'LL SEE YOU THERE.
OKAY, ALI... DON'T GET *TOO* EXCITED. SHE'S BEAUTIFUL. *SO* BEAUTIFUL!
AND SHE *LIKES* YOU! I THINK. WHO KNOWS?
KEEP IT TOGETHER--
IS THAT YOU, HAILEY?

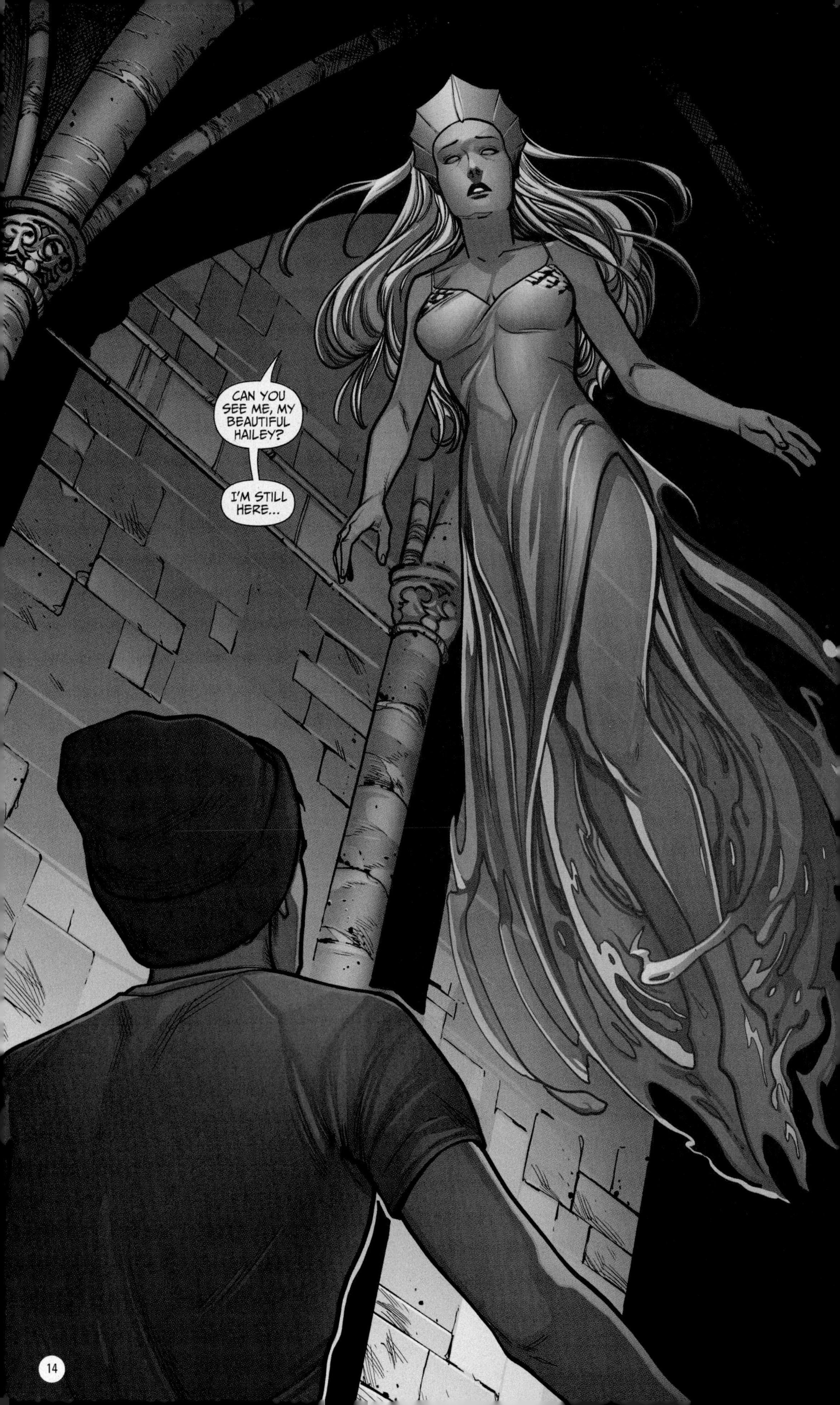
CAN YOU SEE ME, MY BEAUTIFUL HAILEY?
I'M STILL HERE...

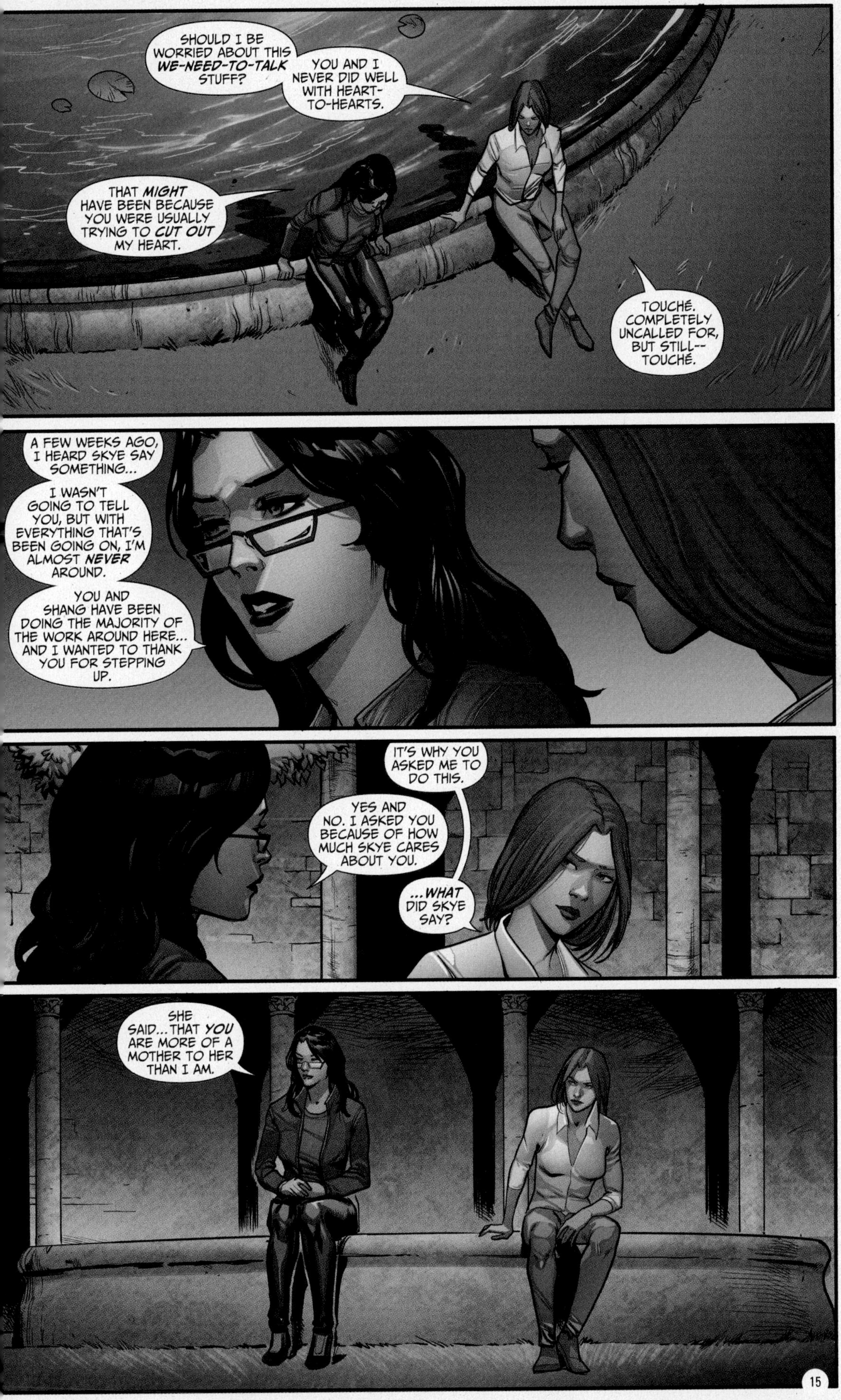
SHOULD I BE WORRIED ABOUT THIS *WE-NEED-TO-TALK* STUFF?
YOU AND I NEVER DID WELL WITH HEART-TO-HEARTS.
THAT *MIGHT* HAVE BEEN BECAUSE YOU WERE USUALLY TRYING TO *CUT OUT* MY HEART.
TOUCHÉ. COMPLETELY UNCALLED FOR, BUT STILL-- TOUCHÉ.
A FEW WEEKS AGO, I HEARD SKYE SAY SOMETHING...
I WASN'T GOING TO TELL YOU, BUT WITH EVERYTHING THAT'S BEEN GOING ON, I'M ALMOST *NEVER* AROUND.
YOU AND SHANG HAVE BEEN DOING THE MAJORITY OF THE WORK AROUND HERE... AND I WANTED TO THANK YOU FOR STEPPING UP.
IT'S WHY YOU ASKED ME TO DO THIS.
YES AND NO. I ASKED YOU BECAUSE OF HOW MUCH SKYE CARES ABOUT YOU.
...WHAT DID SKYE SAY?
SHE SAID...THAT *YOU* ARE MORE OF A MOTHER TO HER THAN I AM.

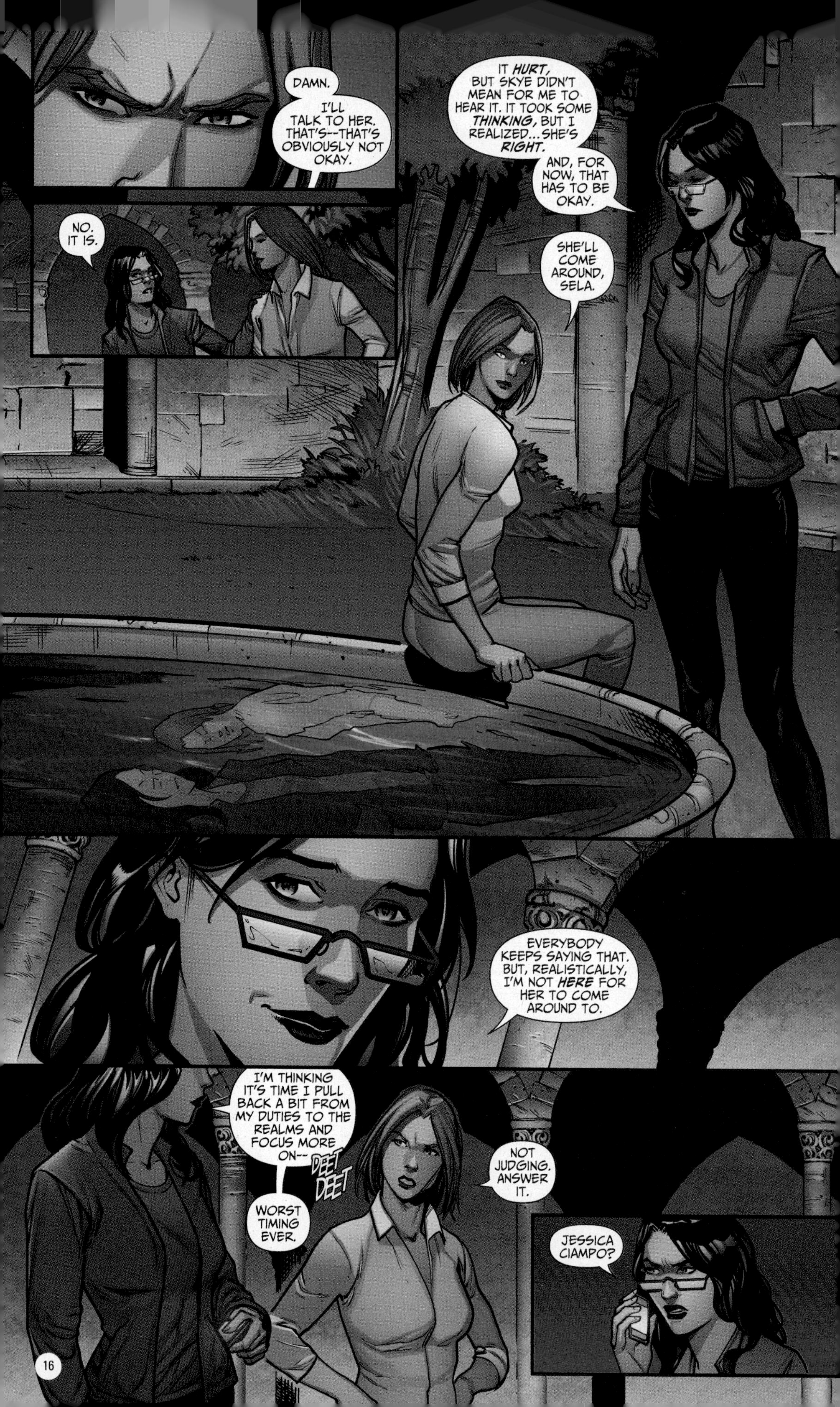
DAMN.
I'LL TALK TO HER. THAT'S--THAT'S OBVIOUSLY NOT OKAY.
NO. IT IS.
IT *HURT*, BUT SKYE DIDN'T MEAN FOR ME TO HEAR IT. IT TOOK SOME *THINKING*, BUT I REALIZED...SHE'S *RIGHT*.
AND, FOR NOW, THAT HAS TO BE OKAY.
SHE'LL COME AROUND, SELA.
EVERYBODY KEEPS SAYING THAT. BUT, REALISTICALLY, I'M NOT *HERE* FOR HER TO COME AROUND TO.
I'M THINKING IT'S TIME I PULL BACK A BIT FROM MY DUTIES TO THE REALMS AND FOCUS MORE ON--
DEET DEET
WORST TIMING EVER.
NOT JUDGING. ANSWER IT.
JESSICA CIAMPO?

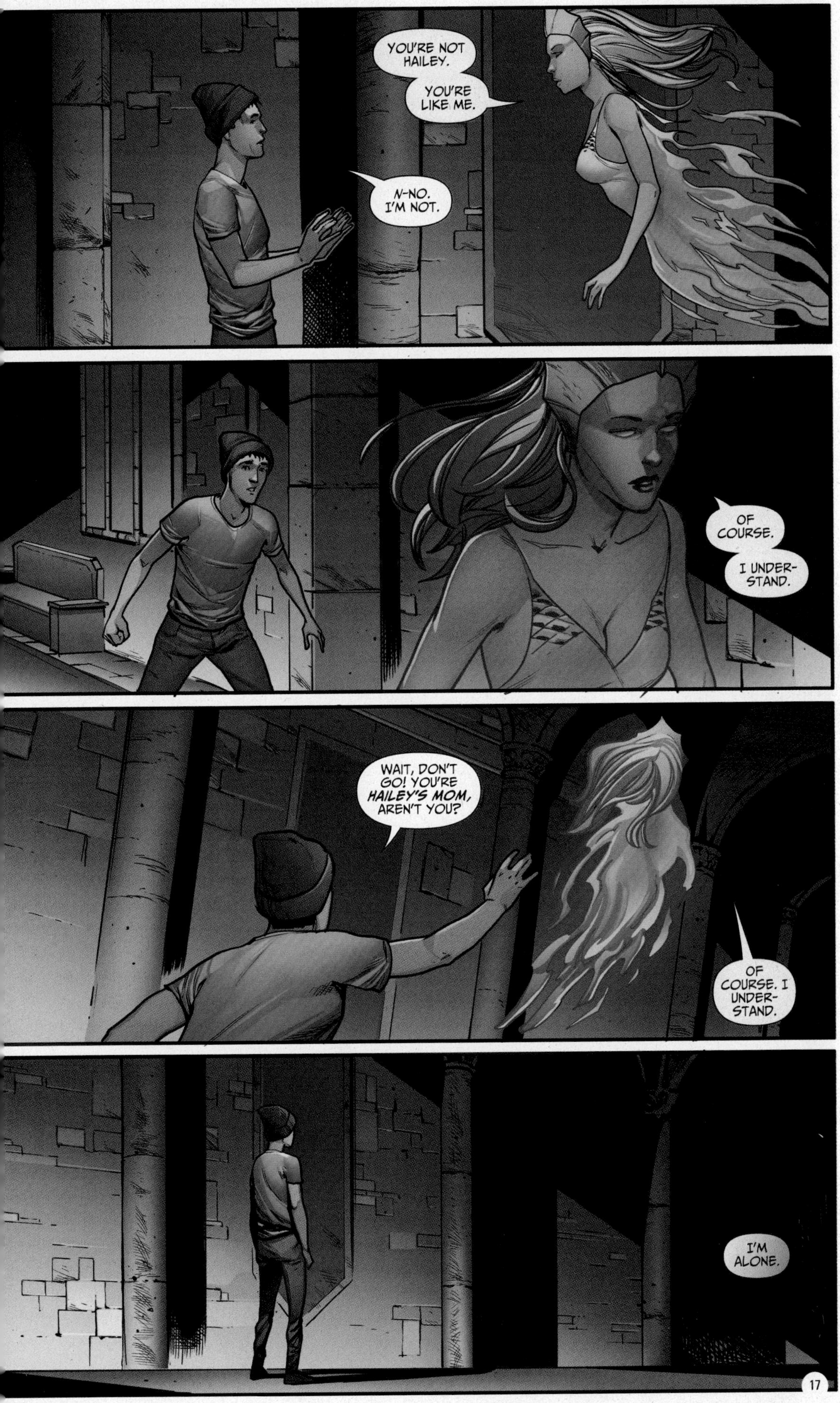
YOU'RE NOT HAILEY.
YOU'RE LIKE ME.
N-NO. I'M NOT.
OF COURSE.
I UNDERSTAND.
WAIT, DON'T GO! YOU'RE HAILEY'S MOM, AREN'T YOU?
OF COURSE. I UNDERSTAND.
I'M ALONE.

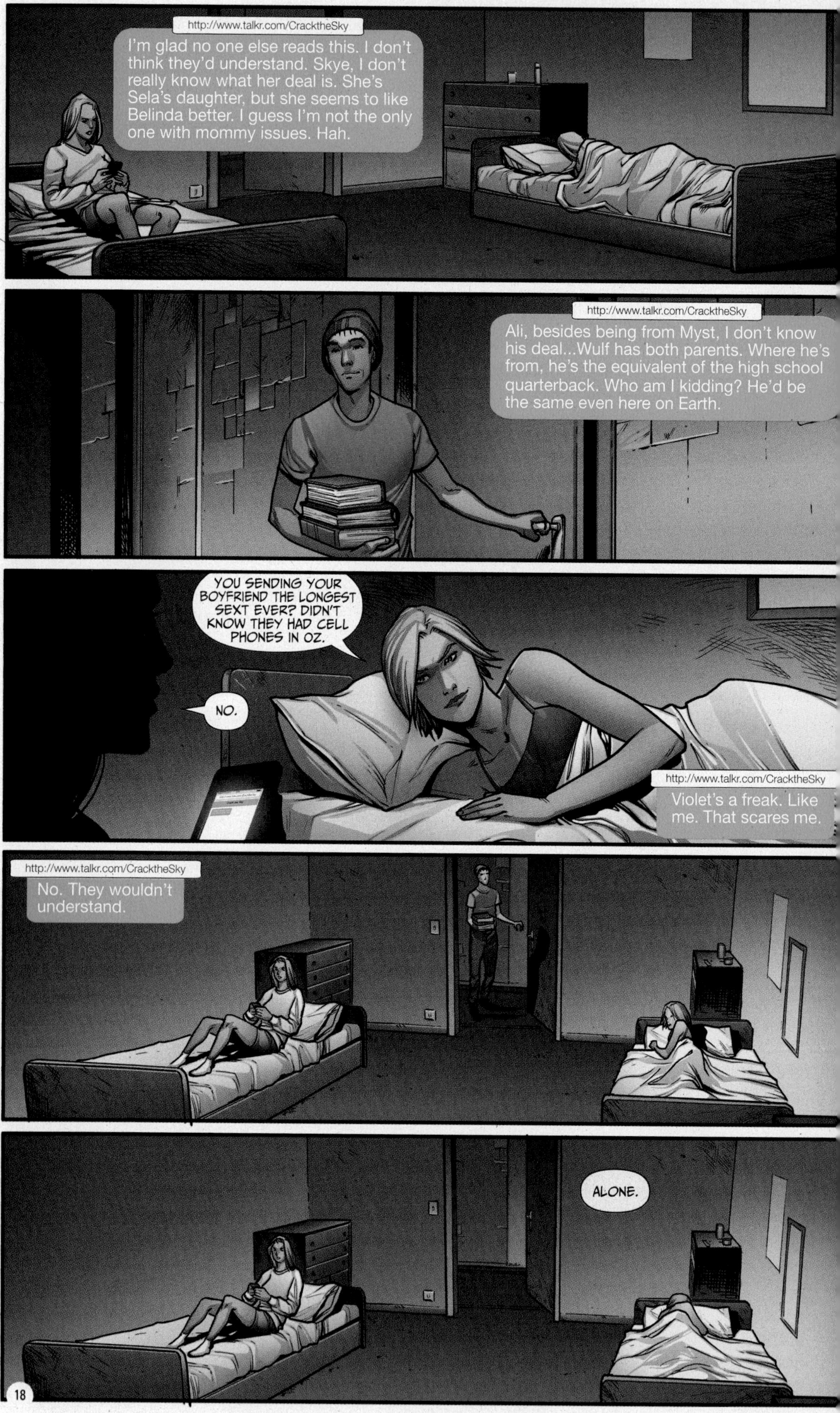

http://www.talkr.com/CracktheSky
I'm glad no one else reads this. I don't think they'd understand. Skye, I don't really know what her deal is. She's Sela's daughter, but she seems to like Belinda better. I guess I'm not the only one with mommy issues. Hah.
http://www.talkr.com/CracktheSky
Ali, besides being from Myst, I don't know his deal...Wulf has both parents. Where he's from, he's the equivalent of the high school quarterback. Who am I kidding? He'd be the same even here on Earth.
YOU SENDING YOUR BOYFRIEND THE LONGEST SEXT EVER? DIDN'T KNOW THEY HAD CELL PHONES IN OZ.
NO.
http://www.talkr.com/CracktheSky
Violet's a freak. Like me. That scares me.
http://www.talkr.com/CracktheSky
No. They wouldn't understand.
ALONE.

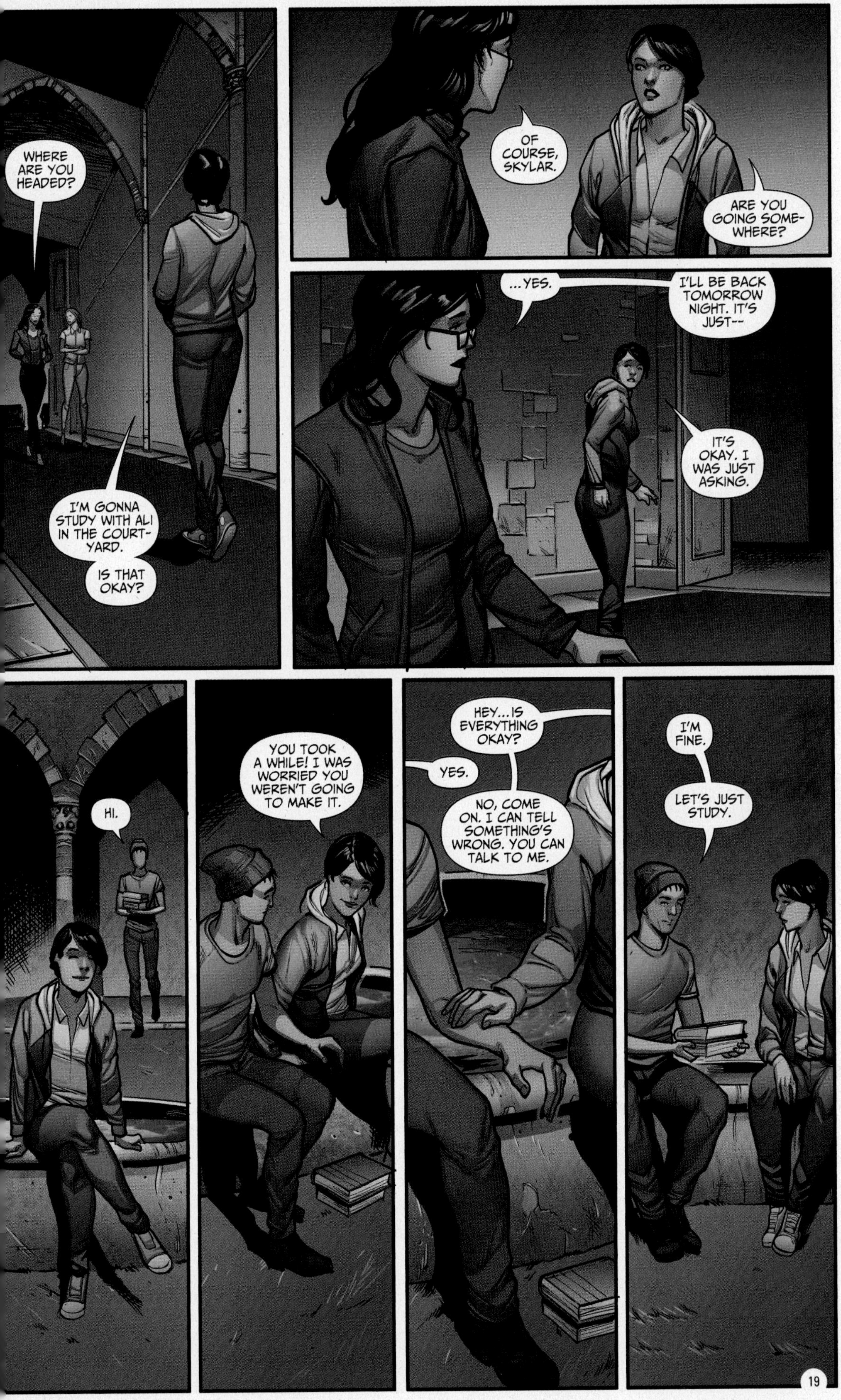

WHERE ARE YOU HEADED?
I'M GONNA STUDY WITH ALI IN THE COURT-YARD.
IS THAT OKAY?
OF COURSE, SKYLAR.
ARE YOU GOING SOME-WHERE?
...YES.
I'LL BE BACK TOMORROW NIGHT. IT'S JUST--
IT'S OKAY. I WAS JUST ASKING.
HI.
YOU TOOK A WHILE! I WAS WORRIED YOU WEREN'T GOING TO MAKE IT.
HEY... IS EVERYTHING OKAY?
YES.
NO, COME ON. I CAN TELL SOMETHING'S WRONG. YOU CAN TALK TO ME.
I'M FINE.
LET'S JUST STUDY.

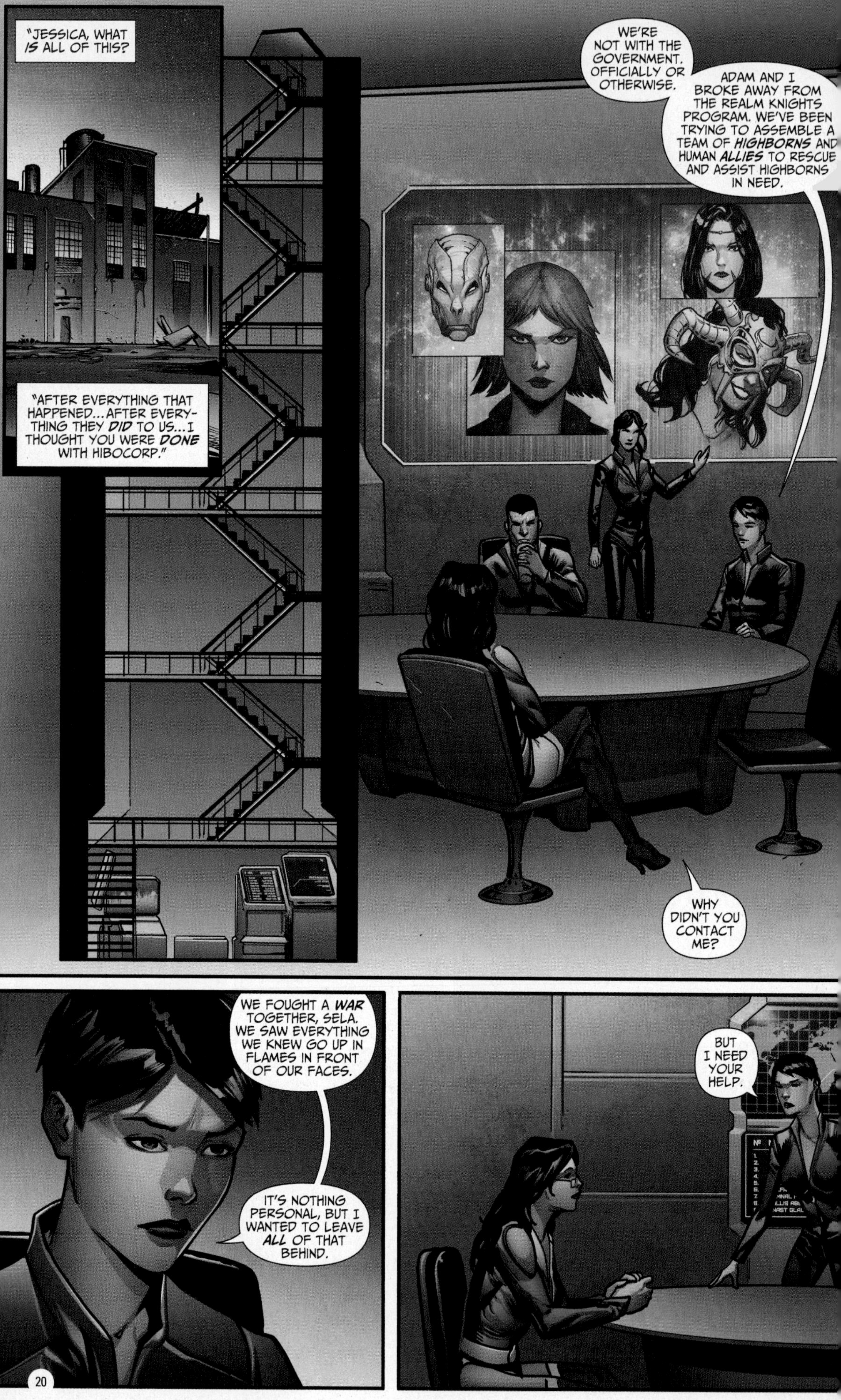
"JESSICA, WHAT IS ALL OF THIS?
"AFTER EVERYTHING THAT HAPPENED... AFTER EVERYTHING THEY DID TO US... I THOUGHT YOU WERE DONE WITH HIBOCORP."
WE'RE NOT WITH THE GOVERNMENT. OFFICIALLY OR OTHERWISE.
ADAM AND I BROKE AWAY FROM THE REALM KNIGHTS PROGRAM. WE'VE BEEN TRYING TO ASSEMBLE A TEAM OF HIGHBORNS AND HUMAN ALLIES TO RESCUE AND ASSIST HIGHBORNS IN NEED.
WHY DIDN'T YOU CONTACT ME?
WE FOUGHT A WAR TOGETHER, SELA. WE SAW EVERYTHING WE KNEW GO UP IN FLAMES IN FRONT OF OUR FACES.
IT'S NOTHING PERSONAL, BUT I WANTED TO LEAVE ALL OF THAT BEHIND.
BUT I NEED YOUR HELP.

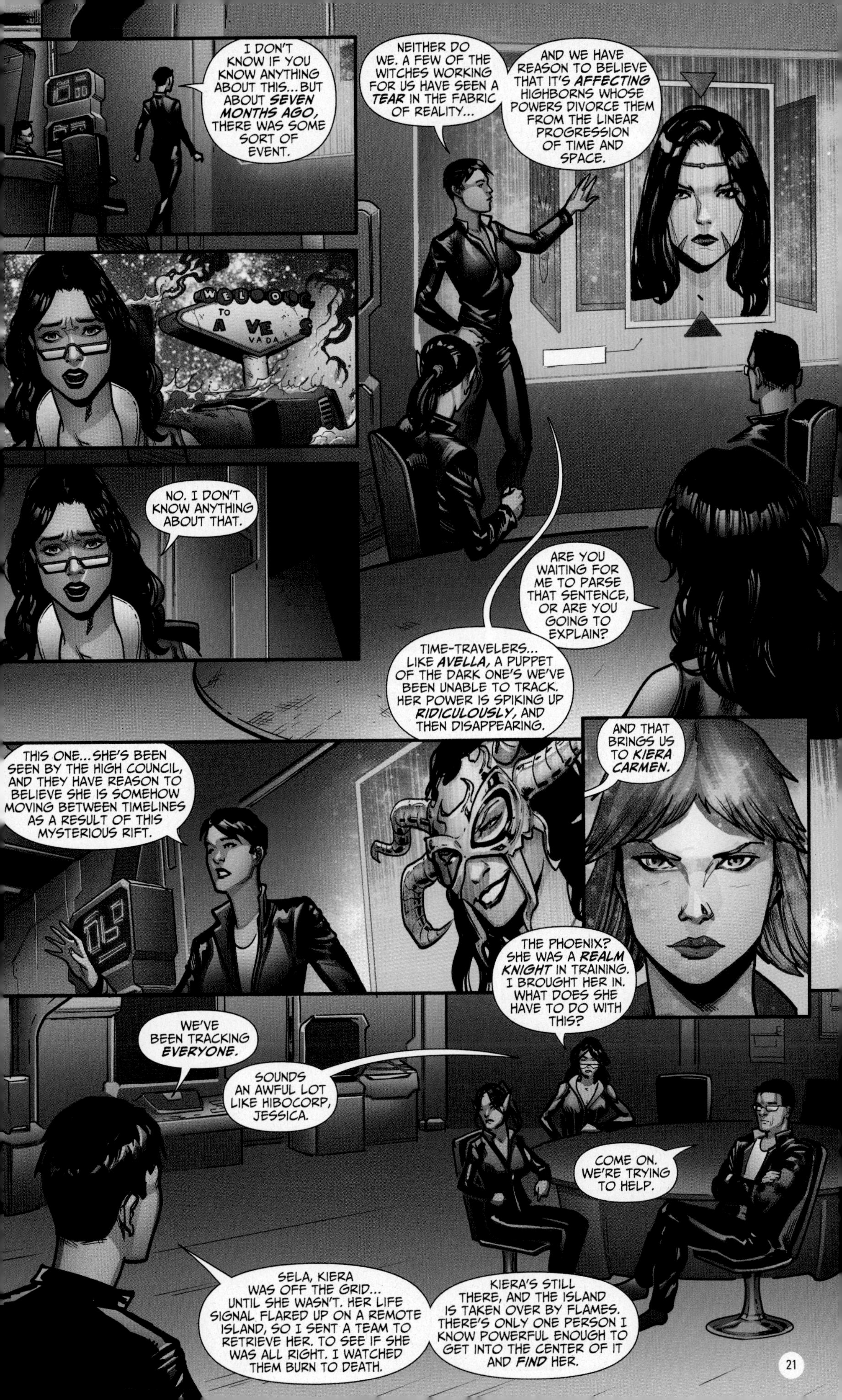

I DON'T KNOW IF YOU KNOW ANYTHING ABOUT THIS... BUT ABOUT SEVEN MONTHS AGO, THERE WAS SOME SORT OF EVENT.
NEITHER DO WE. A FEW OF THE WITCHES WORKING FOR US HAVE SEEN A TEAR IN THE FABRIC OF REALITY...
AND WE HAVE REASON TO BELIEVE THAT IT'S AFFECTING HIGHBORNS WHOSE POWERS DIVORCE THEM FROM THE LINEAR PROGRESSION OF TIME AND SPACE.
NO. I DON'T KNOW ANYTHING ABOUT THAT.
ARE YOU WAITING FOR ME TO PARSE THAT SENTENCE, OR ARE YOU GOING TO EXPLAIN?
TIME-TRAVELERS... LIKE AVELLA, A PUPPET OF THE DARK ONE'S WE'VE BEEN UNABLE TO TRACK. HER POWER IS SPIKING UP RIDICULOUSLY, AND THEN DISAPPEARING.
THIS ONE... SHE'S BEEN SEEN BY THE HIGH COUNCIL, AND THEY HAVE REASON TO BELIEVE SHE IS SOMEHOW MOVING BETWEEN TIMELINES AS A RESULT OF THIS MYSTERIOUS RIFT.
AND THAT BRINGS US TO KIERA CARMEN.
THE PHOENIX? SHE WAS A REALM KNIGHT IN TRAINING. I BROUGHT HER IN. WHAT DOES SHE HAVE TO DO WITH THIS?
WE'VE BEEN TRACKING EVERYONE.
SOUNDS AN AWFUL LOT LIKE HIBOCORP, JESSICA.
COME ON. WE'RE TRYING TO HELP.
SELA, KIERA WAS OFF THE GRID... UNTIL SHE WASN'T. HER LIFE SIGNAL FLARED UP ON A REMOTE ISLAND, SO I SENT A TEAM TO RETRIEVE HER. TO SEE IF SHE WAS ALL RIGHT. I WATCHED THEM BURN TO DEATH.
KIERA'S STILL THERE, AND THE ISLAND IS TAKEN OVER BY FLAMES. THERE'S ONLY ONE PERSON I KNOW POWERFUL ENOUGH TO GET INTO THE CENTER OF IT AND FIND HER.

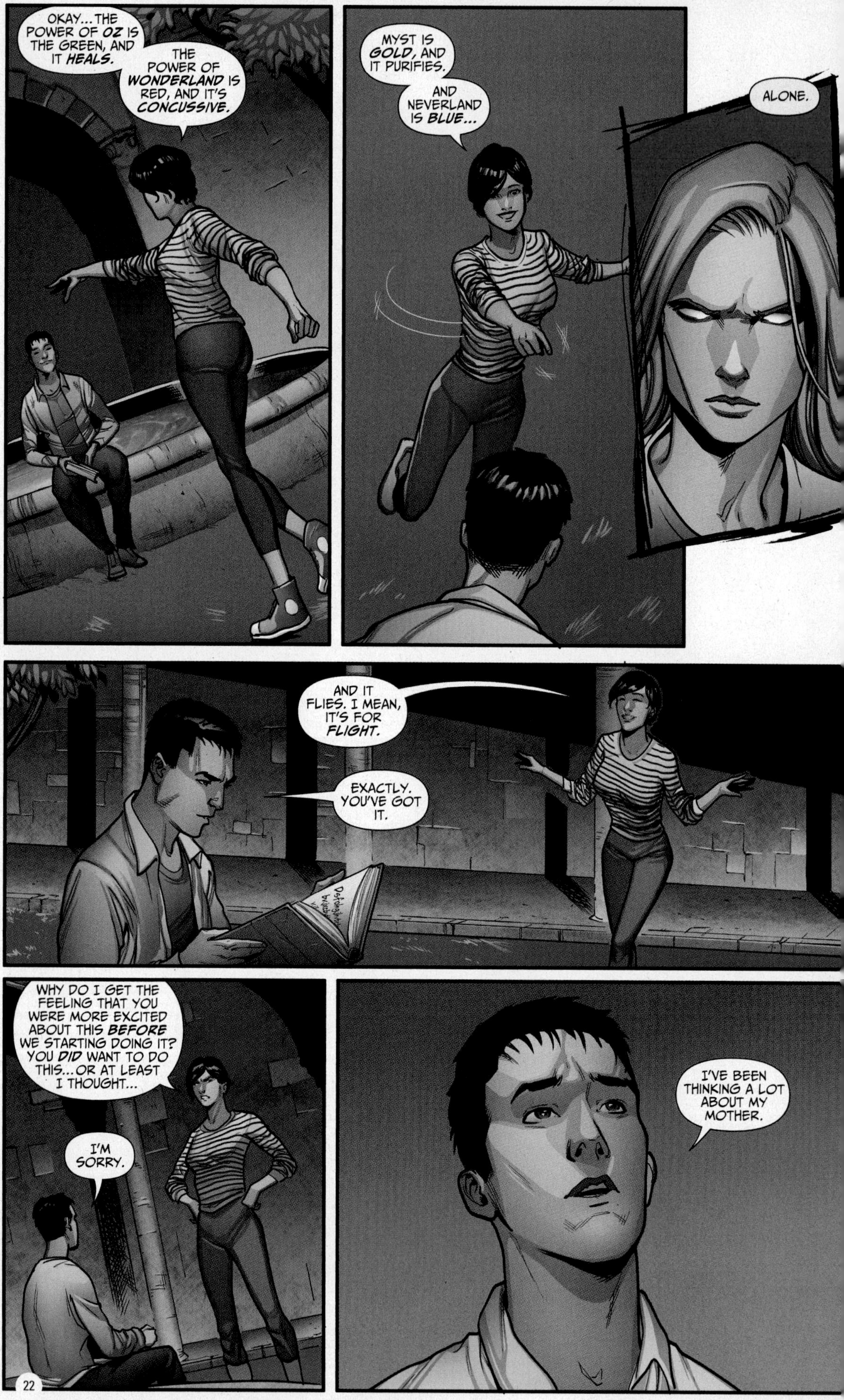

OKAY... THE POWER OF OZ IS THE GREEN, AND IT HEALS.
THE POWER OF WONDERLAND IS RED, AND IT'S CONCUSSIVE.
MYST IS GOLD, AND IT PURIFIES.
AND NEVERLAND IS BLUE...
ALONE.
AND IT FLIES. I MEAN, IT'S FOR FLIGHT.
EXACTLY. YOU'VE GOT IT.
WHY DO I GET THE FEELING THAT YOU WERE MORE EXCITED ABOUT THIS BEFORE WE STARTING DOING IT? YOU DID WANT TO DO THIS... OR AT LEAST I THOUGHT...
I'M SORRY.
I'VE BEEN THINKING A LOT ABOUT MY MOTHER.

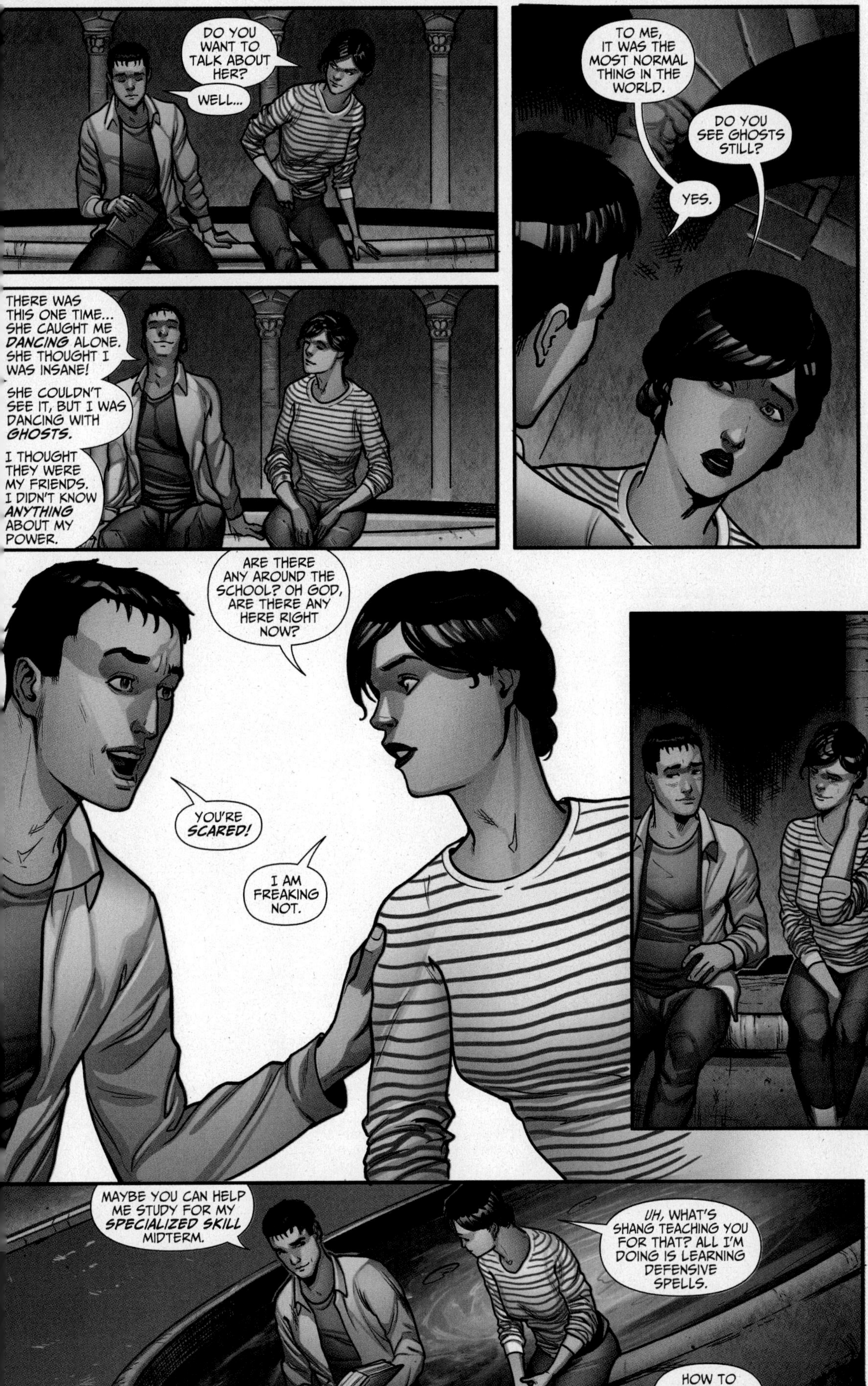
DO YOU WANT TO TALK ABOUT HER?
WELL...
TO ME, IT WAS THE MOST NORMAL THING IN THE WORLD.
DO YOU SEE GHOSTS STILL?
YES.
THERE WAS THIS ONE TIME... SHE CAUGHT ME DANCING ALONE. SHE THOUGHT I WAS INSANE!
SHE COULDN'T SEE IT, BUT I WAS DANCING WITH GHOSTS.
I THOUGHT THEY WERE MY FRIENDS. I DIDN'T KNOW ANYTHING ABOUT MY POWER.
ARE THERE ANY AROUND THE SCHOOL? OH GOD, ARE THERE ANY HERE RIGHT NOW?
YOU'RE SCARED!
I AM FREAKING NOT.
MAYBE YOU CAN HELP ME STUDY FOR MY SPECIALIZED SKILL MIDTERM.
UH, WHAT'S SHANG TEACHING YOU FOR THAT? ALL I'M DOING IS LEARNING DEFENSIVE SPELLS.
HOW TO SUMMON A BENEVOLENT SPIRIT.

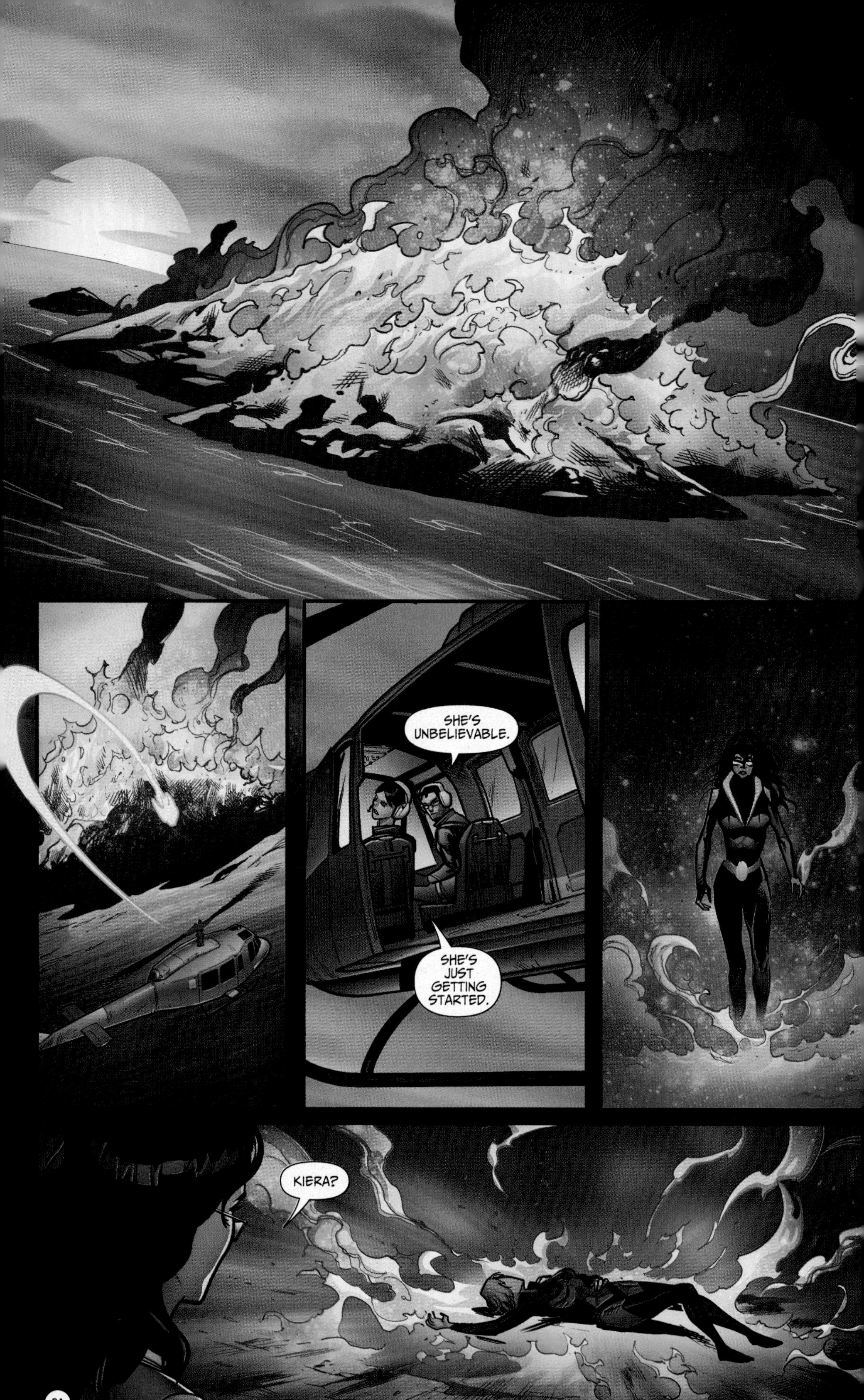
SHE'S UNBELIEVABLE.
SHE'S JUST GETTING STARTED.
KIERA?

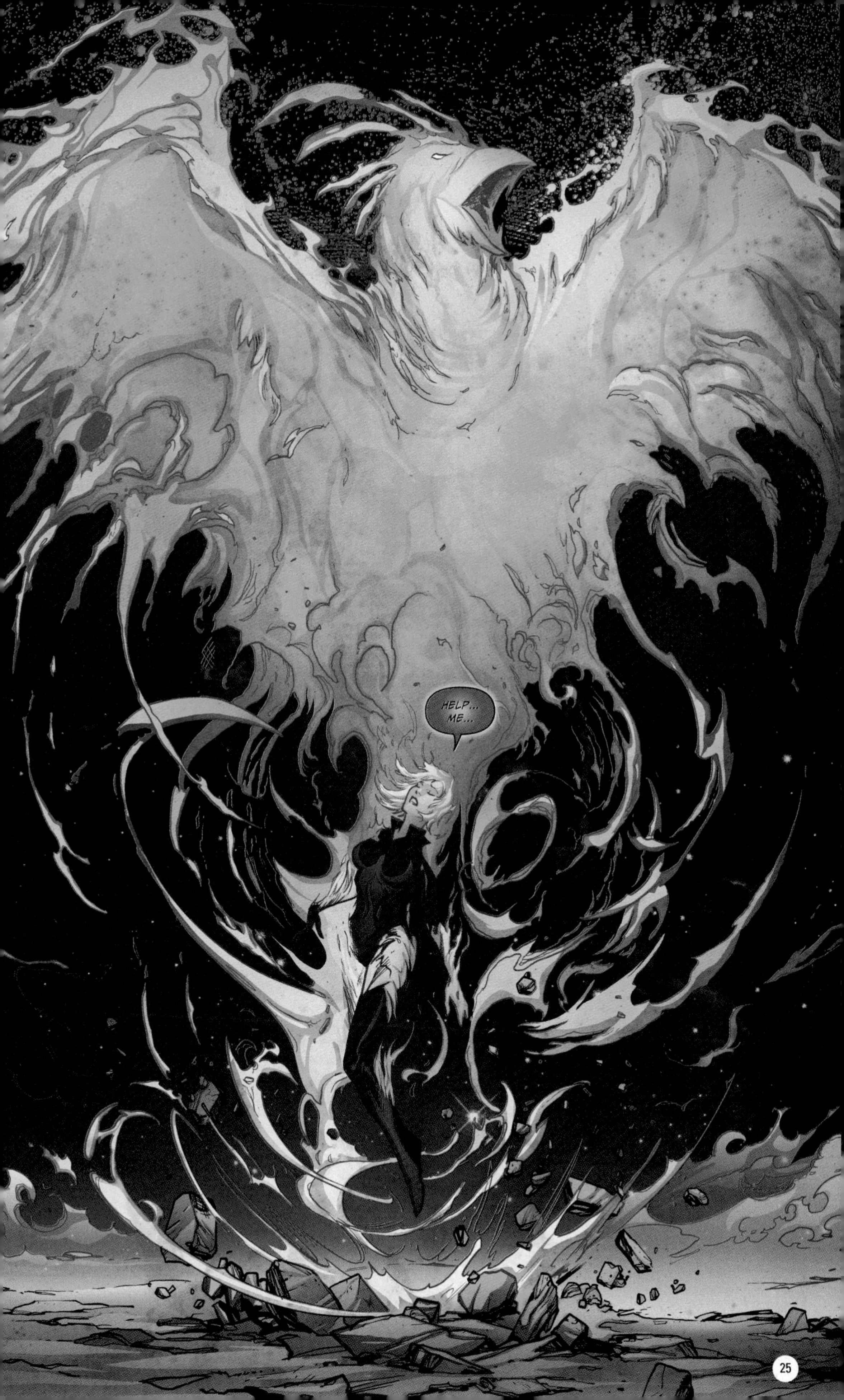
HELP... ME...

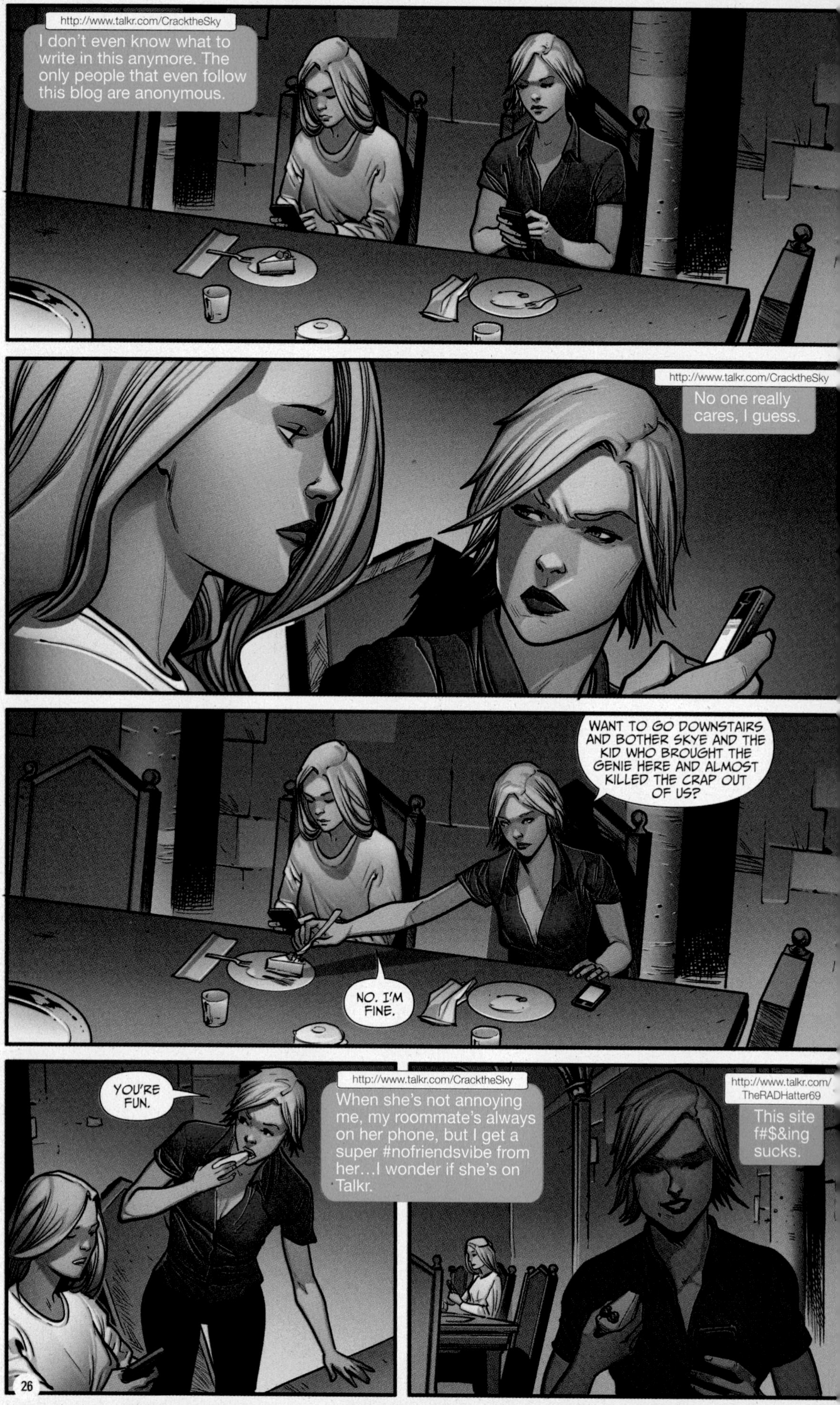
http://www.talkr.com/ConcktheSky
I don't even know what to write in this anymore. The only people that even follow this blog are anonymous.
http://www.talkr.com/CracktheSky
No one really cares, I guess.
WANT TO GO DOWNSTAIRS AND BOTHER SKYE AND THE KID WHO BROUGHT THE GENIE HERE AND ALMOST KILLED THE CRAP OUT OF US?
NO. I'M FINE.
YOU'RE FUN.
http://www.talkr.com/CracktheSky
When she's not annoying me, my roommate's always on her phone, but I get a super #nofriendsvibe from her...I wonder if she's on Talkr.
http://www.talkr.com/TheRADHatter69
This site f#$&ing sucks.

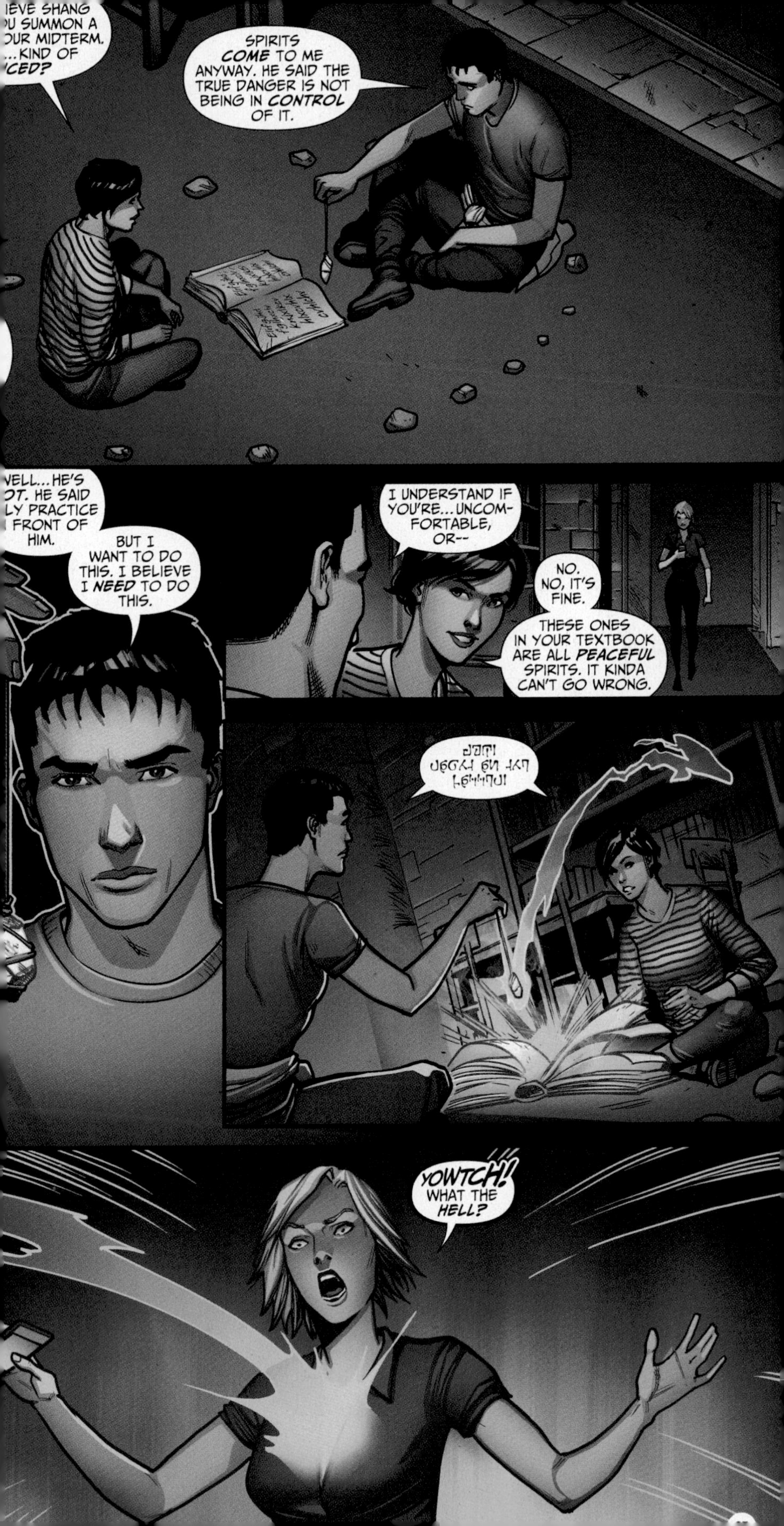

IEVE SHANG OU SUMMON A OUR MIDTERM. ...KIND OF CED?
SPIRITS COME TO ME ANYWAY. HE SAID THE TRUE DANGER IS NOT BEING IN CONTROL OF IT.
WELL... HE'S OT. HE SAID LY PRACTICE FRONT OF HIM.
BUT I WANT TO DO THIS. I BELIEVE I NEED TO DO THIS.
I UNDERSTAND IF YOU'RE... UNCOMFORTABLE, OR--
NO. NO, IT'S FINE.
THESE ONES IN YOUR TEXTBOOK ARE ALL PEACEFUL SPIRITS. IT KINDA CAN'T GO WRONG.
YOWTCH! WHAT THE HELL?

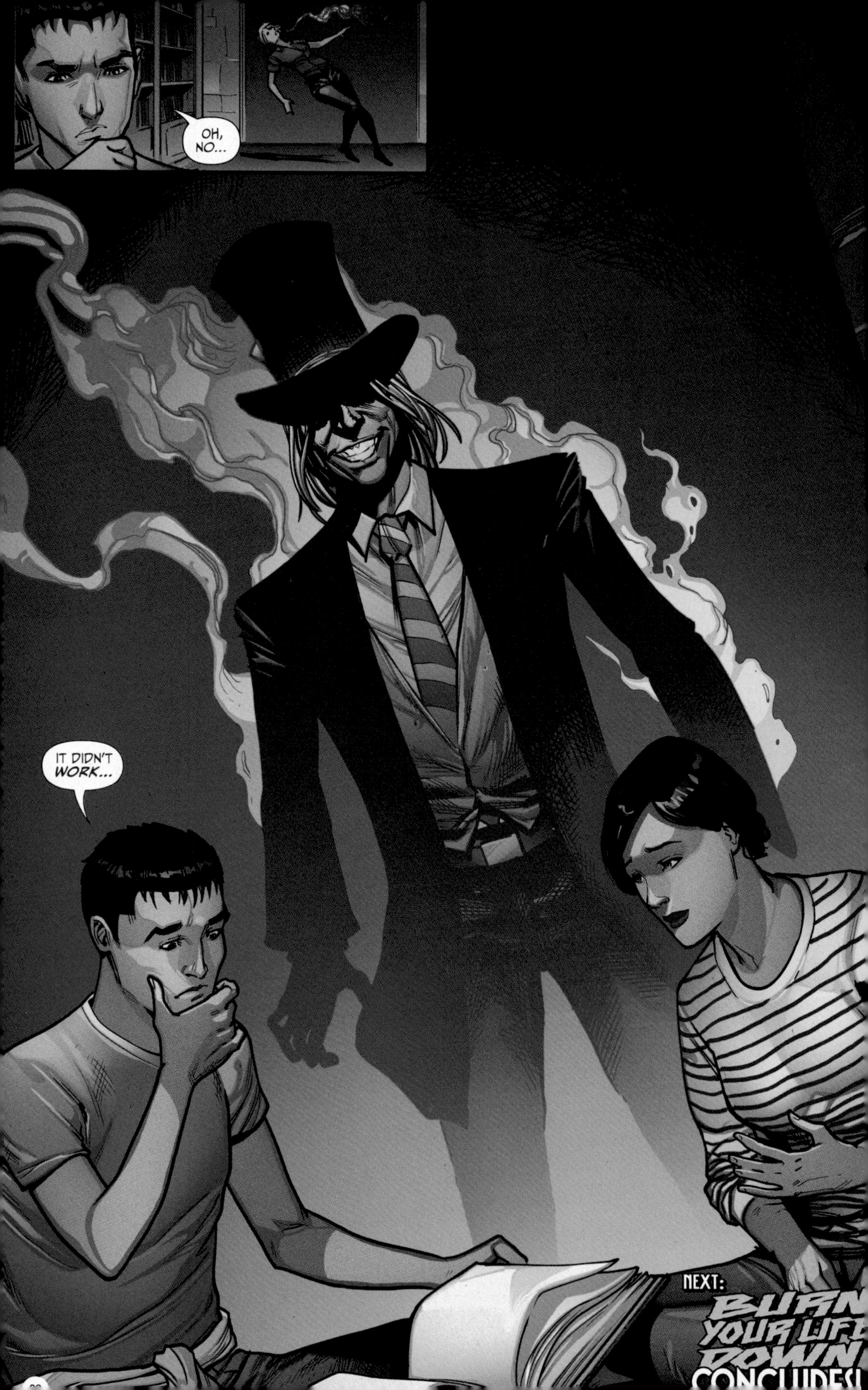
OH, NO...
IT DIDN'T *WORK*...
NEXT:
BURN YOUR LIFE DOWN CONCLUDES!

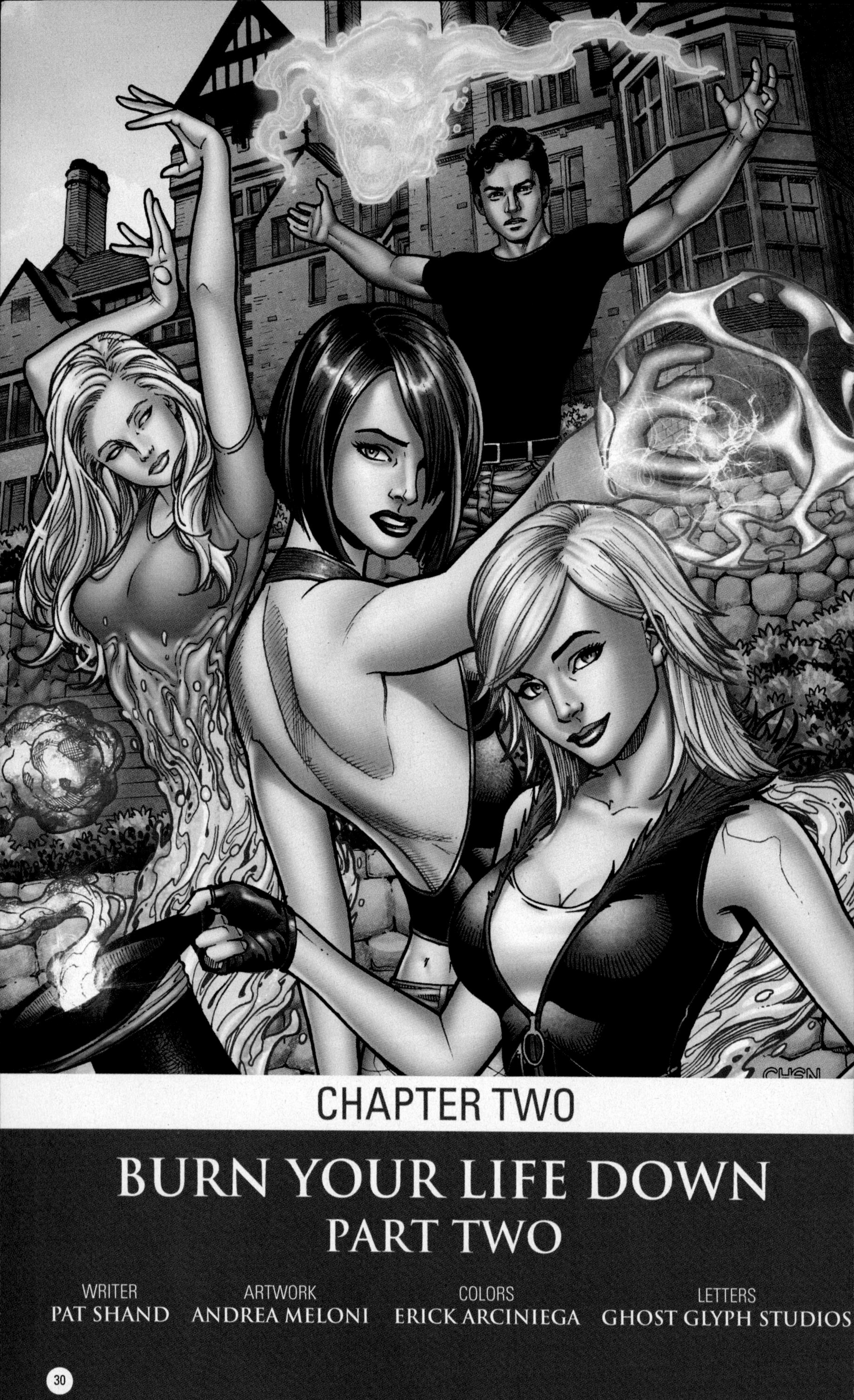

CHAPTER TWO

BURN YOUR LIFE DOWN
PART TWO

WRITER	ARTWORK	COLORS	LETTERS
PAT SHAND	ANDREA MELONI	ERICK ARCINIEGA	GHOST GLYPH STUDIOS

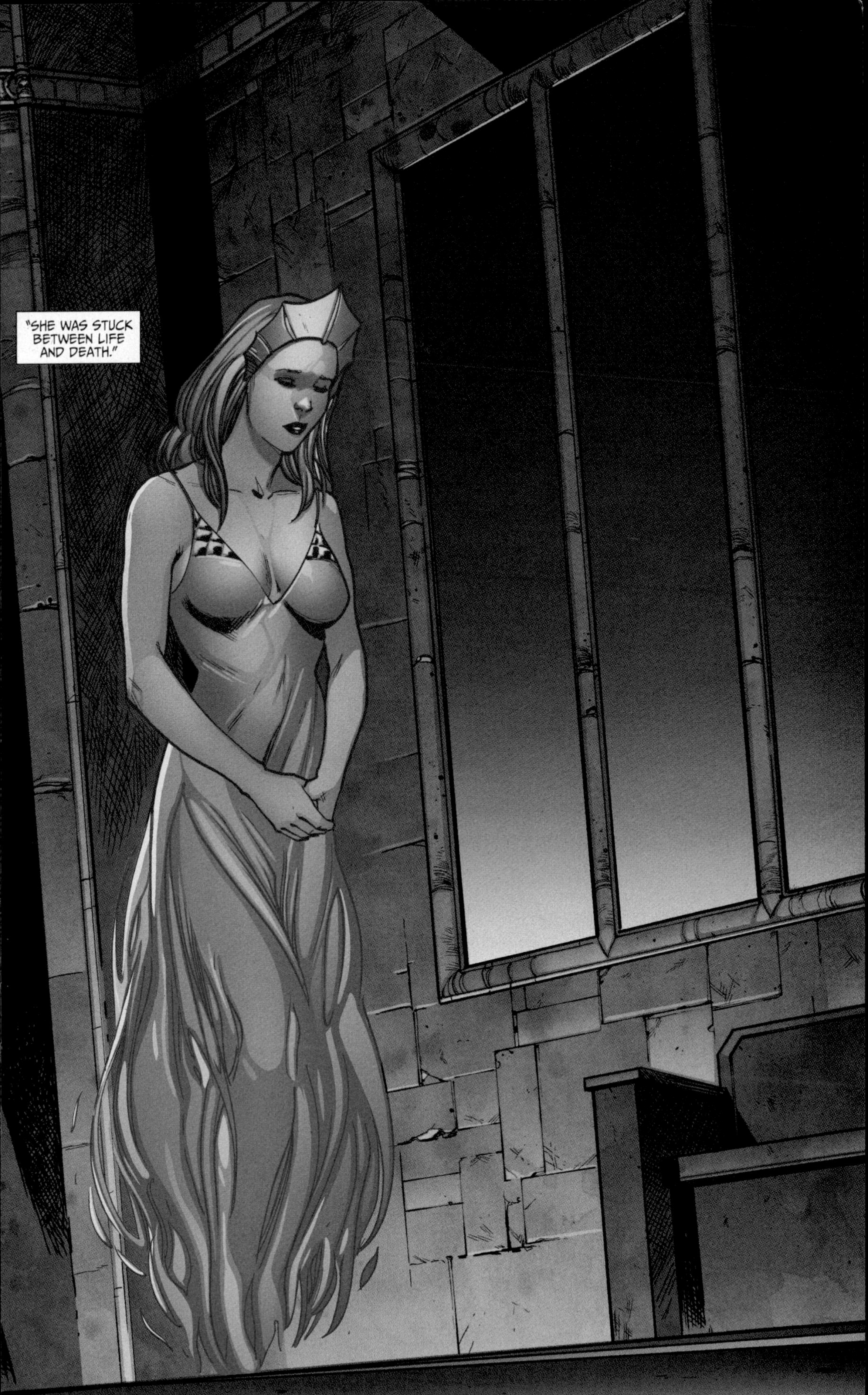
"SHE WAS STUCK BETWEEN LIFE AND DEATH."

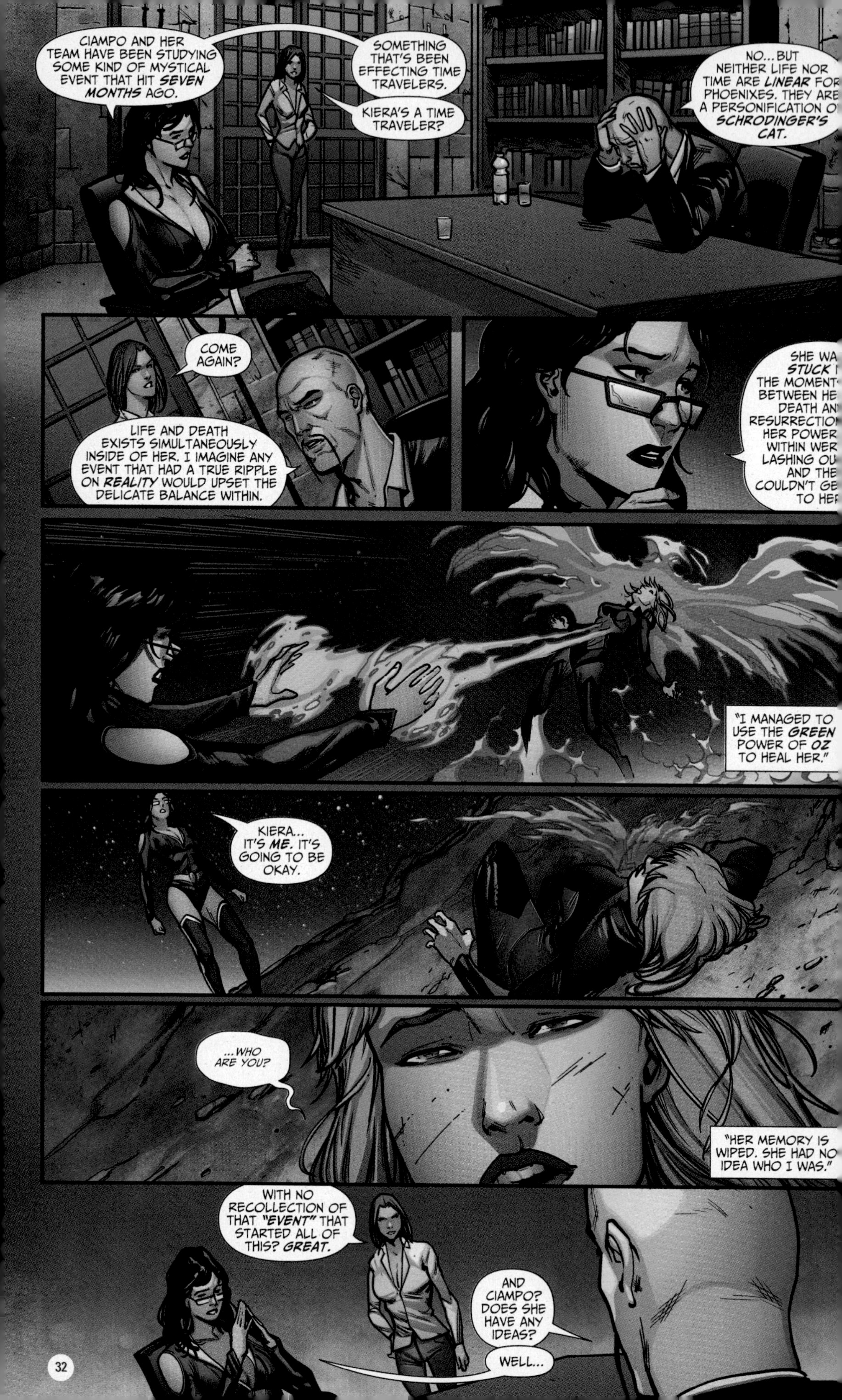

CIAMPO AND HER TEAM HAVE BEEN STUDYING SOME KIND OF MYSTICAL EVENT THAT HIT SEVEN MONTHS AGO.
SOMETHING THAT'S BEEN EFFECTING TIME TRAVELERS.
KIERA'S A TIME TRAVELER?
NO...BUT NEITHER LIFE NOR TIME ARE LINEAR FOR PHOENIXES. THEY ARE A PERSONIFICATION OF SCHRODINGER'S CAT.
COME AGAIN?
LIFE AND DEATH EXISTS SIMULTANEOUSLY INSIDE OF HER. I IMAGINE ANY EVENT THAT HAD A TRUE RIPPLE ON REALITY WOULD UPSET THE DELICATE BALANCE WITHIN.
SHE WA STUCK THE MOMENT BETWEEN HE DEATH AN RESURRECTIO HER POWER WITHIN WER LASHING OU AND THE COULDN'T GE TO HER
"I MANAGED TO USE THE GREEN POWER OF OZ TO HEAL HER."
KIERA... IT'S ME. IT'S GOING TO BE OKAY.
...WHO ARE YOU?
"HER MEMORY IS WIPED. SHE HAD NO IDEA WHO I WAS."
WITH NO RECOLLECTION OF THAT "EVENT" THAT STARTED ALL OF THIS? GREAT.
AND CIAMPO? DOES SHE HAVE ANY IDEAS?
WELL...

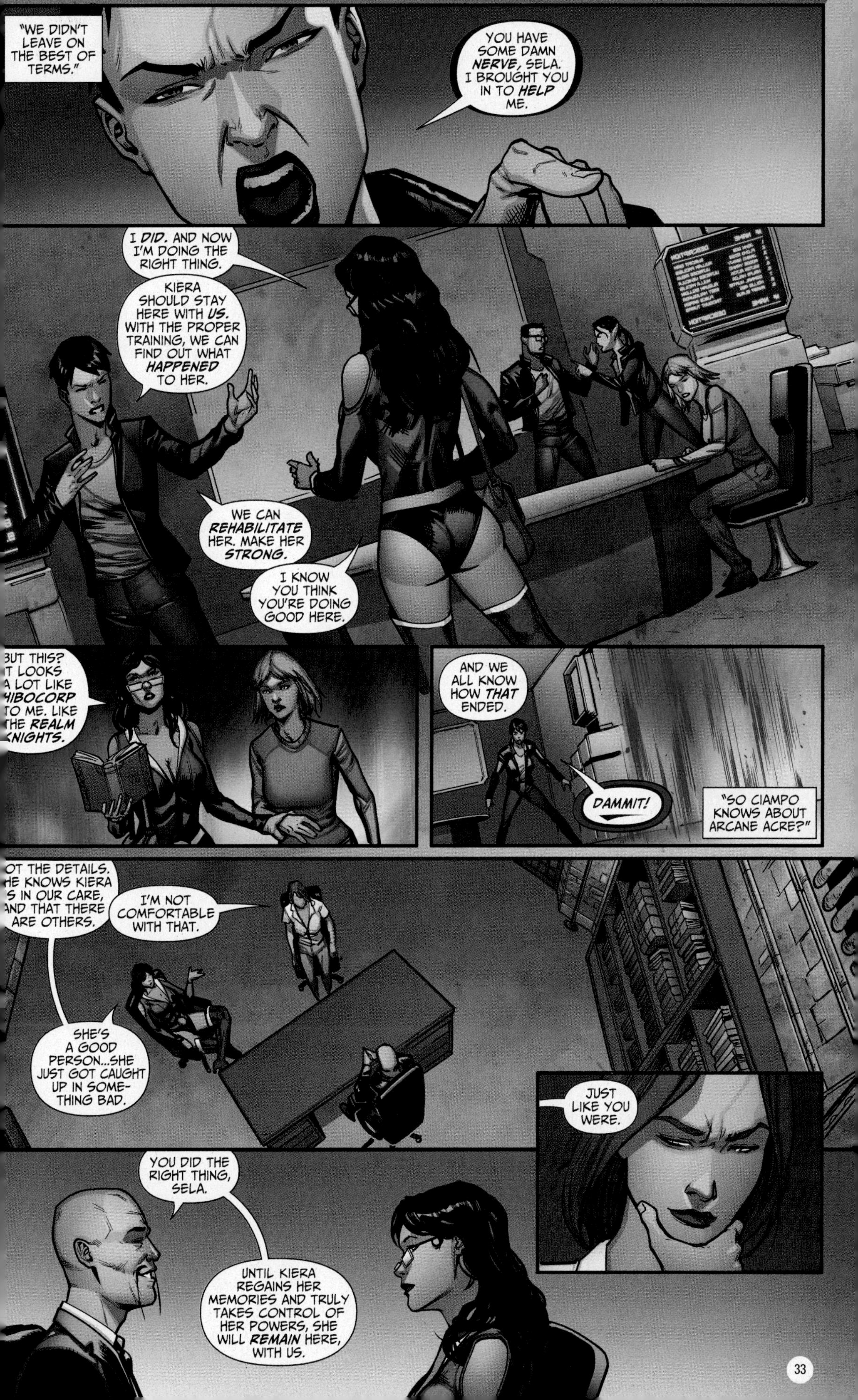
"WE DIDN'T LEAVE ON THE BEST OF TERMS."
YOU HAVE SOME DAMN NERVE, SELA. I BROUGHT YOU IN TO HELP ME.
I DID. AND NOW I'M DOING THE RIGHT THING.
KIERA SHOULD STAY HERE WITH US. WITH THE PROPER TRAINING, WE CAN FIND OUT WHAT HAPPENED TO HER.
WE CAN REHABILITATE HER. MAKE HER STRONG.
I KNOW YOU THINK YOU'RE DOING GOOD HERE.
BUT THIS? IT LOOKS A LOT LIKE HIBOCORP TO ME. LIKE THE REALM KNIGHTS.
AND WE ALL KNOW HOW THAT ENDED.
DAMMIT!
"SO CIAMPO KNOWS ABOUT ARCANE ACRE?"
NOT THE DETAILS. SHE KNOWS KIERA IS IN OUR CARE, AND THAT THERE ARE OTHERS.
I'M NOT COMFORTABLE WITH THAT.
SHE'S A GOOD PERSON...SHE JUST GOT CAUGHT UP IN SOMETHING BAD.
JUST LIKE YOU WERE.
YOU DID THE RIGHT THING, SELA.
UNTIL KIERA REGAINS HER MEMORIES AND TRULY TAKES CONTROL OF HER POWERS, SHE WILL REMAIN HERE, WITH US.

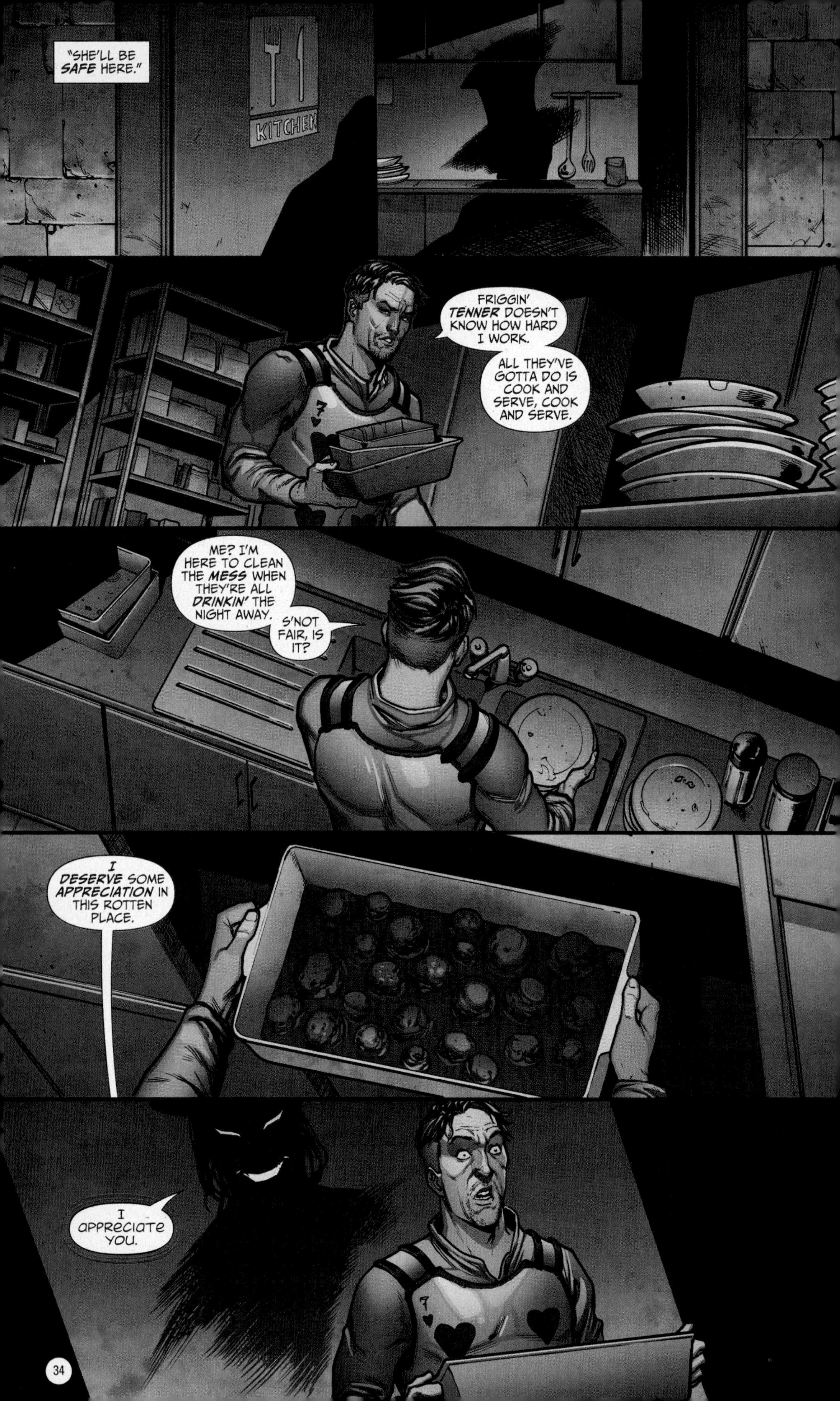

"SHE'LL BE SAFE HERE."
KITCHEN
FRIGGIN' TENNER DOESN'T KNOW HOW HARD I WORK.
ALL THEY'VE GOTTA DO IS COOK AND SERVE, COOK AND SERVE.
ME? I'M HERE TO CLEAN THE MESS WHEN THEY'RE ALL DRINKIN' THE NIGHT AWAY.
S'NOT FAIR, IS IT?
I DESERVE SOME APPRECIATION IN THIS ROTTEN PLACE.
I appreciate you.

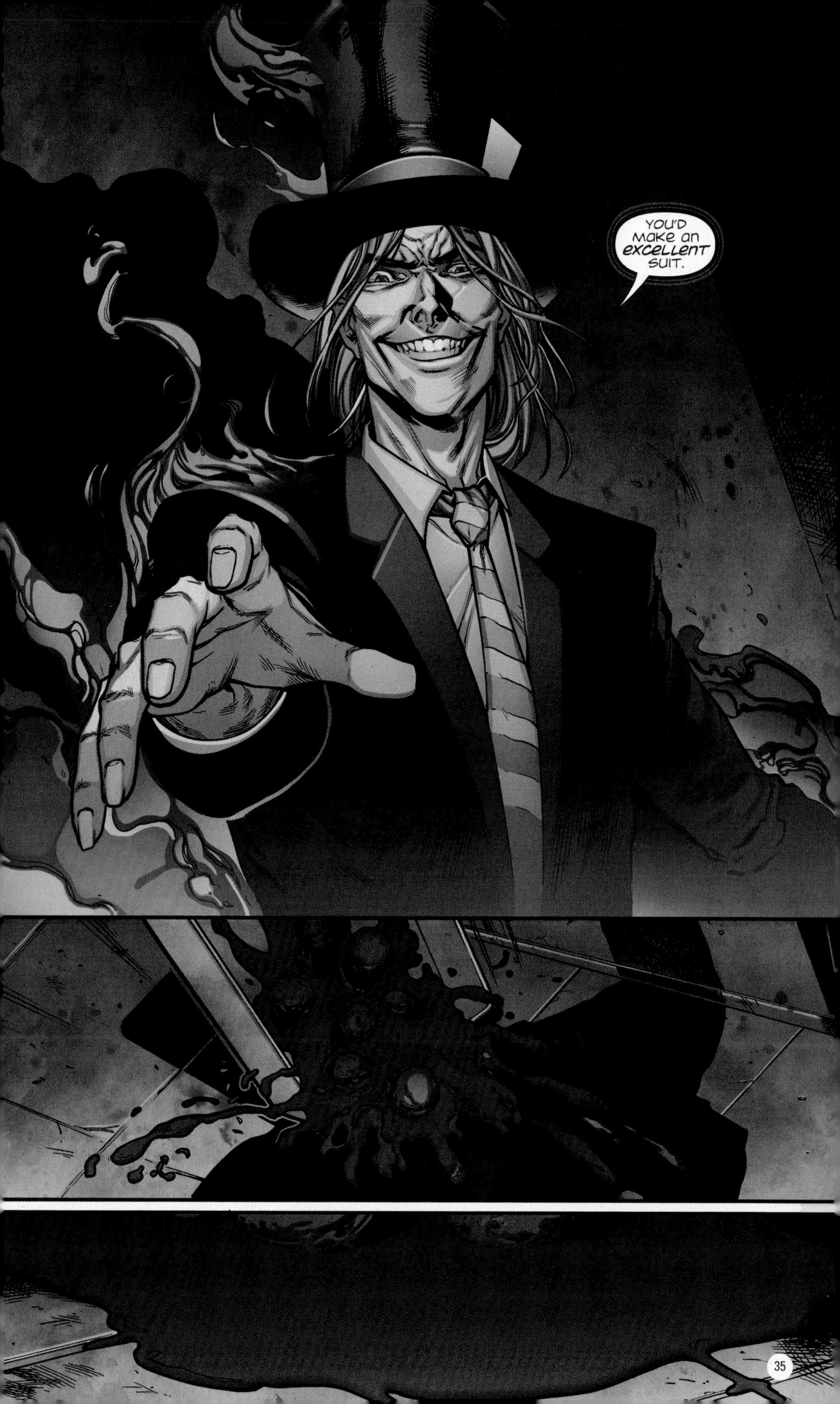
YOU'D MAKE AN EXCELLENT SUIT.

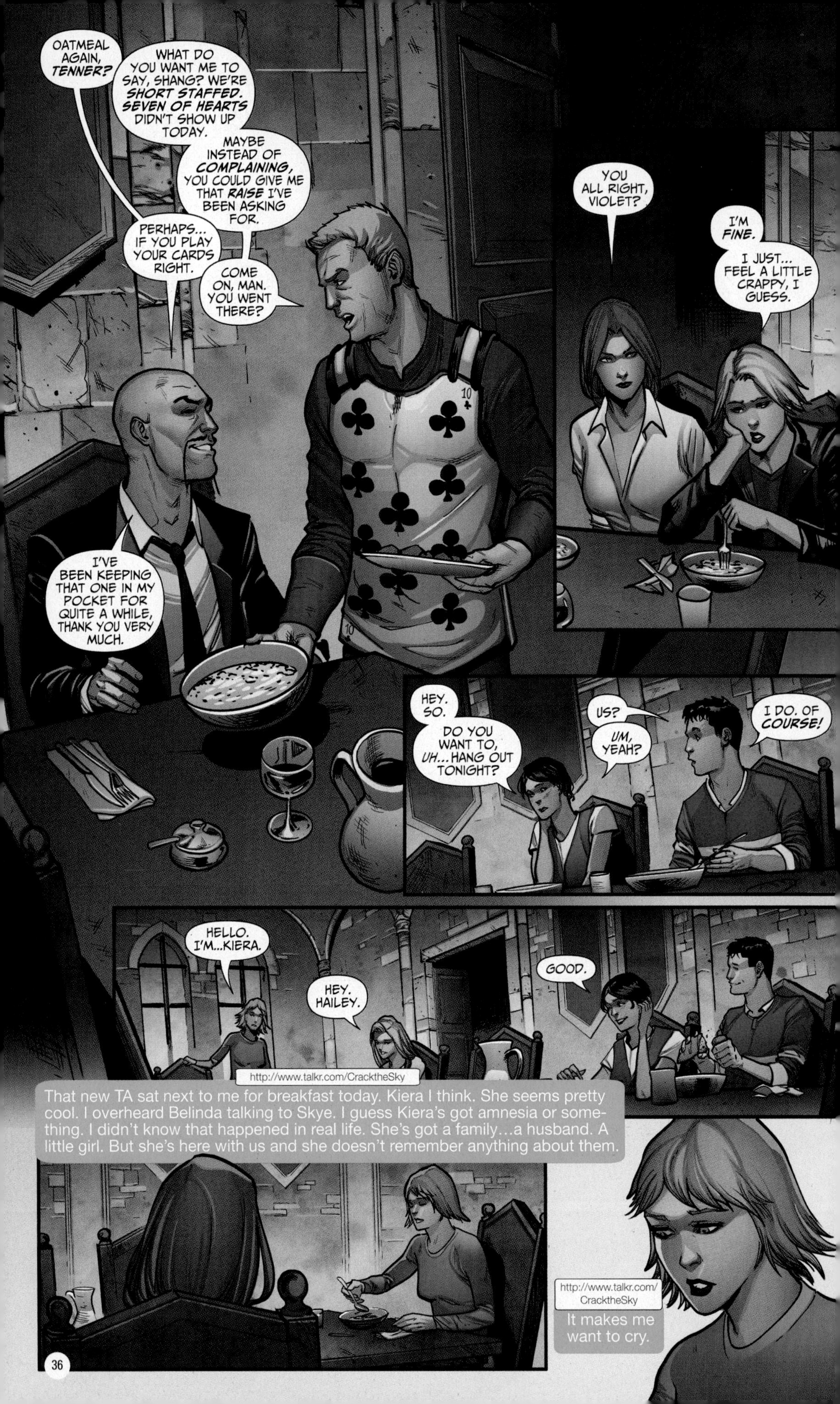

OATMEAL AGAIN, TENNER?
WHAT DO YOU WANT ME TO SAY, SHANG? WE'RE SHORT STAFFED. SEVEN OF HEARTS DIDN'T SHOW UP TODAY.
MAYBE INSTEAD OF COMPLAINING, YOU COULD GIVE ME THAT RAISE I'VE BEEN ASKING FOR.
PERHAPS... IF YOU PLAY YOUR CARDS RIGHT.
COME ON, MAN. YOU WENT THERE?
I'VE BEEN KEEPING THAT ONE IN MY POCKET FOR QUITE A WHILE, THANK YOU VERY MUCH.
YOU ALL RIGHT, VIOLET?
I'M FINE.
I JUST... FEEL A LITTLE CRAPPY, I GUESS.
HEY. SO.
DO YOU WANT TO, UH... HANG OUT TONIGHT?
US?
UM, YEAH?
I DO. OF COURSE!
HELLO. I'M...KIERA.
HEY. HAILEY.
GOOD.
http://www.talkr.com/CracktheSky
That new TA sat next to me for breakfast today. Kiera I think. She seems pretty cool. I overheard Belinda talking to Skye. I guess Kiera's got amnesia or something. I didn't know that happened in real life. She's got a family…a husband. A little girl. But she's here with us and she doesn't remember anything about them.
http://www.talkr.com/CracktheSky
It makes me want to cry.

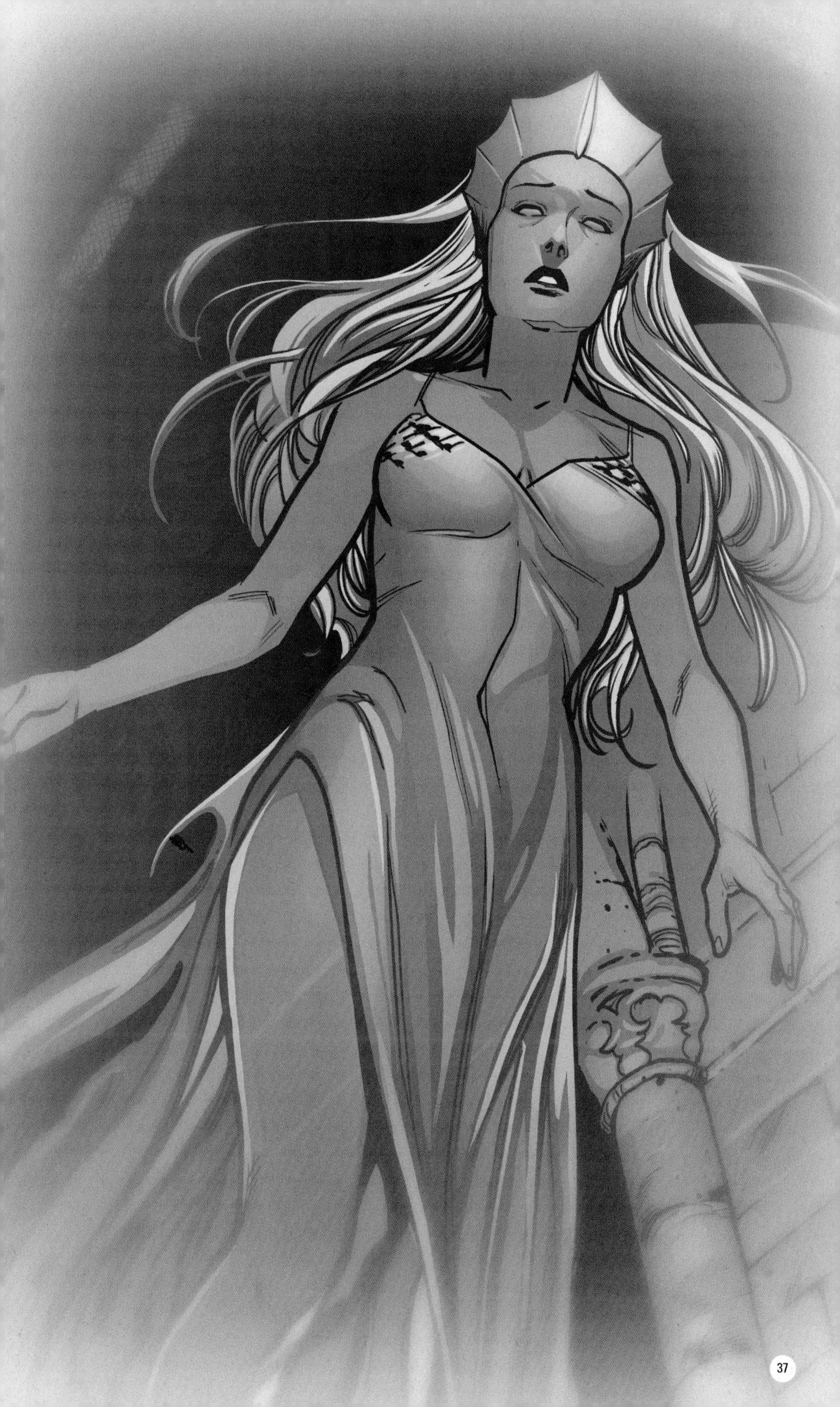

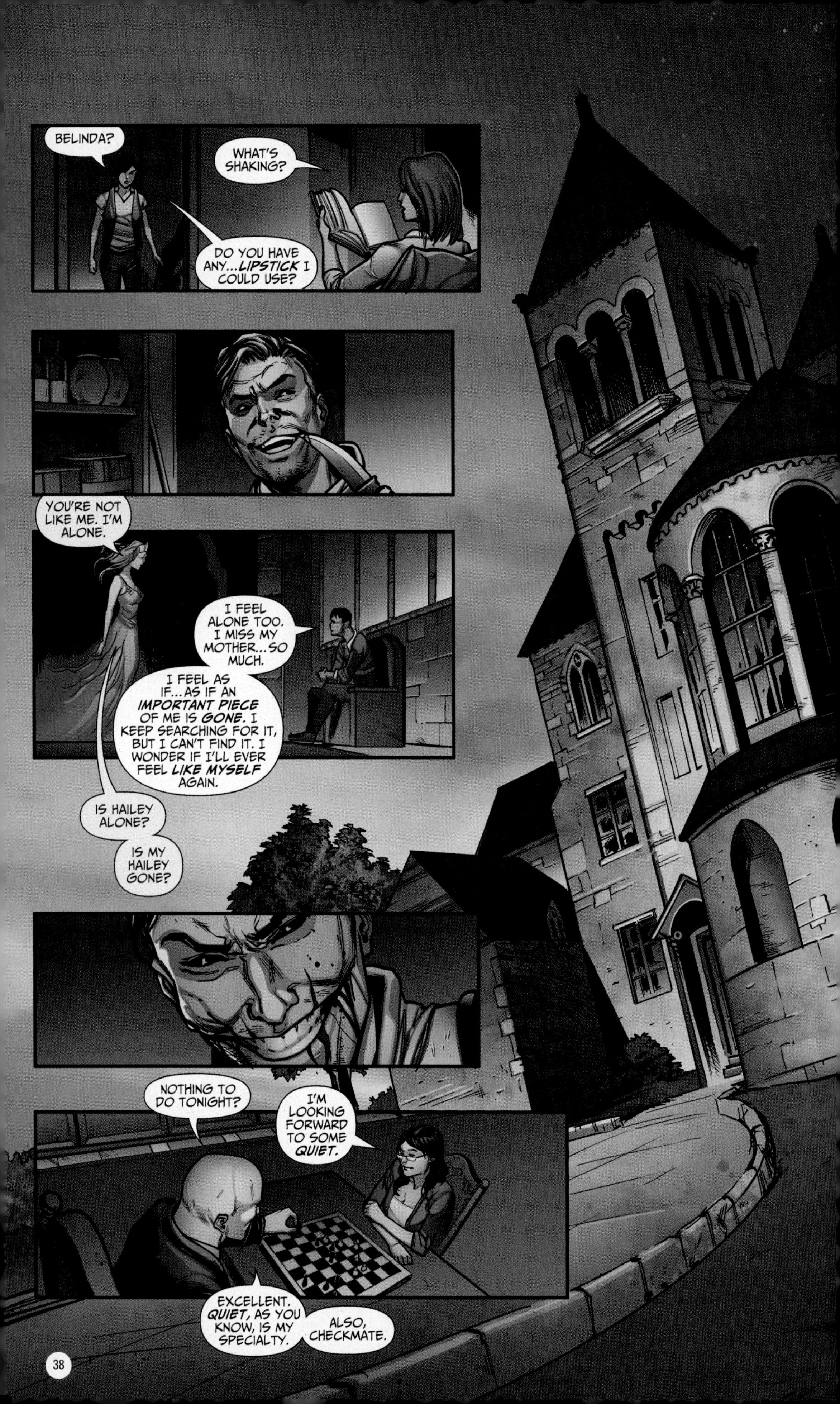
BELINDA?
WHAT'S SHAKING?
DO YOU HAVE ANY...LIPSTICK I COULD USE?
YOU'RE NOT LIKE ME. I'M ALONE.
I FEEL ALONE TOO. I MISS MY MOTHER...SO MUCH.
I FEEL AS IF...AS IF AN IMPORTANT PIECE OF ME IS GONE. I KEEP SEARCHING FOR IT, BUT I CAN'T FIND IT. I WONDER IF I'LL EVER FEEL LIKE MYSELF AGAIN.
IS HAILEY ALONE?
IS MY HAILEY GONE?
NOTHING TO DO TONIGHT?
I'M LOOKING FORWARD TO SOME QUIET.
EXCELLENT. QUIET, AS YOU KNOW, IS MY SPECIALTY.
ALSO, CHECKMATE.

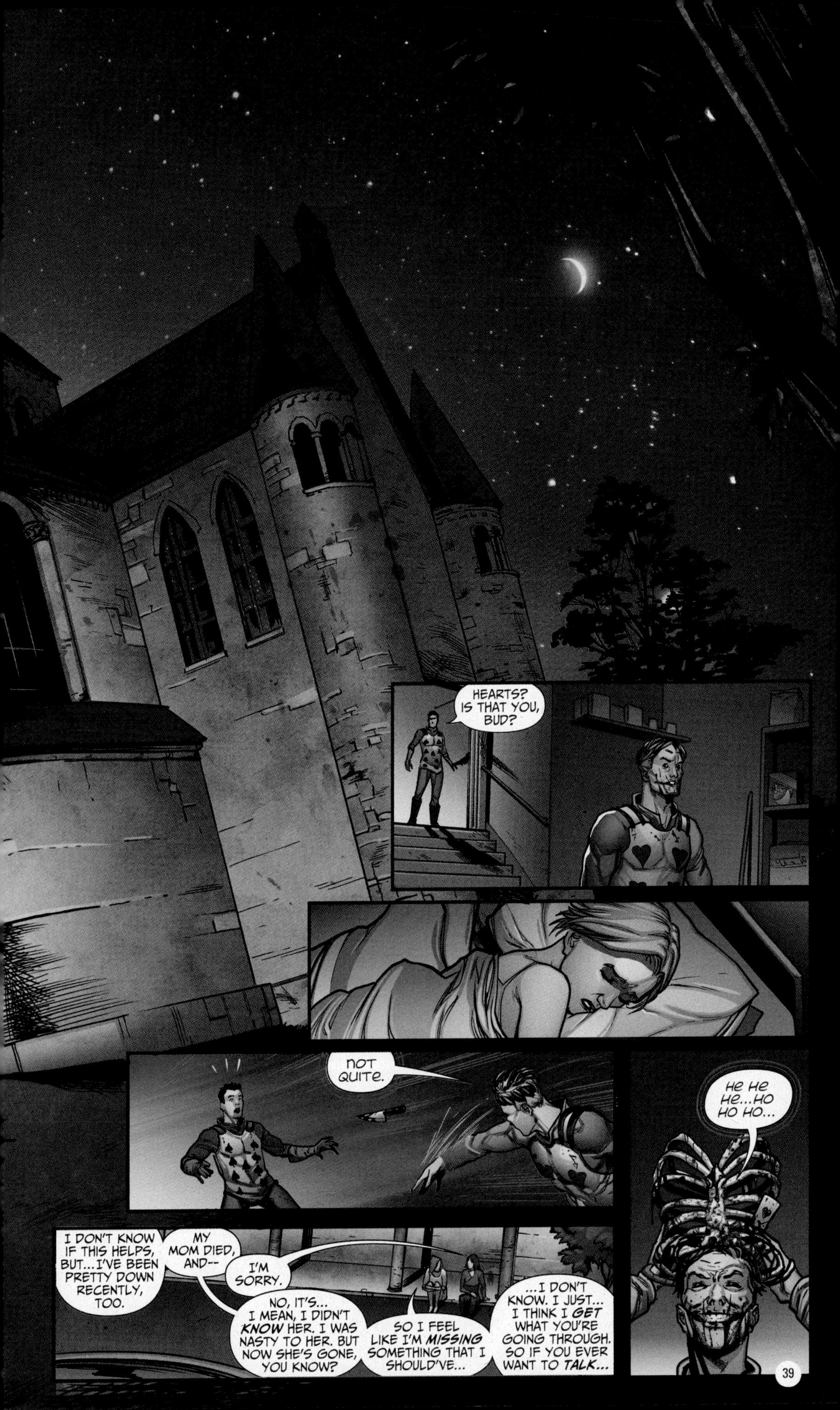

HEARTS? IS THAT YOU, BUD?
NOT QUITE.
HE HE HE...HO HO HO...
I DON'T KNOW IF THIS HELPS, BUT... I'VE BEEN PRETTY DOWN RECENTLY, TOO.
MY MOM DIED, AND--
I'M SORRY.
NO, IT'S... I MEAN, I DIDN'T KNOW HER. I WAS NASTY TO HER. BUT NOW SHE'S GONE, YOU KNOW?
SO I FEEL LIKE I'M MISSING SOMETHING THAT I SHOULD'VE...
...I DON'T KNOW. I JUST... I THINK I GET WHAT YOU'RE GOING THROUGH. SO IF YOU EVER WANT TO TALK...

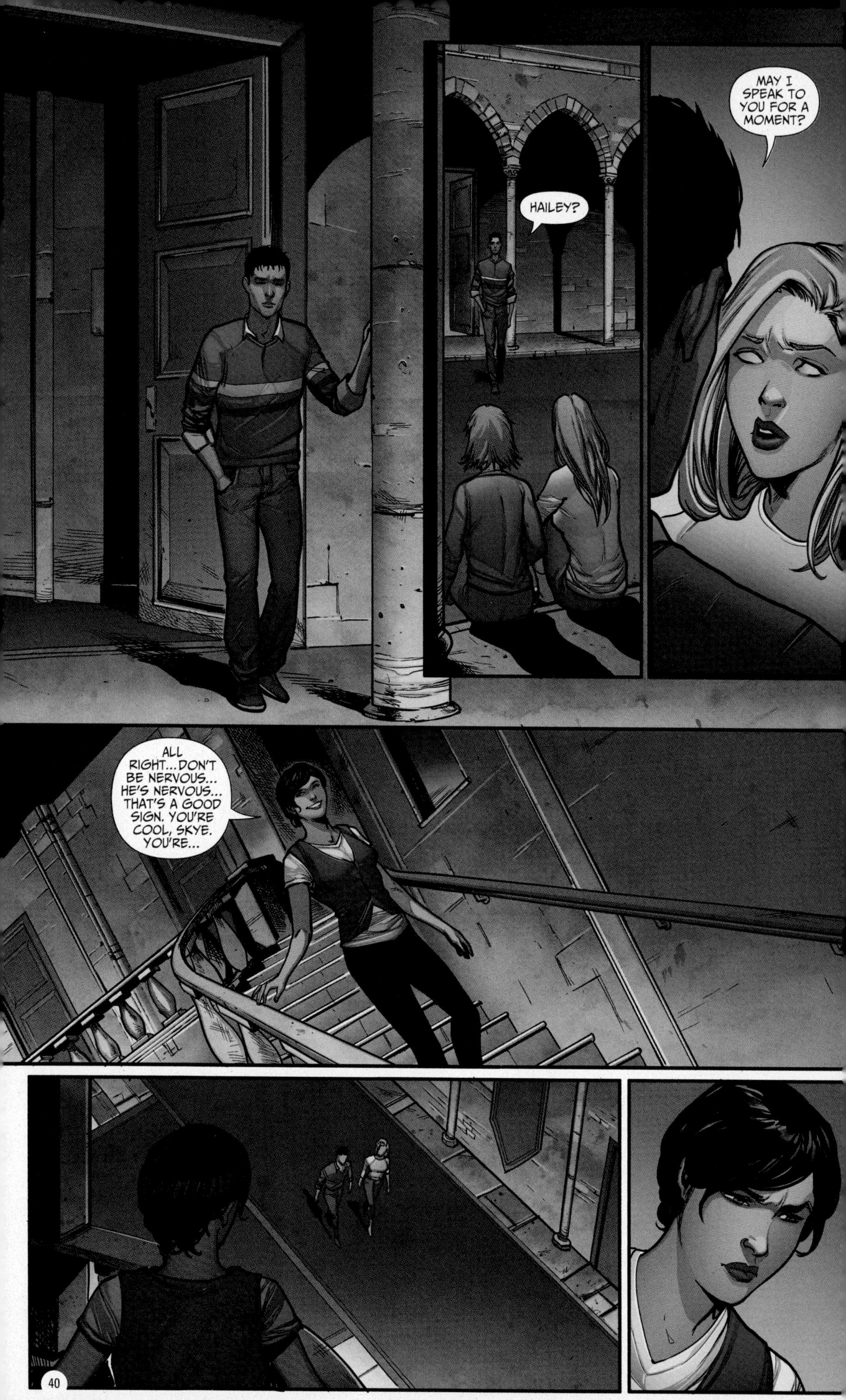
HAILEY?
MAY I SPEAK TO YOU FOR A MOMENT?
ALL RIGHT...DON'T BE NERVOUS... HE'S NERVOUS... THAT'S A GOOD SIGN. YOU'RE COOL, SKYE. YOU'RE...

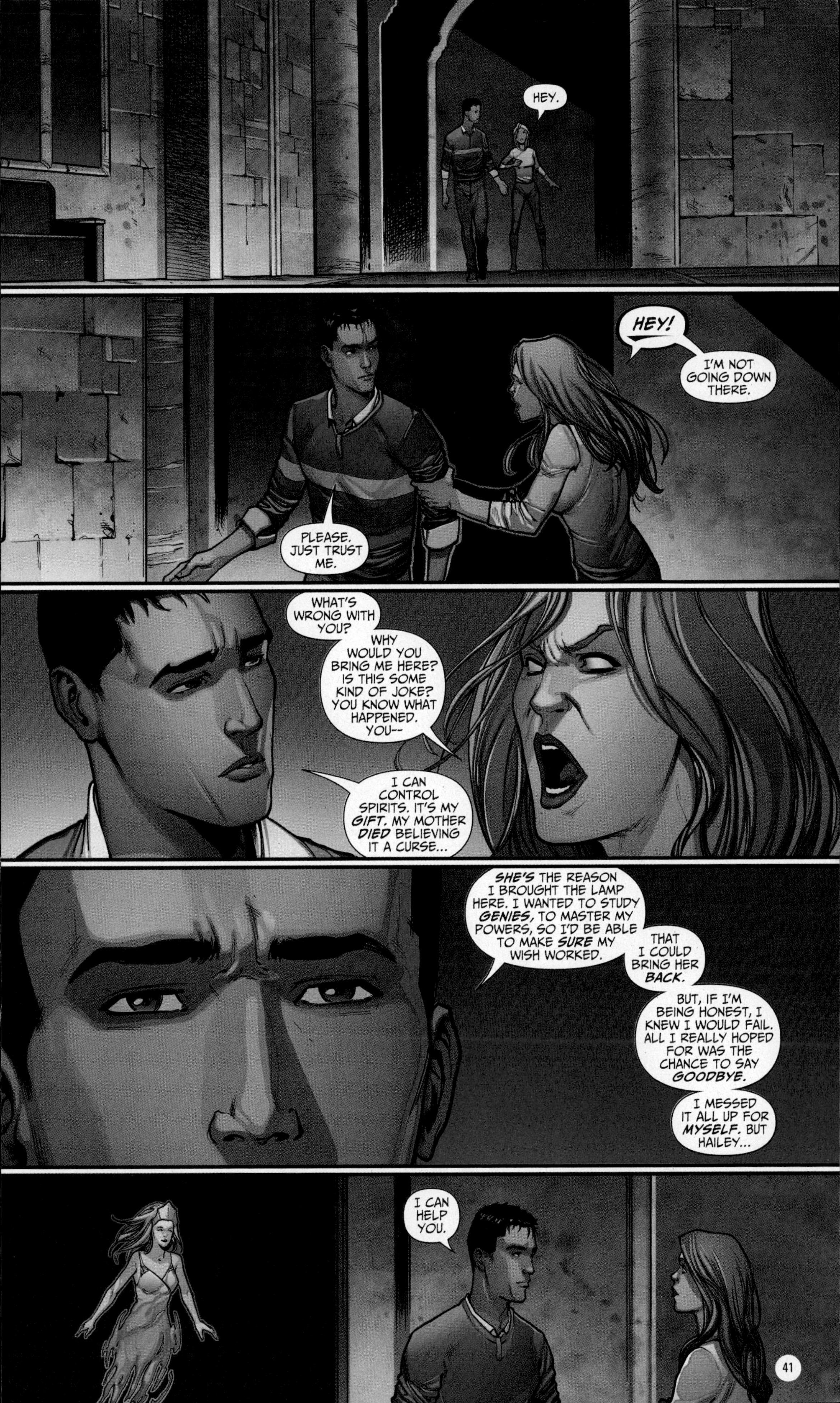
HEY.
HEY!
I'M NOT GOING DOWN THERE.
PLEASE. JUST TRUST ME.
WHAT'S WRONG WITH YOU?
WHY WOULD YOU BRING ME HERE? IS THIS SOME KIND OF JOKE? YOU KNOW WHAT HAPPENED. YOU--
I CAN CONTROL SPIRITS. IT'S MY GIFT. MY MOTHER DIED BELIEVING IT A CURSE...
SHE'S THE REASON I BROUGHT THE LAMP HERE. I WANTED TO STUDY GENIES, TO MASTER MY POWERS, SO I'D BE ABLE TO MAKE SURE MY WISH WORKED.
THAT I COULD BRING HER BACK.
BUT, IF I'M BEING HONEST, I KNEW I WOULD FAIL. ALL I REALLY HOPED FOR WAS THE CHANCE TO SAY GOODBYE.
I MESSED IT ALL UP FOR MYSELF. BUT HAILEY...
I CAN HELP YOU.

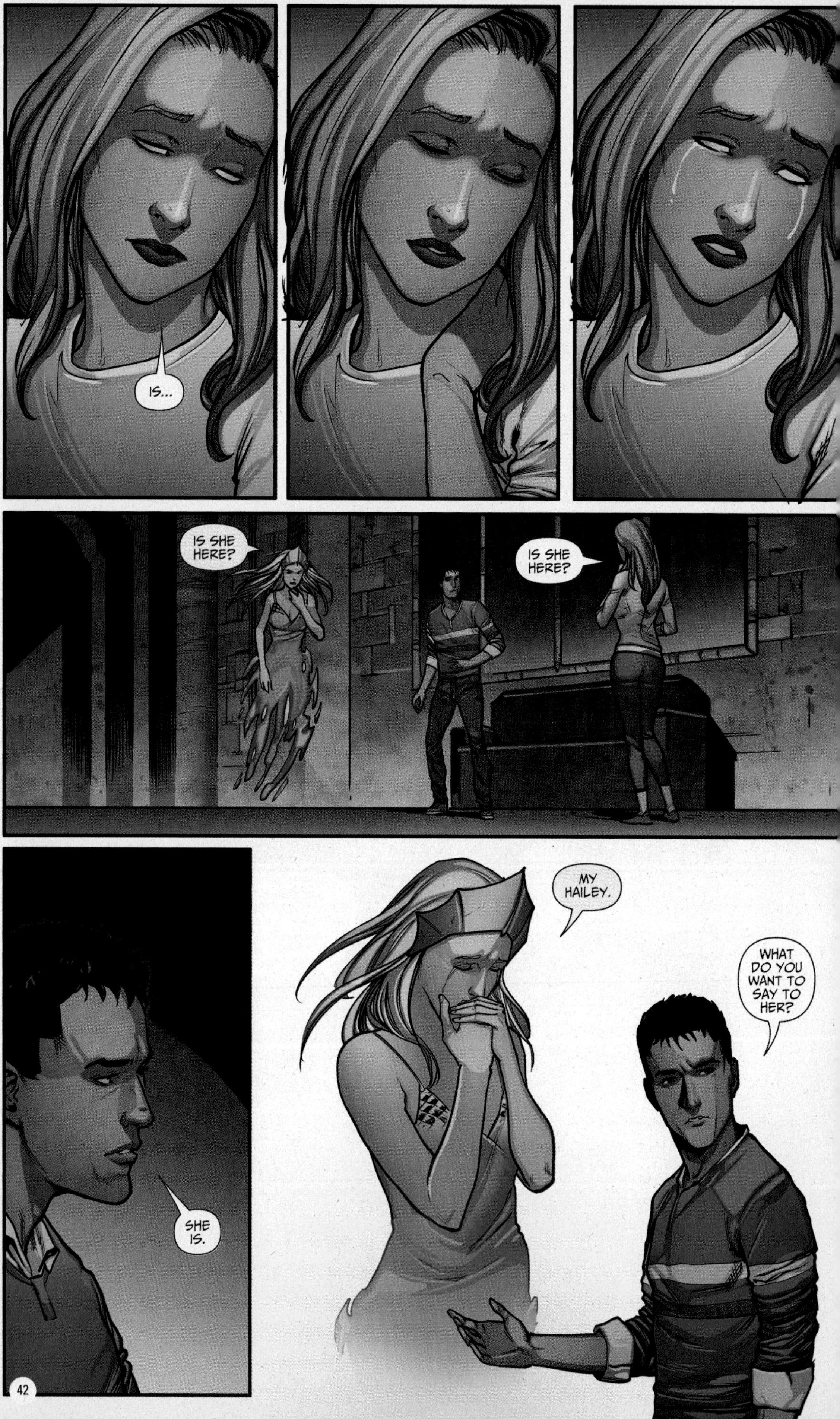
IS...
IS SHE HERE?
IS SHE HERE?
SHE IS.
MY HAILEY.
WHAT DO YOU WANT TO SAY TO HER?

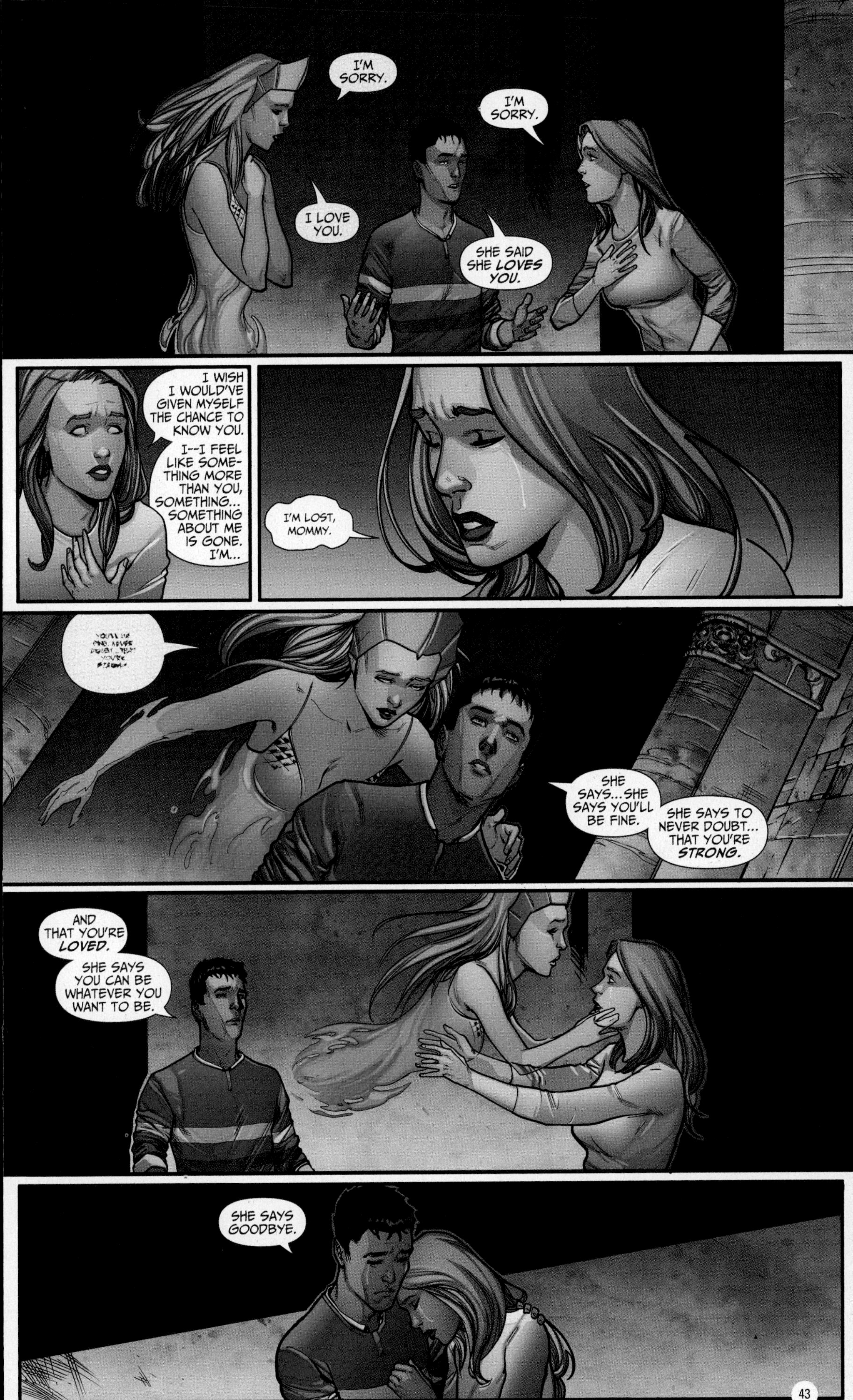
I'M SORRY.
I'M SORRY.
I LOVE YOU.
SHE SAID SHE **LOVES** YOU.
I WISH I WOULD'VE GIVEN MYSELF THE CHANCE TO KNOW YOU.
I--I FEEL LIKE SOMETHING MORE THAN YOU, SOMETHING... SOMETHING ABOUT ME IS GONE. I'M...
I'M LOST, MOMMY.
SHE SAYS...SHE SAYS YOU'LL BE FINE.
SHE SAYS TO NEVER DOUBT... THAT YOU'RE **STRONG.**
AND THAT YOU'RE **LOVED.**
SHE SAYS YOU CAN BE WHATEVER YOU WANT TO BE.
SHE SAYS GOODBYE.

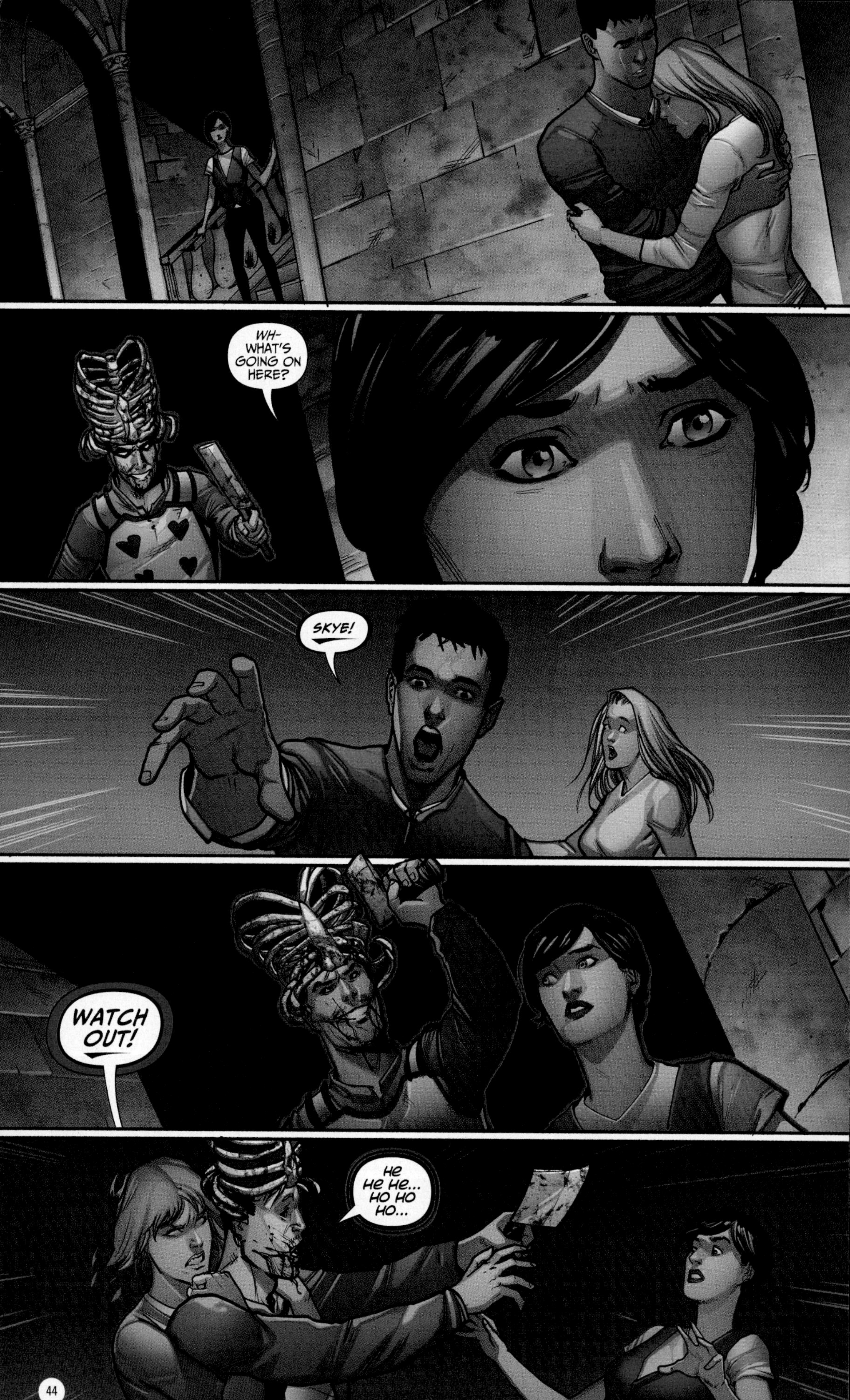
WH- WHAT'S GOING ON HERE?
SKYE!
WATCH OUT!
HE HE HE... HO HO HO...

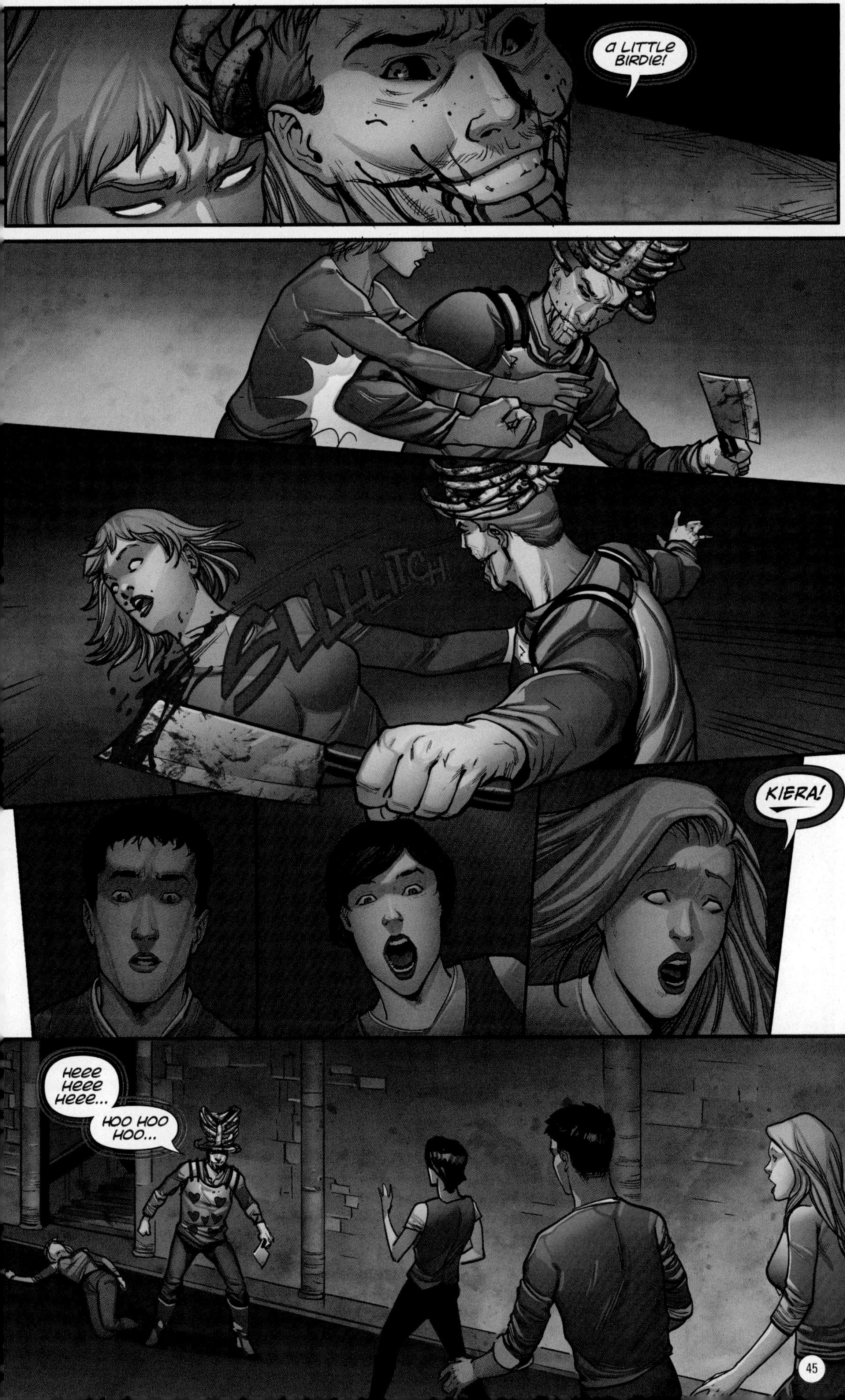

A LITTLE BIRDIE!
SHLLLITCH!
KIERA!
HEEE HEEE HEEE...
HOO HOO HOO...

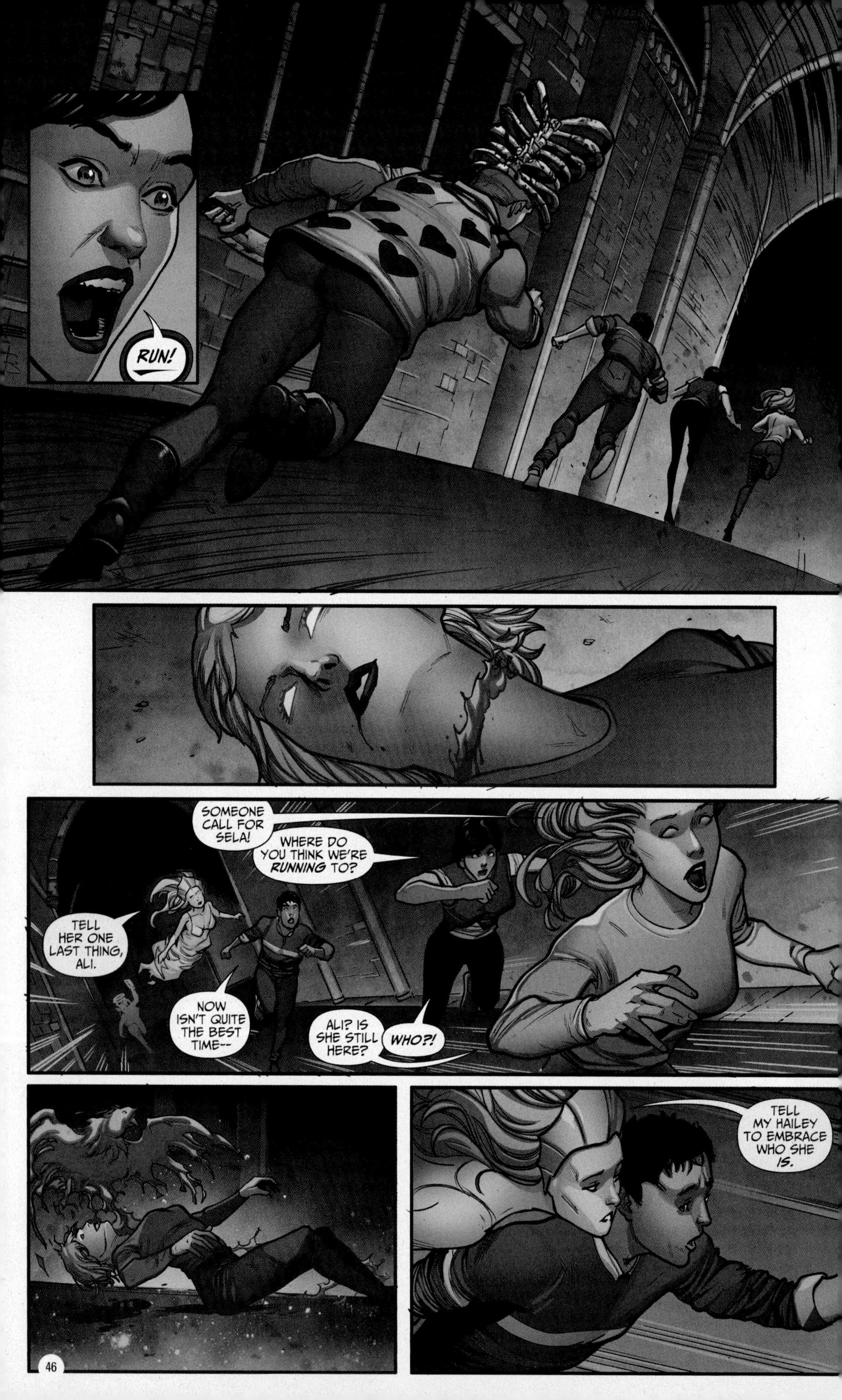

RUN!
SOMEONE CALL FOR SELA!
WHERE DO YOU THINK WE'RE *RUNNING* TO?
TELL HER ONE LAST THING, ALI.
NOW ISN'T QUITE THE BEST TIME--
ALI? IS SHE STILL HERE?
WHO?!
TELL MY HAILEY TO EMBRACE WHO SHE *IS*.

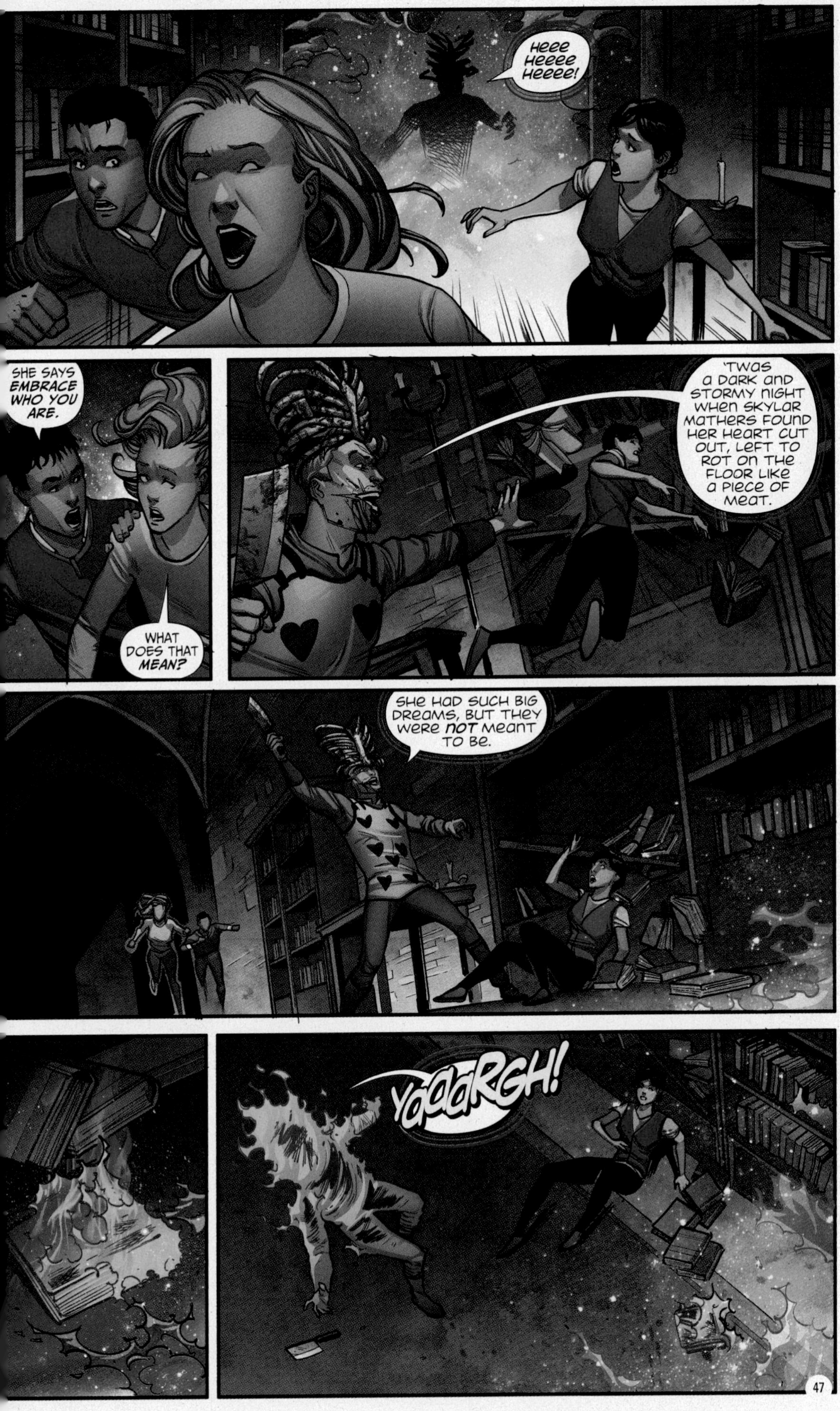

Heee Heeee Heeee!
SHE SAYS EMBRACE WHO YOU ARE.
WHAT DOES THAT MEAN?
'TWAS a DARK and STORMY NIGHT WHEN SKYLAR MATHERS FOUND HER HEART CUT OUT, LEFT TO ROT ON THE FLOOR LIKE a PIECE OF MEAT.
SHE HAD SUCH BIG DREAMS, BUT THEY WERE NOT MEANT TO BE.
YaaaRGH!

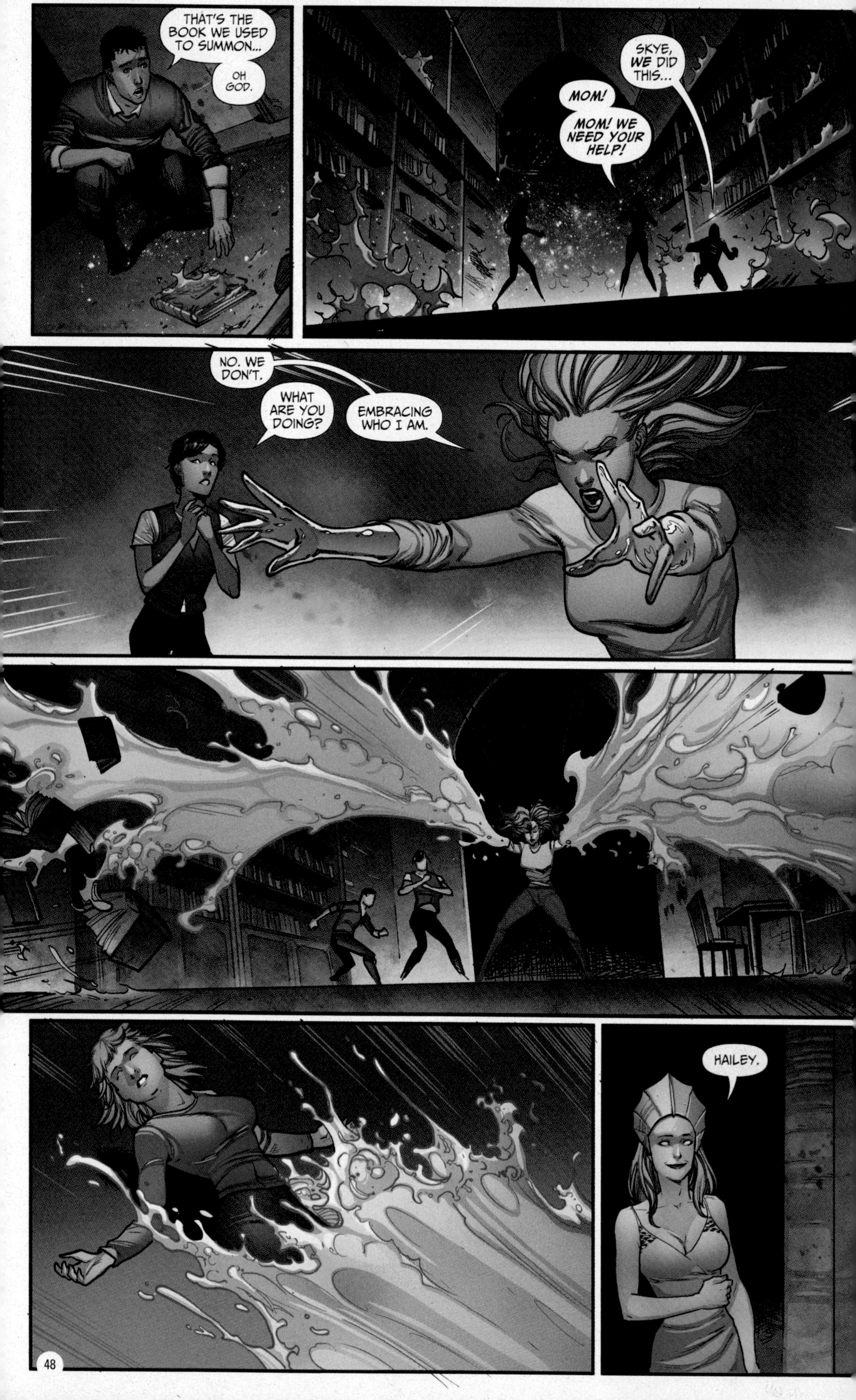
THAT'S THE BOOK WE USED TO SUMMON...
OH GOD.
SKYE, WE DID THIS...
MOM!
MOM! WE NEED YOUR HELP!
NO. WE DON'T.
WHAT ARE YOU DOING?
EMBRACING WHO I AM.
HAILEY.

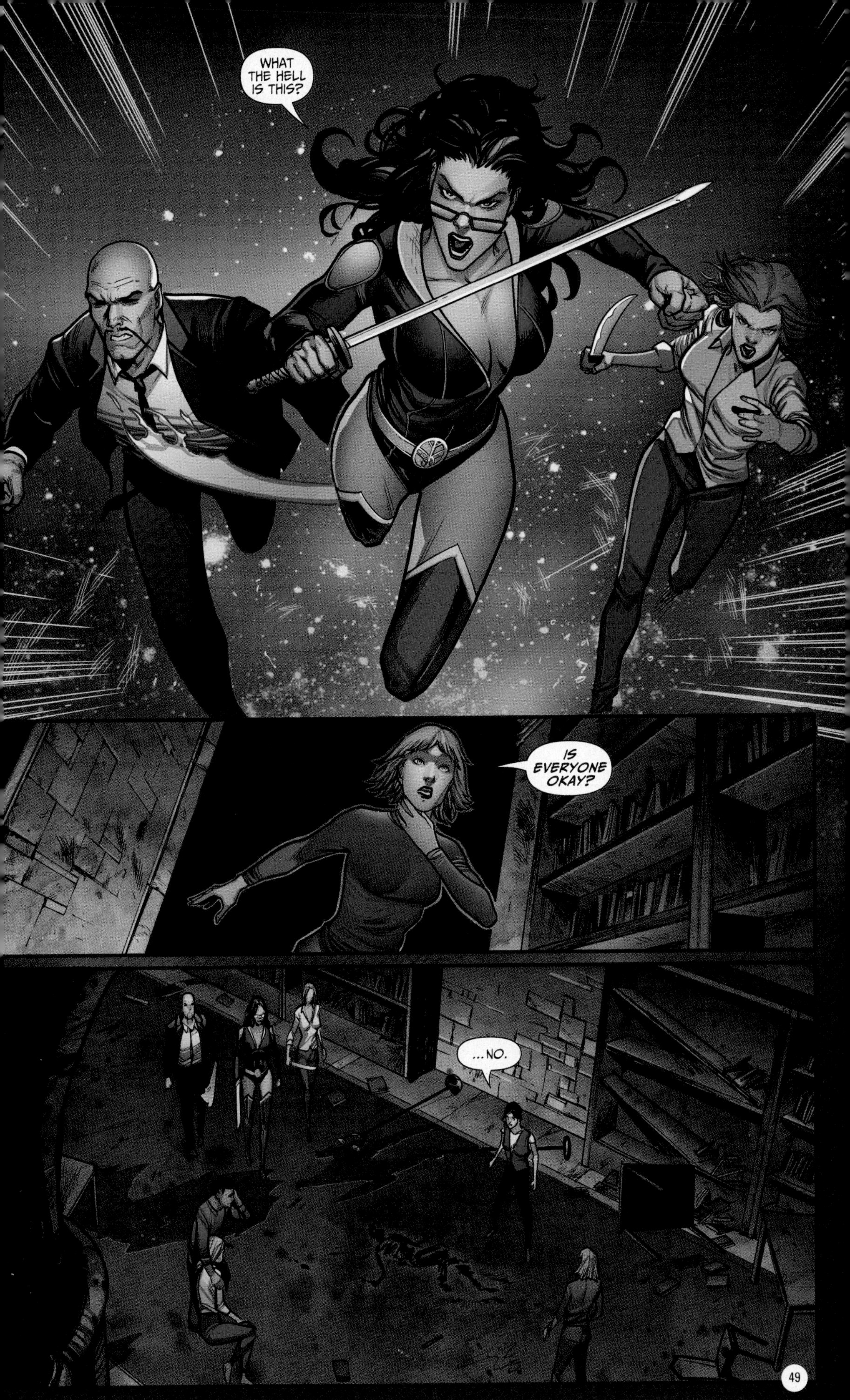
WHAT THE HELL IS THIS?
IS EVERYONE OKAY?
...NO.

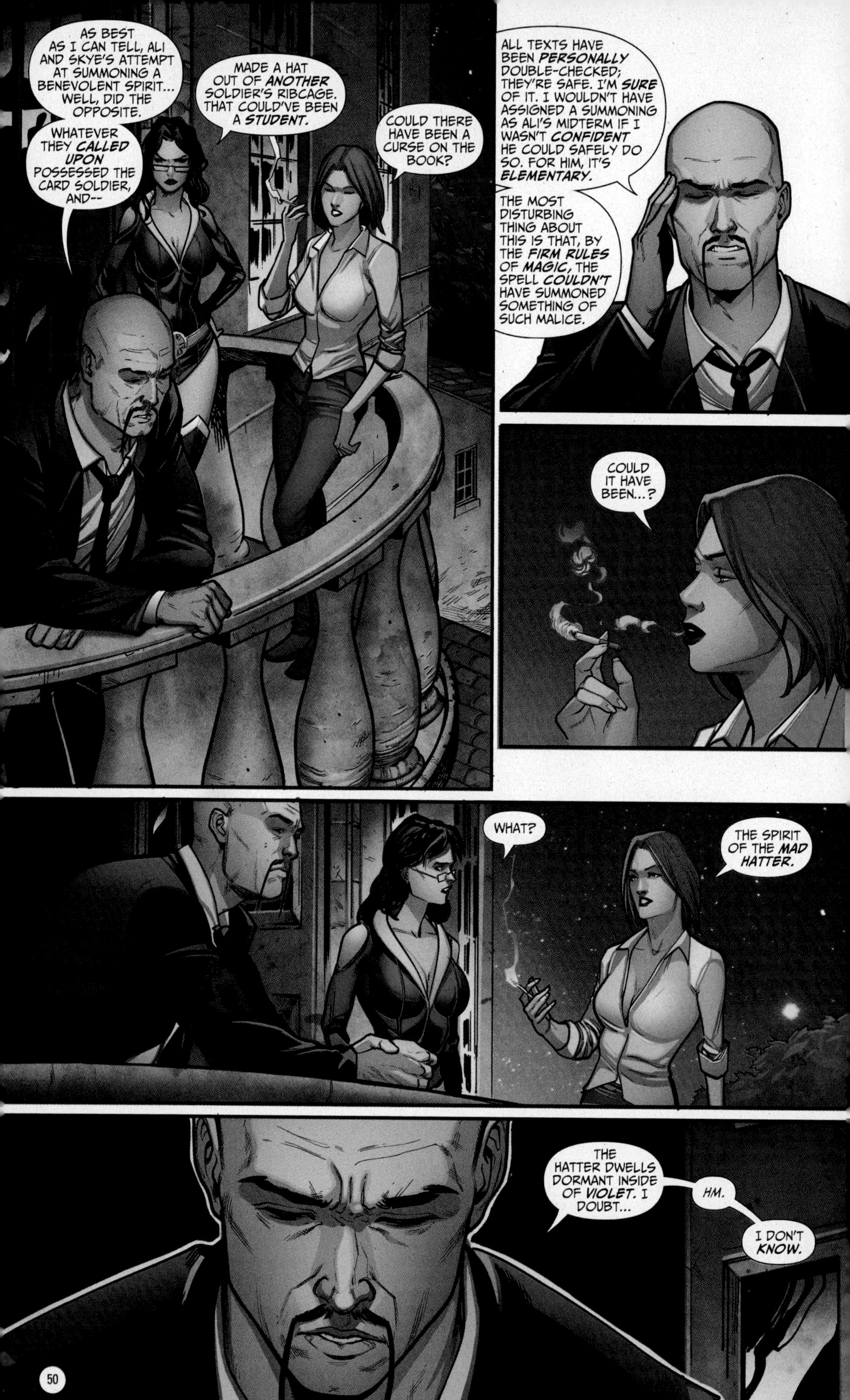
AS BEST AS I CAN TELL, ALI AND SKYE'S ATTEMPT AT SUMMONING A BENEVOLENT SPIRIT... WELL, DID THE OPPOSITE.
WHATEVER THEY CALLED UPON POSSESSED THE CARD SOLDIER, AND--
MADE A HAT OUT OF ANOTHER SOLDIER'S RIBCAGE. THAT COULD'VE BEEN A STUDENT.
COULD THERE HAVE BEEN A CURSE ON THE BOOK?
ALL TEXTS HAVE BEEN PERSONALLY DOUBLE-CHECKED; THEY'RE SAFE. I'M SURE OF IT. I WOULDN'T HAVE ASSIGNED A SUMMONING AS ALI'S MIDTERM IF I WASN'T CONFIDENT HE COULD SAFELY DO SO. FOR HIM, IT'S ELEMENTARY.
THE MOST DISTURBING THING ABOUT THIS IS THAT, BY THE FIRM RULES OF MAGIC, THE SPELL COULDN'T HAVE SUMMONED SOMETHING OF SUCH MALICE.
COULD IT HAVE BEEN...?
WHAT?
THE SPIRIT OF THE MAD HATTER.
THE HATTER DWELLS DORMANT INSIDE OF VIOLET. I DOUBT...
HM.
I DON'T KNOW.

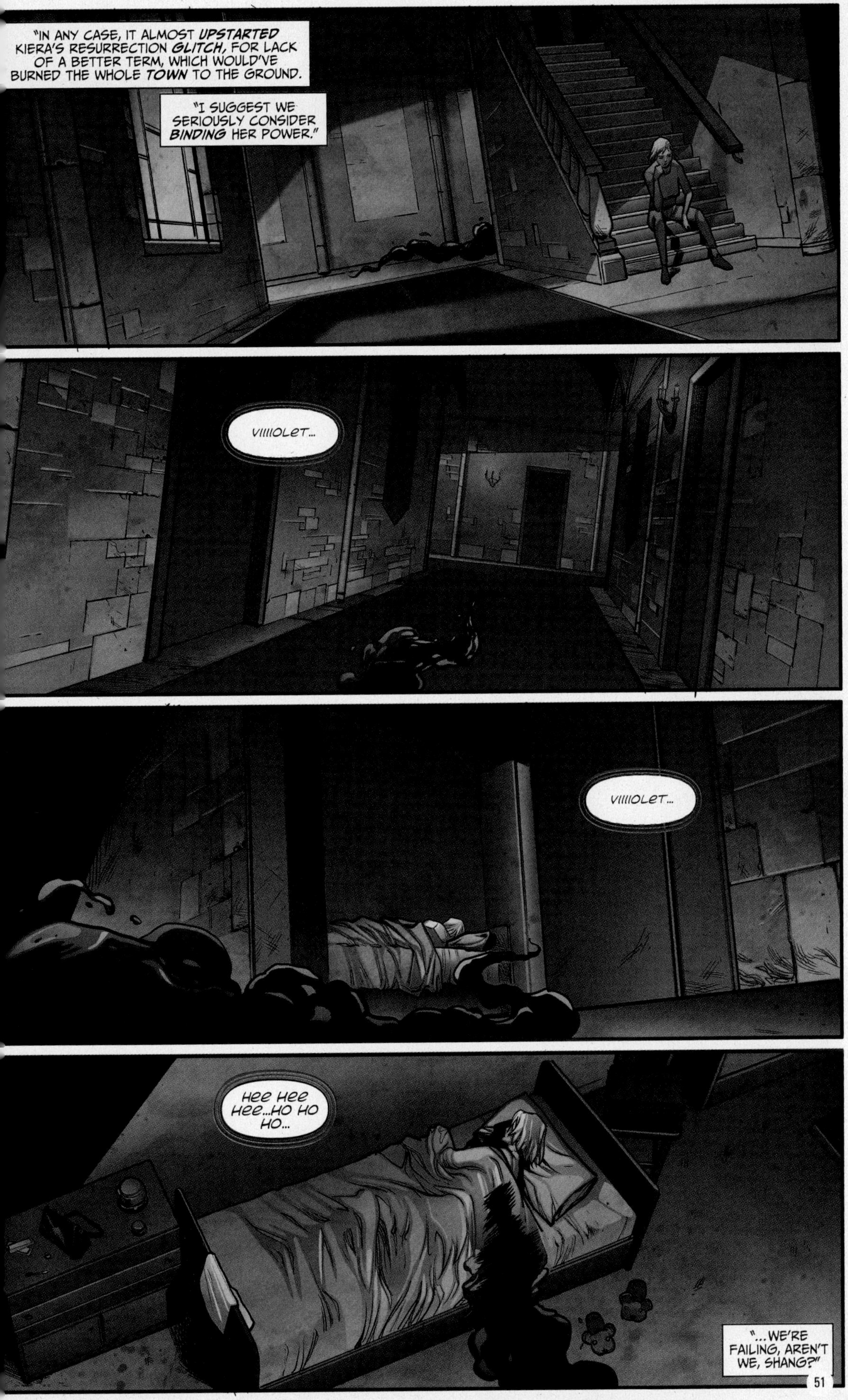
"IN ANY CASE, IT ALMOST UPSTARTED KIERA'S RESURRECTION GLITCH, FOR LACK OF A BETTER TERM, WHICH WOULD'VE BURNED THE WHOLE TOWN TO THE GROUND.
"I SUGGEST WE SERIOUSLY CONSIDER BINDING HER POWER."
VIIIIOLET...
VIIIIOLET...
HEE HEE HEE...HO HO HO...
"...WE'RE FAILING, AREN'T WE, SHANG?"

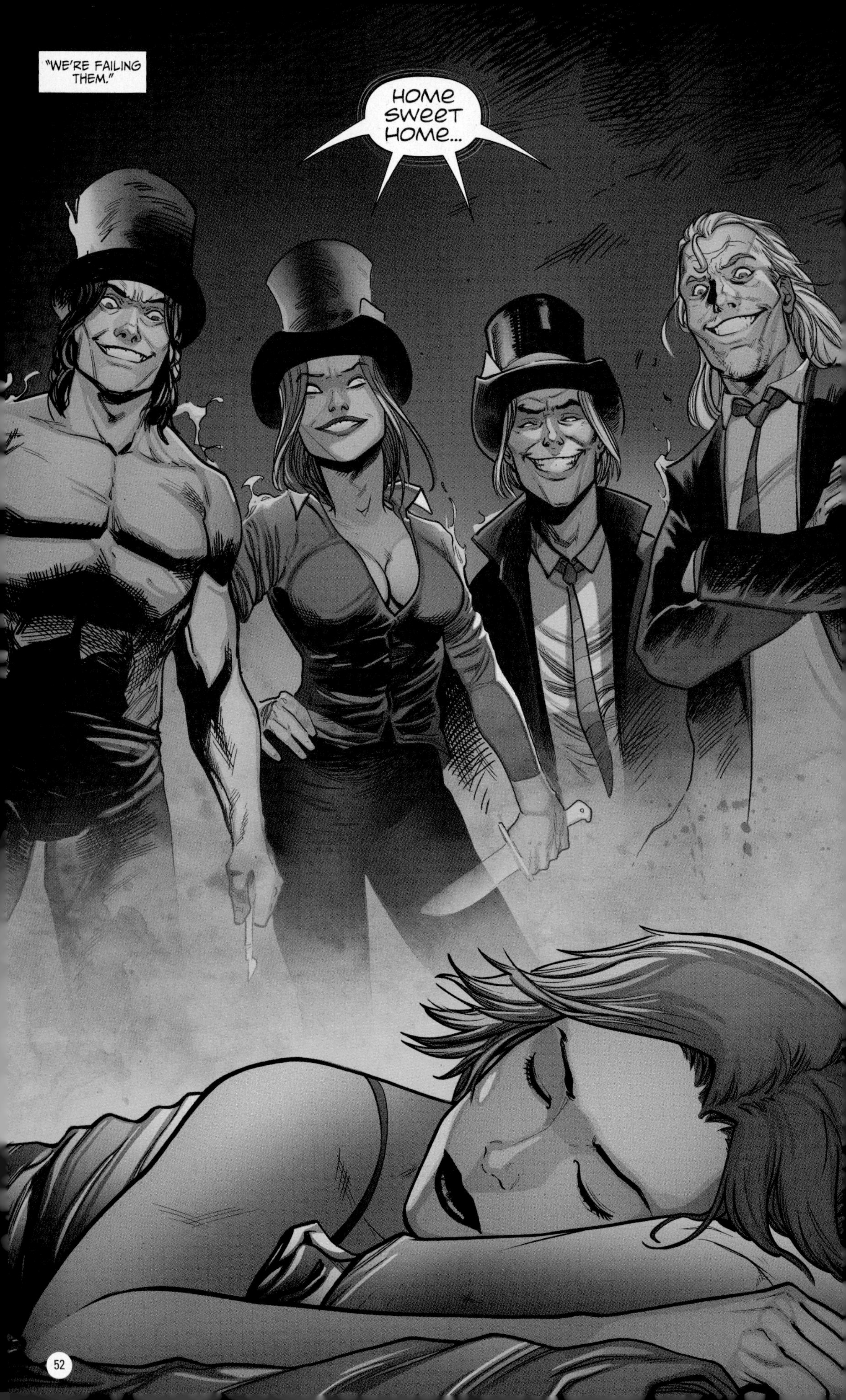
"WE'RE FAILING THEM."
HOME SWEET HOME...

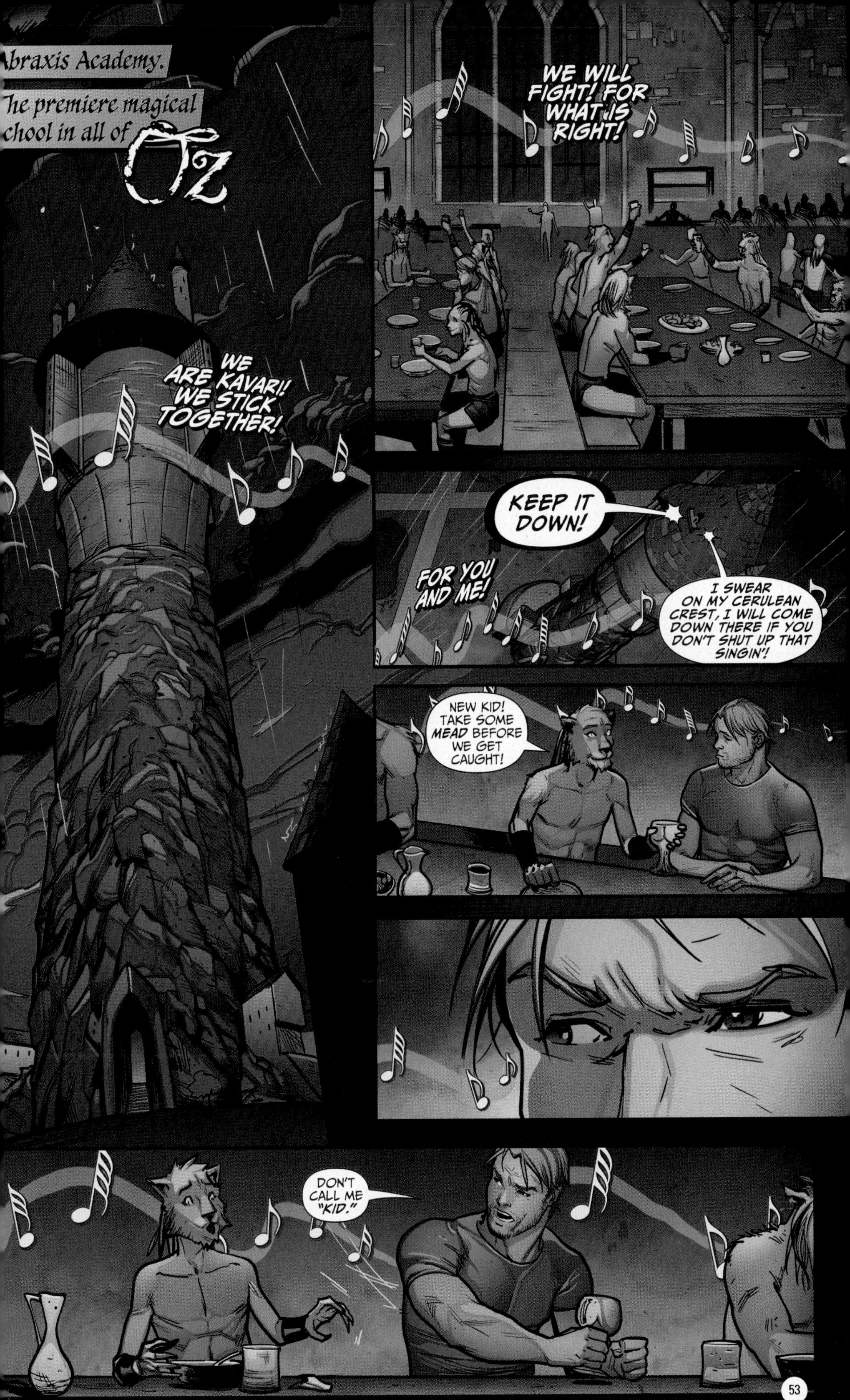

Abraxis Academy.
The premiere magical school in all of Oz
WE ARE KAVARI! WE STICK TOGETHER!
WE WILL FIGHT! FOR WHAT IS RIGHT!
FOR YOU AND ME!
KEEP IT DOWN!
I SWEAR ON MY CERULEAN CREST, I WILL COME DOWN THERE IF YOU DON'T SHUT UP THAT SINGIN'!
NEW KID! TAKE SOME MEAD BEFORE WE GET CAUGHT!
DON'T CALL ME "KID."

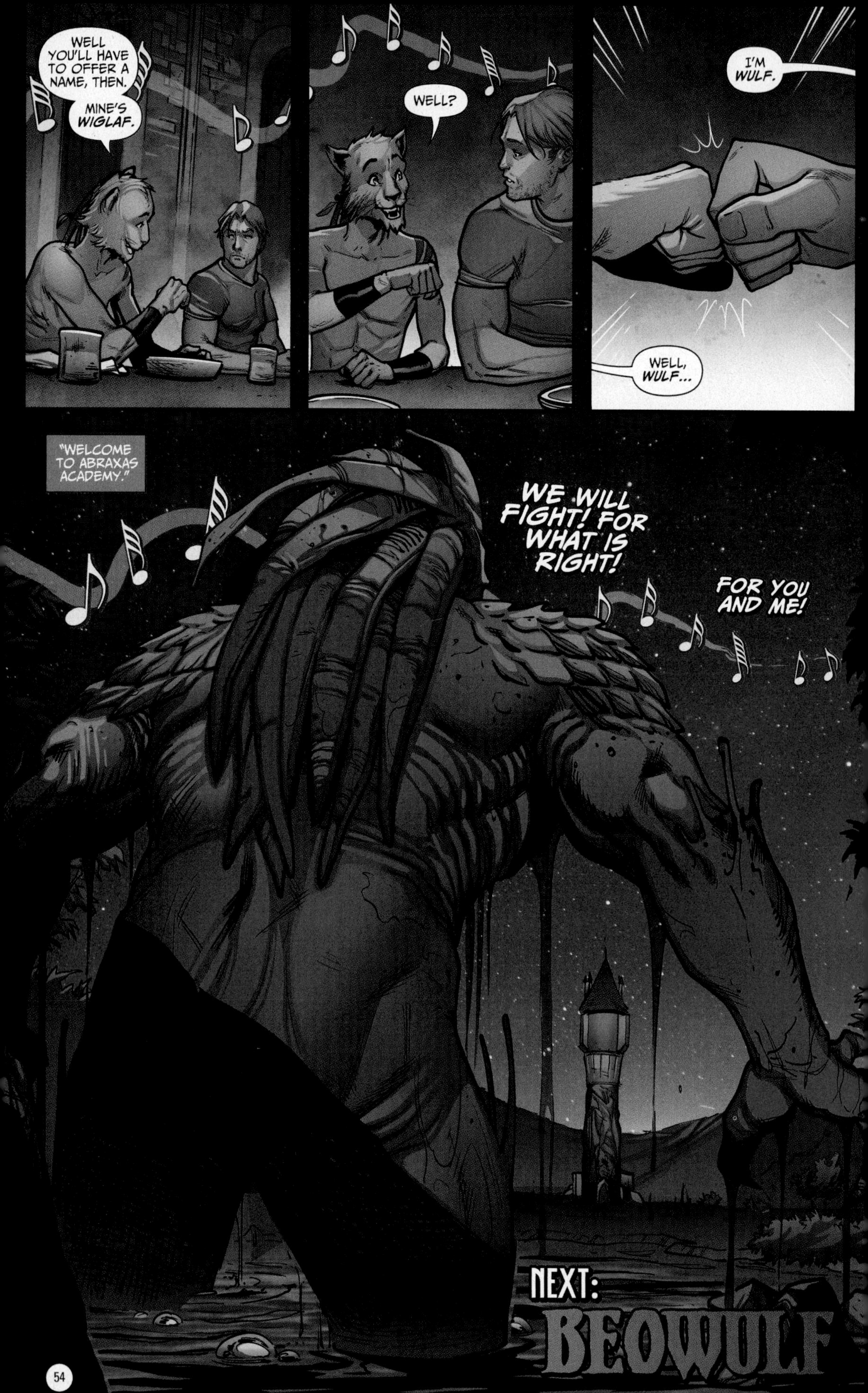
WELL YOU'LL HAVE TO OFFER A NAME, THEN.
MINE'S WIGLAF.
WELL?
I'M WULF.
WELL, WULF...
"WELCOME TO ABRAXAS ACADEMY."
WE WILL FIGHT! FOR WHAT IS RIGHT!
FOR YOU AND ME!
NEXT: BEOWULF

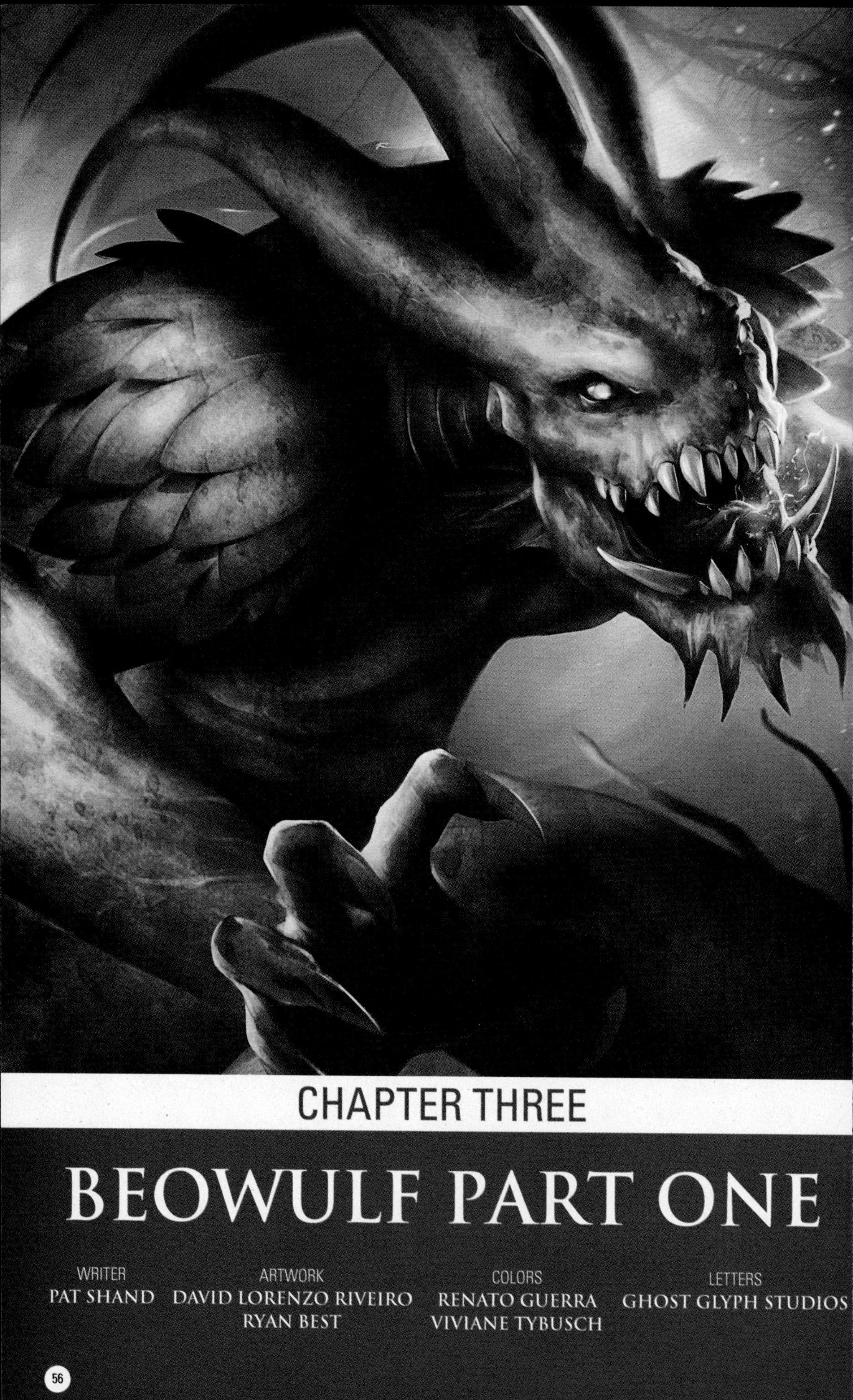

CHAPTER THREE

BEOWULF PART ONE

WRITER
PAT SHAND

ARTWORK
DAVID LORENZO RIVEIRO
RYAN BEST

COLORS
RENATO GUERRA
VIVIANE TYBUSCH

LETTERS
GHOST GLYPH STUDIOS

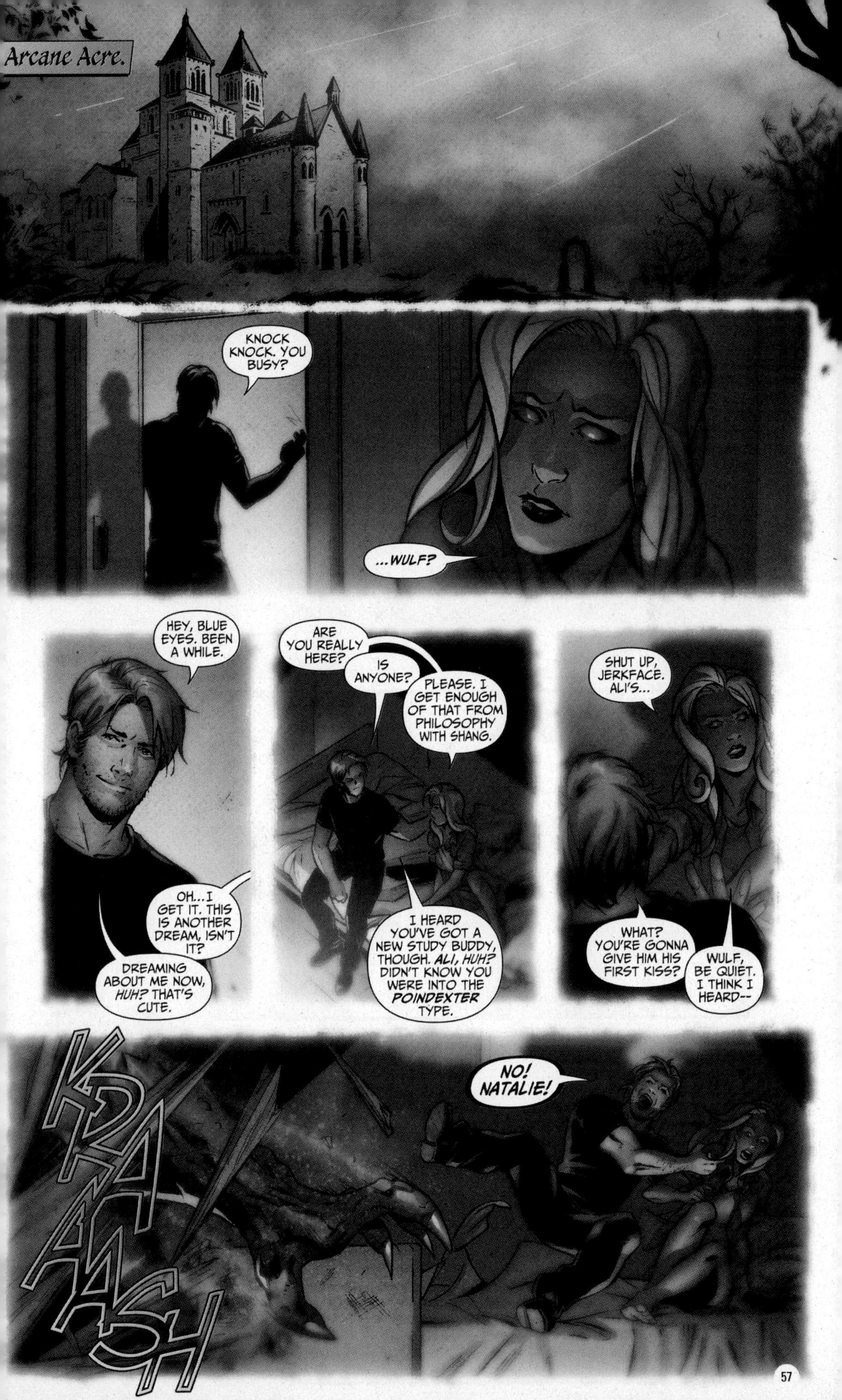

Arcane Acre.
KNOCK KNOCK. YOU BUSY?
...WULF?
HEY, BLUE EYES. BEEN A WHILE.
OH...I GET IT. THIS IS ANOTHER DREAM, ISN'T IT?
DREAMING ABOUT ME NOW, HUH? THAT'S CUTE.
ARE YOU REALLY HERE?
IS ANYONE?
PLEASE. I GET ENOUGH OF THAT FROM PHILOSOPHY WITH SHANG.
I HEARD YOU'VE GOT A NEW STUDY BUDDY, THOUGH. ALI, HUH? DIDN'T KNOW YOU WERE INTO THE POINDEXTER TYPE.
SHUT UP, JERKFACE. ALI'S...
WHAT? YOU'RE GONNA GIVE HIM HIS FIRST KISS?
WULF, BE QUIET. I THINK I HEARD--
KRAAAASH
NO! NATALIE!

WHO... NATALIE...

HAILEY, *WAKE UP.*

SHANG'S BEEN WRITING ON THE BOARD FOR FORTY-FIVE MINUTES. HE'S BOUND TO TURN AROUND WITHIN THE HOUR...

OH... I WASN'T SLEEPING... I WAS...

DROOLING AND SNORING FOR SHOW?

EXISTENTIALISM

KIERKE...

the work of certain
20th-century philosophers...
doctrinal differences...
that philosophical th...
the human subject—not in
ng subject, but the acting, t
an individual...existentialism

YAAAAAWN.

HAHAHA! SHHH.

REMEMBER! YOUR PAPER ON EXISTENTIALISM IS DUE NEXT MEETING!

SOUNDED LIKE YOU WERE HAVING A PRETTY WILD DREAM.

OH. NO, I JUST... I DREAMT I WAS, *UH,* TAYLOR SWIFT. IT WAS PRETTY RAD.

AND TAYLOR SWIFT-YOU... WAS HANGING OUT WITH WULF?

WULF WASN'T IN MY DREAM.

YOU SAID HIS NAME SEVEN TIMES. TRUST ME, I COUNTED.

AND THEN, ODDLY, *"NATALIE,"* WHICH BRINGS UP OTHER QUESTIONS.

I WASN'T... UGH. I DON'T KNOW ANYONE NAMED NATALIE. AND WULF, HE WASN'T...

IT'S OKAY. REALLY. I KNOW YOU LIKED HIM.

IT WASN'T EVEN *LIKE* THAT. I WAS JUST LONELY, AND HE... WHATEVER, YOU KNOW? I DON'T EVEN THINK HE REALLY CARED ABOUT ME MUCH.

I JUST... I KNOW HE'S IN THAT *WEIRD* SCHOOL NOW.

I JUST SOMETIMES WONDER HOW HE IS, YOU KNOW?

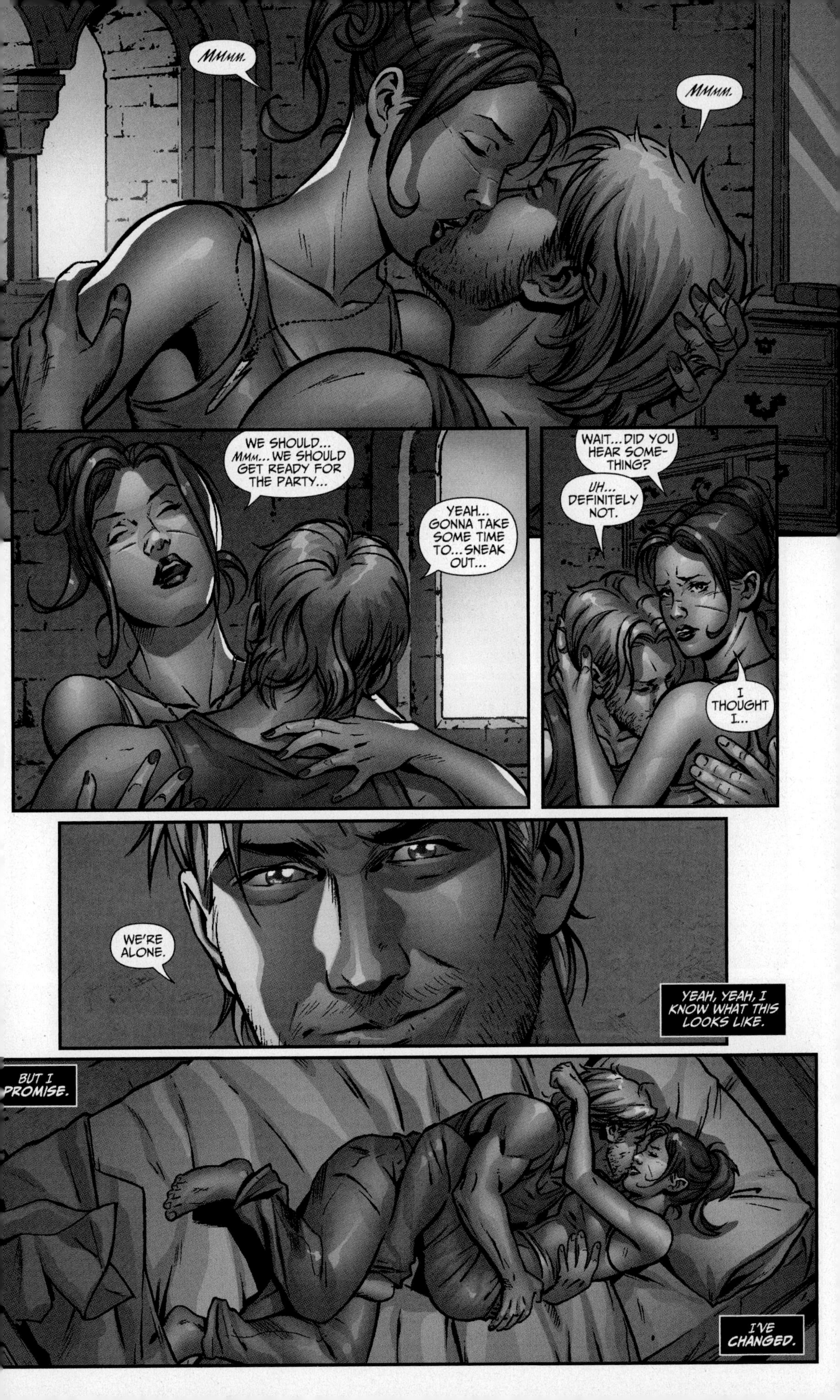
MMMM.
MMMM.
WE SHOULD... MMM... WE SHOULD GET READY FOR THE PARTY...
YEAH... GONNA TAKE SOME TIME TO... SNEAK OUT...
WAIT... DID YOU HEAR SOME-THING?
UH... DEFINITELY NOT.
I THOUGHT I...
WE'RE ALONE.
YEAH, YEAH, I KNOW WHAT THIS LOOKS LIKE.
BUT I PROMISE.
I'VE CHANGED.

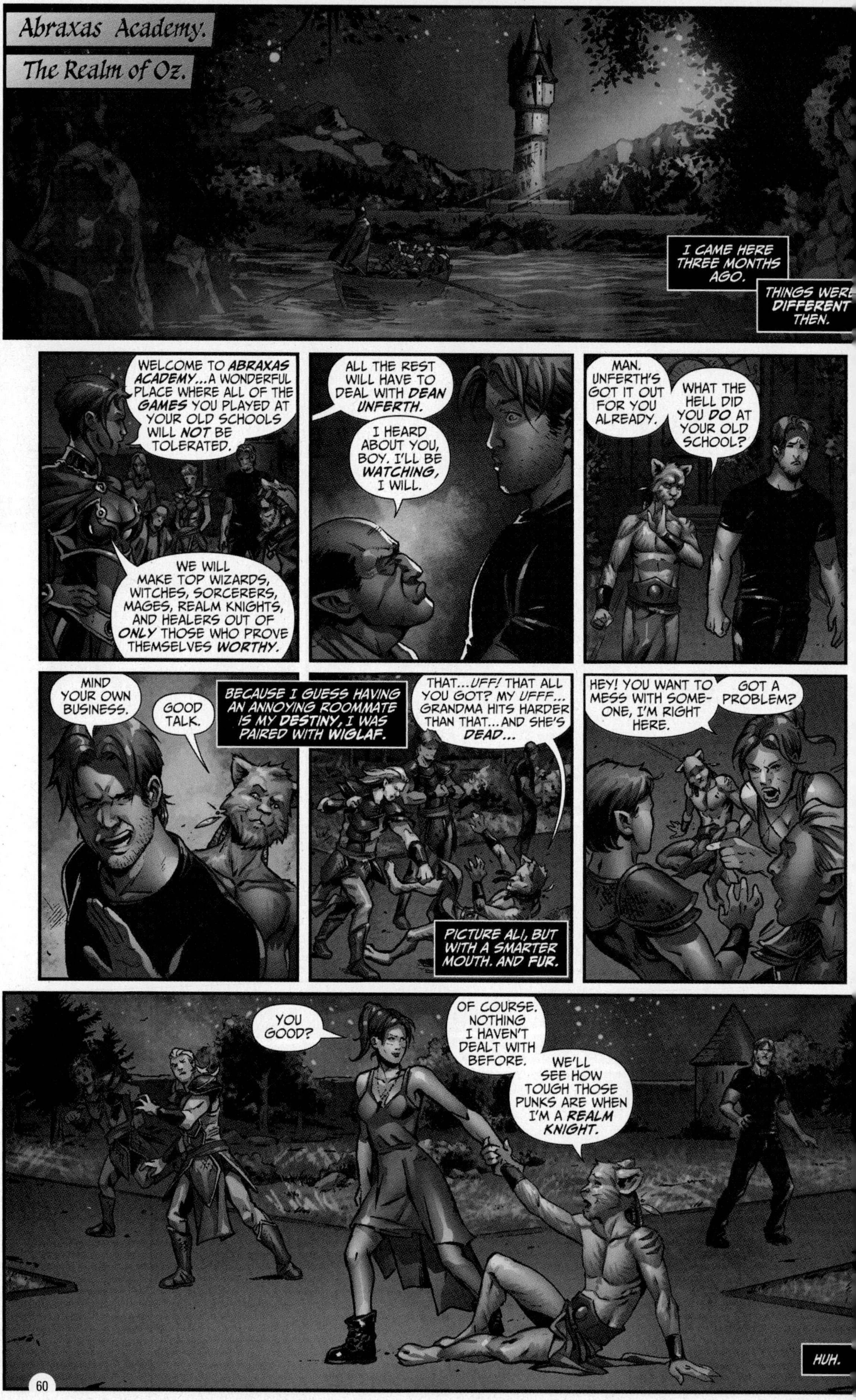

Abraxas Academy.
The Realm of Oz.
I CAME HERE THREE MONTHS AGO.
THINGS WERE DIFFERENT THEN.
WELCOME TO ABRAXAS ACADEMY...A WONDERFUL PLACE WHERE ALL OF THE GAMES YOU PLAYED AT YOUR OLD SCHOOLS WILL NOT BE TOLERATED.
WE WILL MAKE TOP WIZARDS, WITCHES, SORCERERS, MAGES, REALM KNIGHTS, AND HEALERS OUT OF ONLY THOSE WHO PROVE THEMSELVES WORTHY.
ALL THE REST WILL HAVE TO DEAL WITH DEAN UNFERTH.
I HEARD ABOUT YOU, BOY. I'LL BE WATCHING, I WILL.
MAN. UNFERTH'S GOT IT OUT FOR YOU ALREADY.
WHAT THE HELL DID YOU DO AT YOUR OLD SCHOOL?
MIND YOUR OWN BUSINESS.
GOOD TALK.
BECAUSE I GUESS HAVING AN ANNOYING ROOMMATE IS MY DESTINY, I WAS PAIRED WITH WIGLAF.
THAT...UFF! THAT ALL YOU GOT? MY UFFF... GRANDMA HITS HARDER THAN THAT...AND SHE'S DEAD...
PICTURE ALI, BUT WITH A SMARTER MOUTH. AND FUR.
HEY! YOU WANT TO MESS WITH SOME-ONE, I'M RIGHT HERE.
GOT A PROBLEM?
YOU GOOD?
OF COURSE. NOTHING I HAVEN'T DEALT WITH BEFORE.
WE'LL SEE HOW TOUGH THOSE PUNKS ARE WHEN I'M A REALM KNIGHT.
HUH.

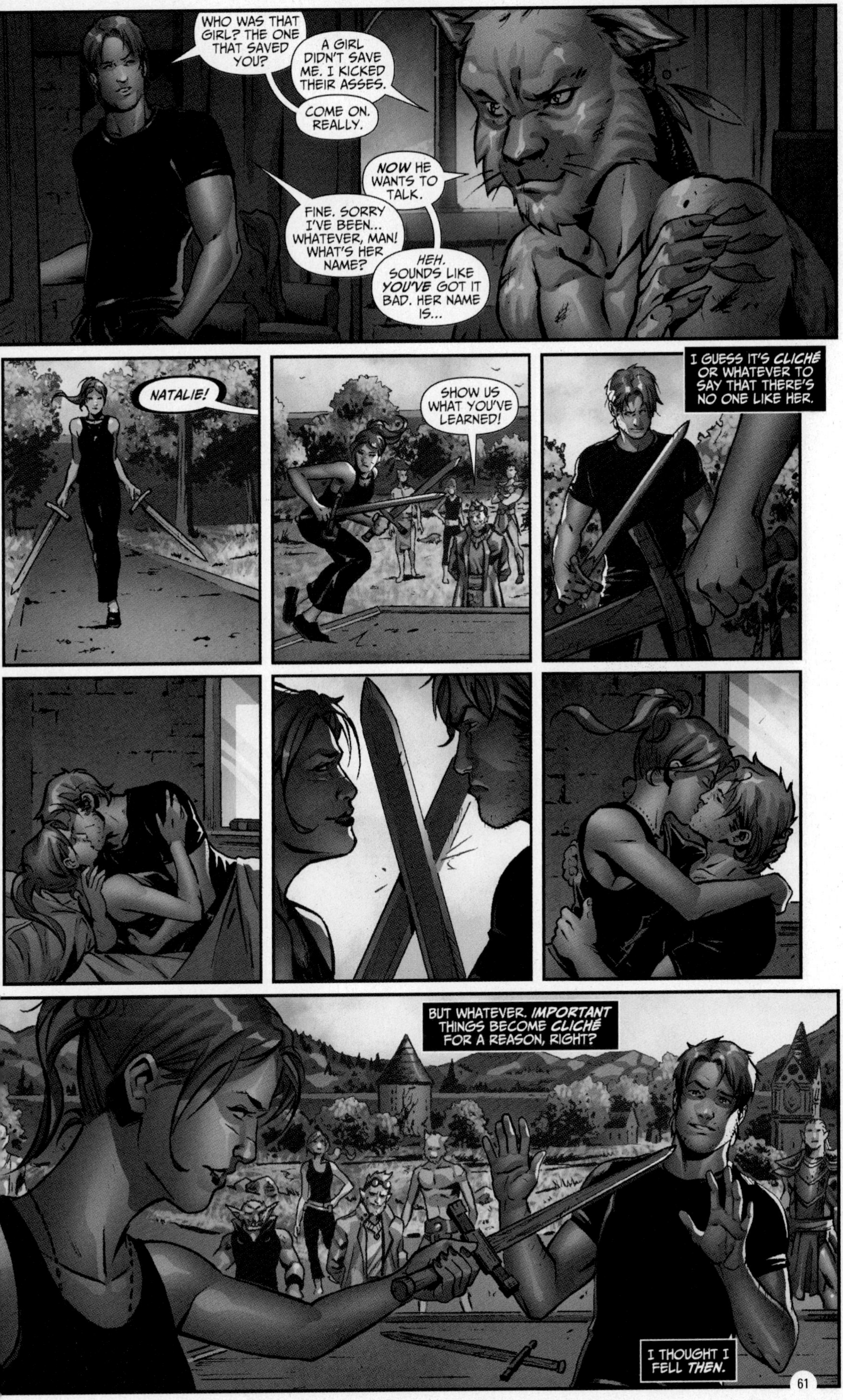

WHO WAS THAT GIRL? THE ONE THAT SAVED YOU?
A GIRL DIDN'T SAVE ME. I KICKED THEIR ASSES.
COME ON. REALLY.
NOW HE WANTS TO TALK.
FINE. SORRY I'VE BEEN... WHATEVER, MAN! WHAT'S HER NAME?
HEH. SOUNDS LIKE YOU'VE GOT IT BAD. HER NAME IS...
NATALIE!
SHOW US WHAT YOU'VE LEARNED!
I GUESS IT'S CLICHÉ OR WHATEVER TO SAY THAT THERE'S NO ONE LIKE HER.
BUT WHATEVER. IMPORTANT THINGS BECOME CLICHÉ FOR A REASON, RIGHT?
I THOUGHT I FELL THEN.

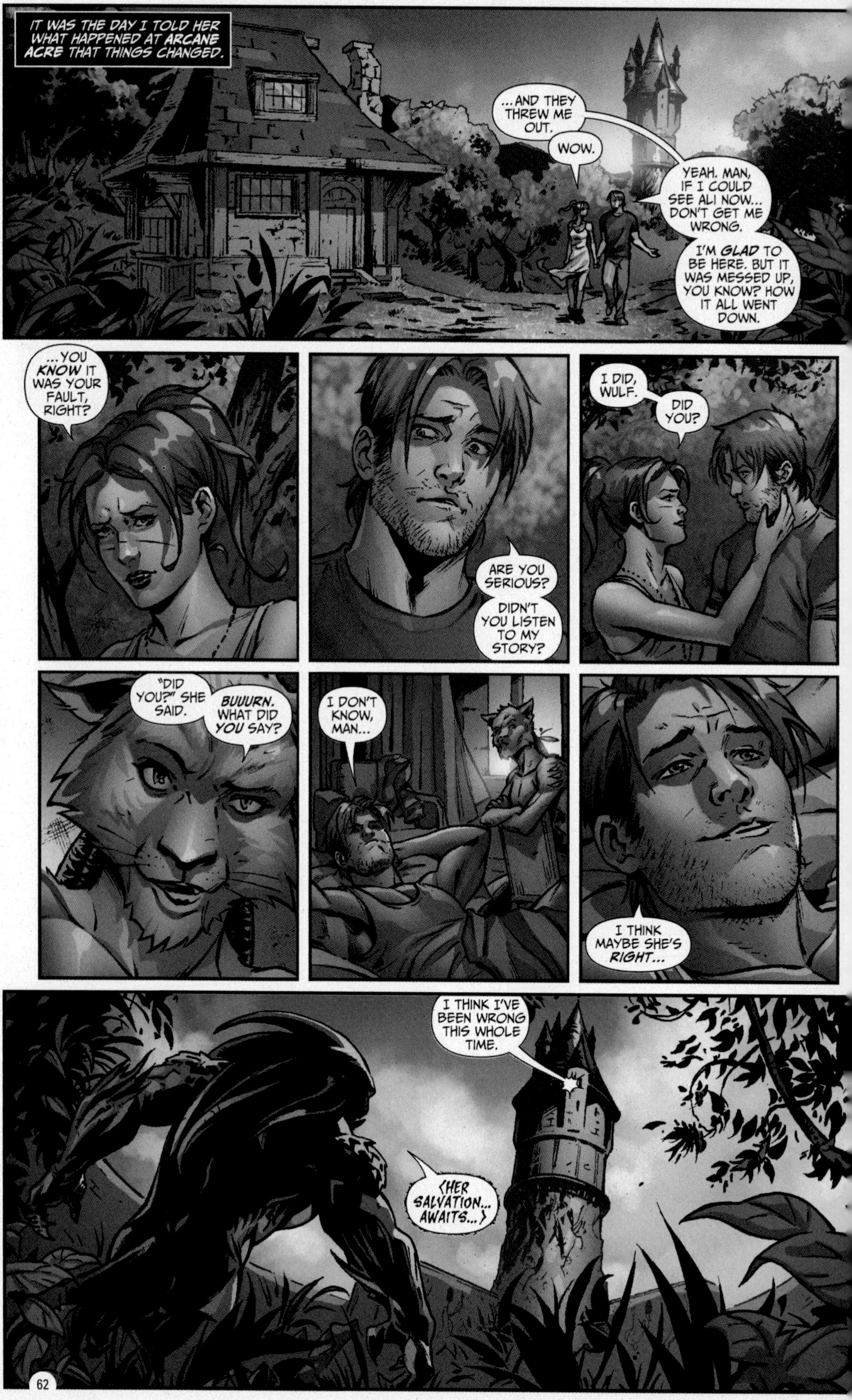
IT WAS THE DAY I TOLD HER WHAT HAPPENED AT ARCANE ACRE THAT THINGS CHANGED.
...AND THEY THREW ME OUT.
WOW.
YEAH. MAN, IF I COULD SEE ALI NOW... DON'T GET ME WRONG.
I'M GLAD TO BE HERE. BUT IT WAS MESSED UP, YOU KNOW? HOW IT ALL WENT DOWN.
...YOU KNOW IT WAS YOUR FAULT, RIGHT?
ARE YOU SERIOUS?
DIDN'T YOU LISTEN TO MY STORY?
I DID, WULF.
DID YOU?
"DID YOU?" SHE SAID.
BUUURN. WHAT DID YOU SAY?
I DON'T KNOW, MAN...
I THINK MAYBE SHE'S RIGHT...
I THINK I'VE BEEN WRONG THIS WHOLE TIME.
‹HER SALVATION... AWAITS...›

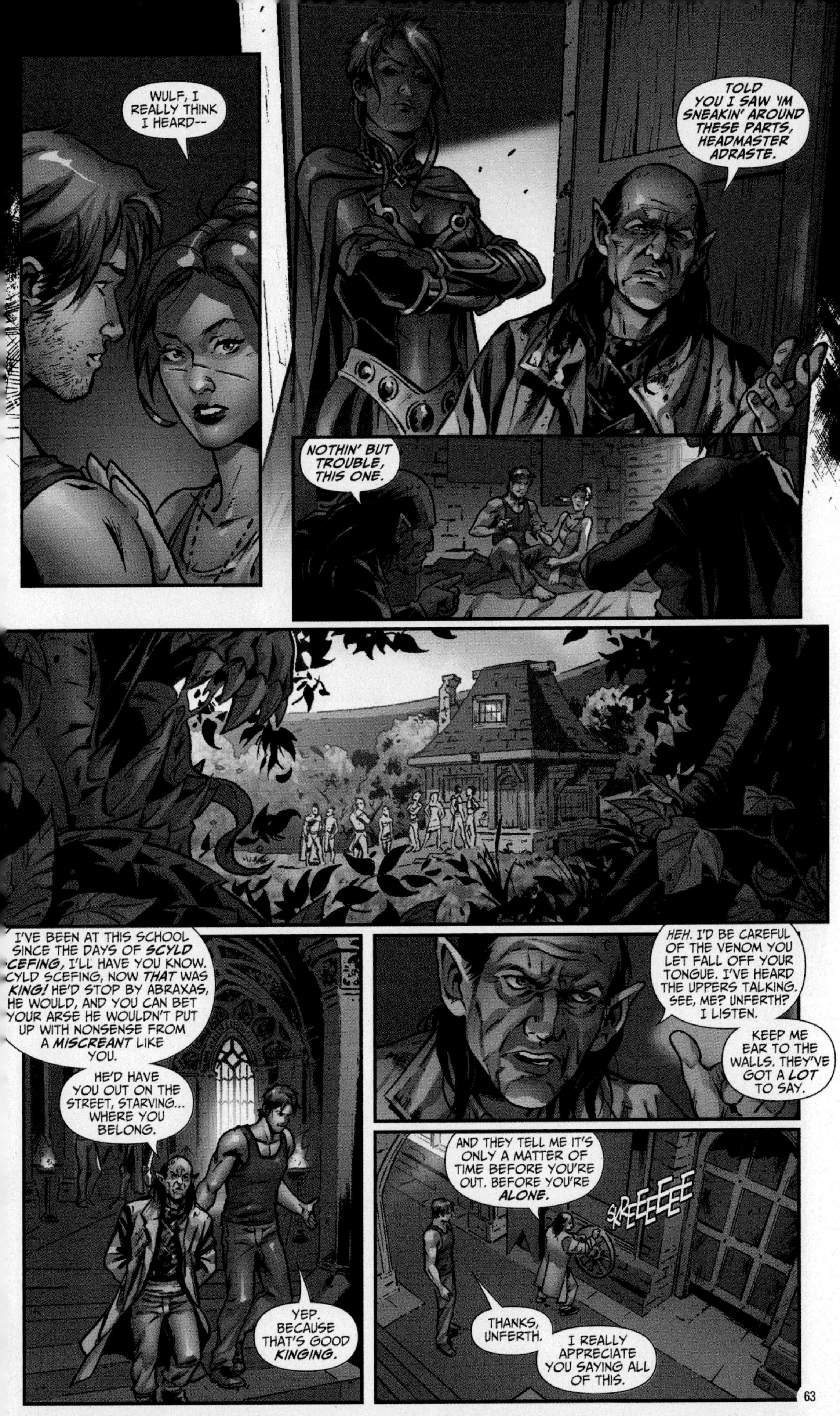
WULF, I REALLY THINK I HEARD--
TOLD YOU I SAW 'IM SNEAKIN' AROUND THESE PARTS, HEADMASTER ADRASTE.
NOTHIN' BUT TROUBLE, THIS ONE.
I'VE BEEN AT THIS SCHOOL SINCE THE DAYS OF SCYLD SCEFING, I'LL HAVE YOU KNOW. SCYLD SCEFING, NOW THAT WAS KING! HE'D STOP BY ABRAXAS, HE WOULD, AND YOU CAN BET YOUR ARSE HE WOULDN'T PUT UP WITH NONSENSE FROM A MISCREANT LIKE YOU.
HE'D HAVE YOU OUT ON THE STREET, STARVING... WHERE YOU BELONG.
YEP. BECAUSE THAT'S GOOD KINGING.
HEH. I'D BE CAREFUL OF THE VENOM YOU LET FALL OFF YOUR TONGUE. I'VE HEARD THE UPPERS TALKING. SEE, ME? UNFERTH? I LISTEN.
KEEP ME EAR TO THE WALLS. THEY'VE GOT A LOT TO SAY.
AND THEY TELL ME IT'S ONLY A MATTER OF TIME BEFORE YOU'RE OUT. BEFORE YOU'RE ALONE.
SKREEEEEEE
THANKS, UNFERTH.
I REALLY APPRECIATE YOU SAYING ALL OF THIS.

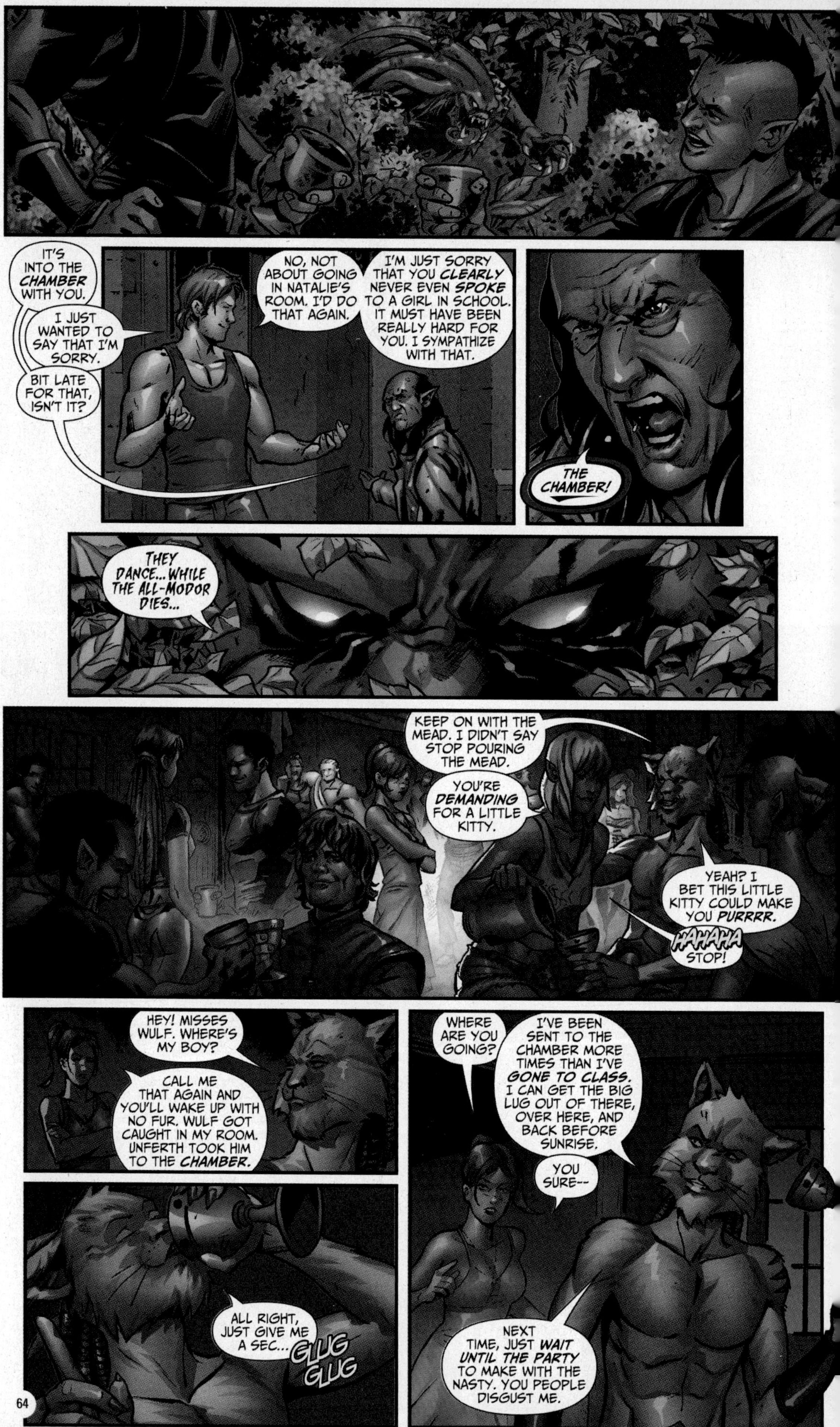
IT'S INTO THE CHAMBER WITH YOU.
I JUST WANTED TO SAY THAT I'M SORRY.
BIT LATE FOR THAT, ISN'T IT?
NO, NOT ABOUT GOING IN NATALIE'S ROOM. I'D DO THAT AGAIN.
I'M JUST SORRY THAT YOU CLEARLY NEVER EVEN SPOKE TO A GIRL IN SCHOOL. IT MUST HAVE BEEN REALLY HARD FOR YOU. I SYMPATHIZE WITH THAT.
THE CHAMBER!
THEY DANCE... WHILE THE ALL-MODOR DIES...
KEEP ON WITH THE MEAD. I DIDN'T SAY STOP POURING THE MEAD.
YOU'RE DEMANDING FOR A LITTLE KITTY.
YEAH? I BET THIS LITTLE KITTY COULD MAKE YOU PURRRR.
HAHAHA
STOP!
HEY! MISSES WULF. WHERE'S MY BOY?
CALL ME THAT AGAIN AND YOU'LL WAKE UP WITH NO FUR. WULF GOT CAUGHT IN MY ROOM. UNFERTH TOOK HIM TO THE CHAMBER.
ALL RIGHT, JUST GIVE ME A SEC...
GLUG GLUG
WHERE ARE YOU GOING?
I'VE BEEN SENT TO THE CHAMBER MORE TIMES THAN I'VE GONE TO CLASS. I CAN GET THE BIG LUG OUT OF THERE, OVER HERE, AND BACK BEFORE SUNRISE.
YOU SURE--
NEXT TIME, JUST WAIT UNTIL THE PARTY TO MAKE WITH THE NASTY. YOU PEOPLE DISGUST ME.

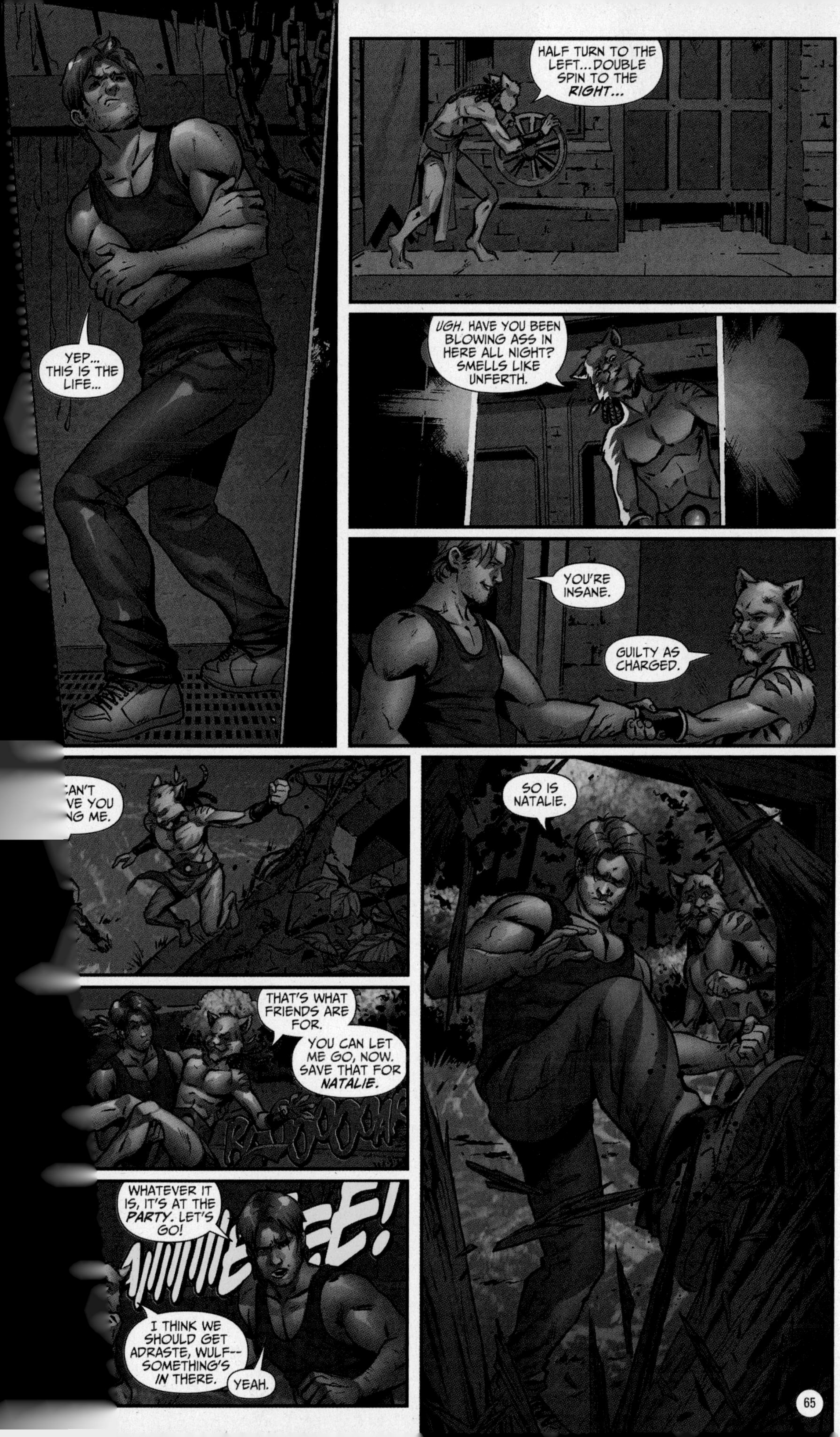
YEP... THIS IS THE LIFE...
HALF TURN TO THE LEFT...DOUBLE SPIN TO THE *RIGHT*...
UGH. HAVE YOU BEEN BLOWING ASS IN HERE ALL NIGHT? SMELLS LIKE UNFERTH.
YOU'RE INSANE.
GUILTY AS CHARGED.
SO IS NATALIE.
THAT'S WHAT FRIENDS ARE FOR.
YOU CAN LET ME GO, NOW. SAVE THAT FOR *NATALIE.*
WHATEVER IT IS, IT'S AT THE *PARTY*. LET'S GO!
I THINK WE SHOULD GET ADRASTE, WULF-- SOMETHING'S *IN* THERE.
YEAH.

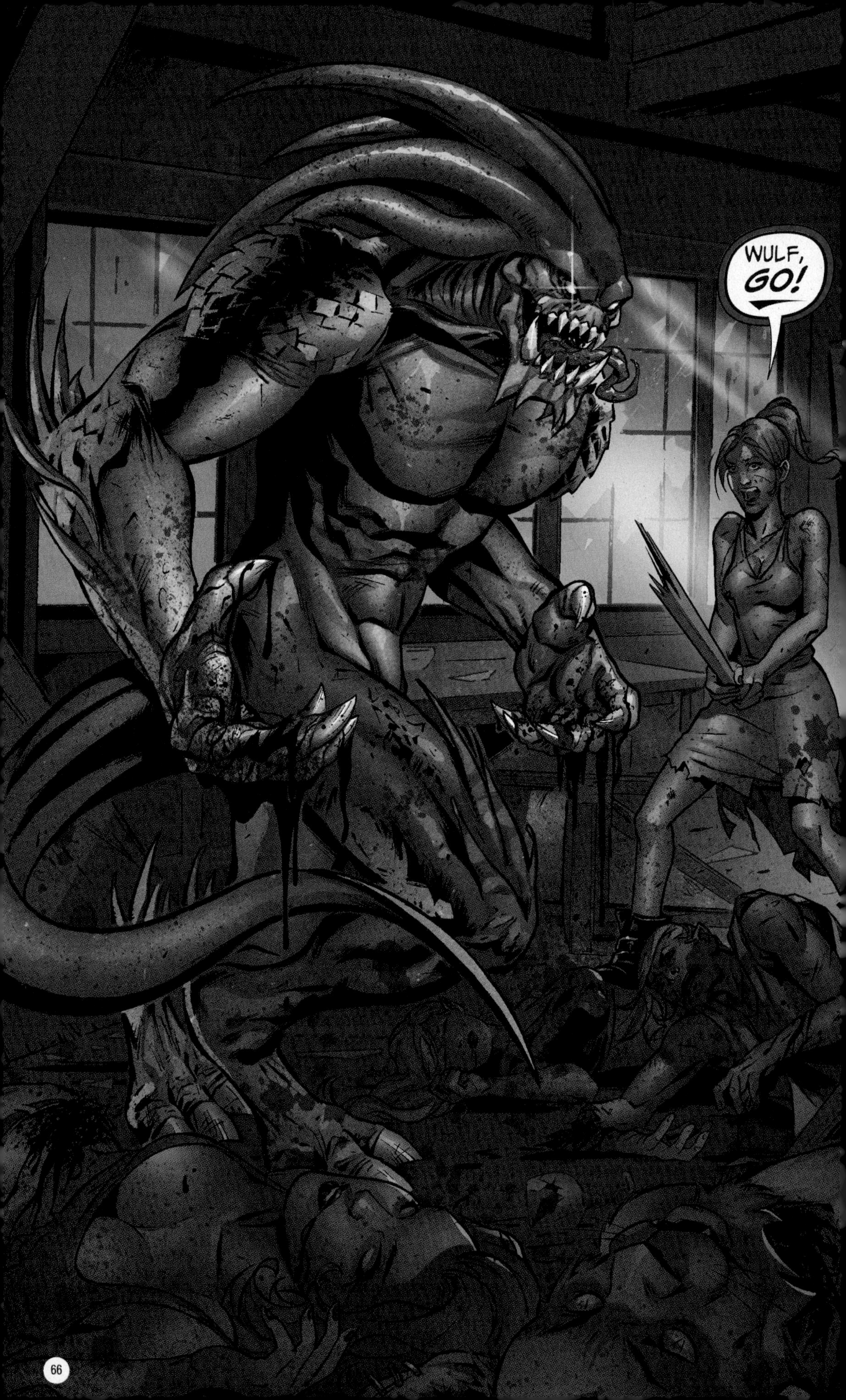
WULF, GO!

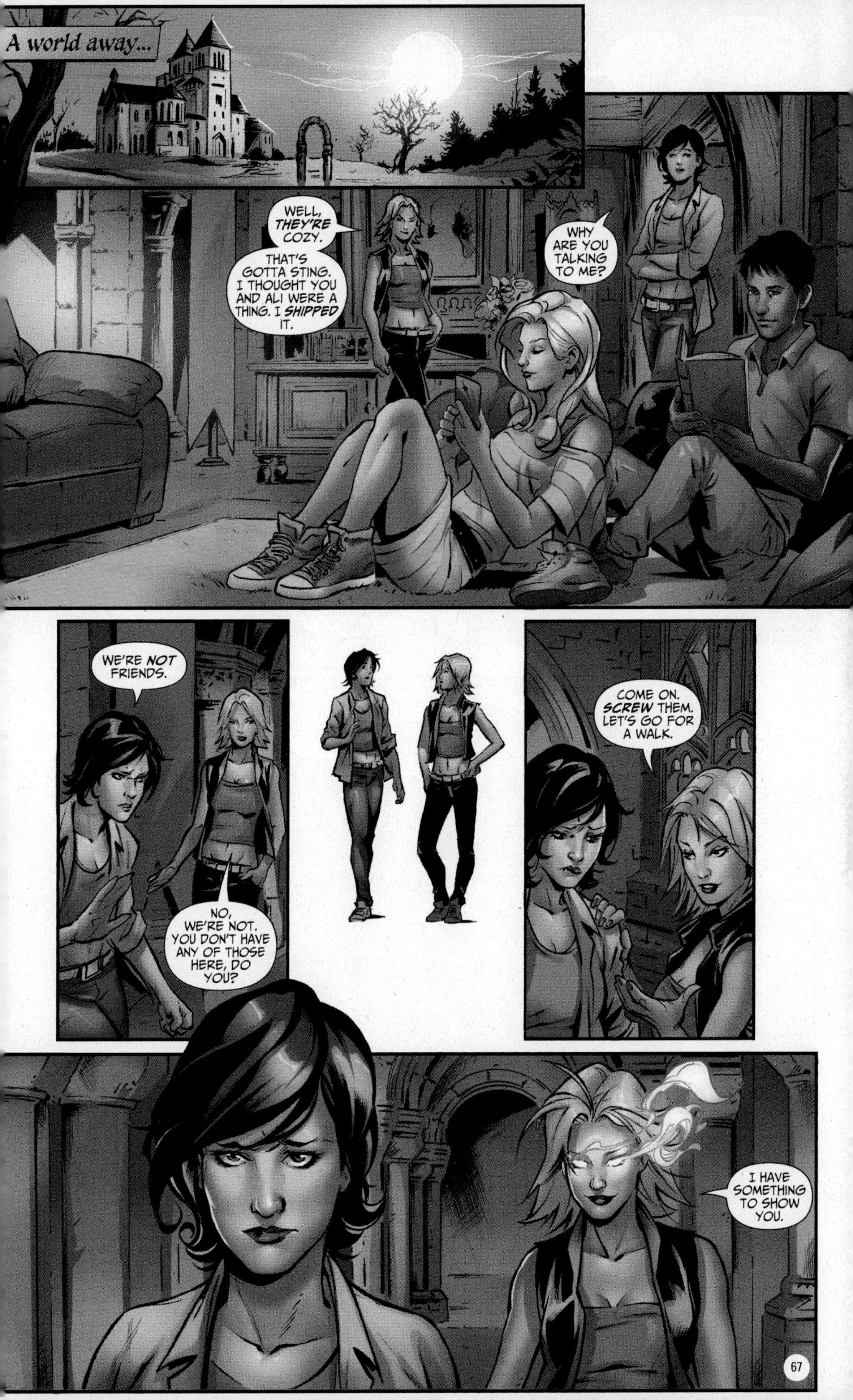
A world away...
WELL, *THEY'RE* COZY.
THAT'S GOTTA STING. I THOUGHT YOU AND ALI WERE A THING. I *SHIPPED* IT.
WHY ARE YOU TALKING TO ME?
WE'RE *NOT* FRIENDS.
NO, WE'RE NOT. YOU DON'T HAVE ANY OF THOSE HERE, DO YOU?
COME ON. *SCREW* THEM. LET'S GO FOR A WALK.
I HAVE SOMETHING TO SHOW YOU.

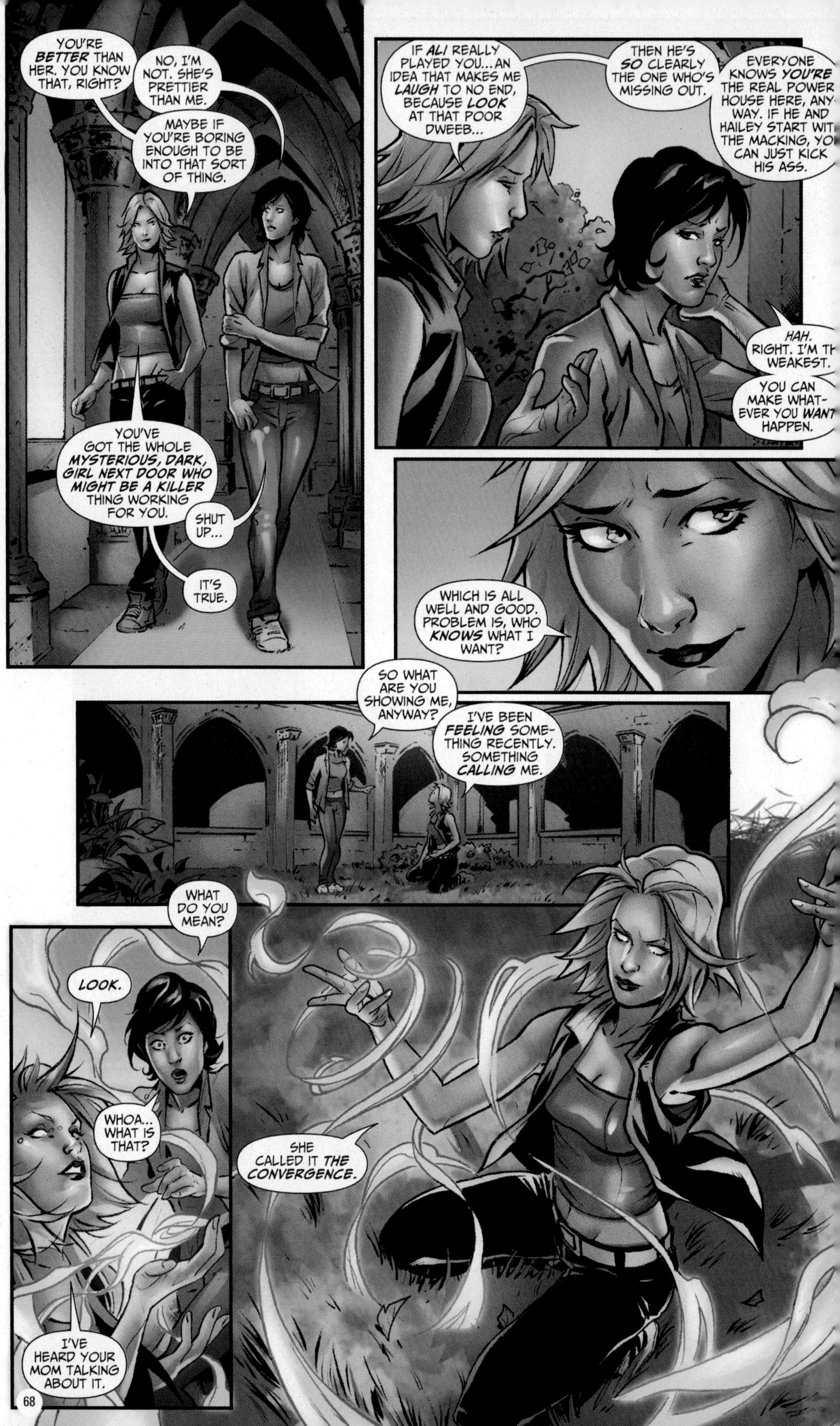
YOU'RE BETTER THAN HER. YOU KNOW THAT, RIGHT?
NO, I'M NOT. SHE'S PRETTIER THAN ME.
MAYBE IF YOU'RE BORING ENOUGH TO BE INTO THAT SORT OF THING.
YOU'VE GOT THE WHOLE MYSTERIOUS, DARK, GIRL NEXT DOOR WHO MIGHT BE A KILLER THING WORKING FOR YOU.
SHUT UP...
IT'S TRUE.
IF ALI REALLY PLAYED YOU... AN IDEA THAT MAKES ME LAUGH TO NO END, BECAUSE LOOK AT THAT POOR DWEEB...
THEN HE'S SO CLEARLY THE ONE WHO'S MISSING OUT.
EVERYONE KNOWS YOU'RE THE REAL POWER HOUSE HERE, ANY WAY. IF HE AND HAILEY START WIT THE MACKING, YO CAN JUST KICK HIS ASS.
HAH. RIGHT. I'M TH WEAKEST.
YOU CAN MAKE WHATEVER YOU WANT HAPPEN.
WHICH IS ALL WELL AND GOOD. PROBLEM IS, WHO KNOWS WHAT I WANT?
SO WHAT ARE YOU SHOWING ME, ANYWAY?
I'VE BEEN FEELING SOMETHING RECENTLY. SOMETHING CALLING ME.
WHAT DO YOU MEAN?
LOOK.
WHOA... WHAT IS THAT?
I'VE HEARD YOUR MOM TALKING ABOUT IT.
SHE CALLED IT THE CONVERGENCE.

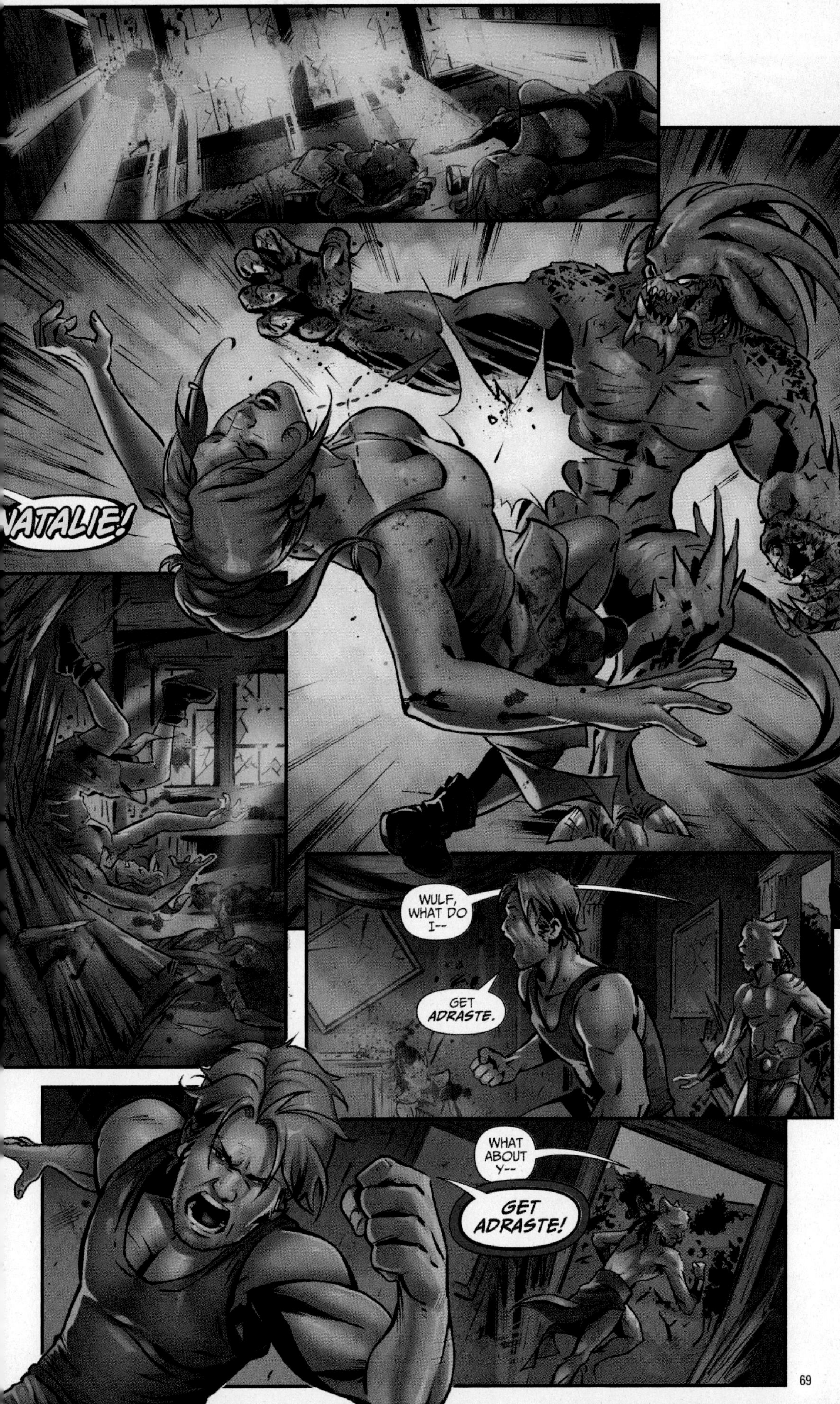
NATALIE!
WULF, WHAT DO I--
GET ADRASTE.
WHAT ABOUT Y--
GET ADRASTE!

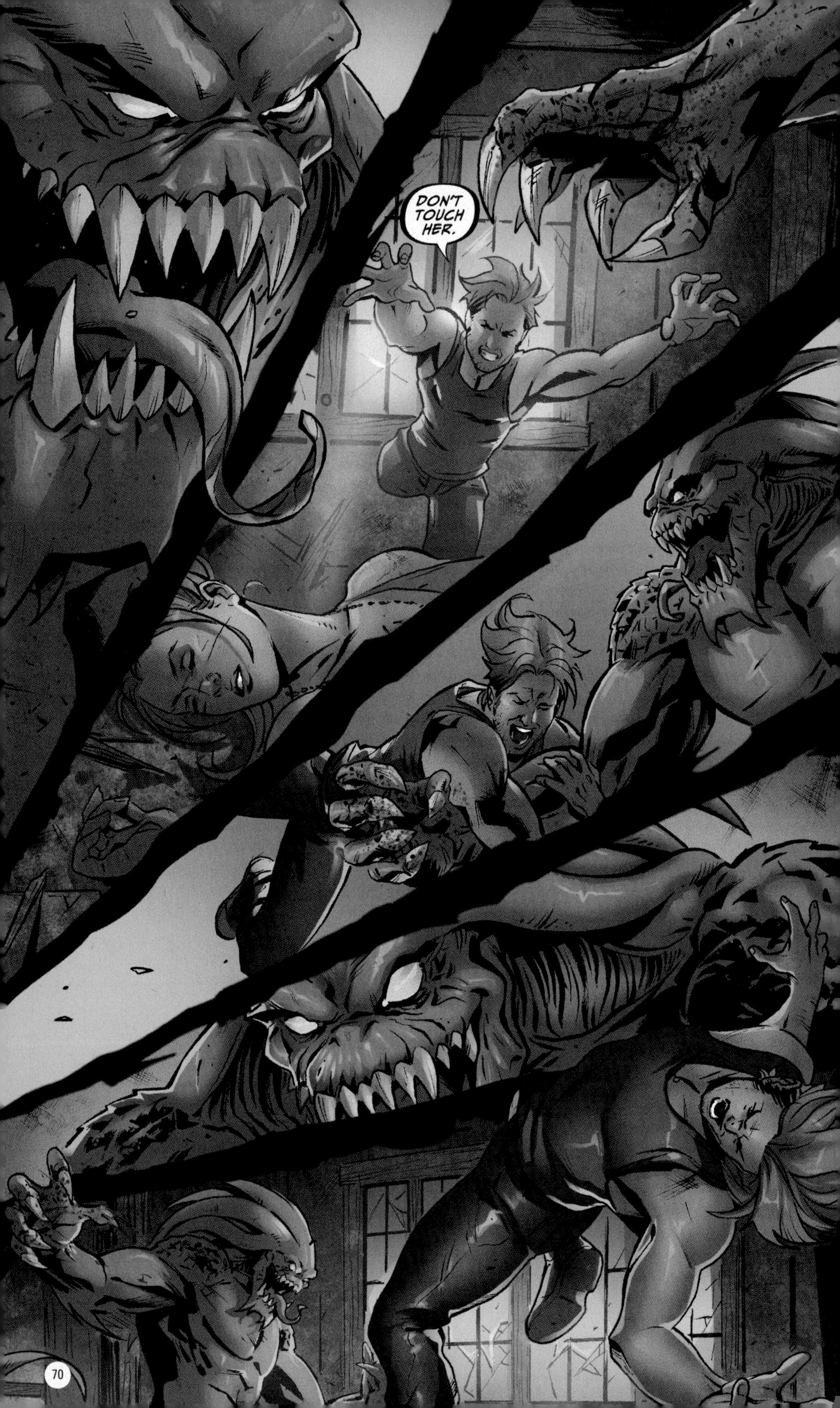
DON'T TOUCH HER.

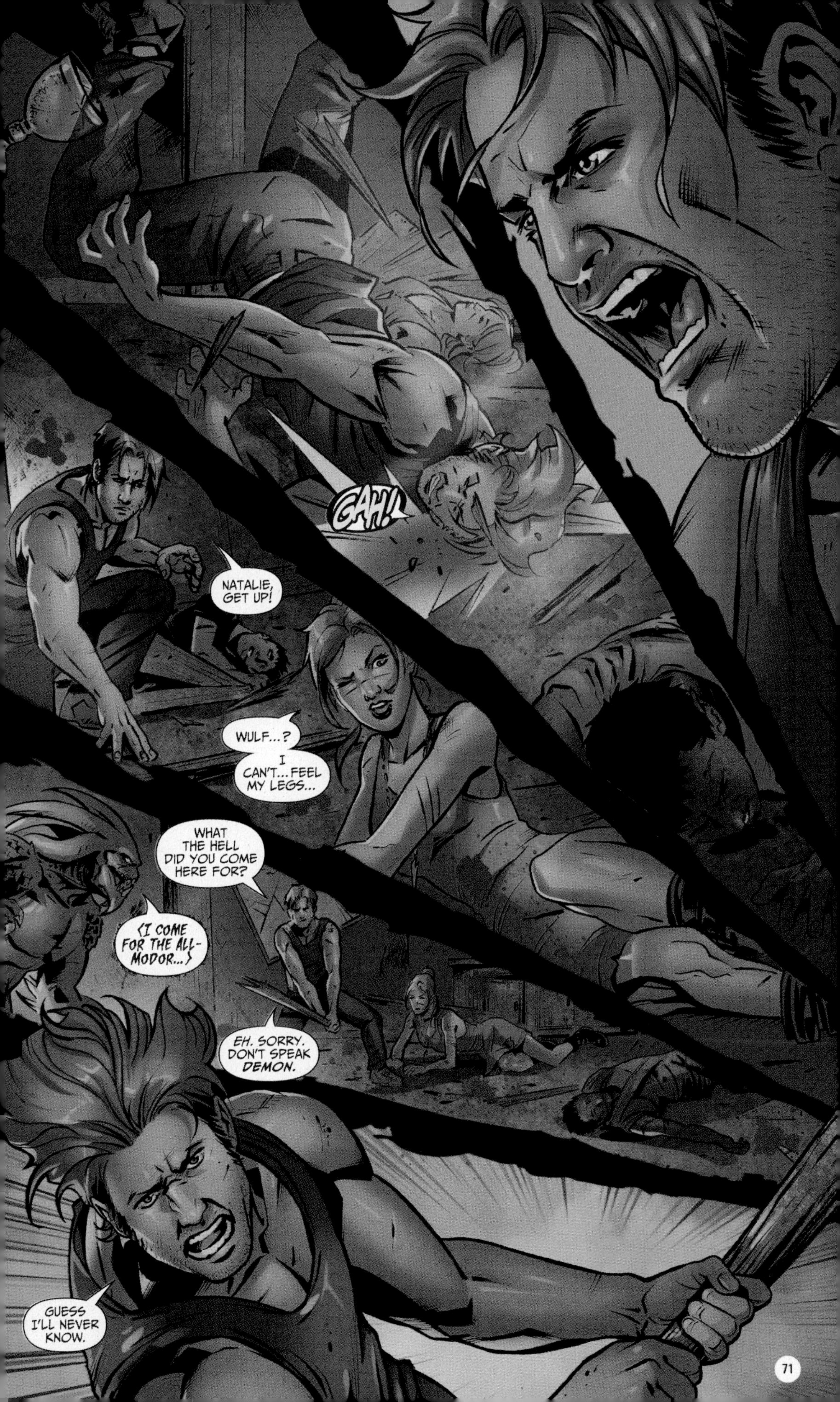
GAH!
NATALIE, GET UP!
WULF...?
I CAN'T...FEEL MY LEGS...
WHAT THE HELL DID YOU COME HERE FOR?
<I COME FOR THE ALL-MODOR...>
EH. SORRY. DON'T SPEAK DEMON.
GUESS I'LL NEVER KNOW.

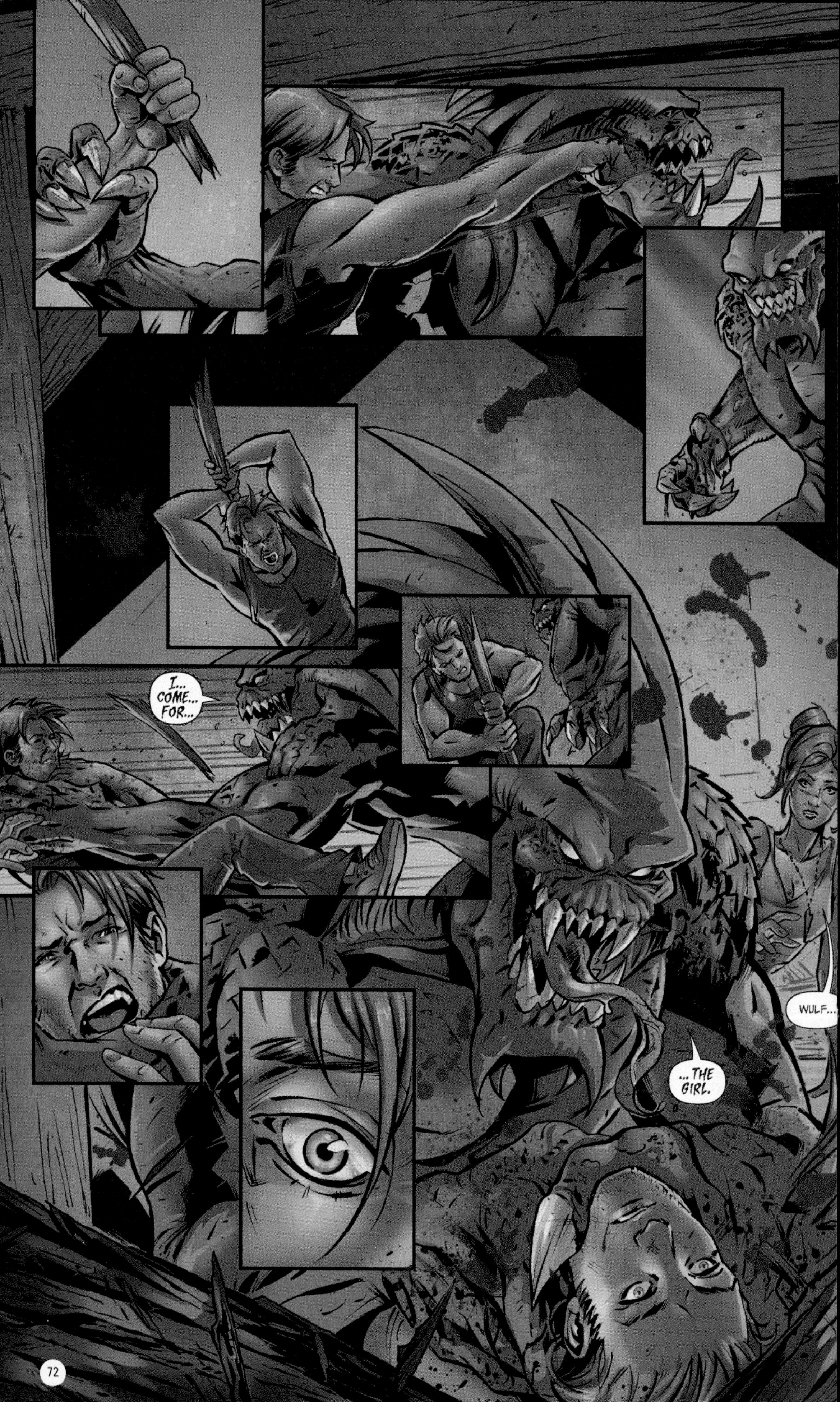
I... COME... FOR...
...THE GIRL.
WULF...

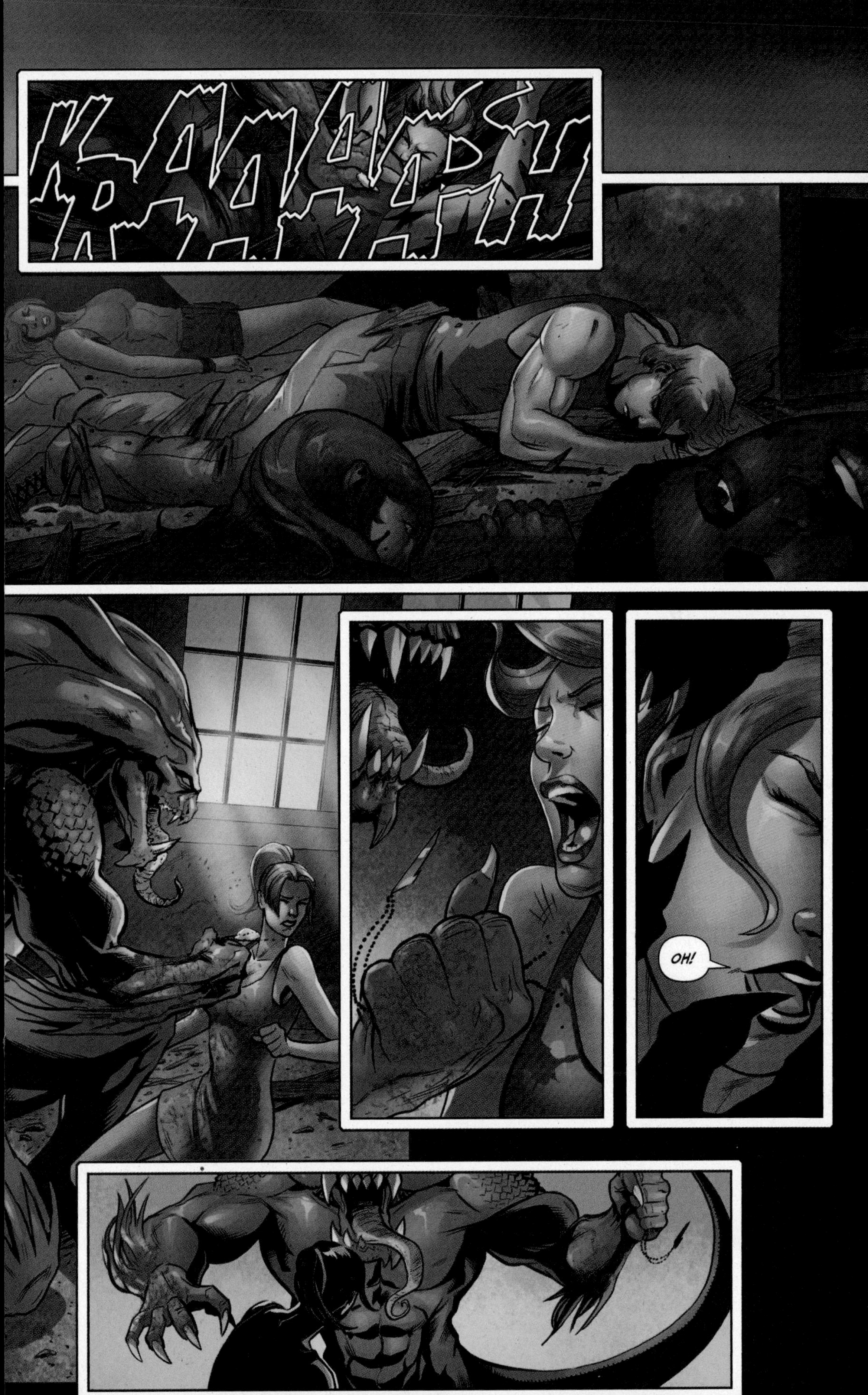
KRAKKOOSH
OH!

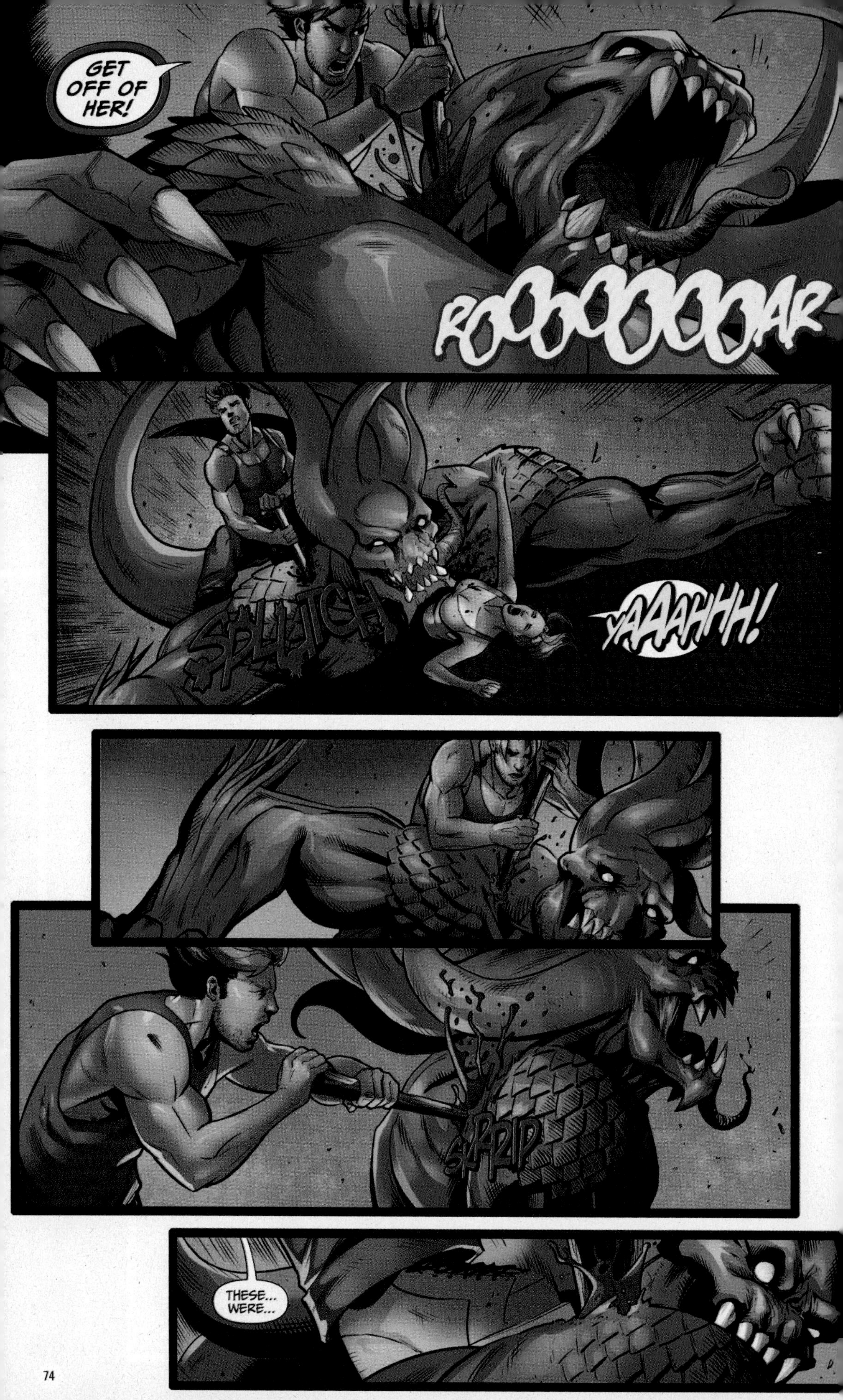
GET OFF OF HER!
ROOOOOOOAR
SPLUTCH
YAAAHHH!
SKRID
THESE... WERE...

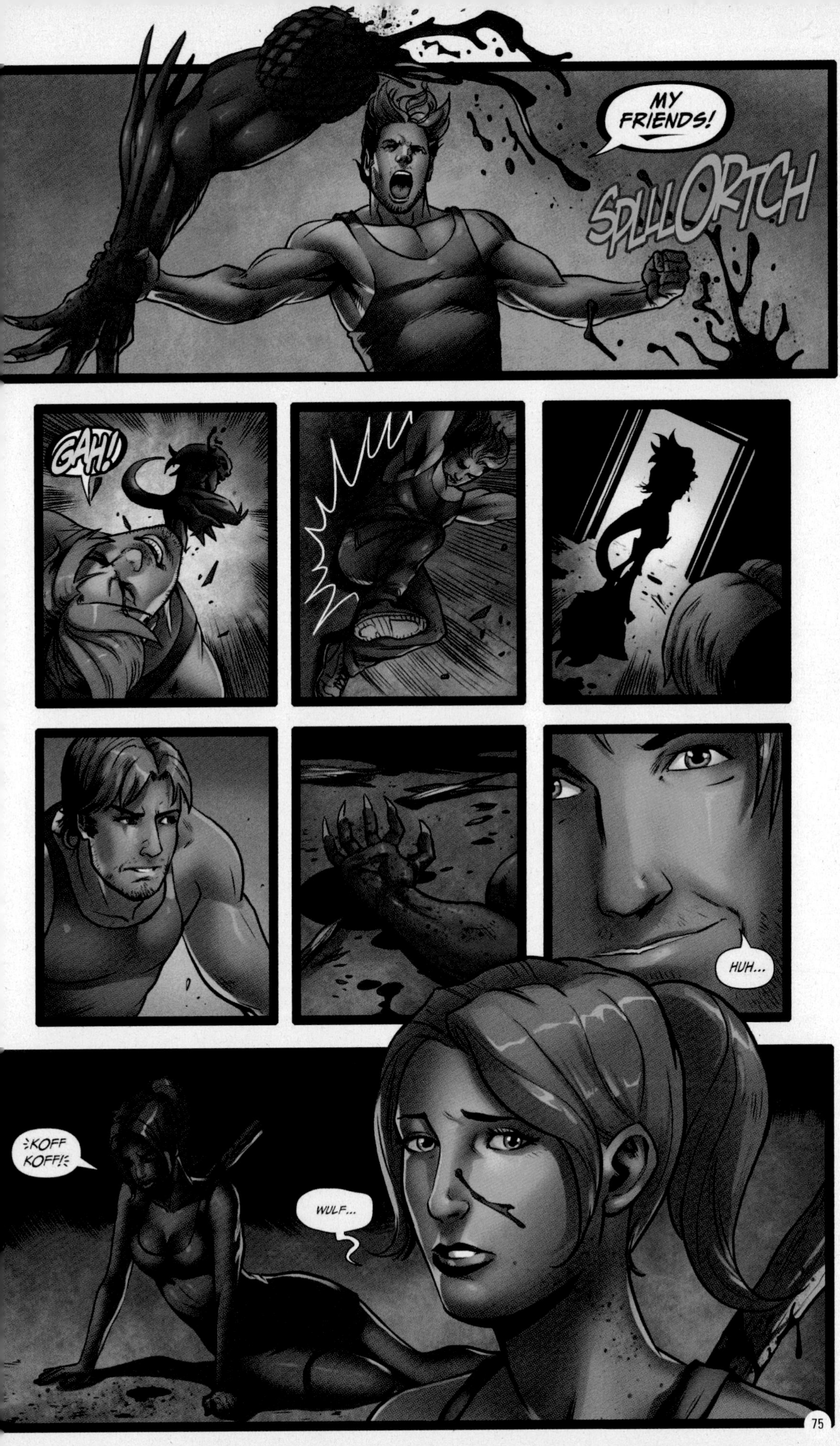

MY FRIENDS!
SPLLLORTCH
GAH!
HUH...
KOFF KOFF!
WULF...

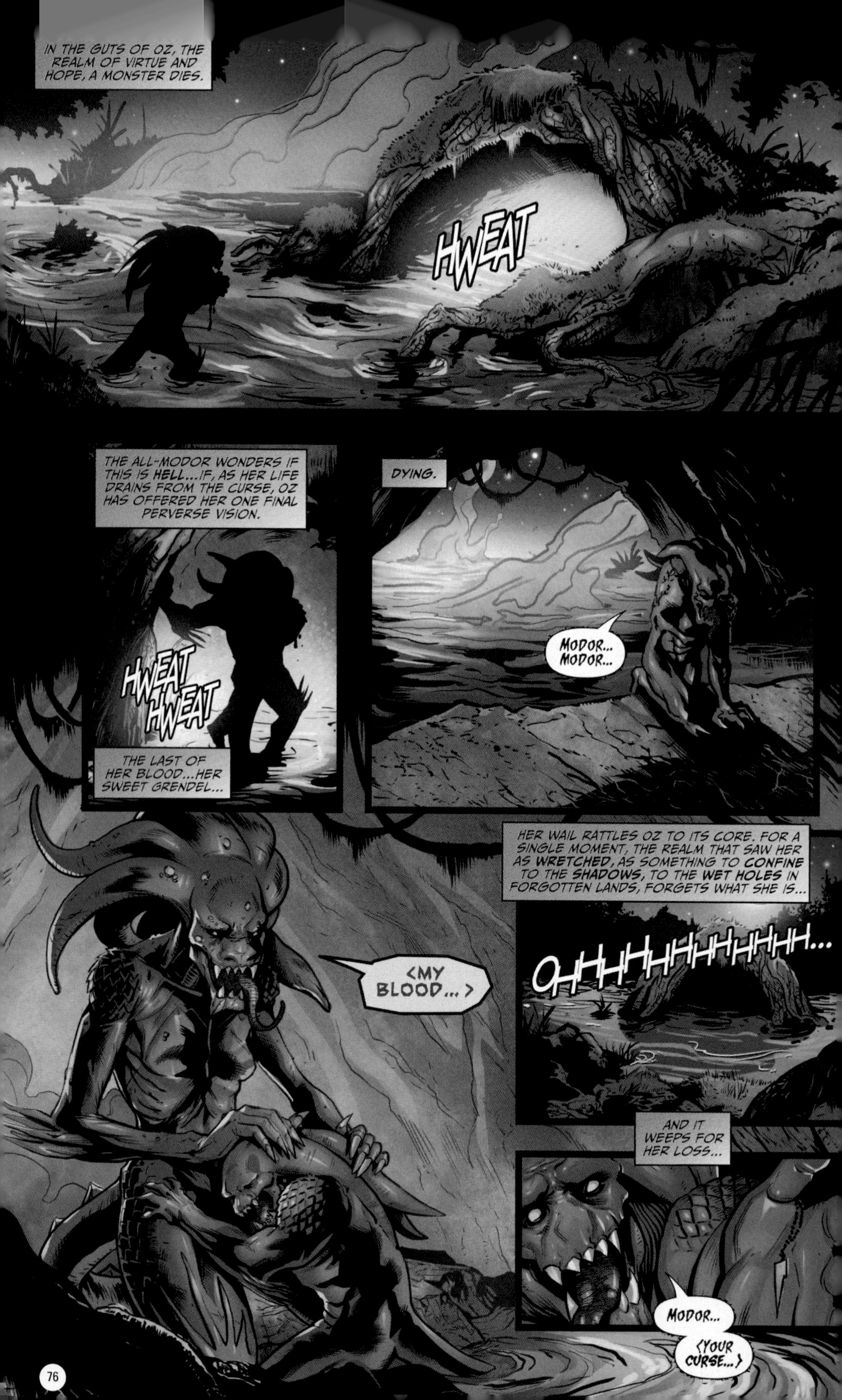

IN THE GUTS OF OZ, THE REALM OF VIRTUE AND HOPE, A MONSTER DIES.
HWEAT
THE ALL-MODOR WONDERS IF THIS IS HELL...IF, AS HER LIFE DRAINS FROM THE CURSE, OZ HAS OFFERED HER ONE FINAL PERVERSE VISION.
HWEAT HWEAT
THE LAST OF HER BLOOD...HER SWEET GRENDEL...
DYING.
MODOR... MODOR...
<MY BLOOD...>
HER WAIL RATTLES OZ TO ITS CORE. FOR A SINGLE MOMENT, THE REALM THAT SAW HER AS WRETCHED, AS SOMETHING TO CONFINE TO THE SHADOWS, TO THE WET HOLES IN FORGOTTEN LANDS, FORGETS WHAT SHE IS...
OHHHHHHHHHHH...
AND IT WEEPS FOR HER LOSS...
MODOR...
<YOUR CURSE...>

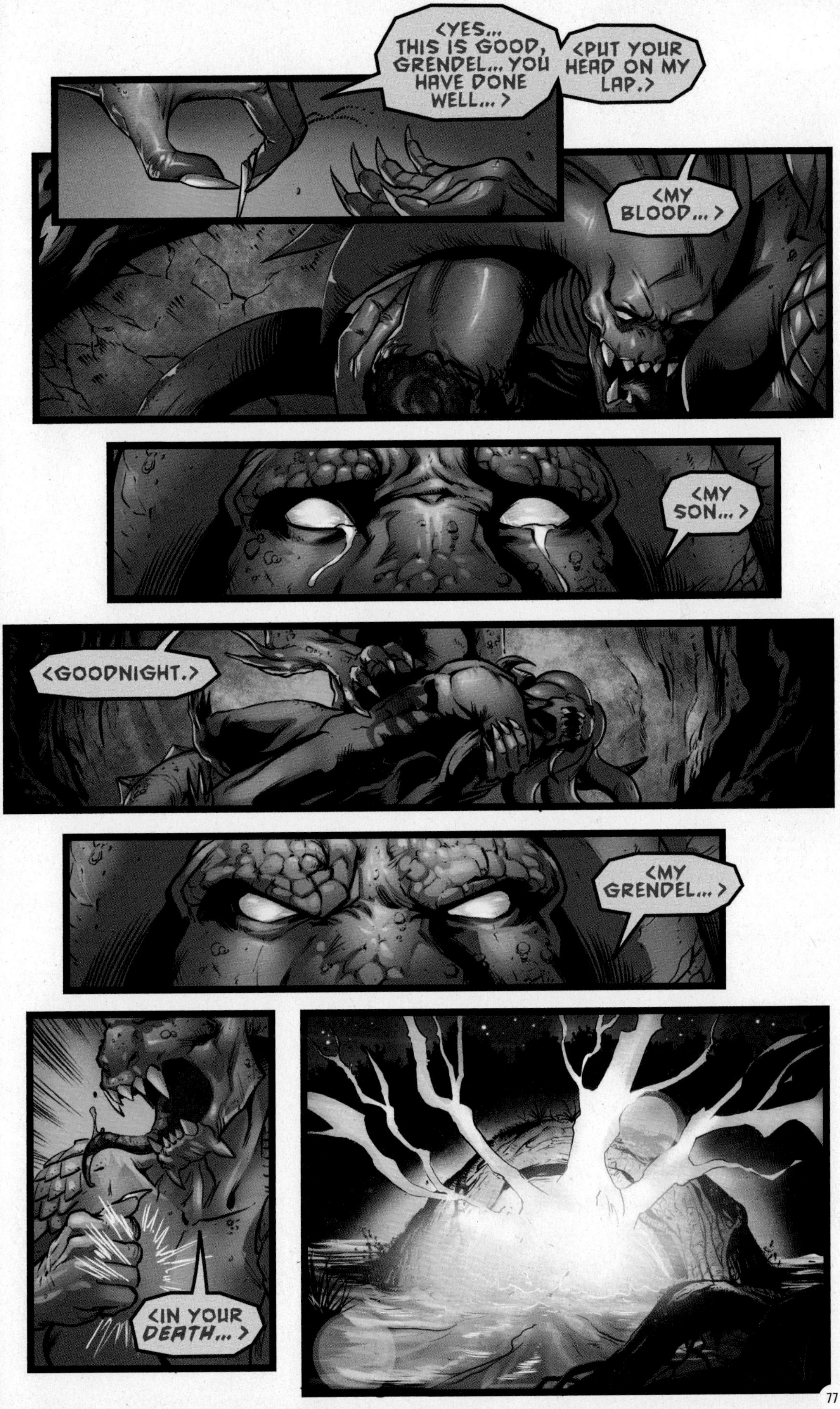
<YES... THIS IS GOOD, GRENDEL... YOU HAVE DONE WELL...>
<PUT YOUR HEAD ON MY LAP.>
<MY BLOOD...>
<MY SON...>
<GOODNIGHT.>
<MY GRENDEL...>
<IN YOUR DEATH...>

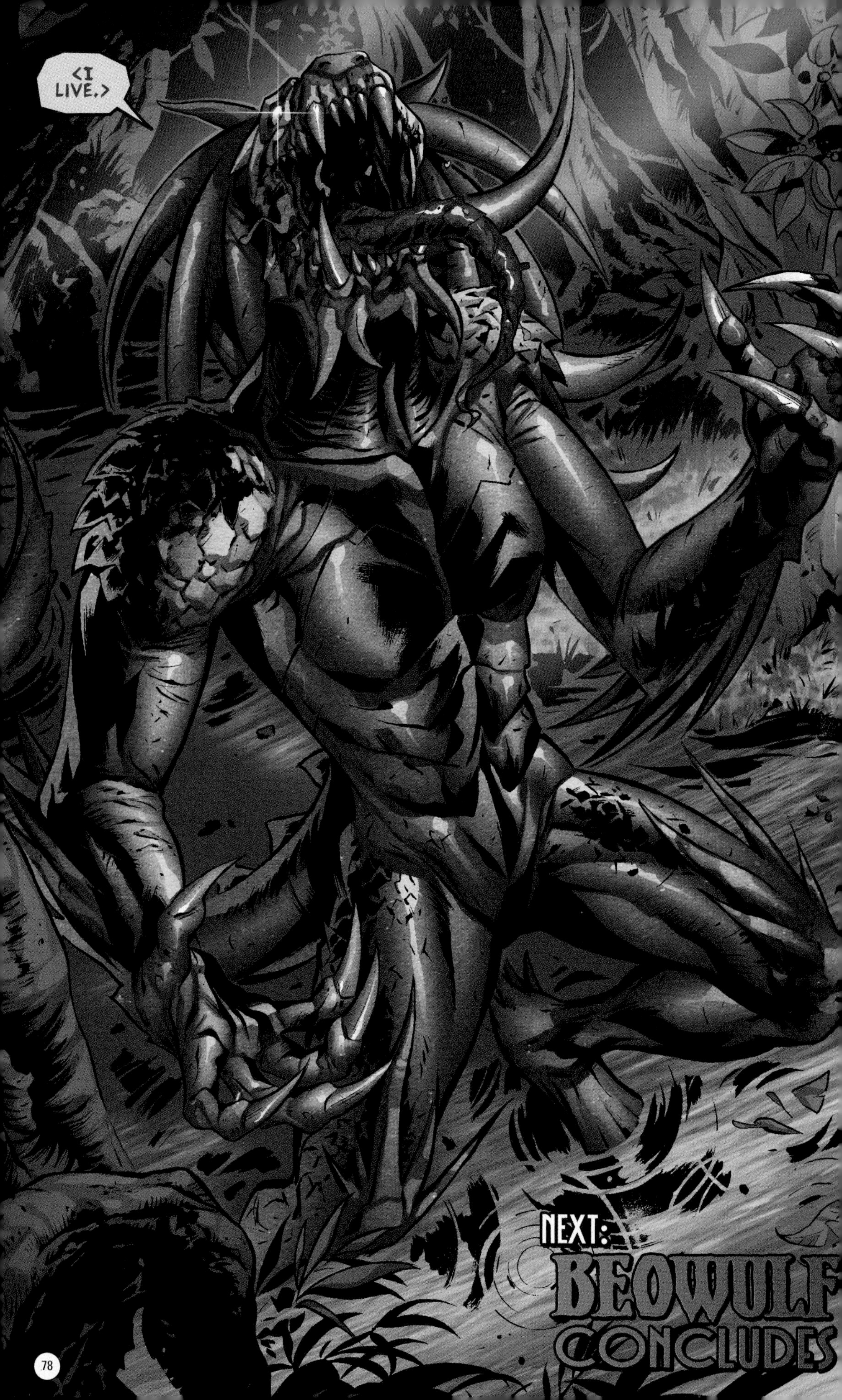
<I LIVE.>
NEXT:
BEOWULF CONCLUDES

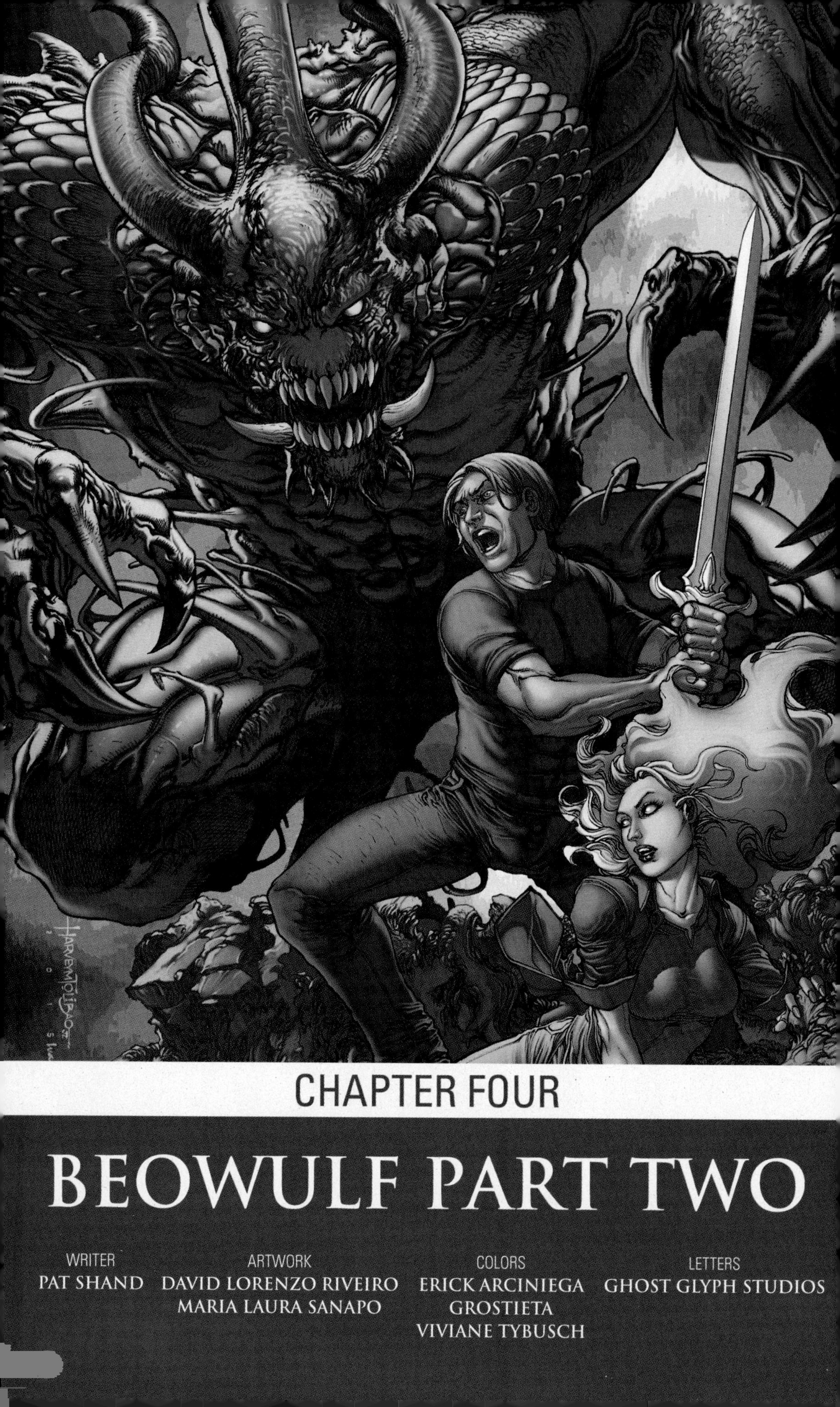

CHAPTER FOUR

BEOWULF PART TWO

WRITER
PAT SHAND

ARTWORK
DAVID LORENZO RIVEIRO
MARIA LAURA SANAPO

COLORS
ERICK ARCINIEGA
GROSTIETA
VIVIANE TYBUSCH

LETTERS
GHOST GLYPH STUDIOS

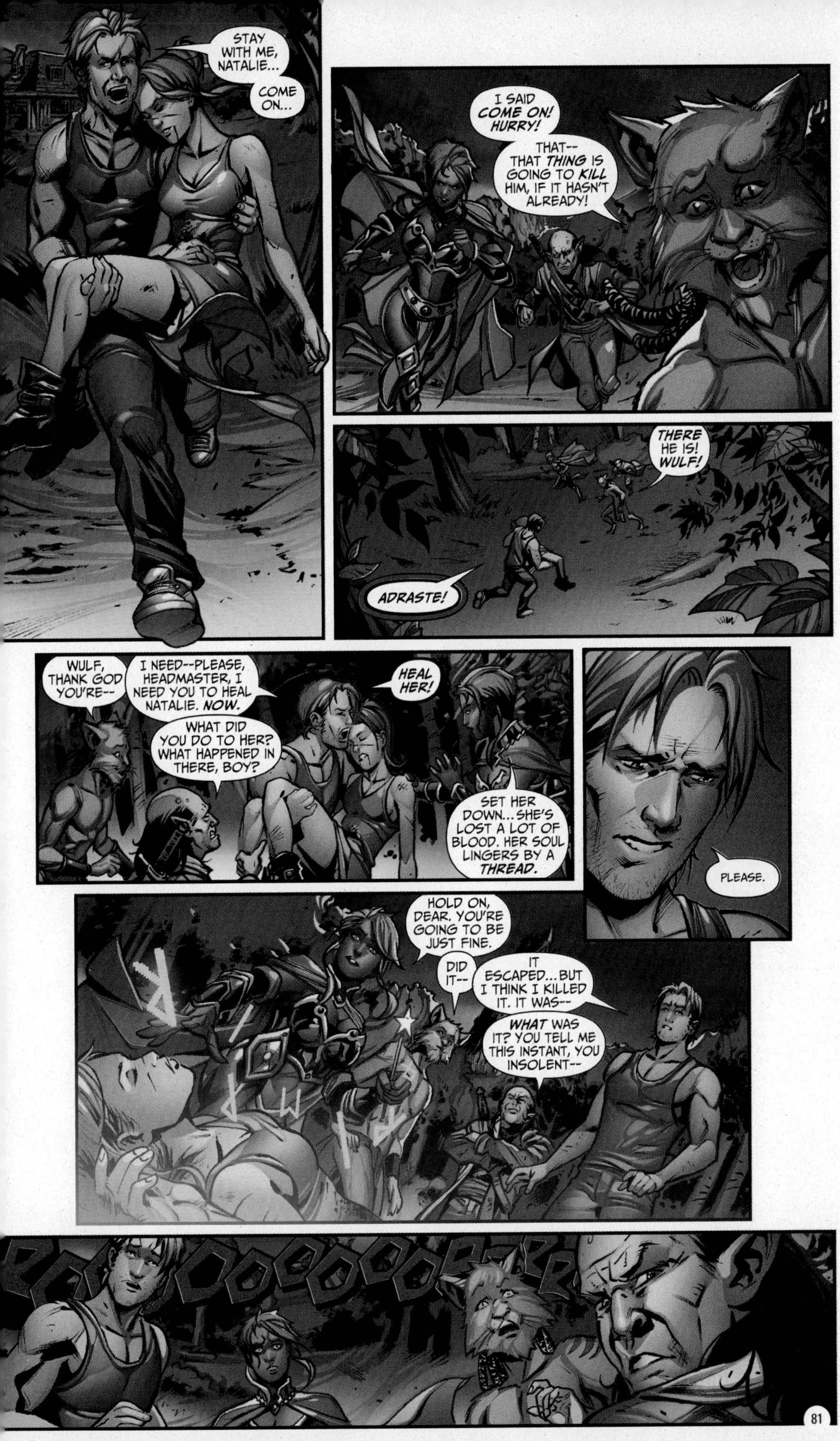

STAY WITH ME, NATALIE...
COME ON...
I SAID COME ON! HURRY!
THAT-- THAT THING IS GOING TO KILL HIM, IF IT HASN'T ALREADY!
THERE HE IS! WULF!
ADRASTE!
WULF, THANK GOD YOU'RE--
I NEED--PLEASE, HEADMASTER, I NEED YOU TO HEAL NATALIE. NOW.
HEAL HER!
WHAT DID YOU DO TO HER? WHAT HAPPENED IN THERE, BOY?
SET HER DOWN... SHE'S LOST A LOT OF BLOOD. HER SOUL LINGERS BY A THREAD.
PLEASE.
HOLD ON, DEAR. YOU'RE GOING TO BE JUST FINE.
DID IT--
IT ESCAPED... BUT I THINK I KILLED IT. IT WAS--
WHAT WAS IT? YOU TELL ME THIS INSTANT, YOU INSOLENT--

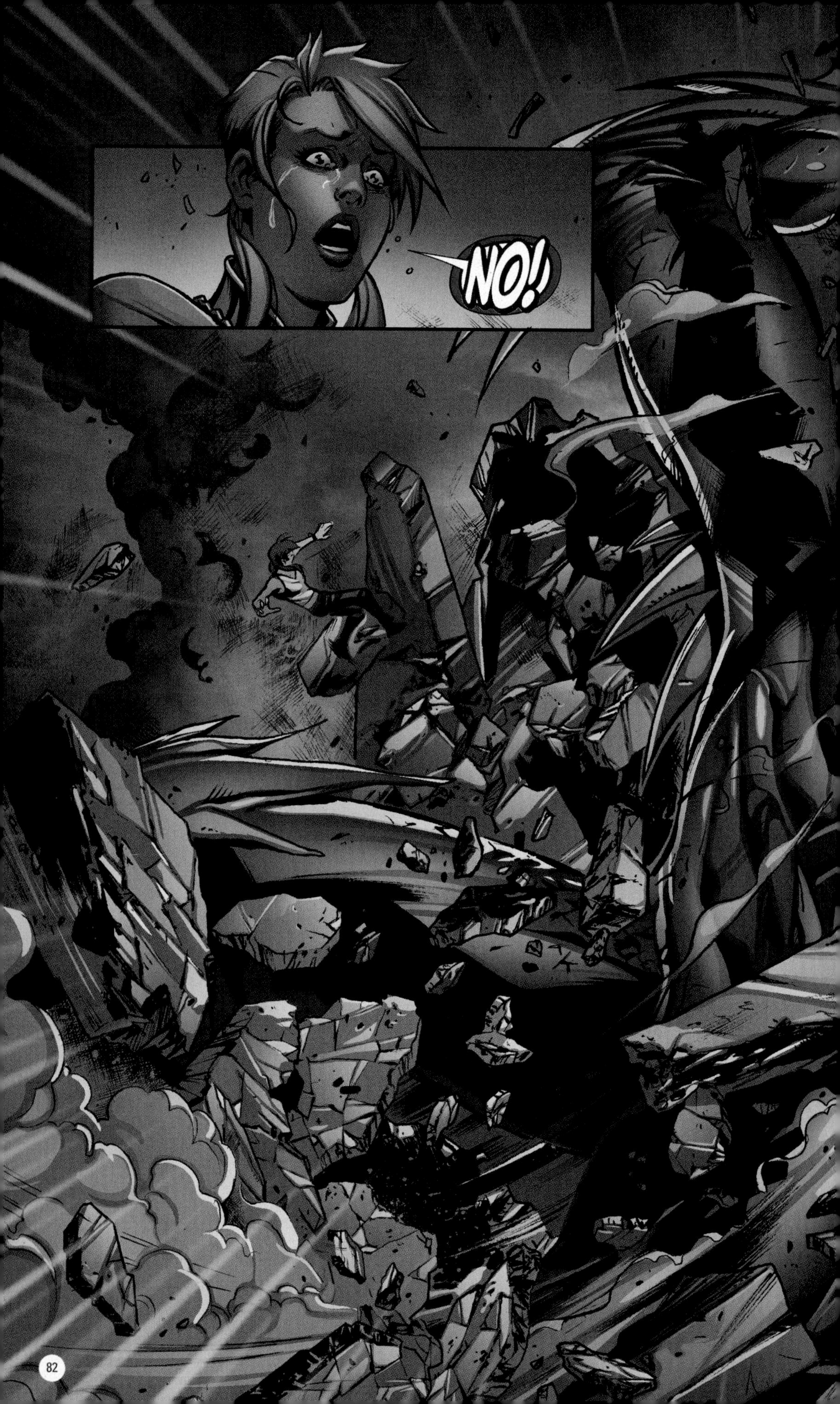
NO!!

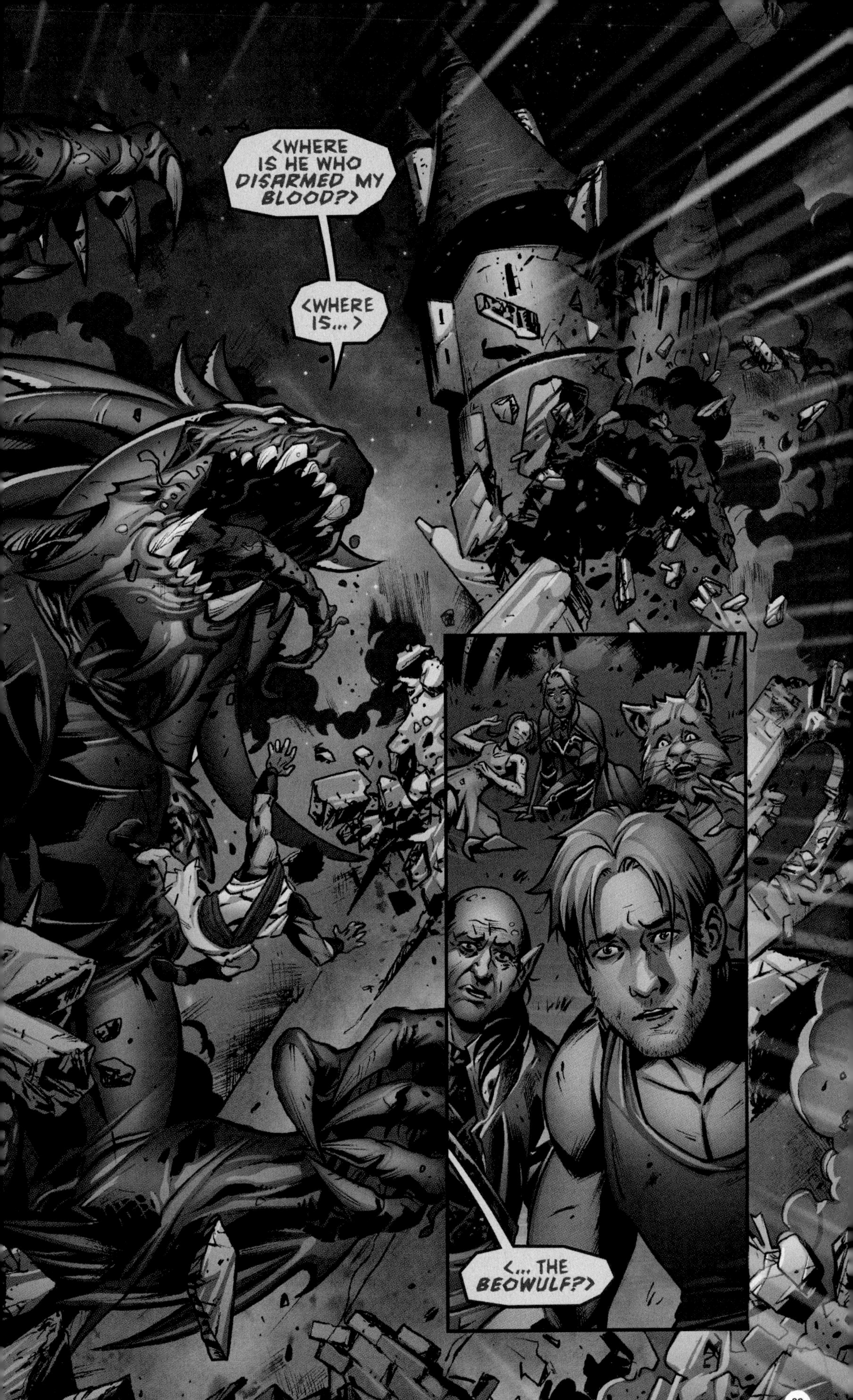
<WHERE IS HE WHO DISARMED MY BLOOD?>
<WHERE IS...>
<... THE BEOWULF?>

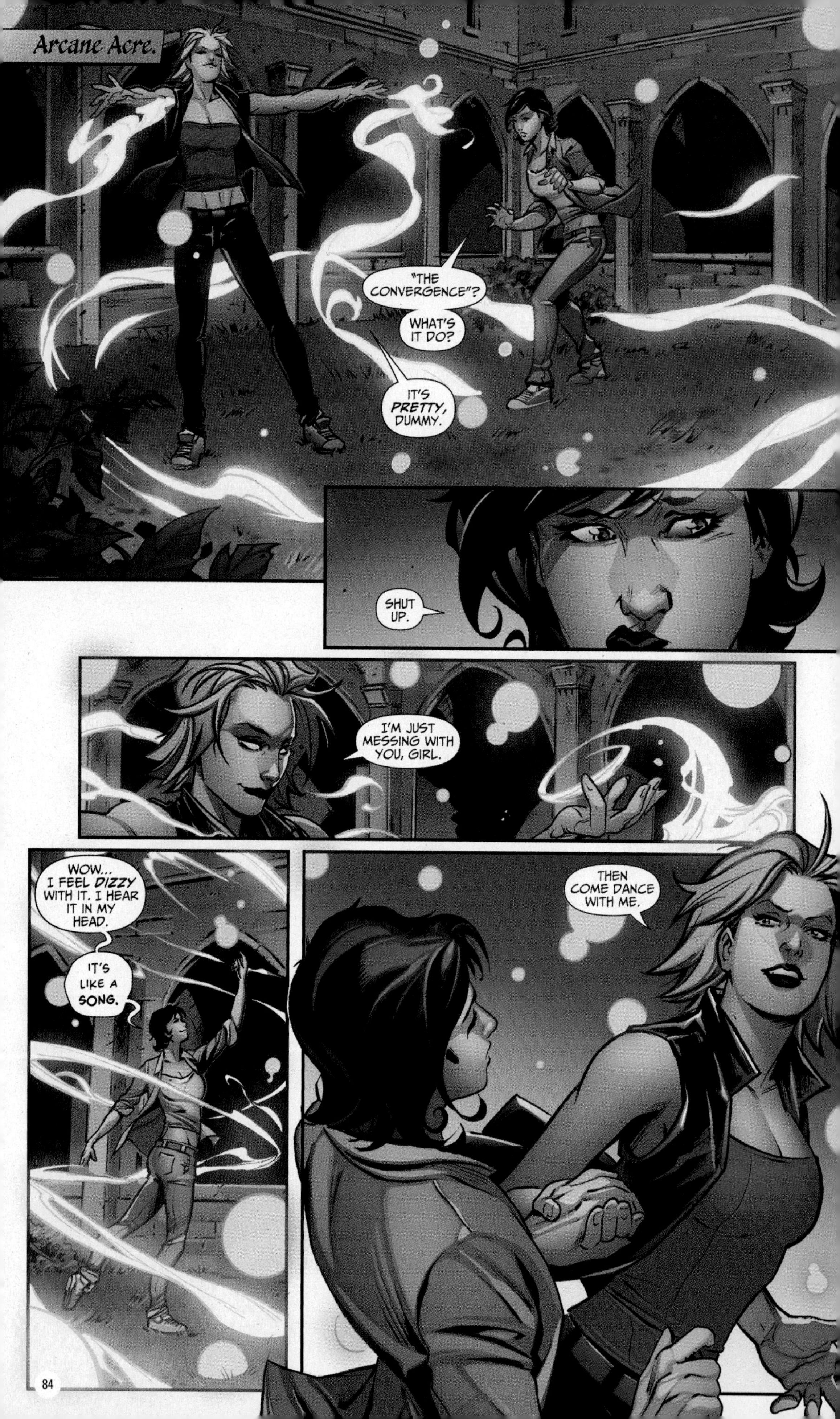
Arcane Acre.
"THE CONVERGENCE"?
WHAT'S IT DO?
IT'S PRETTY, DUMMY.
SHUT UP.
I'M JUST MESSING WITH YOU, GIRL.
WOW... I FEEL DIZZY WITH IT. I HEAR IT IN MY HEAD.
IT'S LIKE A SONG.
THEN COME DANCE WITH ME.

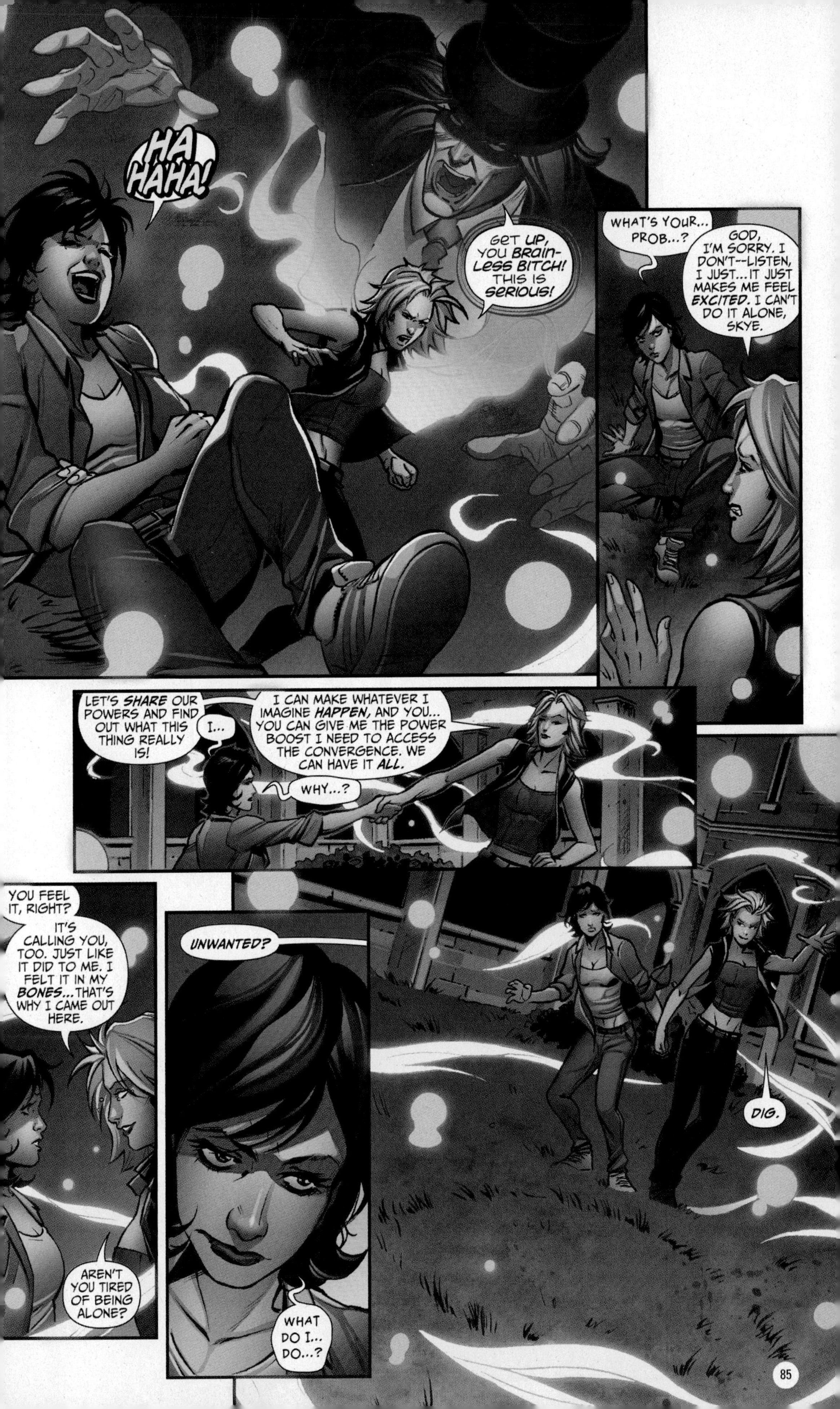

HA HAHA!
GET UP, YOU BRAIN-LESS BITCH! THIS IS SERIOUS!
WHAT'S YOUR... PROB...?
GOD, I'M SORRY. I DON'T--LISTEN, I JUST...IT JUST MAKES ME FEEL EXCITED. I CAN'T DO IT ALONE, SKYE.
LET'S SHARE OUR POWERS AND FIND OUT WHAT THIS THING REALLY IS!
I...
I CAN MAKE WHATEVER I IMAGINE HAPPEN, AND YOU... YOU CAN GIVE ME THE POWER BOOST I NEED TO ACCESS THE CONVERGENCE. WE CAN HAVE IT ALL.
WHY...?
YOU FEEL IT, RIGHT?
IT'S CALLING YOU, TOO. JUST LIKE IT DID TO ME. I FELT IT IN MY BONES...THAT'S WHY I CAME OUT HERE.
AREN'T YOU TIRED OF BEING ALONE?
UNWANTED?
WHAT DO I... DO...?
DIG.

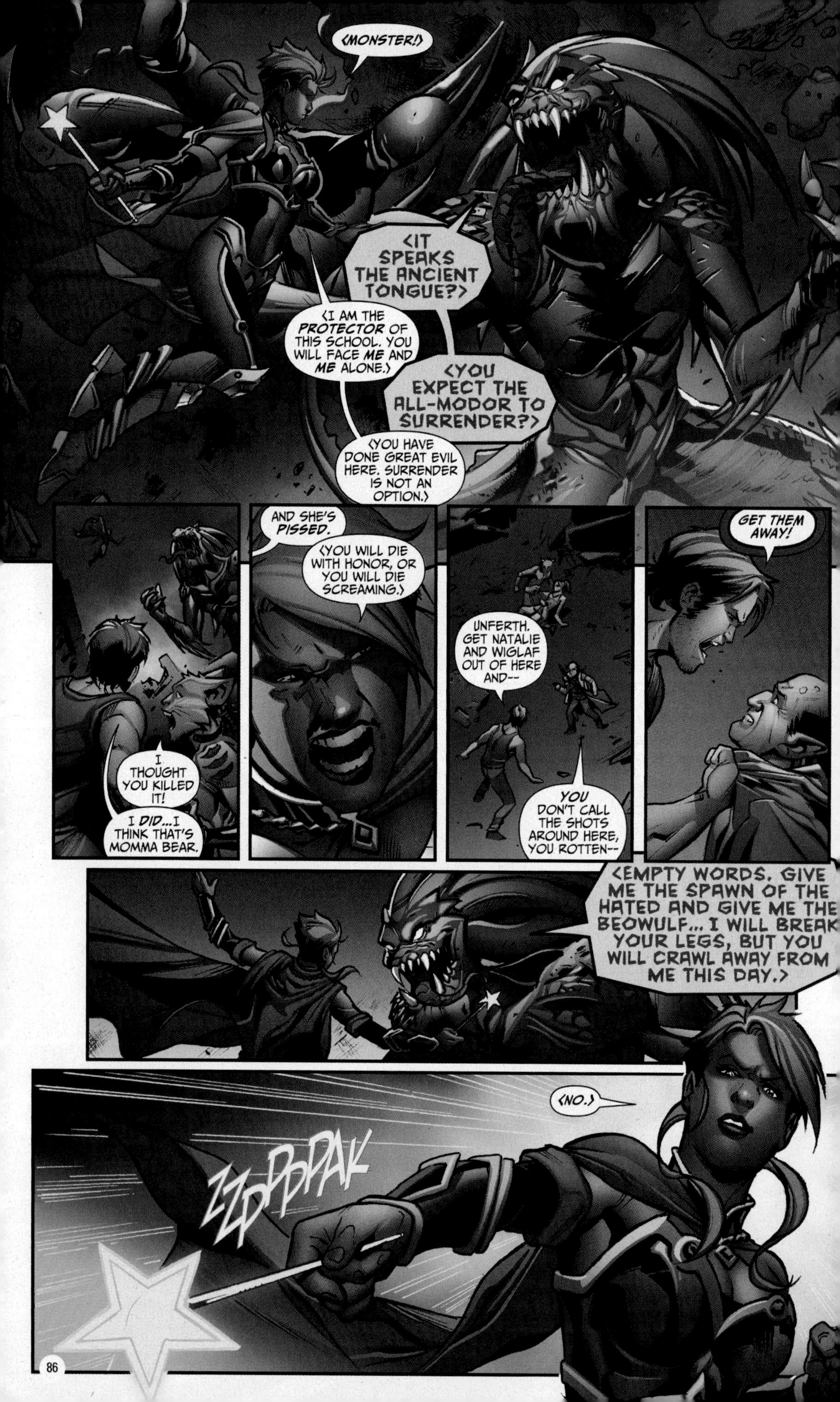

<MONSTER!>
<IT SPEAKS THE ANCIENT TONGUE?>
<I AM THE PROTECTOR OF THIS SCHOOL. YOU WILL FACE ME AND ME ALONE.>
<YOU EXPECT THE ALL-MODOR TO SURRENDER?>
<YOU HAVE DONE GREAT EVIL HERE. SURRENDER IS NOT AN OPTION.>
I THOUGHT YOU KILLED IT!
I DID...I THINK THAT'S MOMMA BEAR.
AND SHE'S PISSED.
<YOU WILL DIE WITH HONOR, OR YOU WILL DIE SCREAMING.>
UNFERTH. GET NATALIE AND WIGLAF OUT OF HERE AND--
YOU DON'T CALL THE SHOTS AROUND HERE, YOU ROTTEN--
GET THEM AWAY!
<EMPTY WORDS. GIVE ME THE SPAWN OF THE HATED AND GIVE ME THE BEOWULF... I WILL BREAK YOUR LEGS, BUT YOU WILL CRAWL AWAY FROM ME THIS DAY.>
<NO.>
ZZDPDPAK

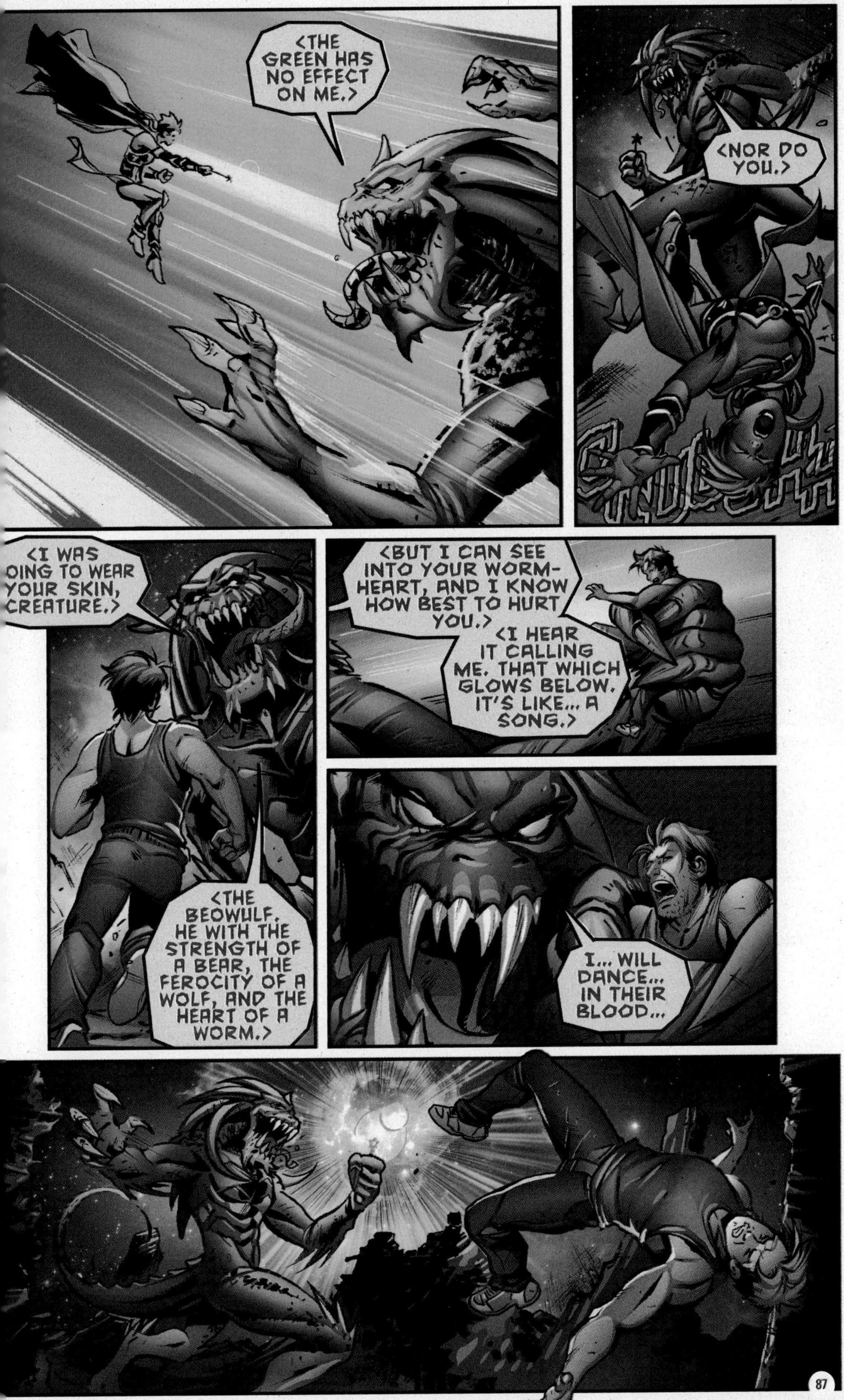
<THE GREEN HAS NO EFFECT ON ME.>
<NOR DO YOU.>
<I WAS OING TO WEAR YOUR SKIN, CREATURE.>
<THE BEOWULF. HE WITH THE STRENGTH OF A BEAR, THE FEROCITY OF A WOLF, AND THE HEART OF A WORM.>
<BUT I CAN SEE INTO YOUR WORM-HEART, AND I KNOW HOW BEST TO HURT YOU.>
<I HEAR IT CALLING ME. THAT WHICH GLOWS BELOW. IT'S LIKE... A SONG.>
I... WILL DANCE... IN THEIR BLOOD...

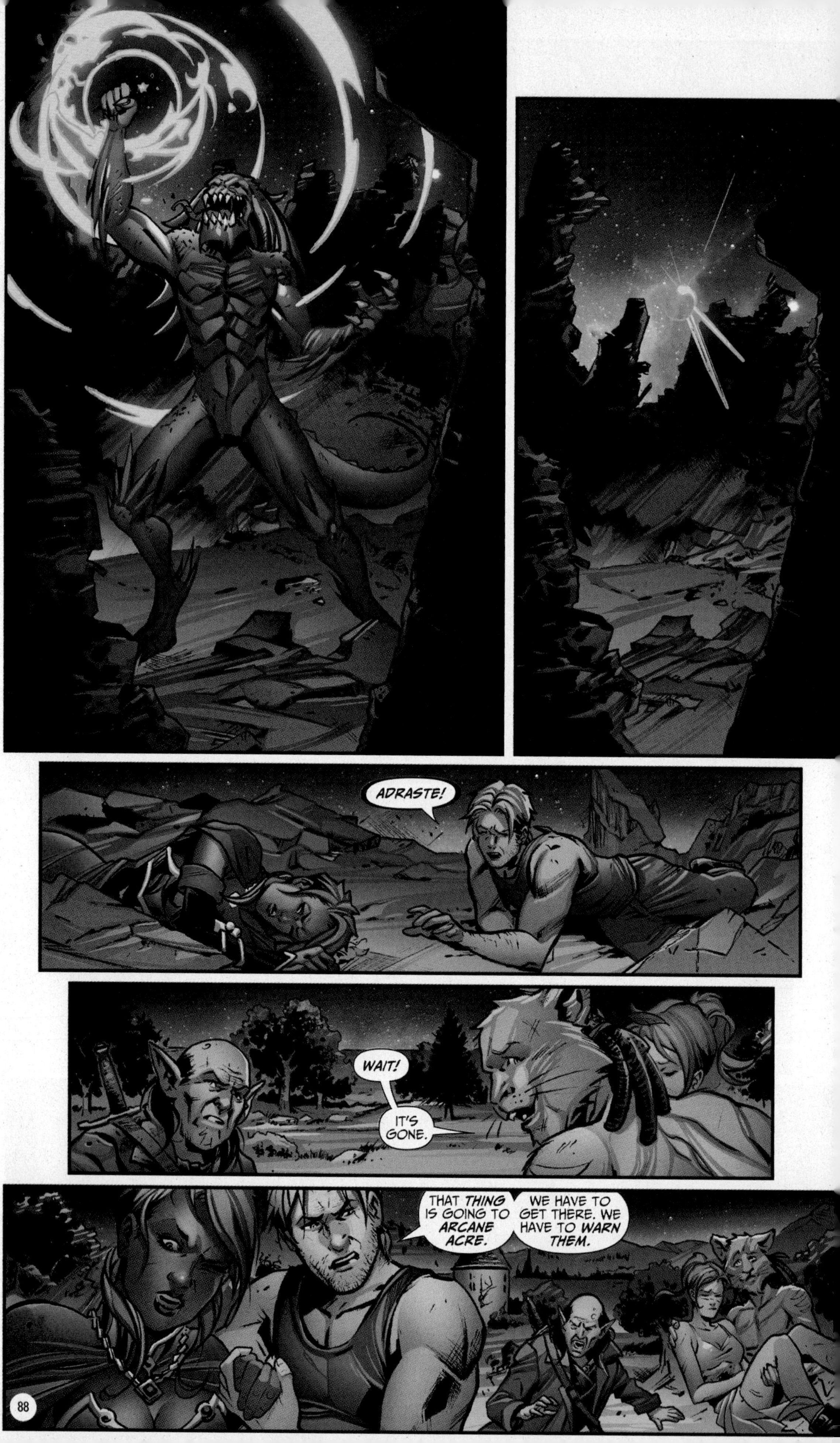
ADRASTE!
WAIT!
IT'S GONE.
THAT *THING* IS GOING TO *ARCANE ACRE.*
WE HAVE TO GET THERE. WE HAVE TO *WARN THEM.*

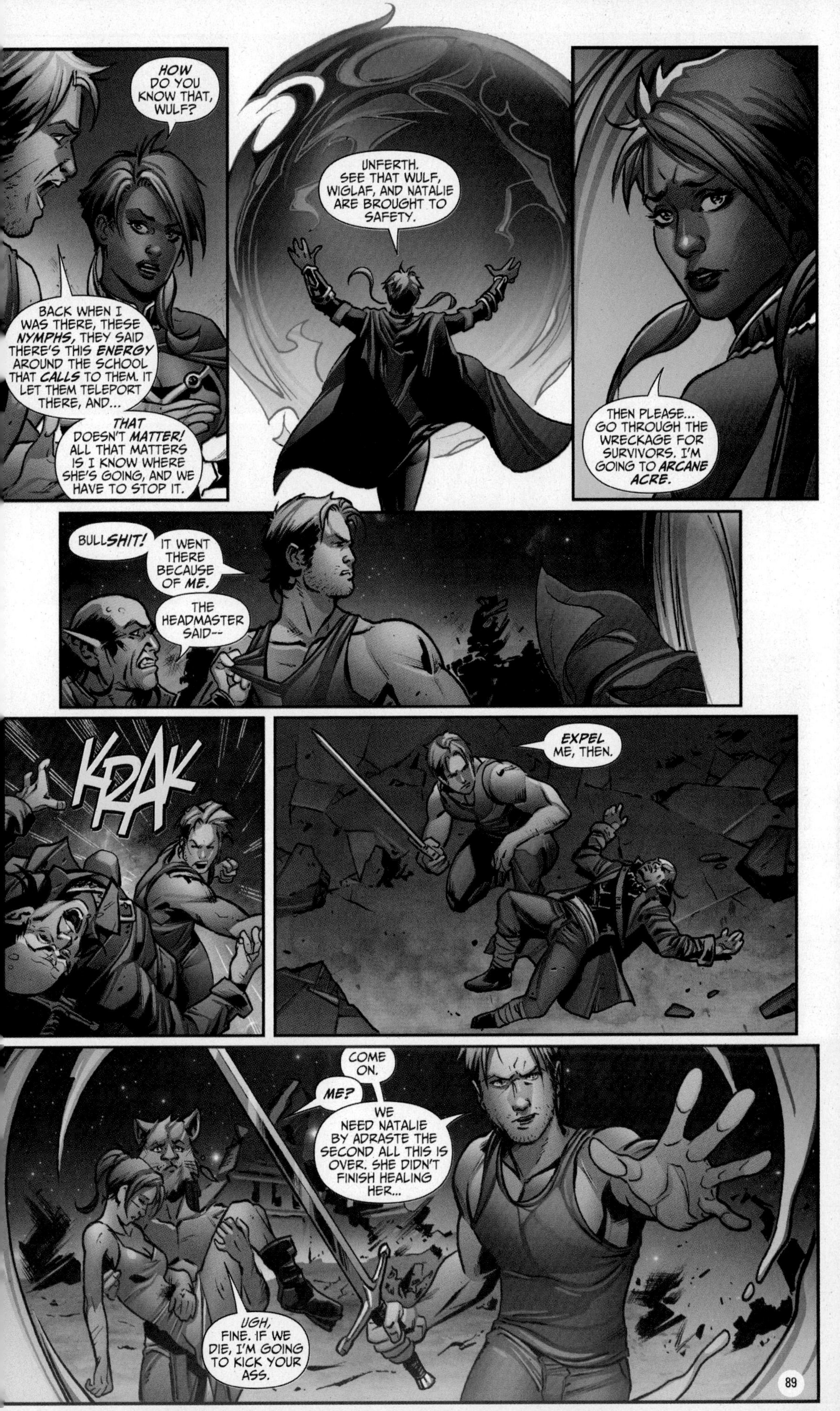
HOW DO YOU KNOW THAT, WULF?
BACK WHEN I WAS THERE, THESE NYMPHS, THEY SAID THERE'S THIS ENERGY AROUND THE SCHOOL THAT CALLS TO THEM. IT LET THEM TELEPORT THERE, AND...
THAT DOESN'T MATTER! ALL THAT MATTERS IS I KNOW WHERE SHE'S GOING, AND WE HAVE TO STOP IT.
UNFERTH. SEE THAT WULF, WIGLAF, AND NATALIE ARE BROUGHT TO SAFETY.
THEN PLEASE... GO THROUGH THE WRECKAGE FOR SURVIVORS. I'M GOING TO ARCANE ACRE.
BULLSHIT!
IT WENT THERE BECAUSE OF ME.
THE HEADMASTER SAID--
KRAK
EXPEL ME, THEN.
COME ON.
ME?
WE NEED NATALIE BY ADRASTE THE SECOND ALL THIS IS OVER. SHE DIDN'T FINISH HEALING HER...
UGH, FINE. IF WE DIE, I'M GOING TO KICK YOUR ASS.

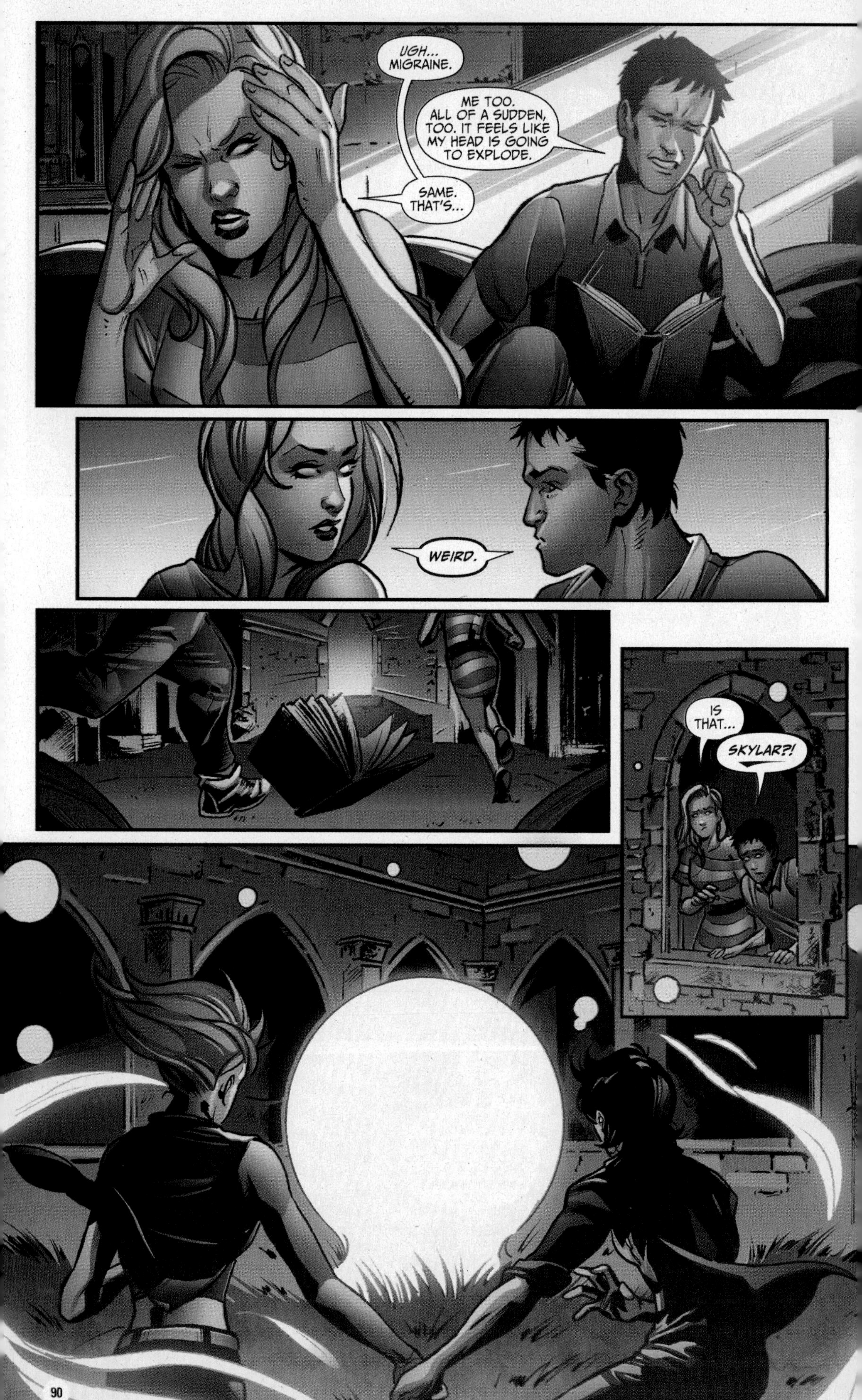
UGH... MIGRAINE.
ME TOO. ALL OF A SUDDEN, TOO. IT FEELS LIKE MY HEAD IS GOING TO EXPLODE.
SAME. THAT'S...
WEIRD.
IS THAT...
SKYLAR?!

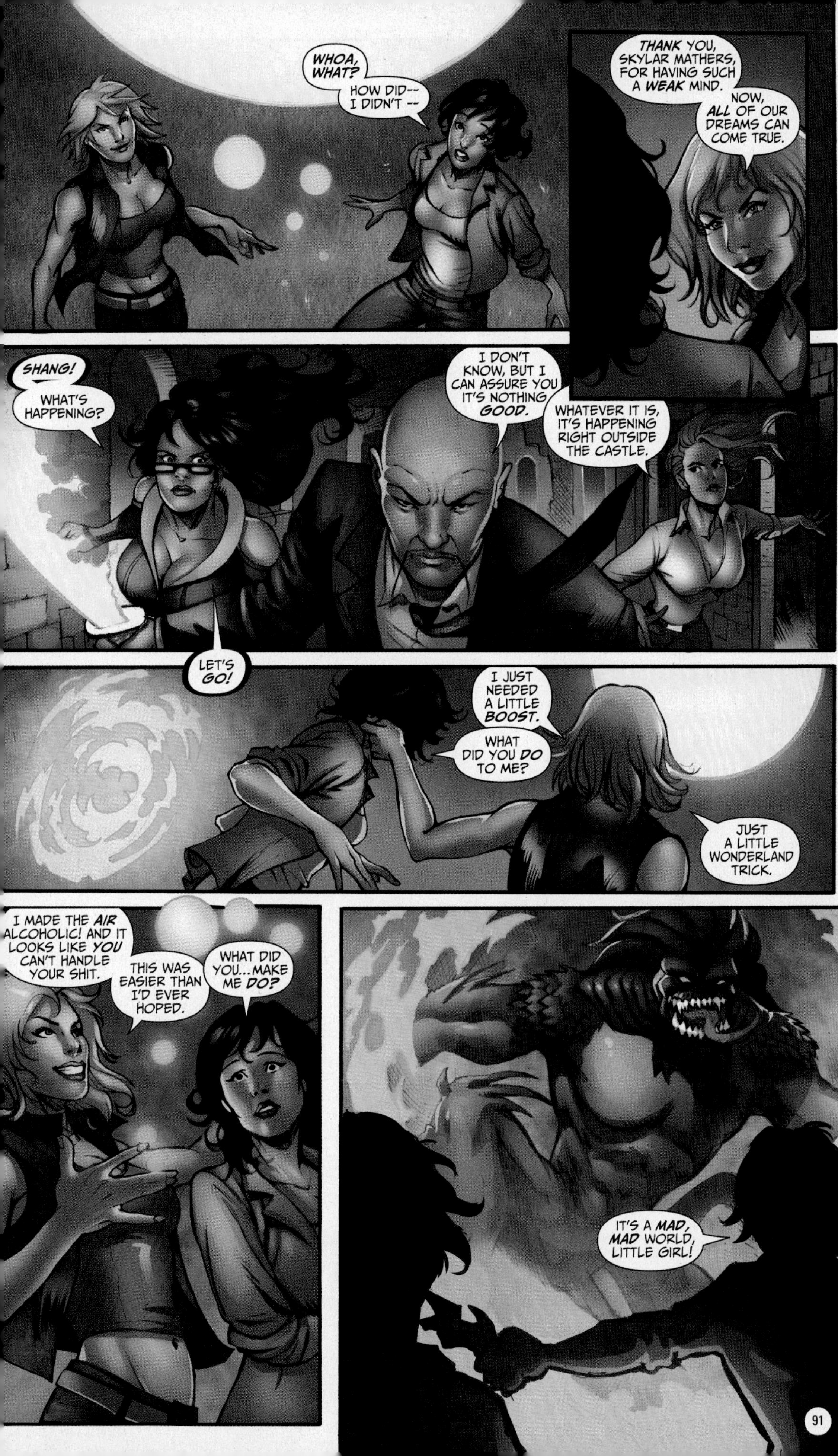
WHOA, WHAT?
HOW DID-- I DIDN'T --
THANK YOU, SKYLAR MATHERS, FOR HAVING SUCH A WEAK MIND.
NOW, ALL OF OUR DREAMS CAN COME TRUE.
SHANG!
WHAT'S HAPPENING?
I DON'T KNOW, BUT I CAN ASSURE YOU IT'S NOTHING GOOD.
WHATEVER IT IS, IT'S HAPPENING RIGHT OUTSIDE THE CASTLE.
LET'S GO!
I JUST NEEDED A LITTLE BOOST.
WHAT DID YOU DO TO ME?
JUST A LITTLE WONDERLAND TRICK.
I MADE THE AIR ALCOHOLIC! AND IT LOOKS LIKE YOU CAN'T HANDLE YOUR SHIT.
THIS WAS EASIER THAN I'D EVER HOPED.
WHAT DID YOU...MAKE ME DO?
IT'S A MAD, MAD WORLD, LITTLE GIRL!

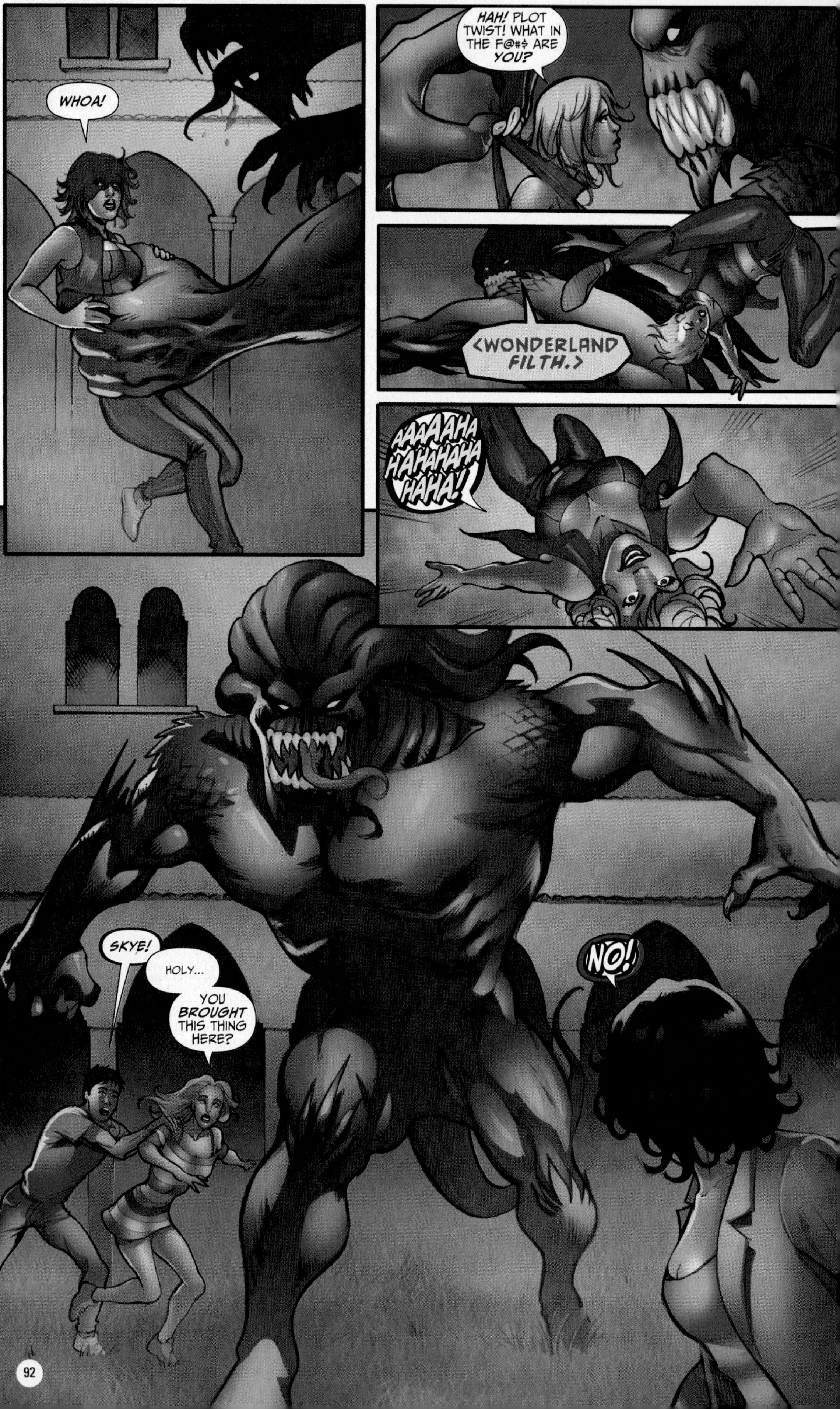
WHOA!
HAH! PLOT TWIST! WHAT IN THE F@#$ ARE YOU?
<WONDERLAND FILTH.>
AAAAAHA HAHAHAHA HAHA!
SKYE!
HOLY...
YOU BROUGHT THIS THING HERE?
NO!

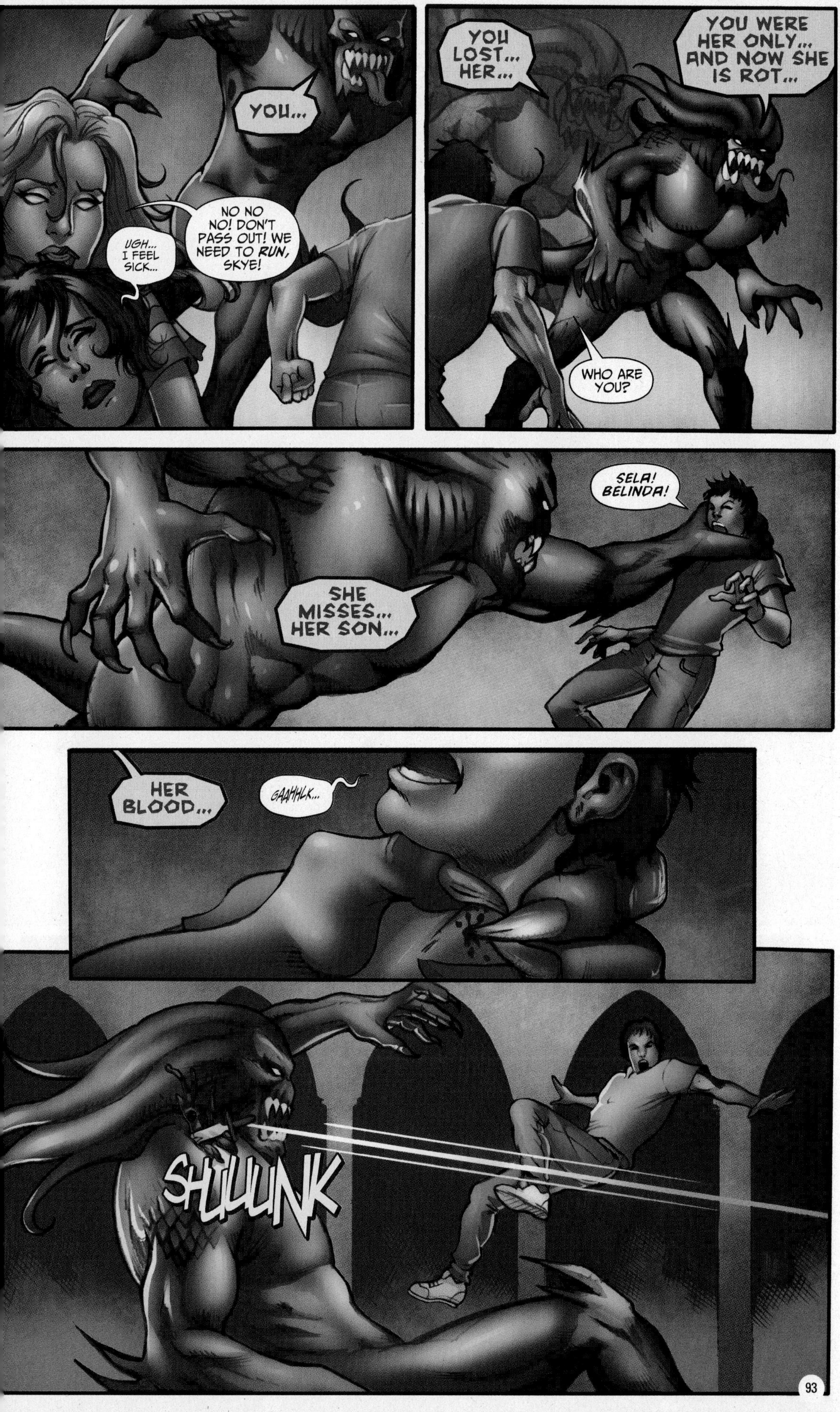
YOU...
UGH... I FEEL SICK...
NO NO NO! DON'T PASS OUT! WE NEED TO RUN, SKYE!
YOU LOST... HER...
YOU WERE HER ONLY... AND NOW SHE IS ROT...
WHO ARE YOU?
SELA! BELINDA!
SHE MISSES... HER SON...
HER BLOOD...
GAAHHLK...
SHUUUNK

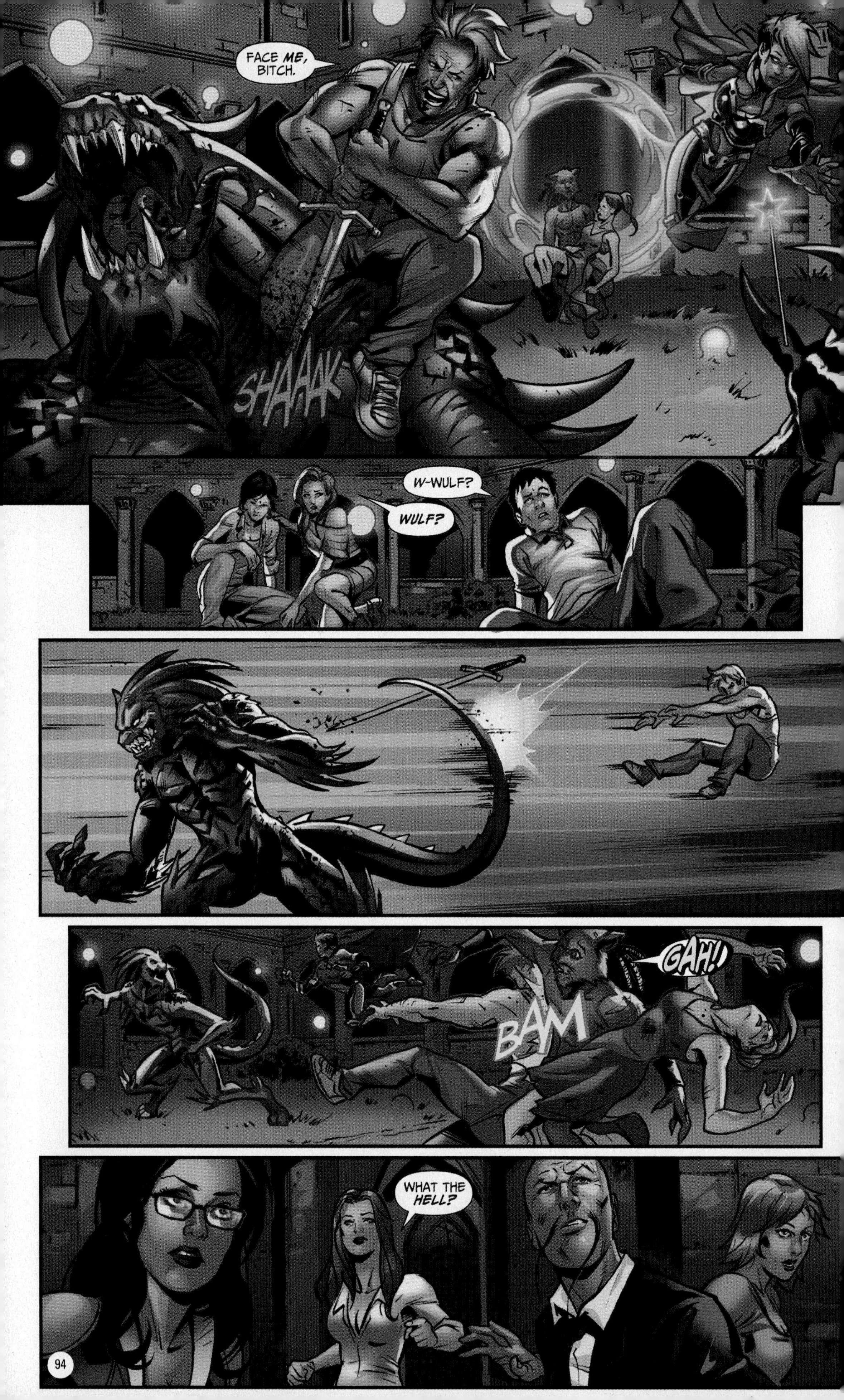
FACE ME, BITCH.
SHAAAK
W-WULF?
WULF?
GAH!!
BAM
WHAT THE HELL?

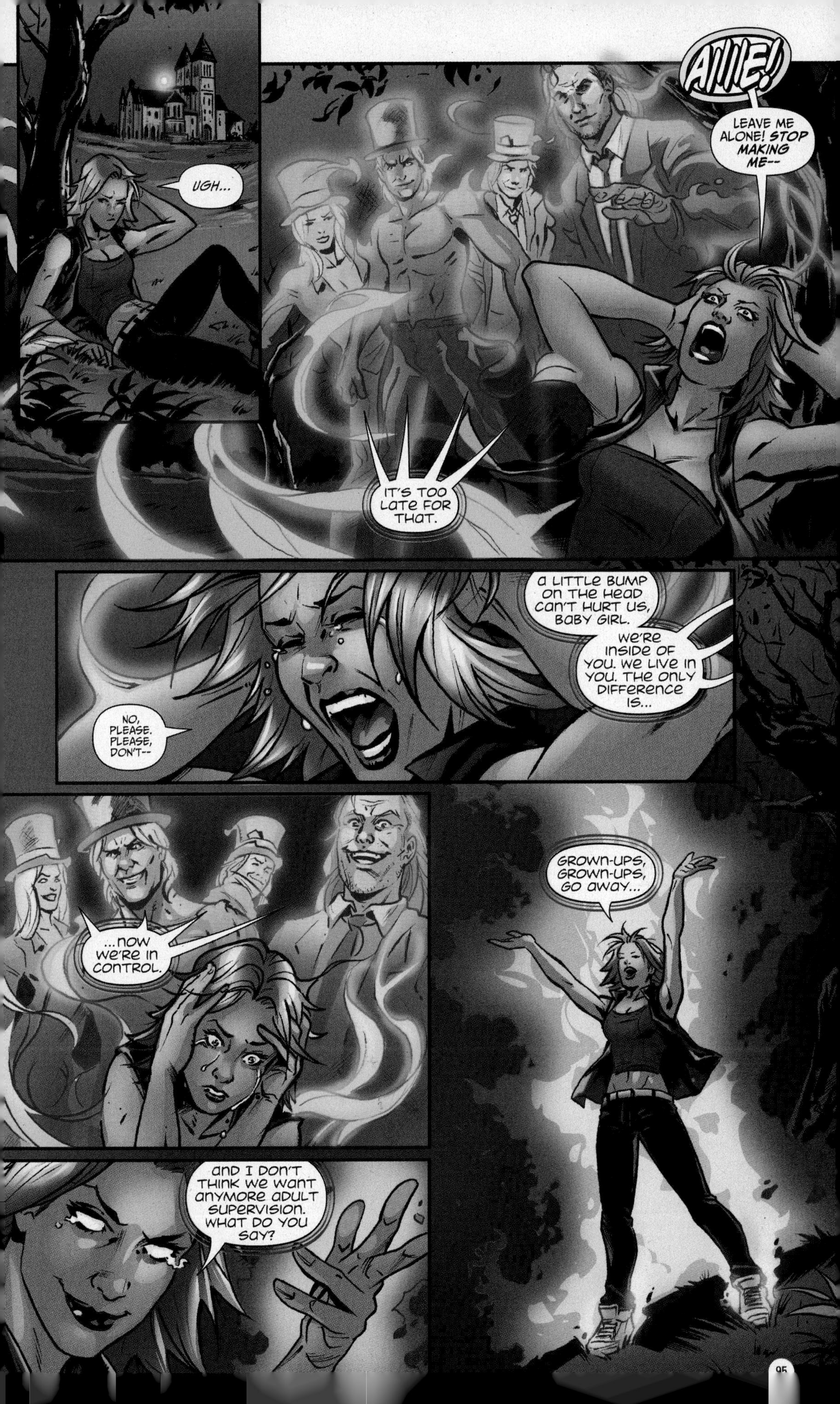
UGH...
AIIIE!!
LEAVE ME ALONE! STOP MAKING ME--
IT'S TOO LATE FOR THAT.
A LITTLE BUMP ON THE HEAD CAN'T HURT US, BABY GIRL.
WE'RE INSIDE OF YOU. WE LIVE IN YOU. THE ONLY DIFFERENCE IS...
NO, PLEASE. PLEASE, DON'T--
...NOW WE'RE IN CONTROL.
AND I DON'T THINK WE WANT ANYMORE ADULT SUPERVISION. WHAT DO YOU SAY?
GROWN-UPS, GROWN-UPS, GO AWAY...

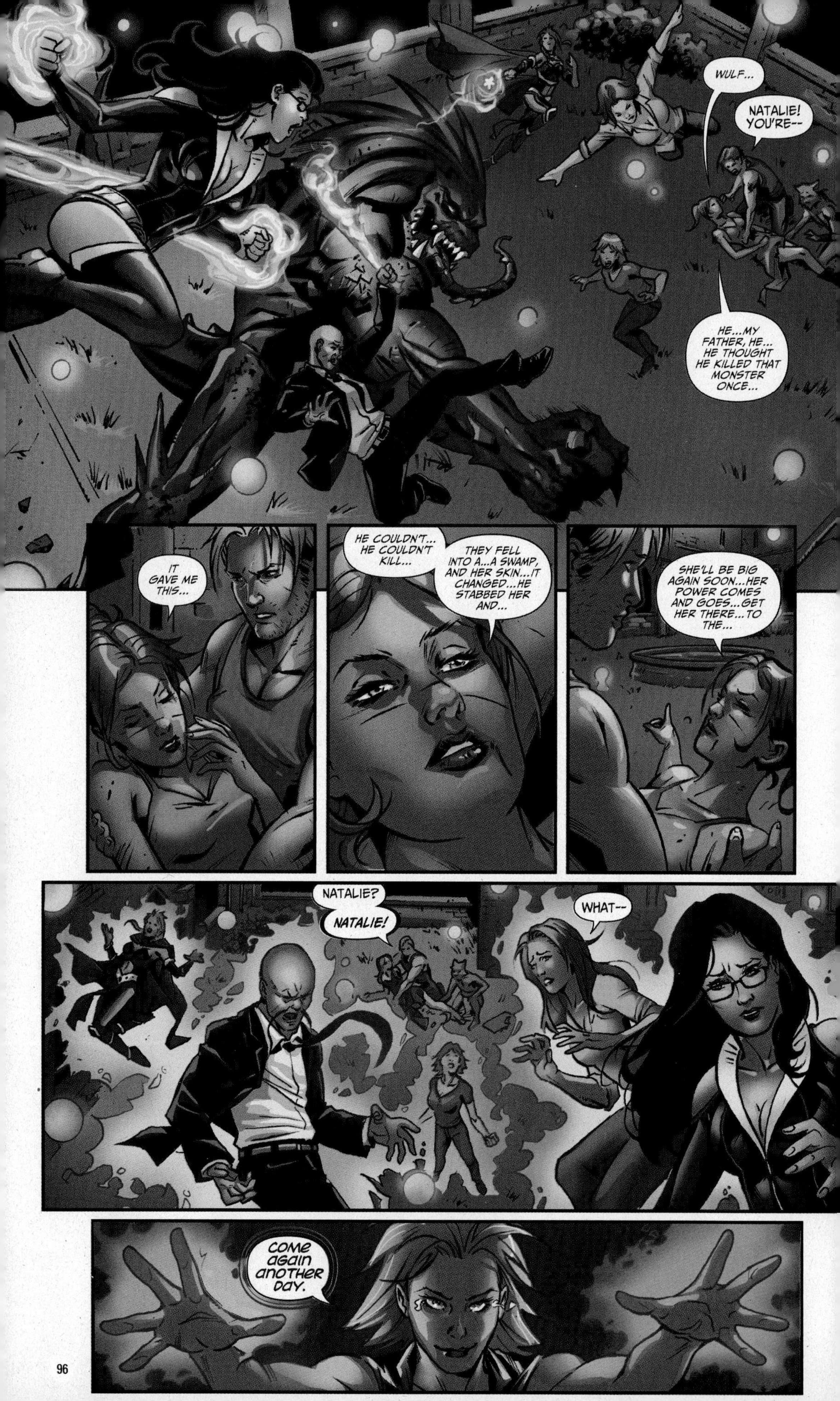
WULF...
NATALIE! YOU'RE--
HE...MY FATHER, HE... HE THOUGHT HE KILLED THAT MONSTER ONCE...
IT GAVE ME THIS...
HE COULDN'T... HE COULDN'T KILL...
THEY FELL INTO A...A SWAMP, AND HER SKIN...IT CHANGED...HE STABBED HER AND...
SHE'LL BE BIG AGAIN SOON...HER POWER COMES AND GOES...GET HER THERE...TO THE...
NATALIE?
NATALIE!
WHAT--
COME AGAIN ANOTHER DAY.

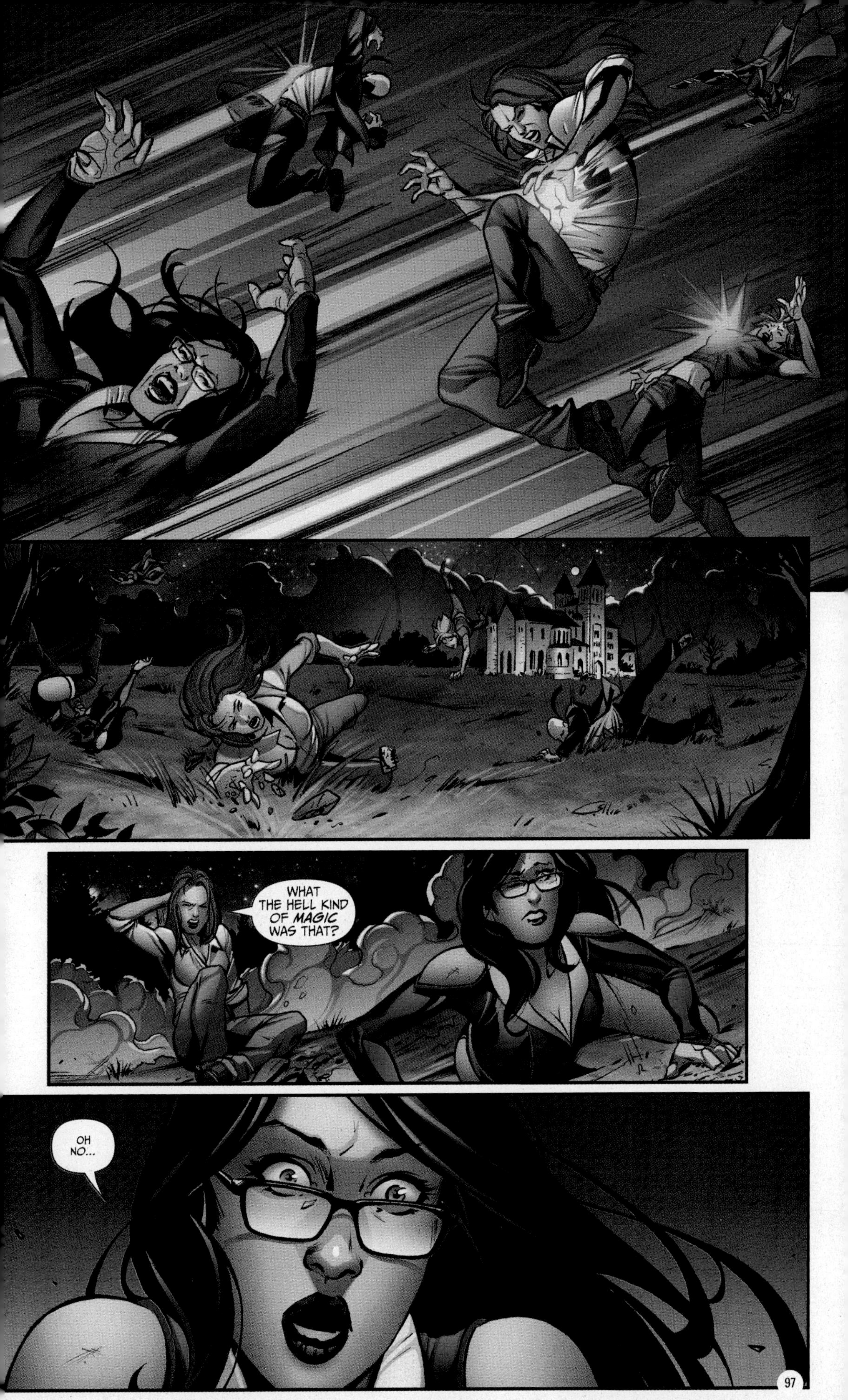
WHAT THE HELL KIND OF MAGIC WAS THAT?
OH NO...

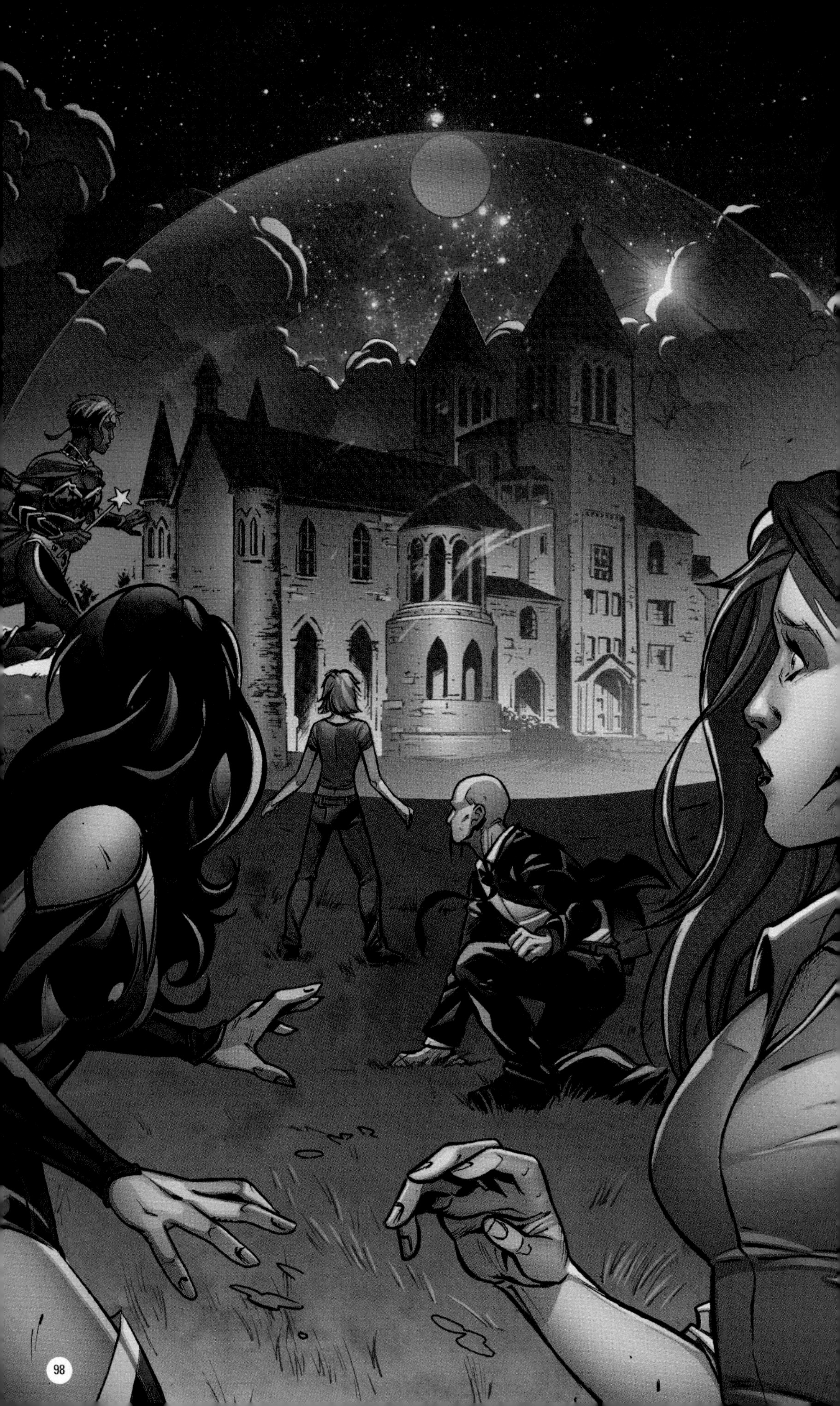

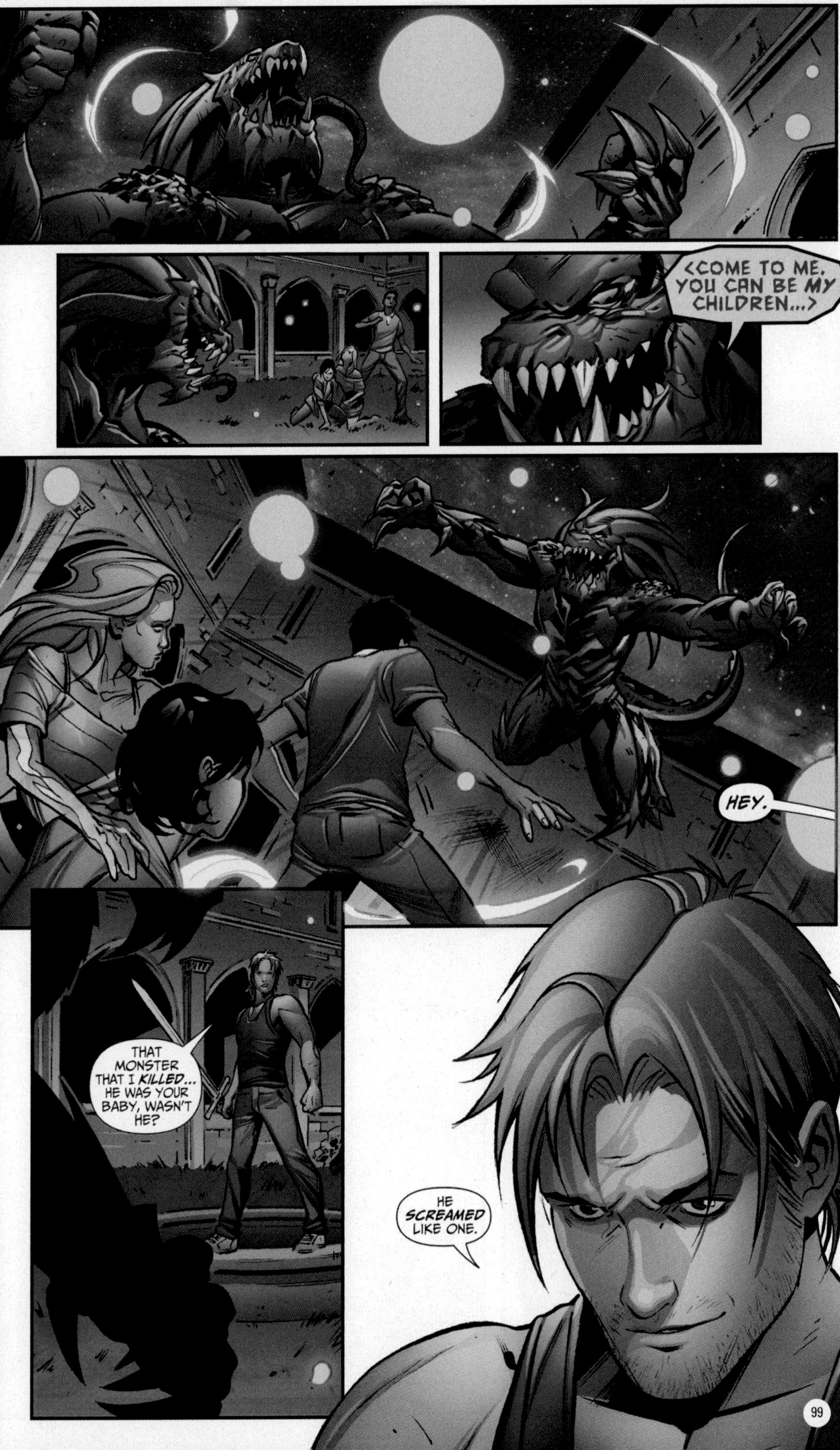

<COME TO ME. YOU CAN BE MY CHILDREN...>
HEY.
THAT MONSTER THAT I KILLED... HE WAS YOUR BABY, WASN'T HE?
HE SCREAMED LIKE ONE.

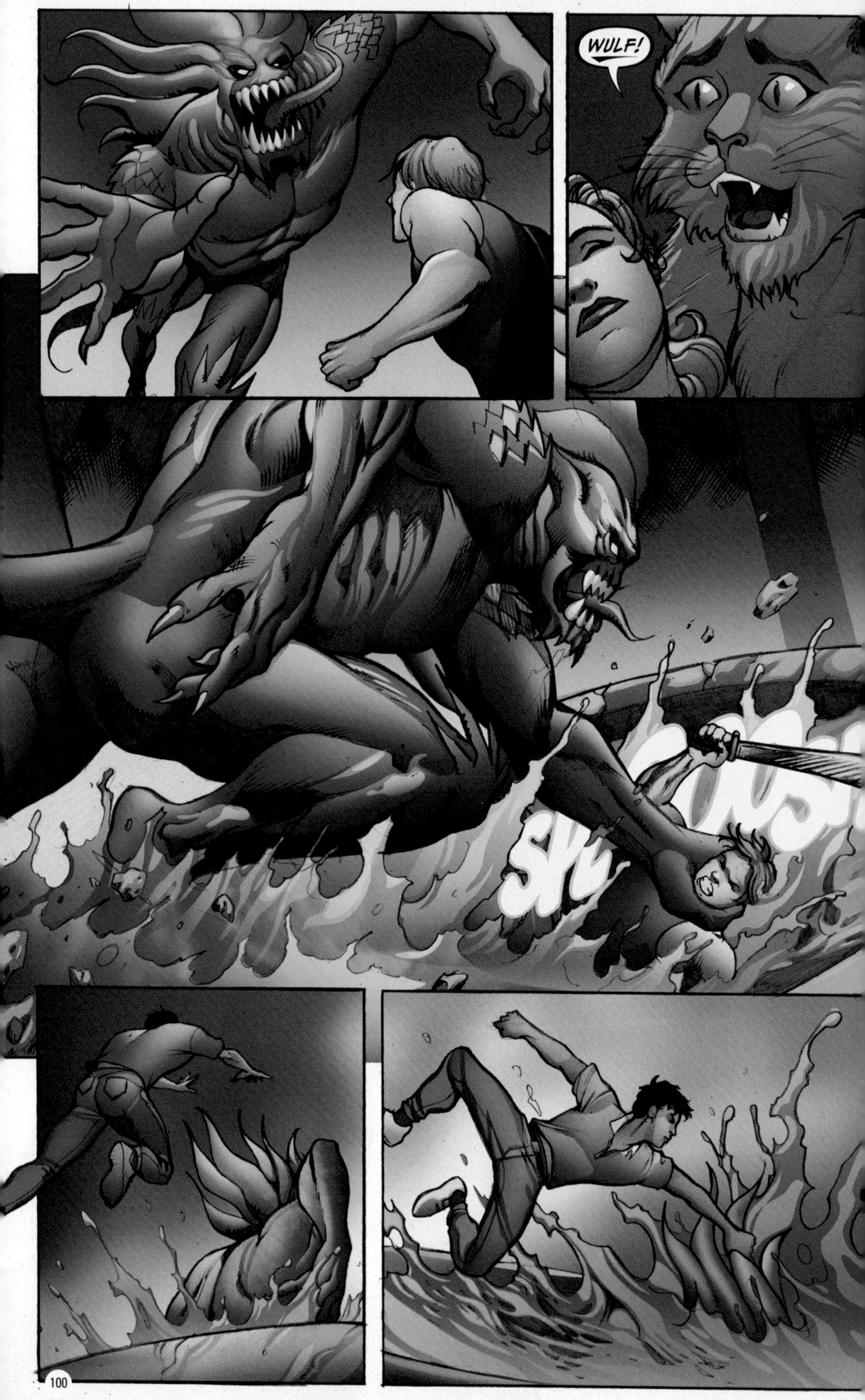
WULF!

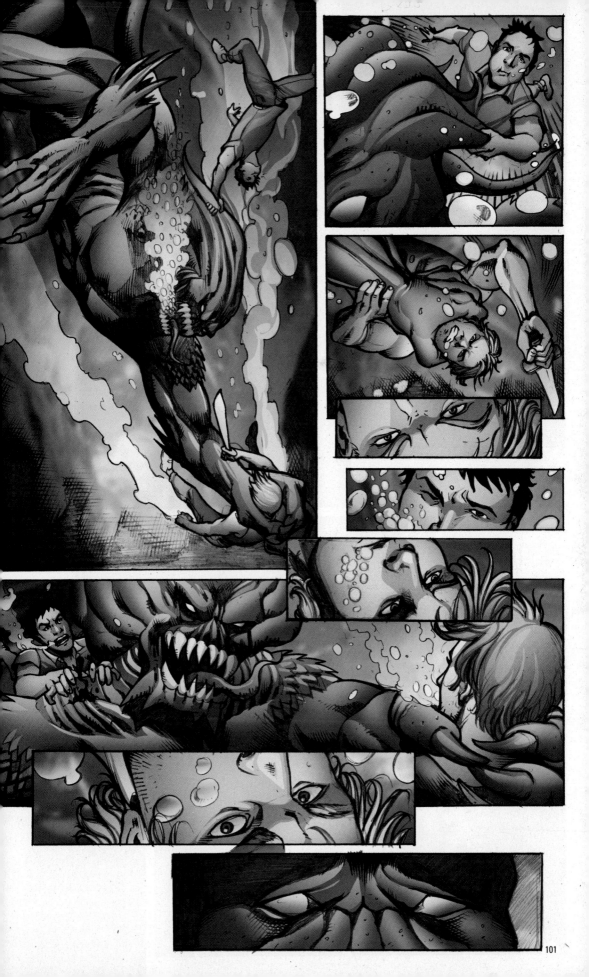

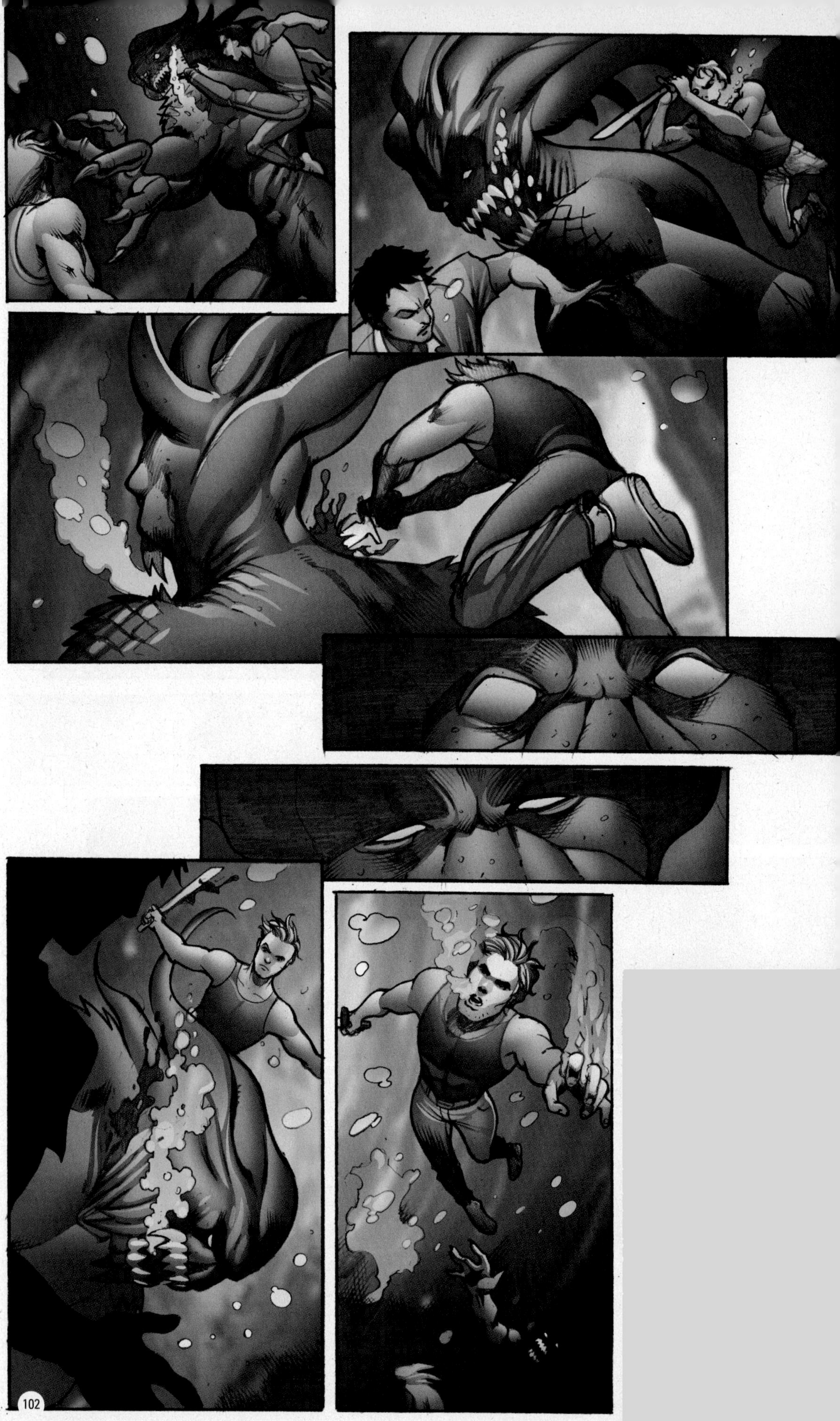

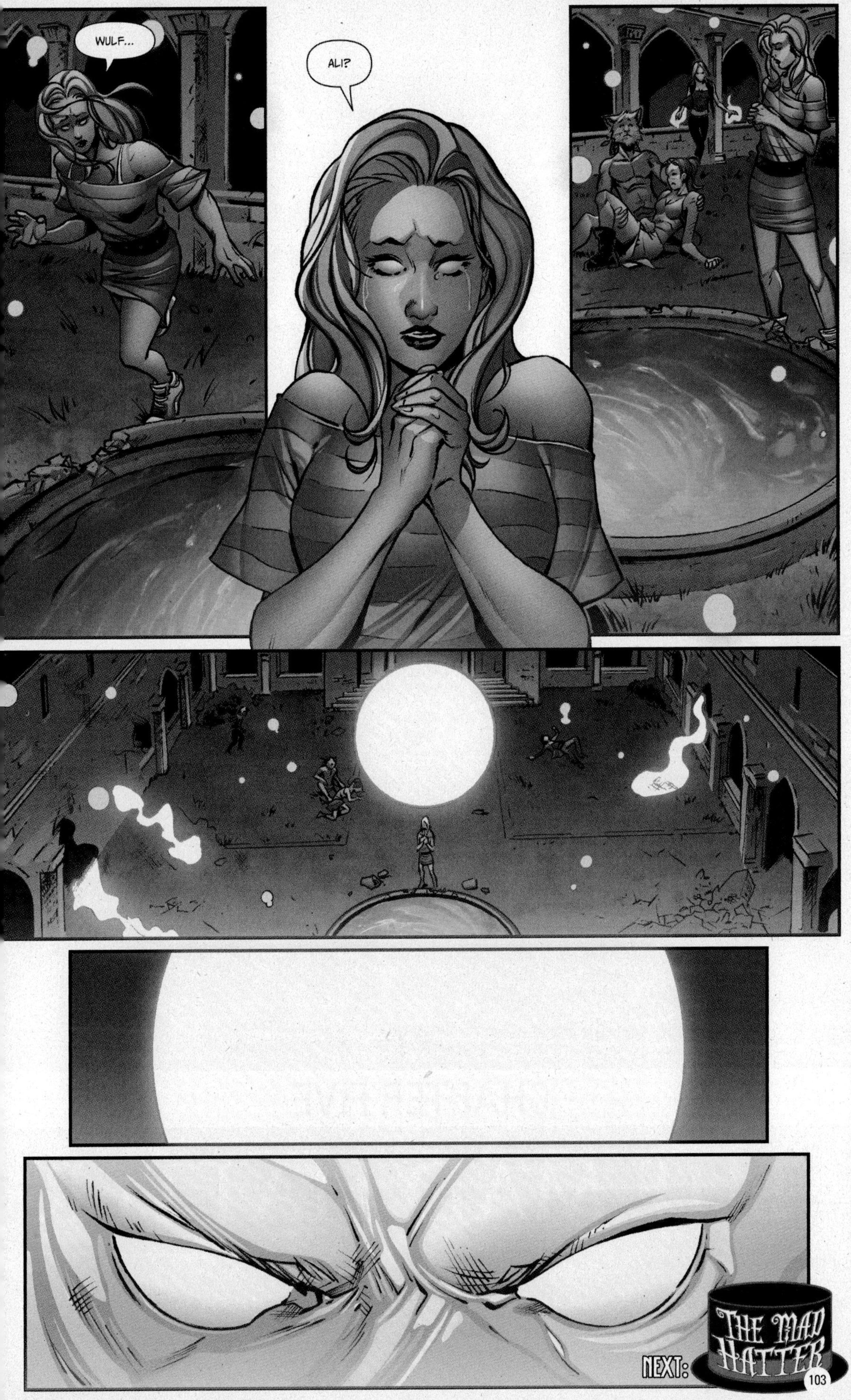
WULF...
ALI?
NEXT:
THE MAD HATTER

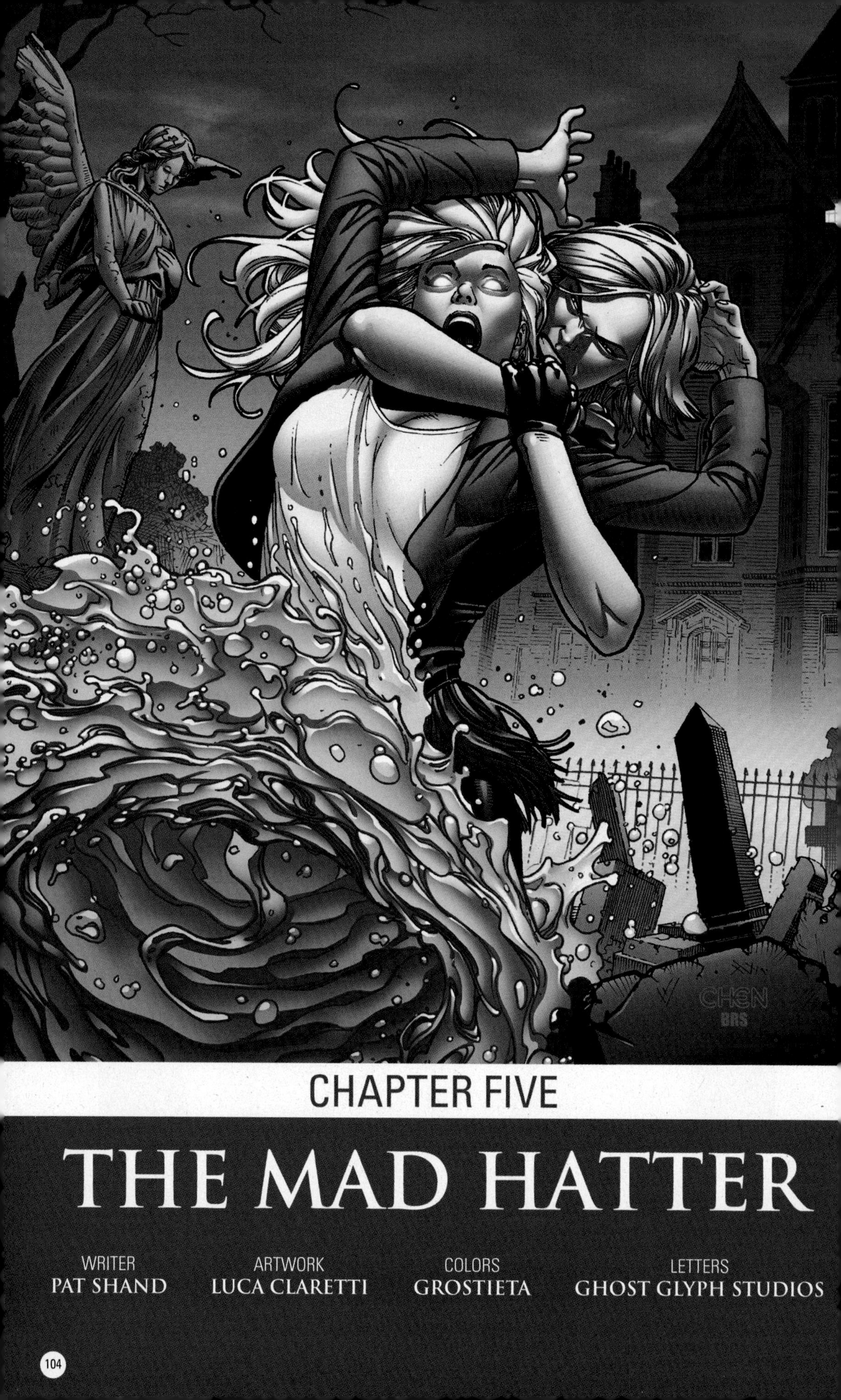
CHEN
BRS

CHAPTER FIVE

THE MAD HATTER

WRITER
PAT SHAND

ARTWORK
LUCA CLARETTI

COLORS
GROSTIETA

LETTERS
GHOST GLYPH STUDIOS

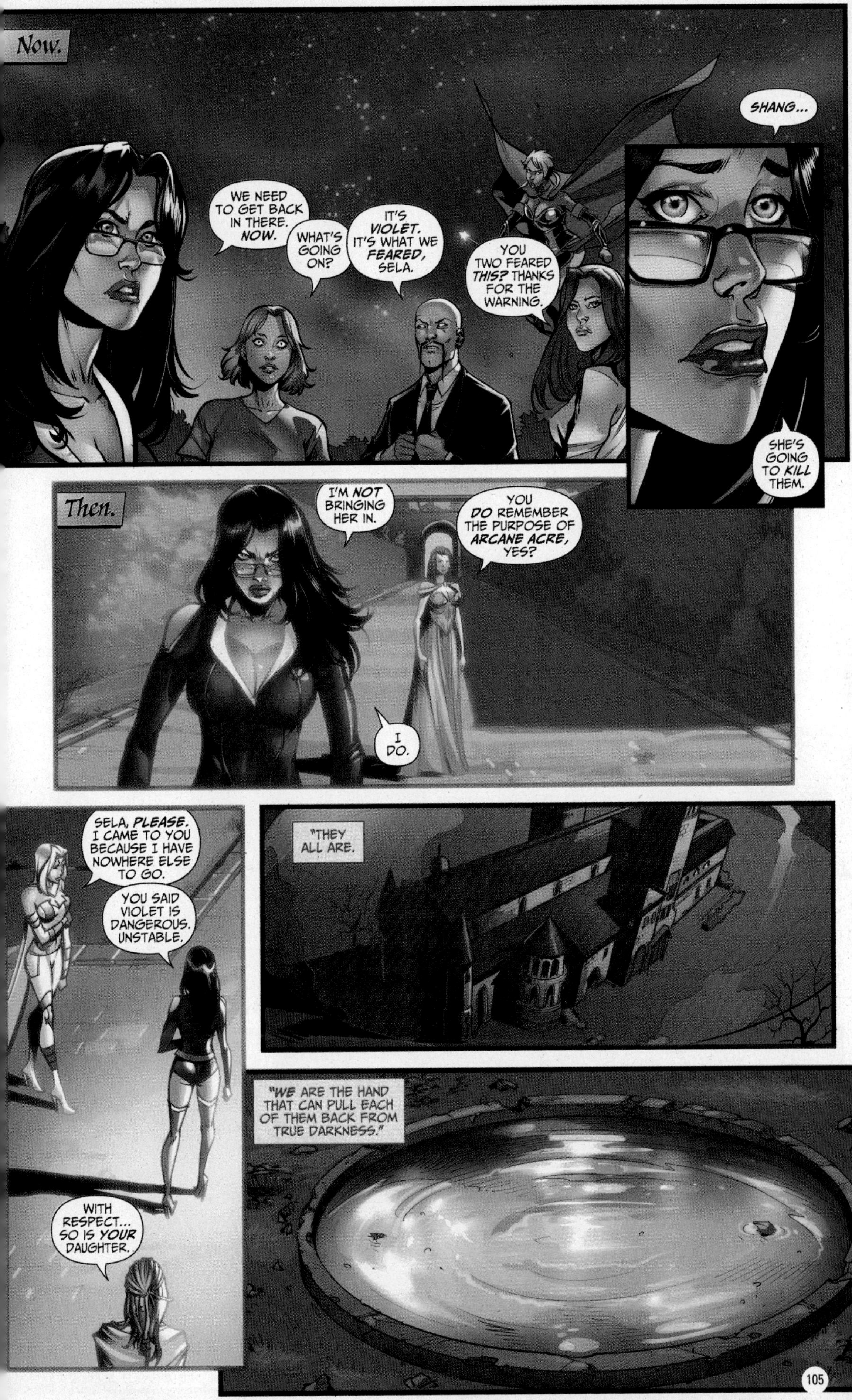
Now.
WE NEED TO GET BACK IN THERE. NOW.
WHAT'S GOING ON?
IT'S VIOLET. IT'S WHAT WE FEARED, SELA.
YOU TWO FEARED THIS? THANKS FOR THE WARNING.
SHANG...
SHE'S GOING TO KILL THEM.
Then.
I'M NOT BRINGING HER IN.
YOU DO REMEMBER THE PURPOSE OF ARCANE ACRE, YES?
I DO.
SELA, PLEASE. I CAME TO YOU BECAUSE I HAVE NOWHERE ELSE TO GO.
YOU SAID VIOLET IS DANGEROUS. UNSTABLE.
WITH RESPECT... SO IS YOUR DAUGHTER.
"THEY ALL ARE.
"WE ARE THE HAND THAT CAN PULL EACH OF THEM BACK FROM TRUE DARKNESS."

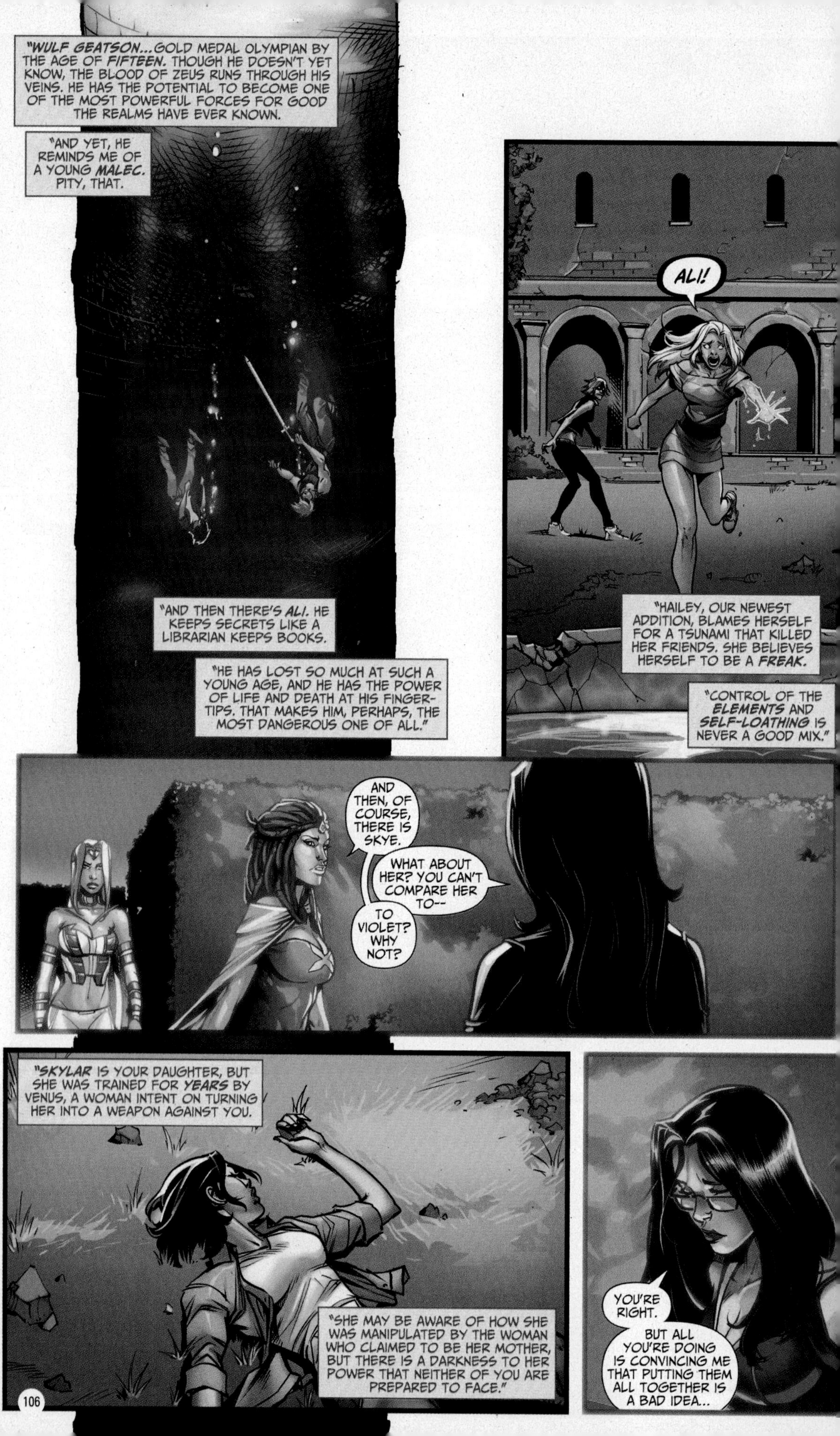

"WULF GEATSON...GOLD MEDAL OLYMPIAN BY THE AGE OF FIFTEEN. THOUGH HE DOESN'T YET KNOW, THE BLOOD OF ZEUS RUNS THROUGH HIS VEINS. HE HAS THE POTENTIAL TO BECOME ONE OF THE MOST POWERFUL FORCES FOR GOOD THE REALMS HAVE EVER KNOWN.
"AND YET, HE REMINDS ME OF A YOUNG MALEC. PITY, THAT.
"AND THEN THERE'S ALI. HE KEEPS SECRETS LIKE A LIBRARIAN KEEPS BOOKS.
"HE HAS LOST SO MUCH AT SUCH A YOUNG AGE, AND HE HAS THE POWER OF LIFE AND DEATH AT HIS FINGER-TIPS. THAT MAKES HIM, PERHAPS, THE MOST DANGEROUS ONE OF ALL."
ALI!
"HAILEY, OUR NEWEST ADDITION, BLAMES HERSELF FOR A TSUNAMI THAT KILLED HER FRIENDS. SHE BELIEVES HERSELF TO BE A FREAK.
"CONTROL OF THE ELEMENTS AND SELF-LOATHING IS NEVER A GOOD MIX."
AND THEN, OF COURSE, THERE IS SKYE.
WHAT ABOUT HER? YOU CAN'T COMPARE HER TO--
TO VIOLET? WHY NOT?
"SKYLAR IS YOUR DAUGHTER, BUT SHE WAS TRAINED FOR YEARS BY VENUS, A WOMAN INTENT ON TURNING HER INTO A WEAPON AGAINST YOU.
"SHE MAY BE AWARE OF HOW SHE WAS MANIPULATED BY THE WOMAN WHO CLAIMED TO BE HER MOTHER, BUT THERE IS A DARKNESS TO HER POWER THAT NEITHER OF YOU ARE PREPARED TO FACE."
YOU'RE RIGHT.
BUT ALL YOU'RE DOING IS CONVINCING ME THAT PUTTING THEM ALL TOGETHER IS A BAD IDEA...

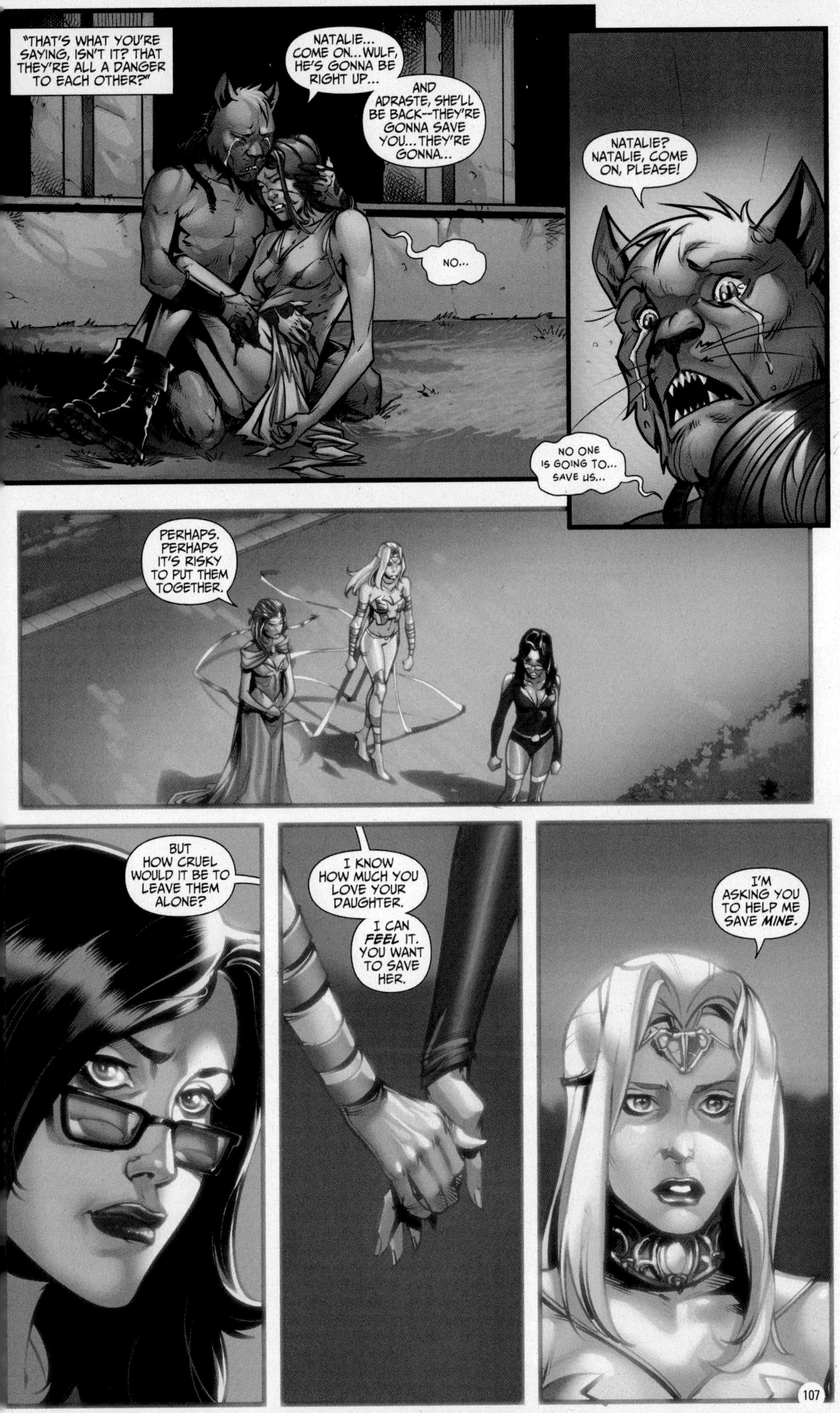
"THAT'S WHAT YOU'RE SAYING, ISN'T IT? THAT THEY'RE ALL A DANGER TO EACH OTHER?"
NATALIE... COME ON...WULF, HE'S GONNA BE RIGHT UP...
AND ADRASTE, SHE'LL BE BACK--THEY'RE GONNA SAVE YOU...THEY'RE GONNA...
NO...
NATALIE? NATALIE, COME ON, PLEASE!
NO ONE IS GOING TO... SAVE US...
PERHAPS. PERHAPS IT'S RISKY TO PUT THEM TOGETHER.
BUT HOW CRUEL WOULD IT BE TO LEAVE THEM ALONE?
I KNOW HOW MUCH YOU LOVE YOUR DAUGHTER.
I CAN *FEEL* IT. YOU WANT TO SAVE HER.
I'M ASKING YOU TO HELP ME SAVE *MINE*.

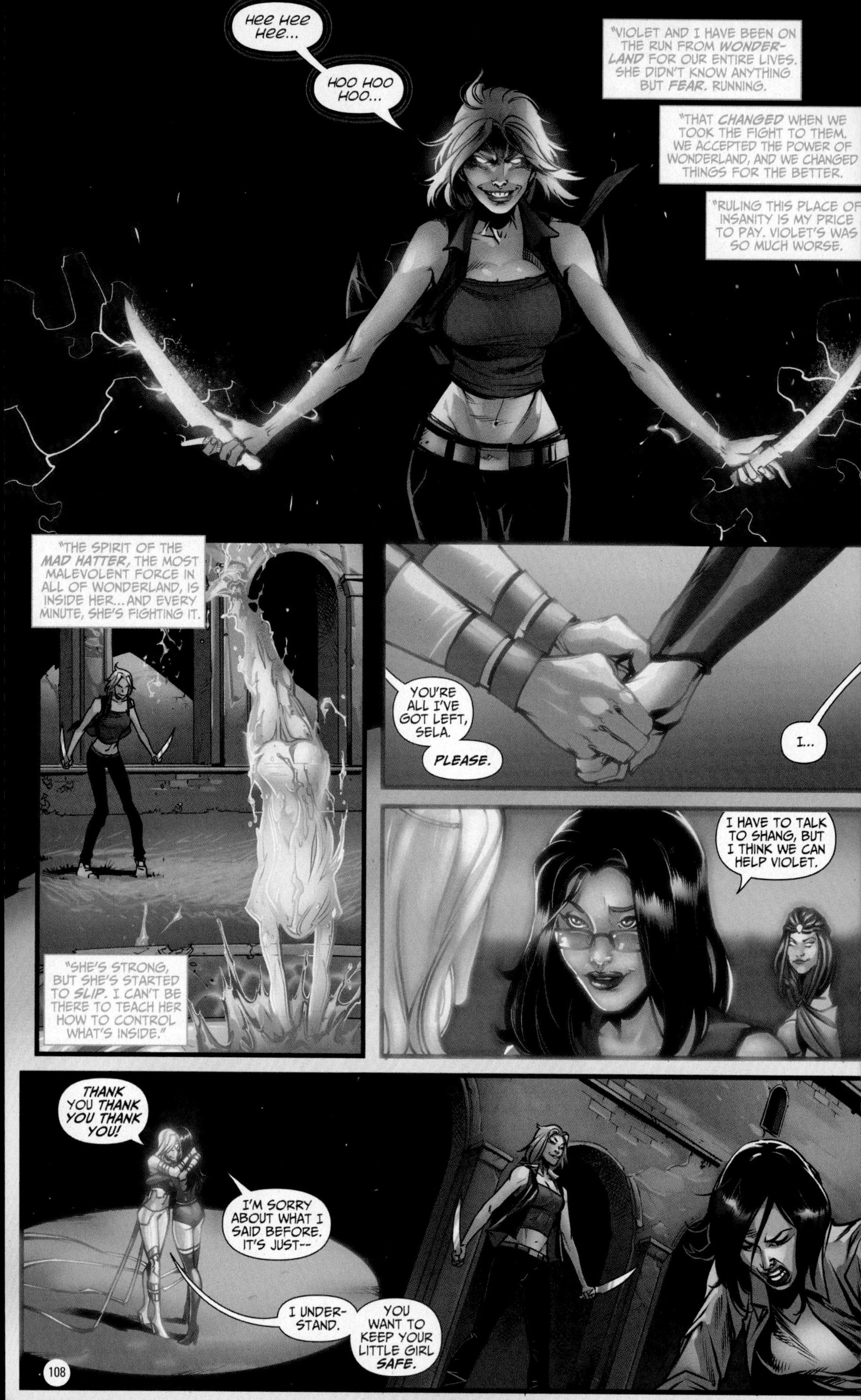
HEE HEE HEE...
HOO HOO HOO...
"VIOLET AND I HAVE BEEN ON THE RUN FROM WONDERLAND FOR OUR ENTIRE LIVES. SHE DIDN'T KNOW ANYTHING BUT FEAR. RUNNING.
"THAT CHANGED WHEN WE TOOK THE FIGHT TO THEM. WE ACCEPTED THE POWER OF WONDERLAND, AND WE CHANGED THINGS FOR THE BETTER.
"RULING THIS PLACE OF INSANITY IS MY PRICE TO PAY. VIOLET'S WAS SO MUCH WORSE.
"THE SPIRIT OF THE MAD HATTER, THE MOST MALEVOLENT FORCE IN ALL OF WONDERLAND, IS INSIDE HER...AND EVERY MINUTE, SHE'S FIGHTING IT.
"SHE'S STRONG, BUT SHE'S STARTED TO SLIP. I CAN'T BE THERE TO TEACH HER HOW TO CONTROL WHAT'S INSIDE."
YOU'RE ALL I'VE GOT LEFT, SELA.
PLEASE.
I...
I HAVE TO TALK TO SHANG, BUT I THINK WE CAN HELP VIOLET.
THANK YOU THANK YOU THANK YOU!
I'M SORRY ABOUT WHAT I SAID BEFORE. IT'S JUST--
I UNDERSTAND.
YOU WANT TO KEEP YOUR LITTLE GIRL SAFE.

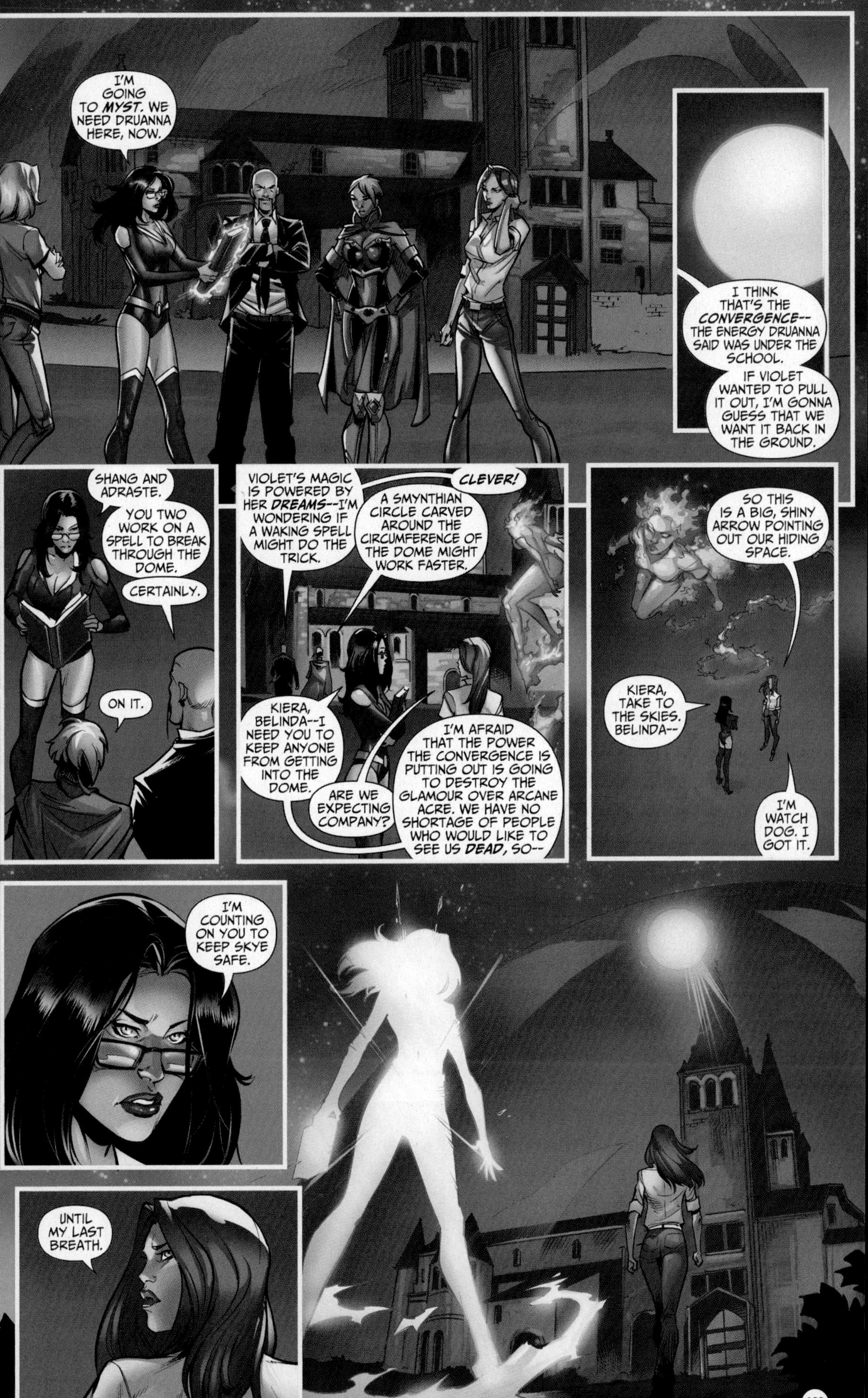
I'M GOING TO MYST. WE NEED DRUANNA HERE, NOW.
I THINK THAT'S THE CONVERGENCE-- THE ENERGY DRUANNA SAID WAS UNDER THE SCHOOL.
IF VIOLET WANTED TO PULL IT OUT, I'M GONNA GUESS THAT WE WANT IT BACK IN THE GROUND.
SHANG AND ADRASTE.
YOU TWO WORK ON A SPELL TO BREAK THROUGH THE DOME.
CERTAINLY.
ON IT.
VIOLET'S MAGIC IS POWERED BY HER DREAMS--I'M WONDERING IF A WAKING SPELL MIGHT DO THE TRICK.
CLEVER!
A SMYNTHIAN CIRCLE CARVED AROUND THE CIRCUMFERENCE OF THE DOME MIGHT WORK FASTER.
KIERA, BELINDA--I NEED YOU TO KEEP ANYONE FROM GETTING INTO THE DOME.
ARE WE EXPECTING COMPANY?
I'M AFRAID THAT THE POWER THE CONVERGENCE IS PUTTING OUT IS GOING TO DESTROY THE GLAMOUR OVER ARCANE ACRE. WE HAVE NO SHORTAGE OF PEOPLE WHO WOULD LIKE TO SEE US DEAD, SO--
SO THIS IS A BIG, SHINY ARROW POINTING OUT OUR HIDING SPACE.
KIERA, TAKE TO THE SKIES. BELINDA--
I'M WATCH DOG. I GOT IT.
I'M COUNTING ON YOU TO KEEP SKYE SAFE.
UNTIL MY LAST BREATH.

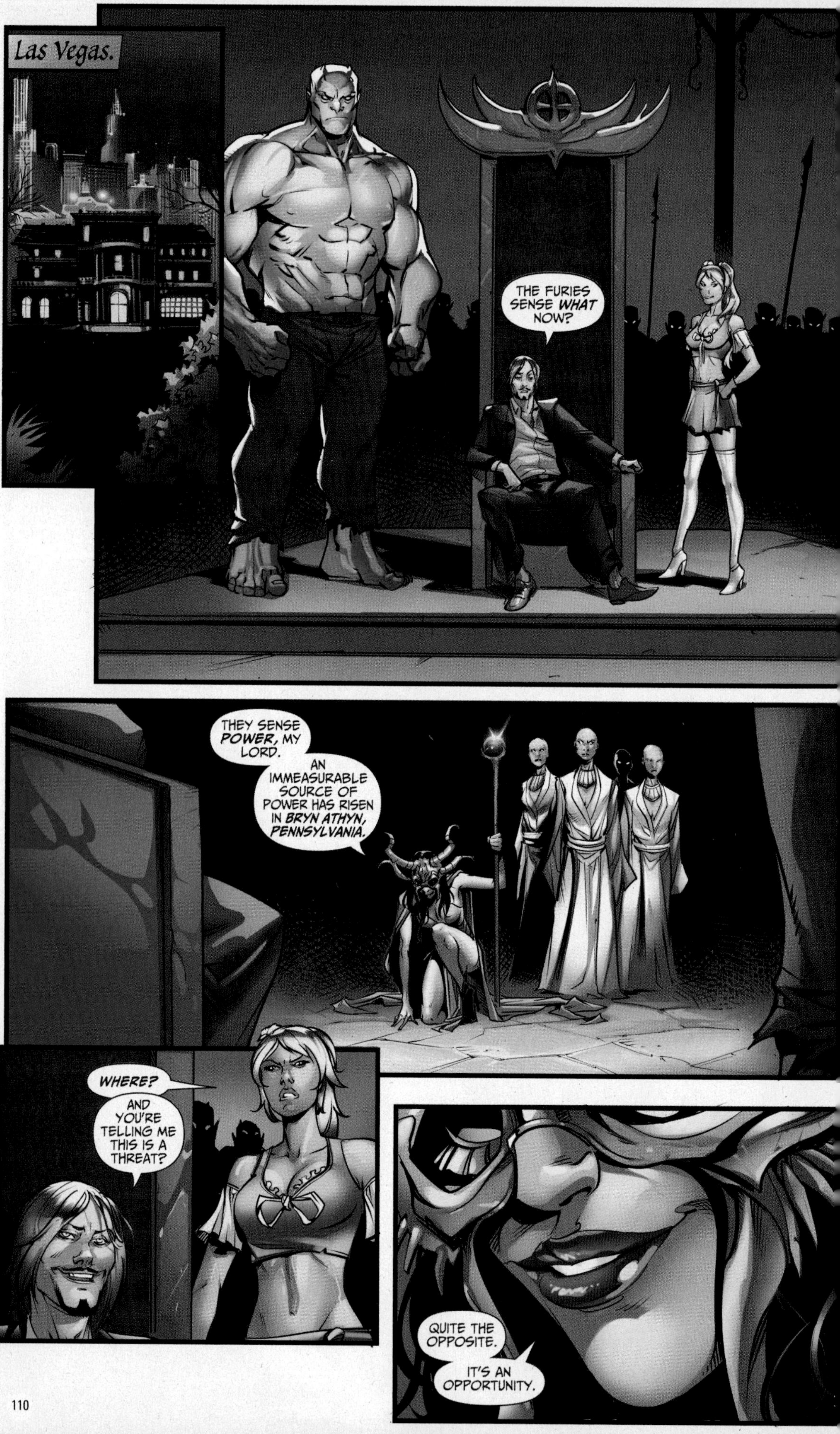

Las Vegas.
THE FURIES SENSE WHAT NOW?
THEY SENSE POWER, MY LORD.
AN IMMEASURABLE SOURCE OF POWER HAS RISEN IN BRYN ATHYN, PENNSYLVANIA.
WHERE?
AND YOU'RE TELLING ME THIS IS A THREAT?
QUITE THE OPPOSITE.
IT'S AN OPPORTUNITY.

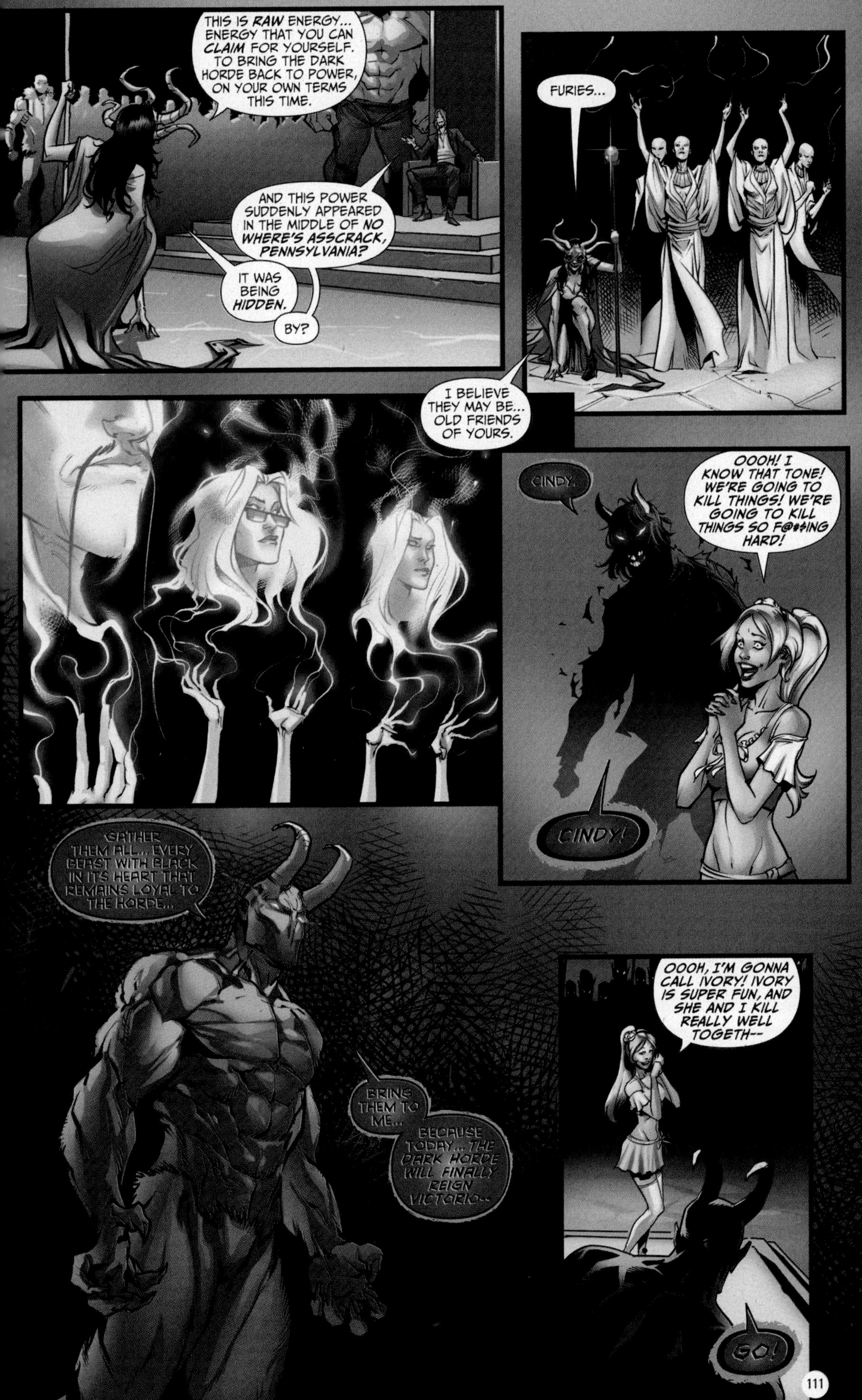

THIS IS *RAW* ENERGY... ENERGY THAT YOU CAN *CLAIM* FOR YOURSELF. TO BRING THE DARK HORDE BACK TO POWER, ON YOUR OWN TERMS THIS TIME.
AND THIS POWER SUDDENLY APPEARED IN THE MIDDLE OF *NO WHERE'S ASSCRACK, PENNSYLVANIA?*
IT WAS BEING *HIDDEN.*
BY?
FURIES...
I BELIEVE THEY MAY BE... OLD FRIENDS OF YOURS.
CINDY.
OOOH! I KNOW THAT TONE! WE'RE GOING TO KILL THINGS! WE'RE GOING TO KILL THINGS SO F@#$ING HARD!
CINDY!
GATHER THEM ALL... EVERY BEAST WITH BLACK IN ITS HEART THAT REMAINS LOYAL TO THE HORDE...
BRING THEM TO ME...
BECAUSE TODAY... THE *DARK HORDE WILL FINALLY REIGN* VICTORIO...
OOOH, I'M GONNA CALL IVORY! IVORY IS SUPER FUN, AND SHE AND I KILL REALLY WELL TOGETH--
GO!

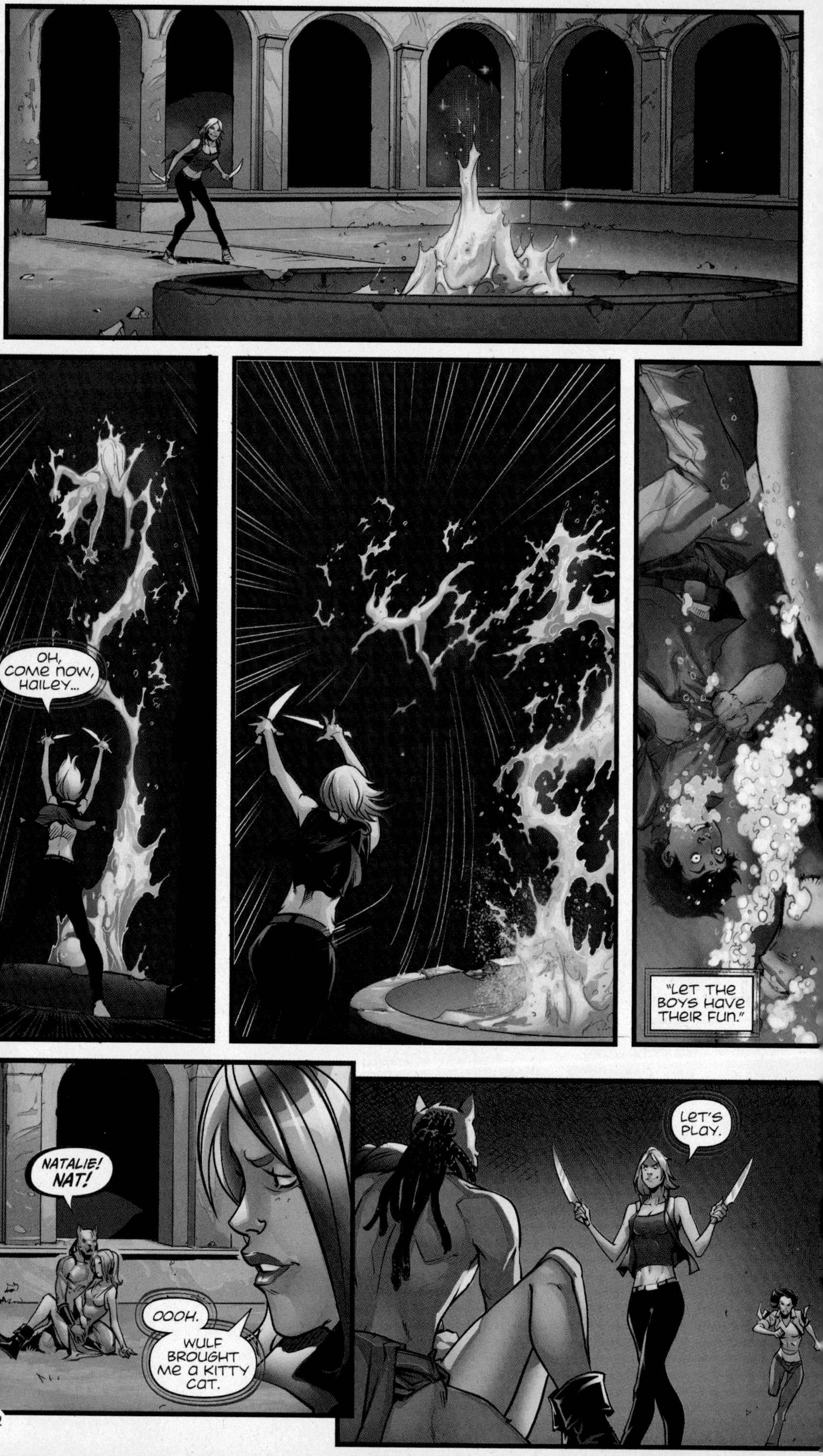

OH, COME NOW, HAILEY...
"LET THE BOYS HAVE THEIR FUN."
NATALIE! NAT!
OOOH.
WULF BROUGHT ME A KITTY CAT.
LET'S PLAY.

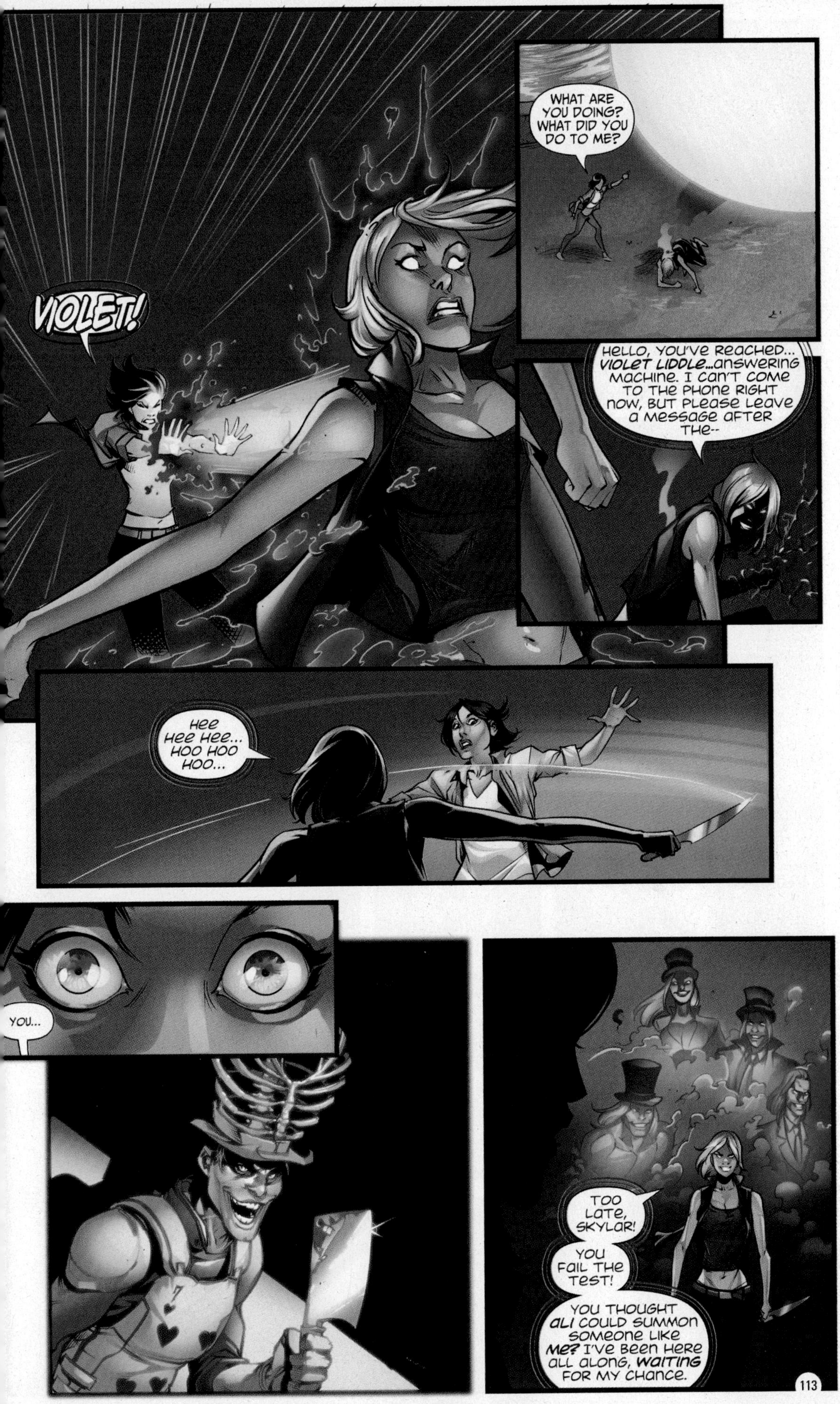
VIOLET!
WHAT ARE YOU DOING? WHAT DID YOU DO TO ME?
HELLO, YOU'VE REACHED... VIOLET LIDDLE...ANSWERING MACHINE. I CAN'T COME TO THE PHONE RIGHT NOW, BUT PLEASE LEAVE A MESSAGE AFTER THE--
HEE HEE HEE... HOO HOO HOO...
YOU...
TOO LATE, SKYLAR!
YOU FAIL THE TEST!
YOU THOUGHT ALI COULD SUMMON SOMEONE LIKE ME? I'VE BEEN HERE ALL ALONG, WAITING FOR MY CHANCE.

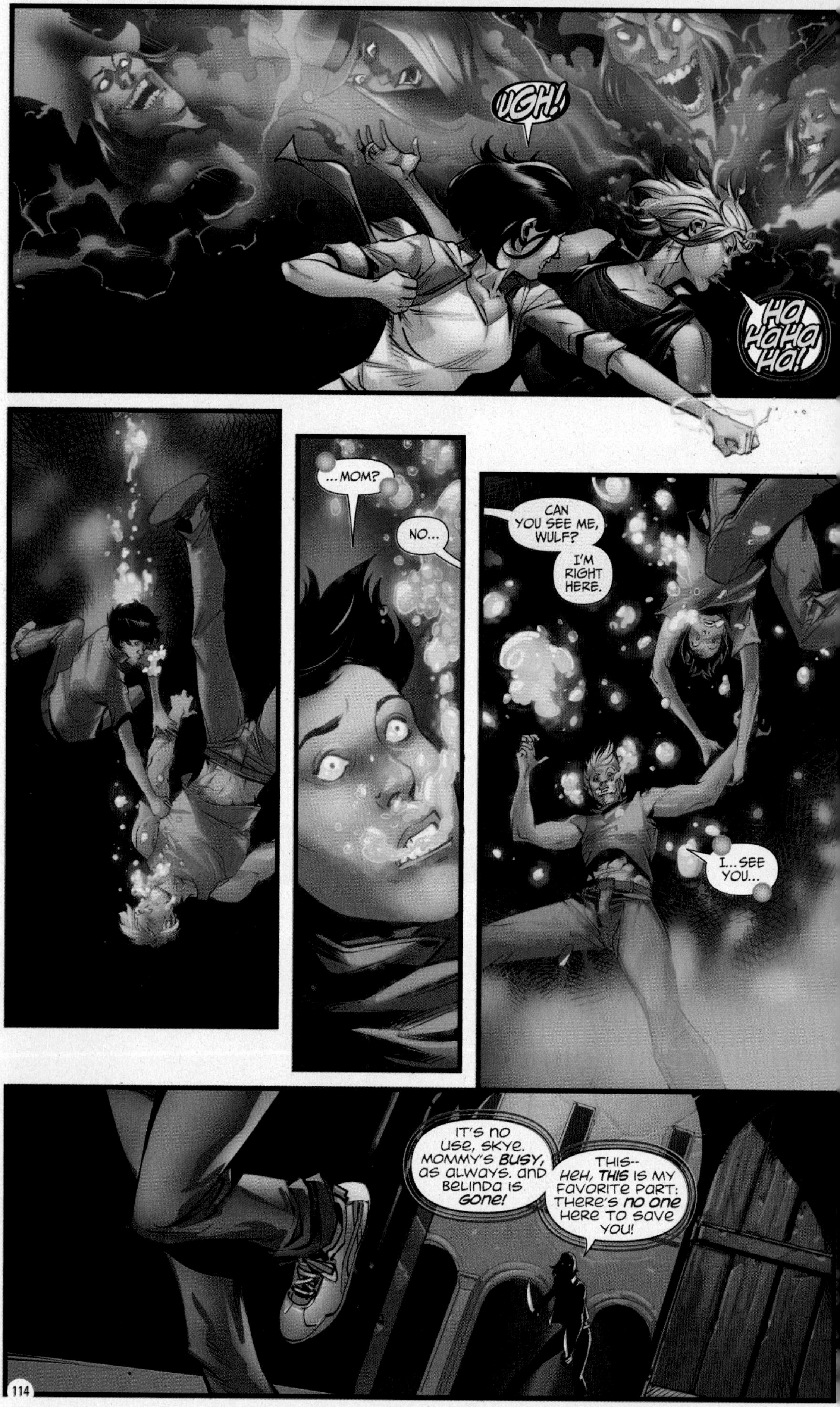
UGH!
HA HAHA HA HA!
...MOM?
NO...
CAN YOU SEE ME, WULF?
I'M RIGHT HERE.
I...SEE YOU...
IT'S NO USE, SKYE. MOMMY'S BUSY, AS ALWAYS. AND BELINDA IS GONE!
THIS-- HEH, THIS IS MY FAVORITE PART: THERE'S NO ONE HERE TO SAVE YOU!

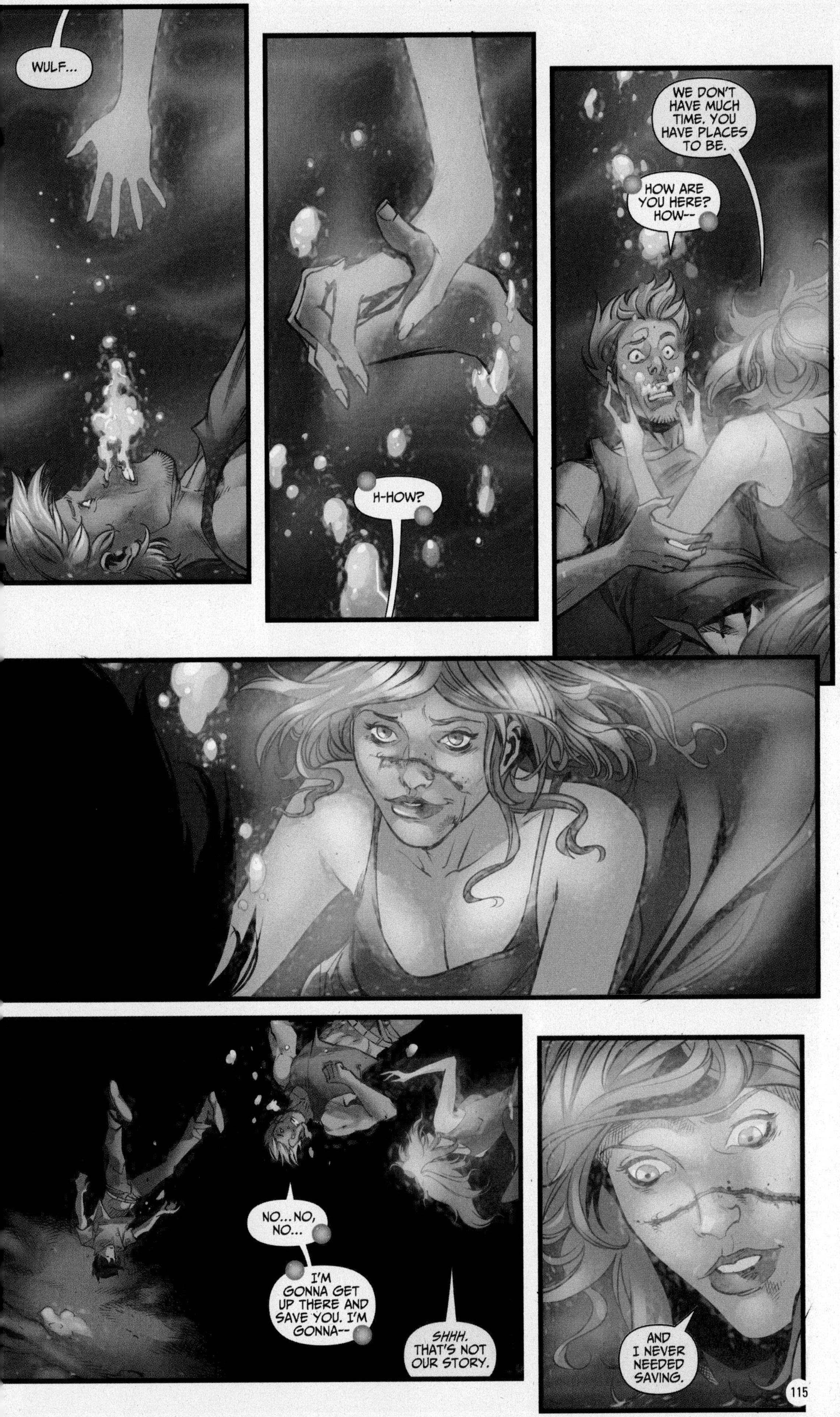
WULF...
H-HOW?
WE DON'T HAVE MUCH TIME. YOU HAVE PLACES TO BE.
HOW ARE YOU HERE? HOW--
NO...NO, NO...
I'M GONNA GET UP THERE AND SAVE YOU. I'M GONNA--
SHHH. THAT'S NOT OUR STORY.
AND I NEVER NEEDED SAVING.

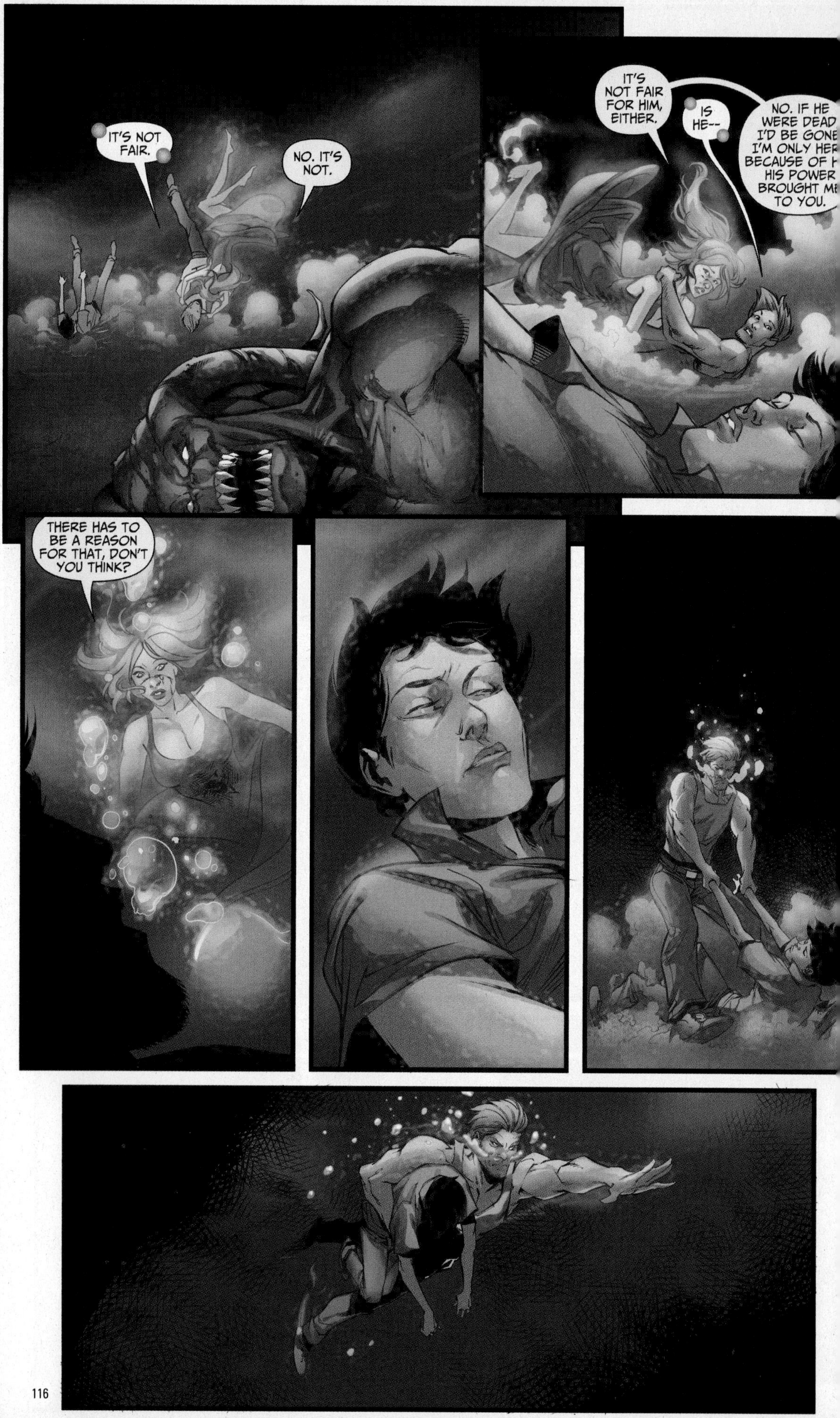
IT'S NOT FAIR.
NO. IT'S NOT.
IT'S NOT FAIR FOR HIM, EITHER.
IS HE--
NO. IF HE WERE DEAD I'D BE GONE
THERE HAS TO BE A REASON FOR THAT, DON'T YOU THINK?

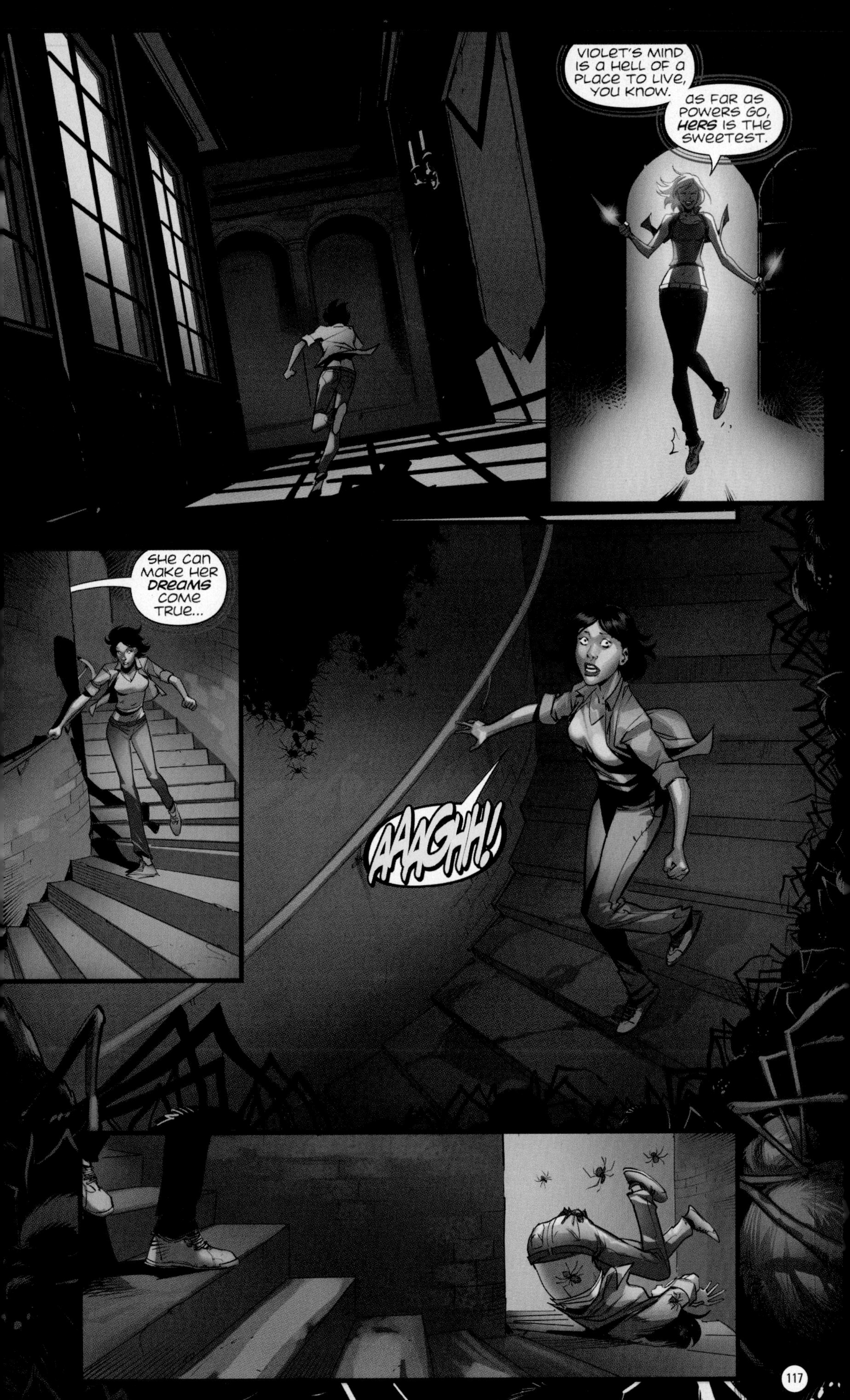
VIOLET'S MIND IS A HELL OF A PLACE TO LIVE, YOU KNOW.
AS FAR AS POWERS GO, HERS IS THE SWEETEST.
SHE CAN MAKE HER DREAMS COME TRUE...
AAAGHH!

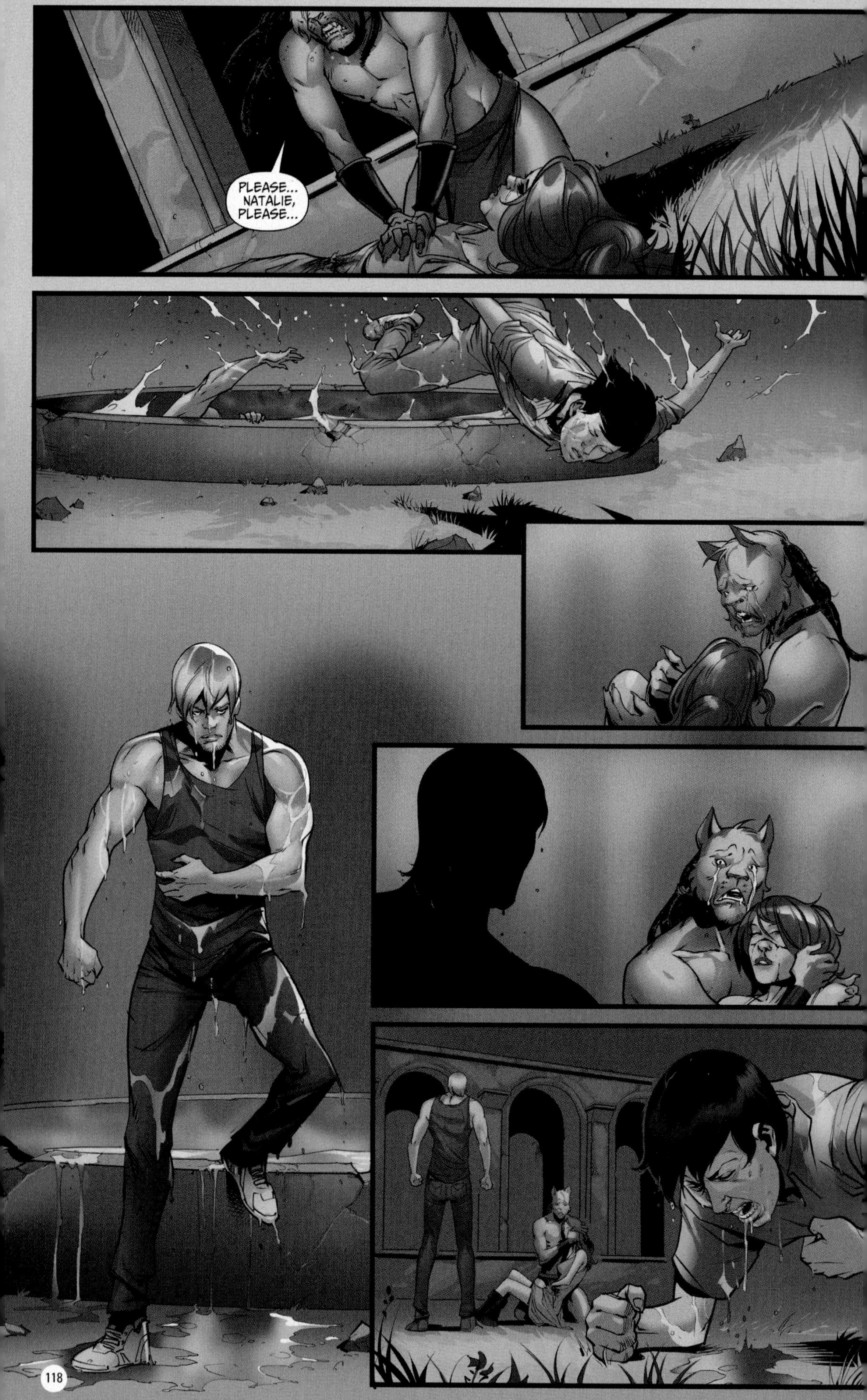
PLEASE... NATALIE, PLEASE...

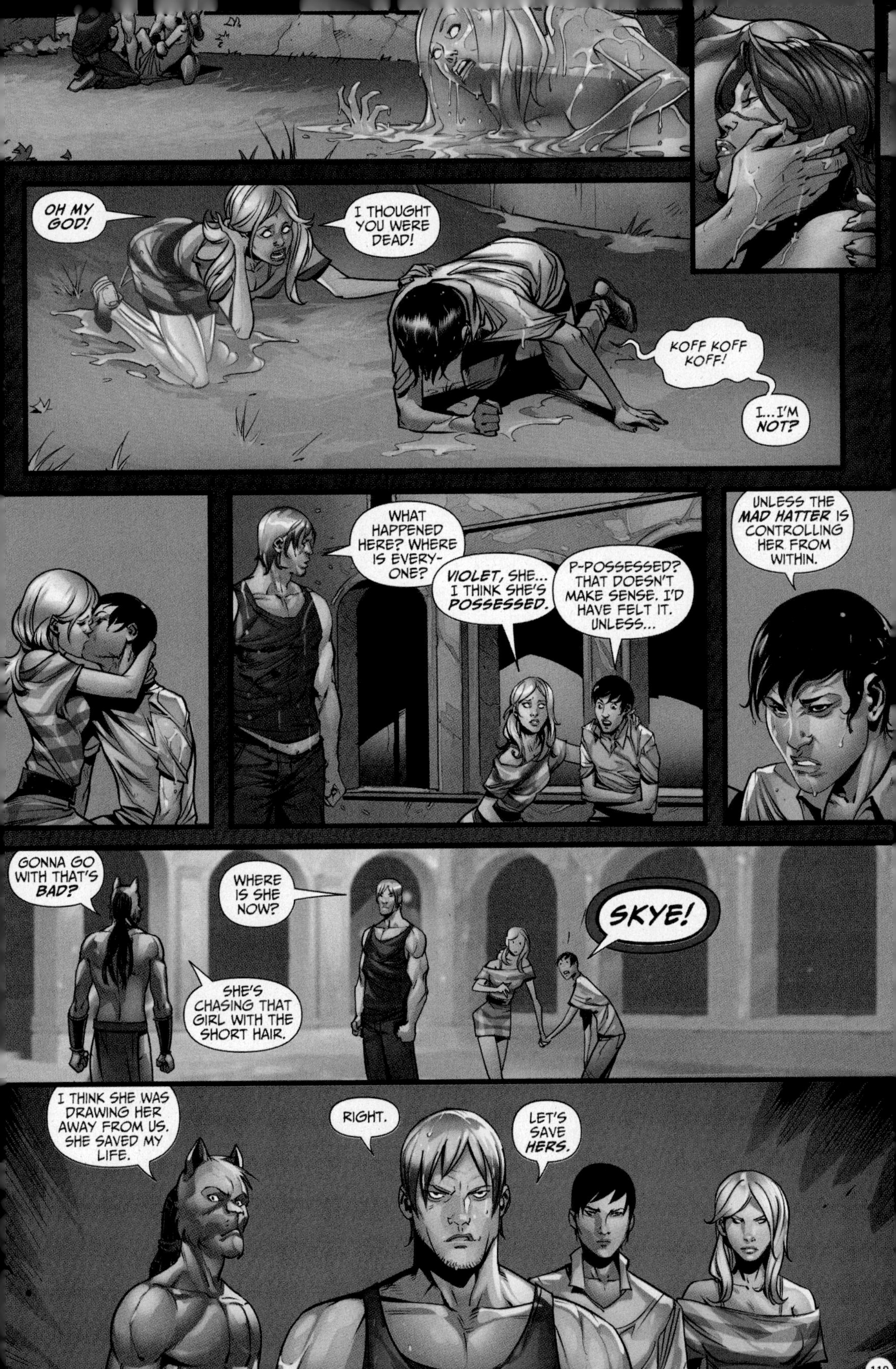
OH MY GOD!
I THOUGHT YOU WERE DEAD!
KOFF KOFF KOFF!
I...I'M NOT?
WHAT HAPPENED HERE? WHERE IS EVERY-ONE?
VIOLET, SHE... I THINK SHE'S POSSESSED.
P-POSSESSED? THAT DOESN'T MAKE SENSE. I'D HAVE FELT IT. UNLESS...
UNLESS THE MAD HATTER IS CONTROLLING HER FROM WITHIN.
GONNA GO WITH THAT'S BAD?
WHERE IS SHE NOW?
SHE'S CHASING THAT GIRL WITH THE SHORT HAIR.
SKYE!
I THINK SHE WAS DRAWING HER AWAY FROM US. SHE SAVED MY LIFE.
RIGHT.
LET'S SAVE HERS.

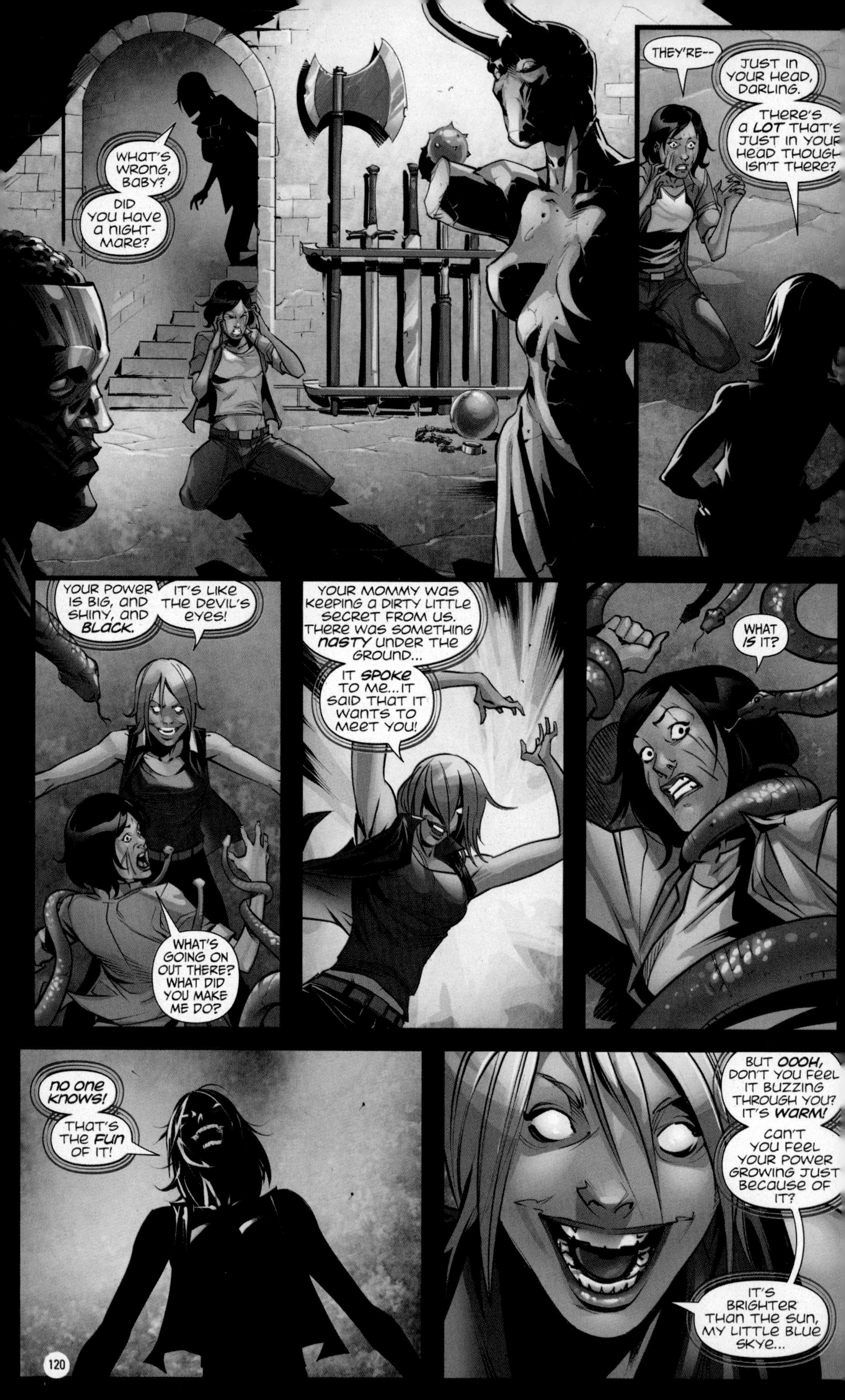

WHAT'S WRONG, BABY?
DID YOU HAVE A NIGHT-MARE?
THEY'RE--
JUST IN YOUR HEAD, DARLING.
THERE'S A LOT THAT'S JUST IN YOUR HEAD THOUGH ISN'T THERE?
YOUR POWER IS BIG, AND SHINY, AND BLACK.
IT'S LIKE THE DEVIL'S EYES!
WHAT'S GOING ON OUT THERE? WHAT DID YOU MAKE ME DO?
YOUR MOMMY WAS KEEPING A DIRTY LITTLE SECRET FROM US. THERE WAS SOMETHING NASTY UNDER THE GROUND...
IT SPOKE TO ME...IT SAID THAT IT WANTS TO MEET YOU!
WHAT IS IT?
NO ONE KNOWS!
THAT'S THE FUN OF IT!
BUT OOOH, DON'T YOU FEEL IT BUZZING THROUGH YOU? IT'S WARM!
CAN'T YOU FEEL YOUR POWER GROWING JUST BECAUSE OF IT?
IT'S BRIGHTER THAN THE SUN, MY LITTLE BLUE SKYE...

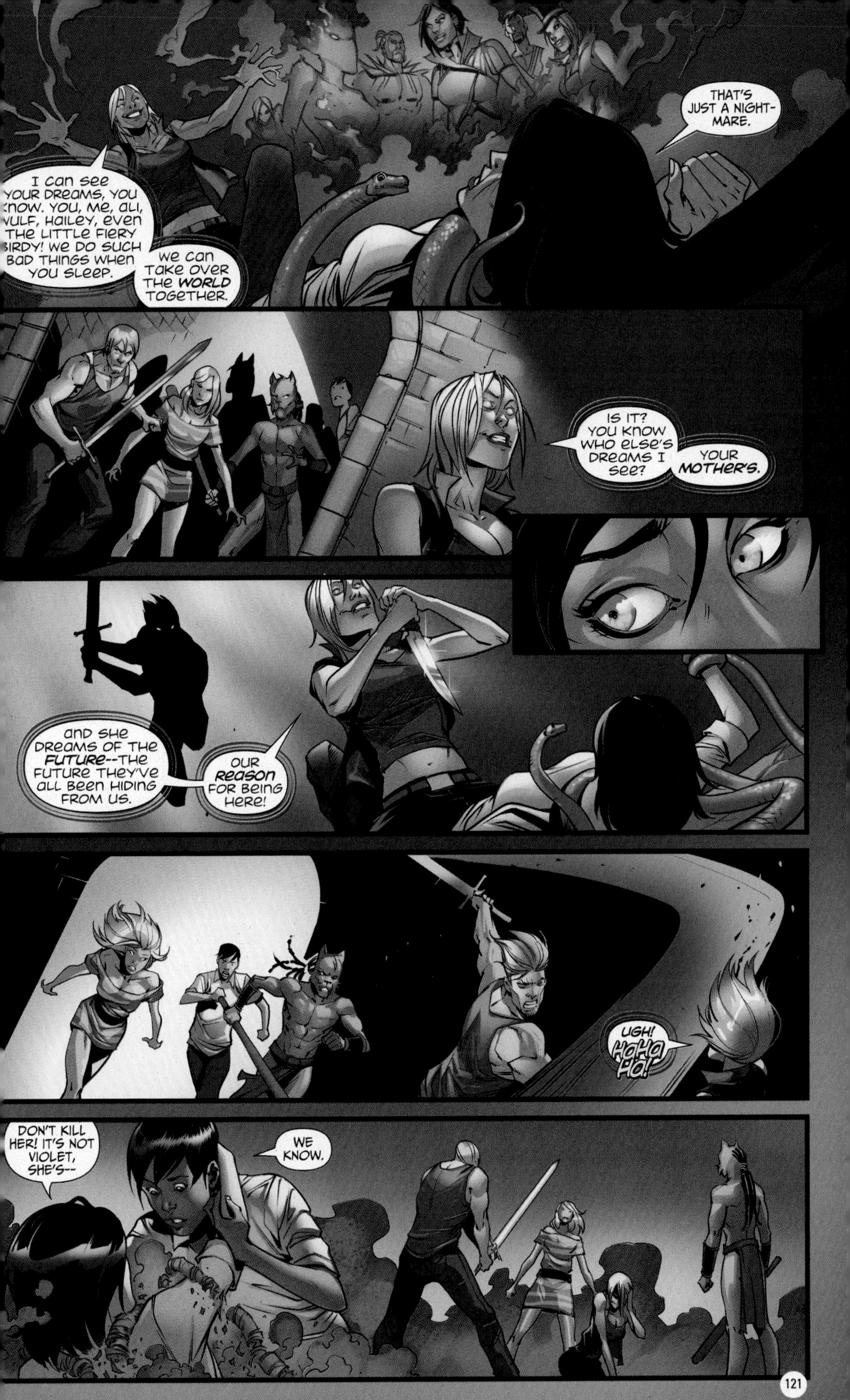
I can see your dreams, you know. You, me, Ali, Wulf, Hailey, even the little fiery birdy! We do such bad things when you sleep.
We can take over the WORLD together.
THAT'S JUST A NIGHTMARE.
IS IT? YOU KNOW WHO ELSE'S DREAMS I SEE?
YOUR MOTHER'S.
and she dreams of the FUTURE--the future they've all been hiding from us.
OUR REASON FOR BEING HERE!
UGH! HaHa Ha!
DON'T KILL HER! IT'S NOT VIOLET, SHE'S--
WE KNOW.

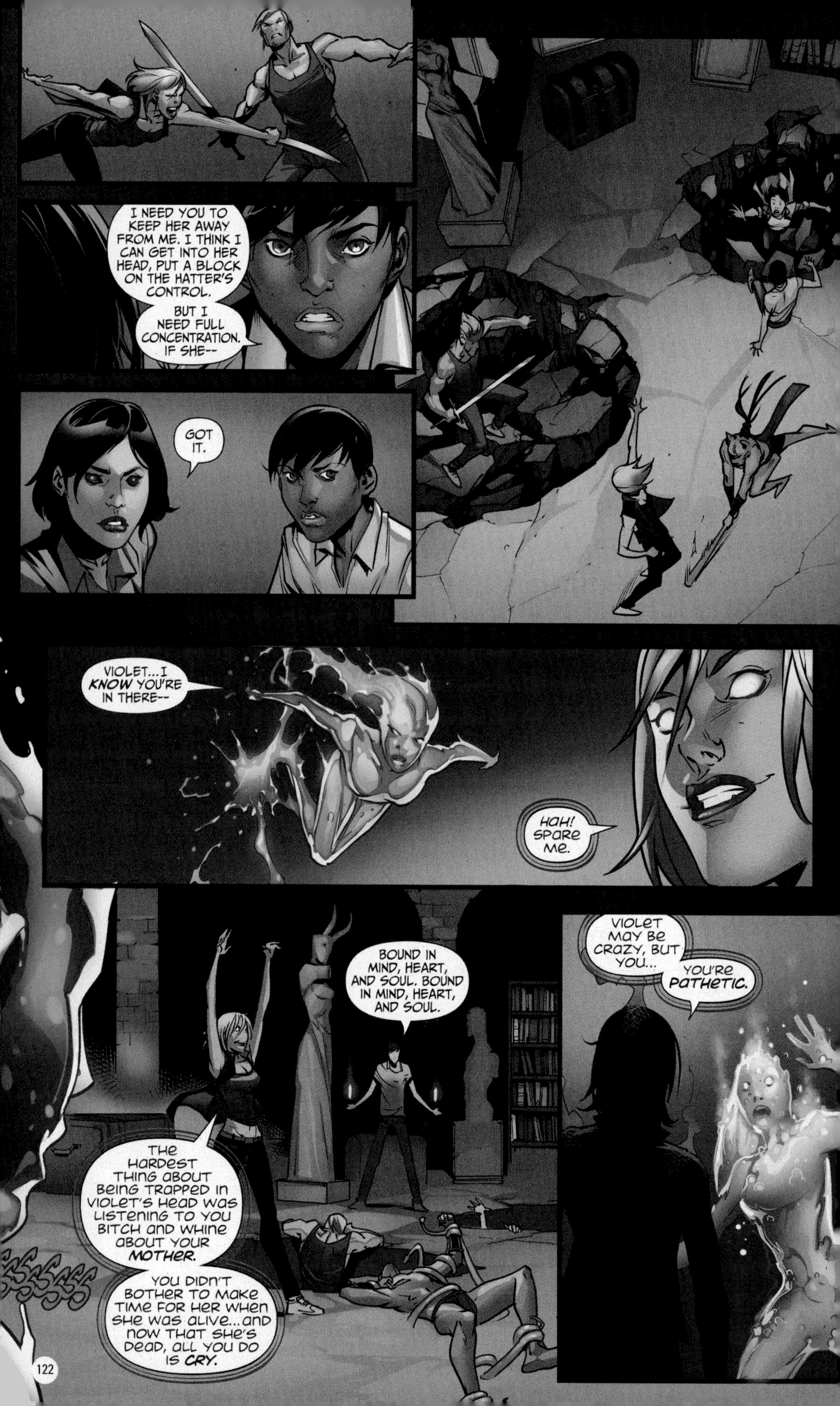
I NEED YOU TO KEEP HER AWAY FROM ME. I THINK I CAN GET INTO HER HEAD, PUT A BLOCK ON THE HATTER'S CONTROL.
BUT I NEED FULL CONCENTRATION. IF SHE--
GOT IT.
VIOLET...I KNOW YOU'RE IN THERE--
HAH! SPARE ME.
BOUND IN MIND, HEART, AND SOUL. BOUND IN MIND, HEART, AND SOUL.
THE HARDEST THING ABOUT BEING TRAPPED IN VIOLET'S HEAD WAS LISTENING TO YOU BITCH AND WHINE ABOUT YOUR MOTHER.
YOU DIDN'T BOTHER TO MAKE TIME FOR HER WHEN SHE WAS ALIVE...AND NOW THAT SHE'S DEAD, ALL YOU DO IS CRY.
SSSSSSSS
VIOLET MAY BE CRAZY, BUT YOU...
YOU'RE PATHETIC.

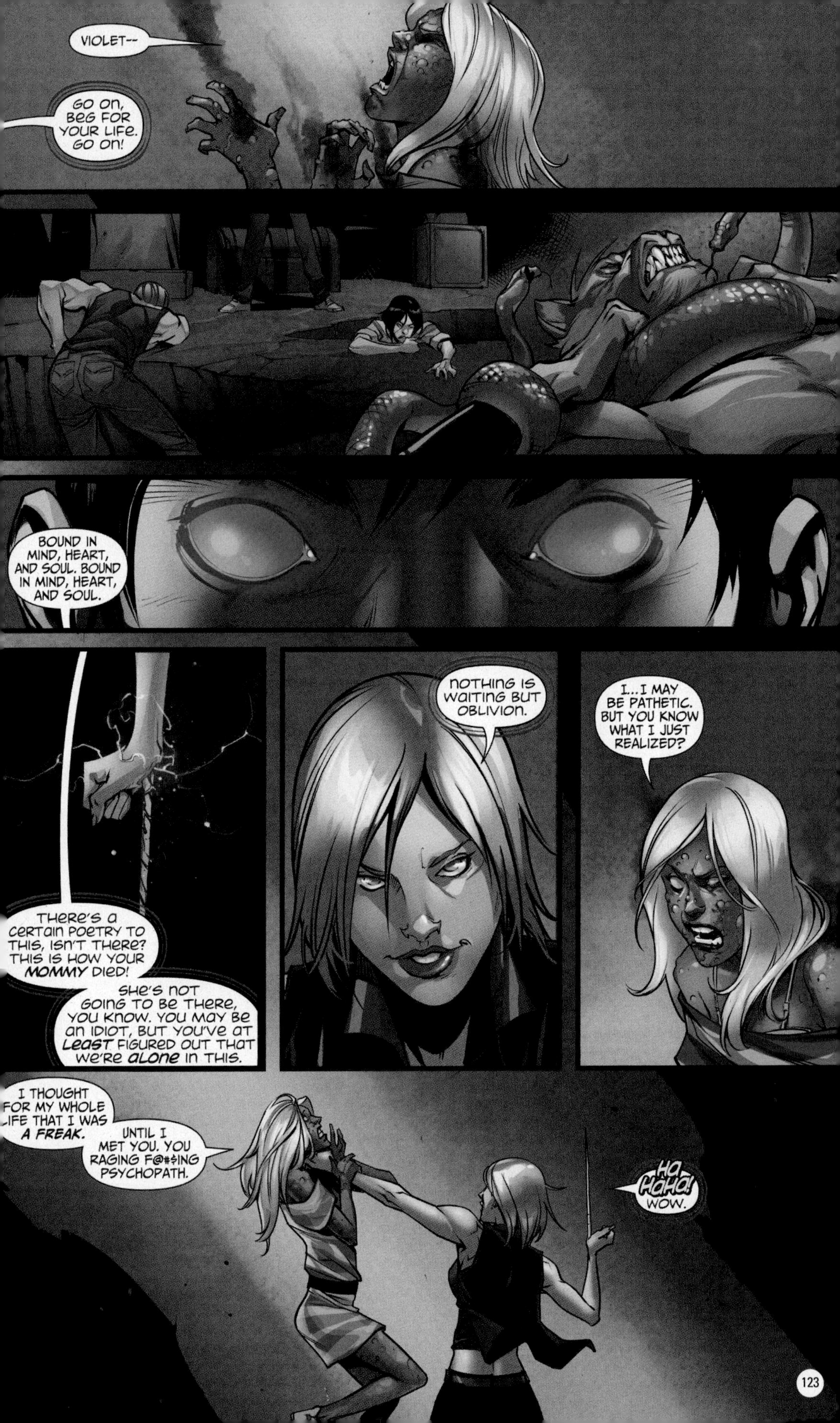
VIOLET--
GO ON, BEG FOR YOUR LIFE. GO ON!
BOUND IN MIND, HEART, AND SOUL. BOUND IN MIND, HEART, AND SOUL.
THERE'S A CERTAIN POETRY TO THIS, ISN'T THERE? THIS IS HOW YOUR MOMMY DIED!
SHE'S NOT GOING TO BE THERE, YOU KNOW. YOU MAY BE AN IDIOT, BUT YOU'VE AT LEAST FIGURED OUT THAT WE'RE ALONE IN THIS.
NOTHING IS WAITING BUT OBLIVION.
I...I MAY BE PATHETIC. BUT YOU KNOW WHAT I JUST REALIZED?
I THOUGHT FOR MY WHOLE LIFE THAT I WAS A FREAK.
UNTIL I MET YOU. YOU RAGING F@#$ING PSYCHOPATH.
HA HAHA! WOW.

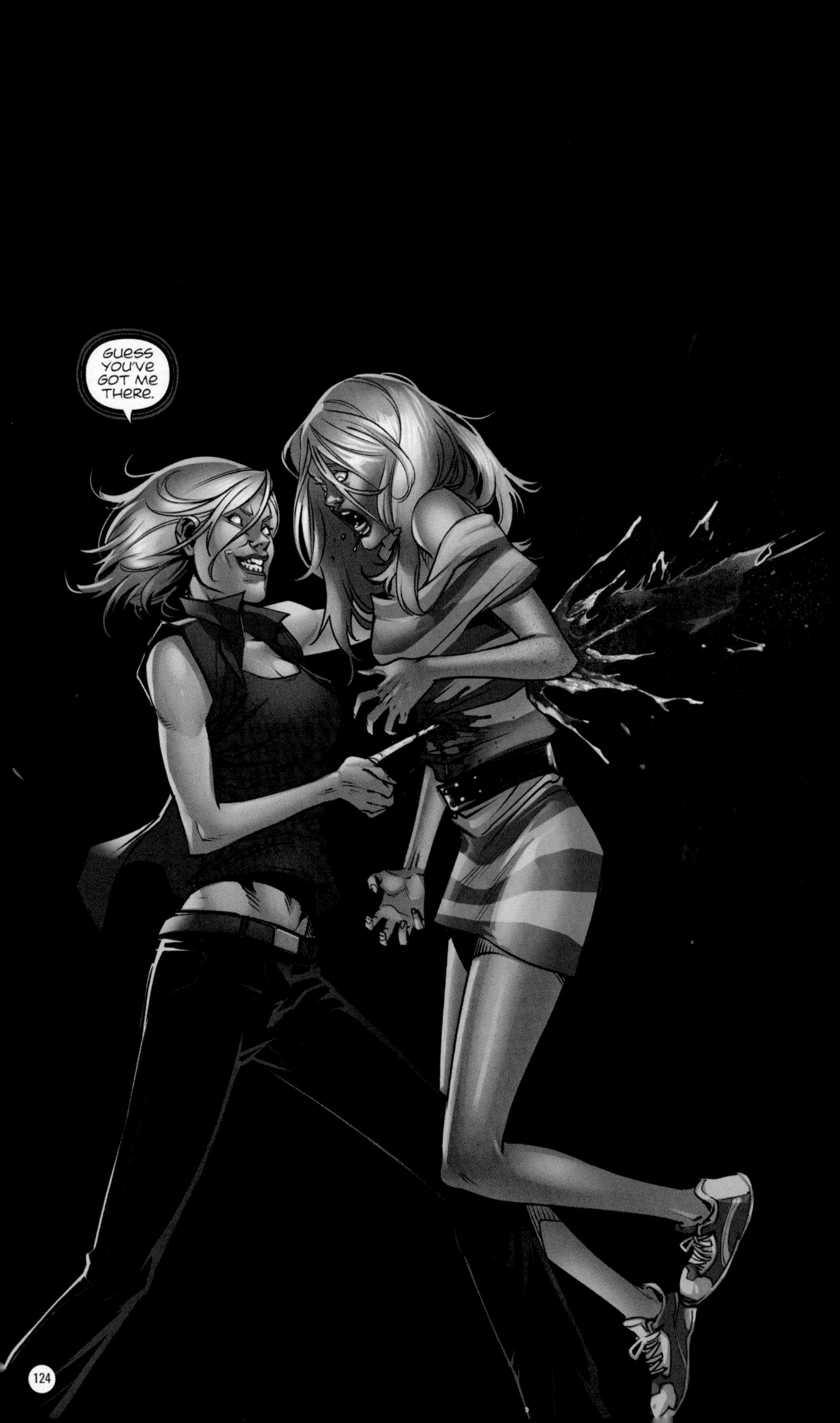
GUESS YOU'VE GOT ME THERE.

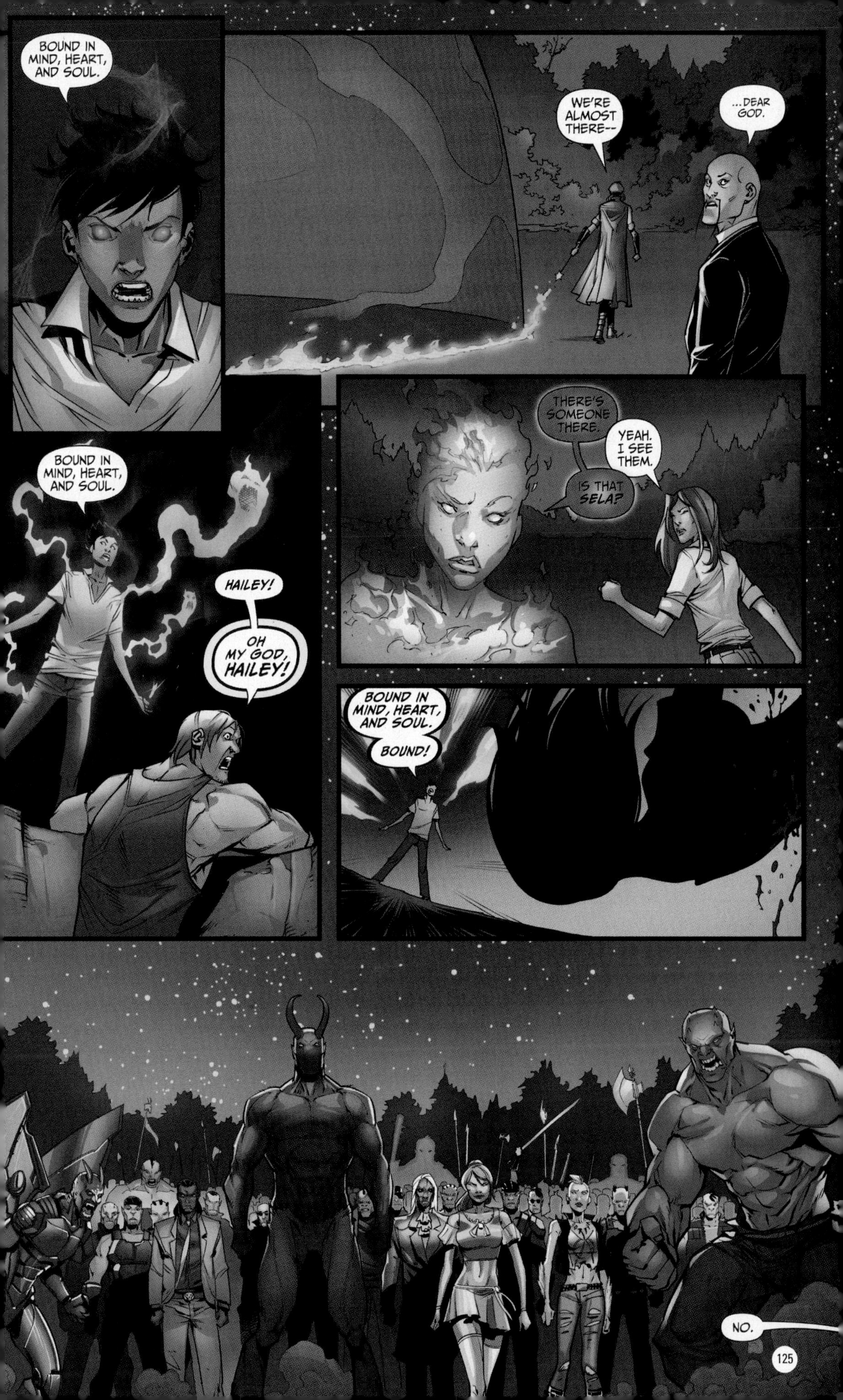

BOUND IN MIND, HEART, AND SOUL.
WE'RE ALMOST THERE--
...DEAR GOD.
BOUND IN MIND, HEART, AND SOUL.
HAILEY!
OH MY GOD, HAILEY!
THERE'S SOMEONE THERE.
YEAH. I SEE THEM.
IS THAT SELA?
BOUND IN MIND, HEART, AND SOUL.
BOUND!
NO.

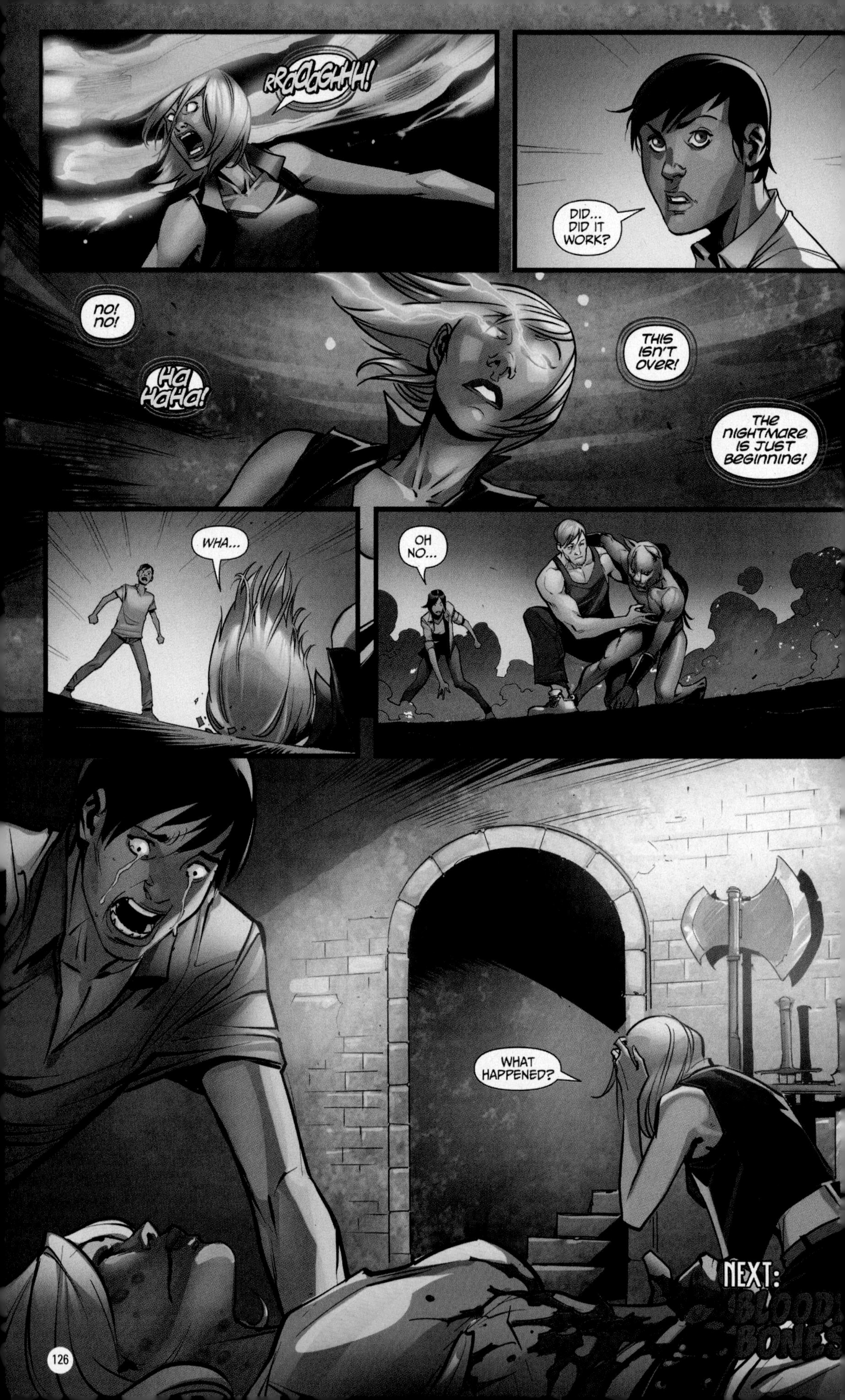
RRAAAGHHH!
DID... DID IT WORK?
NO! NO!
HA HAHA!
THIS ISN'T OVER!
THE NIGHTMARE IS JUST BEGINNING!
WHA...
OH NO...
WHAT HAPPENED?
NEXT: BLOOD & BONES

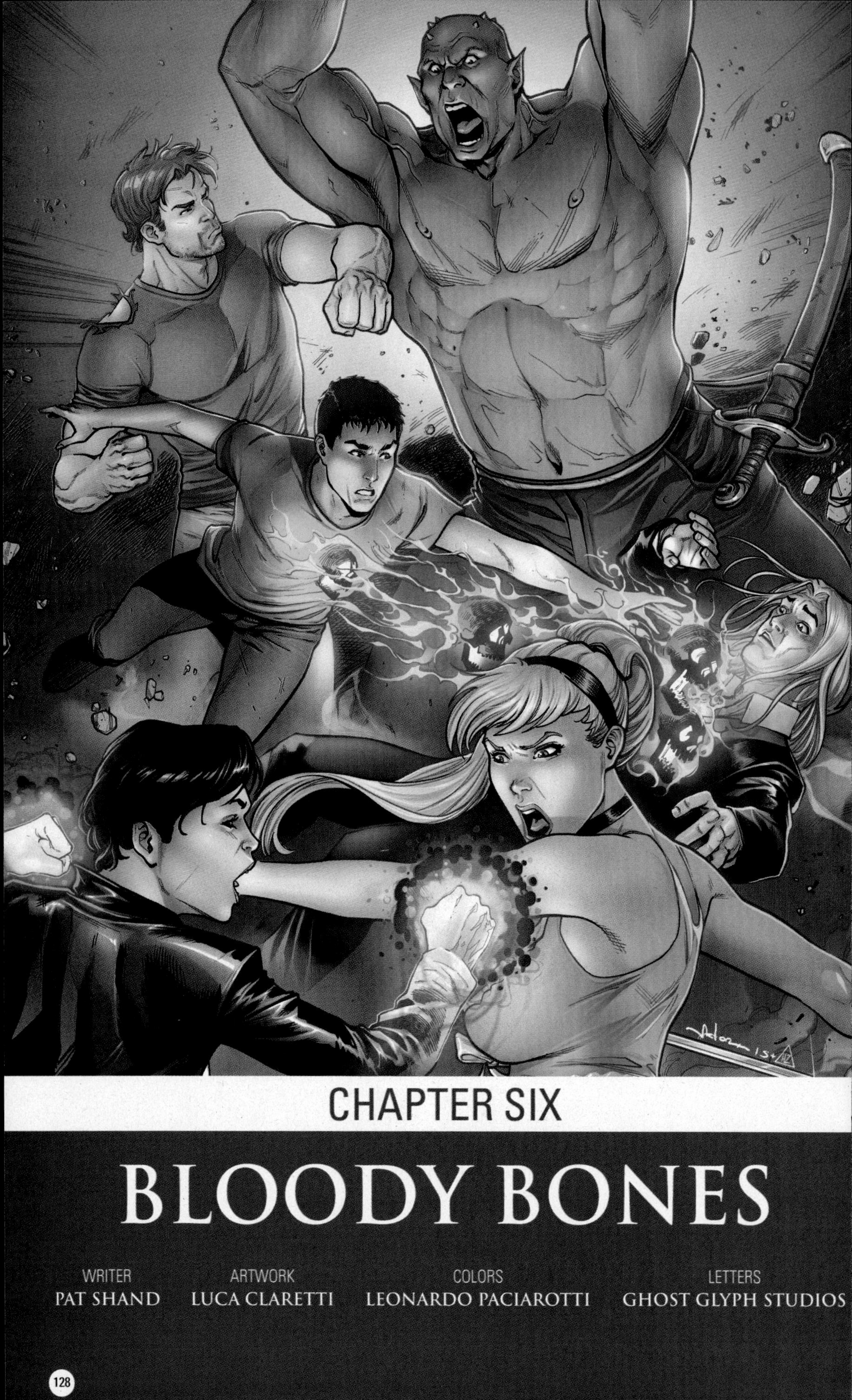

CHAPTER SIX

BLOODY BONES

WRITER
PAT SHAND

ARTWORK
LUCA CLARETTI

COLORS
LEONARDO PACIAROTTI

LETTERS
GHOST GLYPH STUDIOS

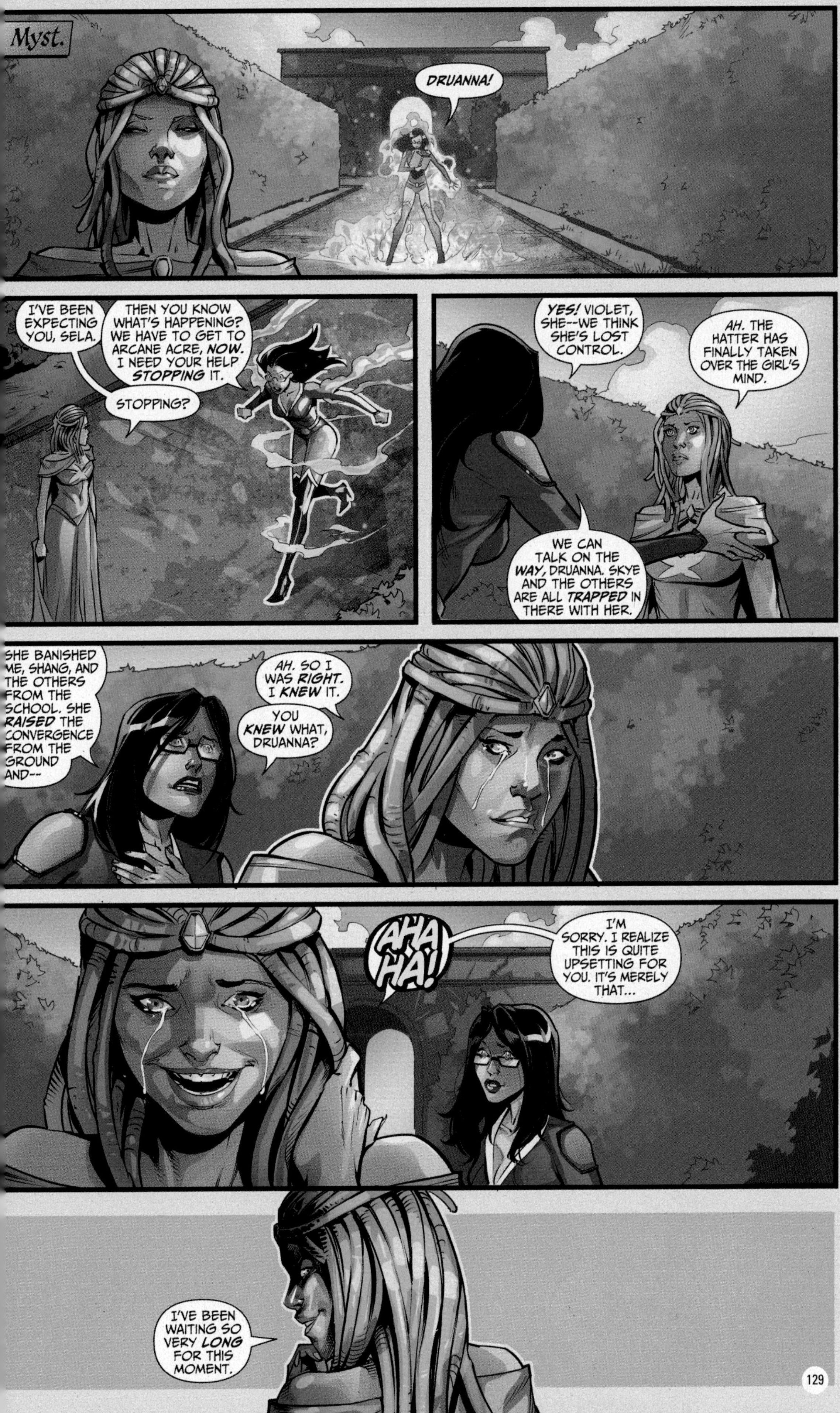
Myst.
DRUANNA!
I'VE BEEN EXPECTING YOU, SELA.
THEN YOU KNOW WHAT'S HAPPENING? WE HAVE TO GET TO ARCANE ACRE, NOW. I NEED YOUR HELP STOPPING IT.
STOPPING?
YES! VIOLET, SHE--WE THINK SHE'S LOST CONTROL.
AH. THE HATTER HAS FINALLY TAKEN OVER THE GIRL'S MIND.
WE CAN TALK ON THE WAY, DRUANNA. SKYE AND THE OTHERS ARE ALL TRAPPED IN THERE WITH HER.
SHE BANISHED ME, SHANG, AND THE OTHERS FROM THE SCHOOL. SHE RAISED THE CONVERGENCE FROM THE GROUND AND--
AH. SO I WAS RIGHT. I KNEW IT.
YOU KNEW WHAT, DRUANNA?
AHA HA!
I'M SORRY. I REALIZE THIS IS QUITE UPSETTING FOR YOU. IT'S MERELY THAT...
I'VE BEEN WAITING SO VERY LONG FOR THIS MOMENT.

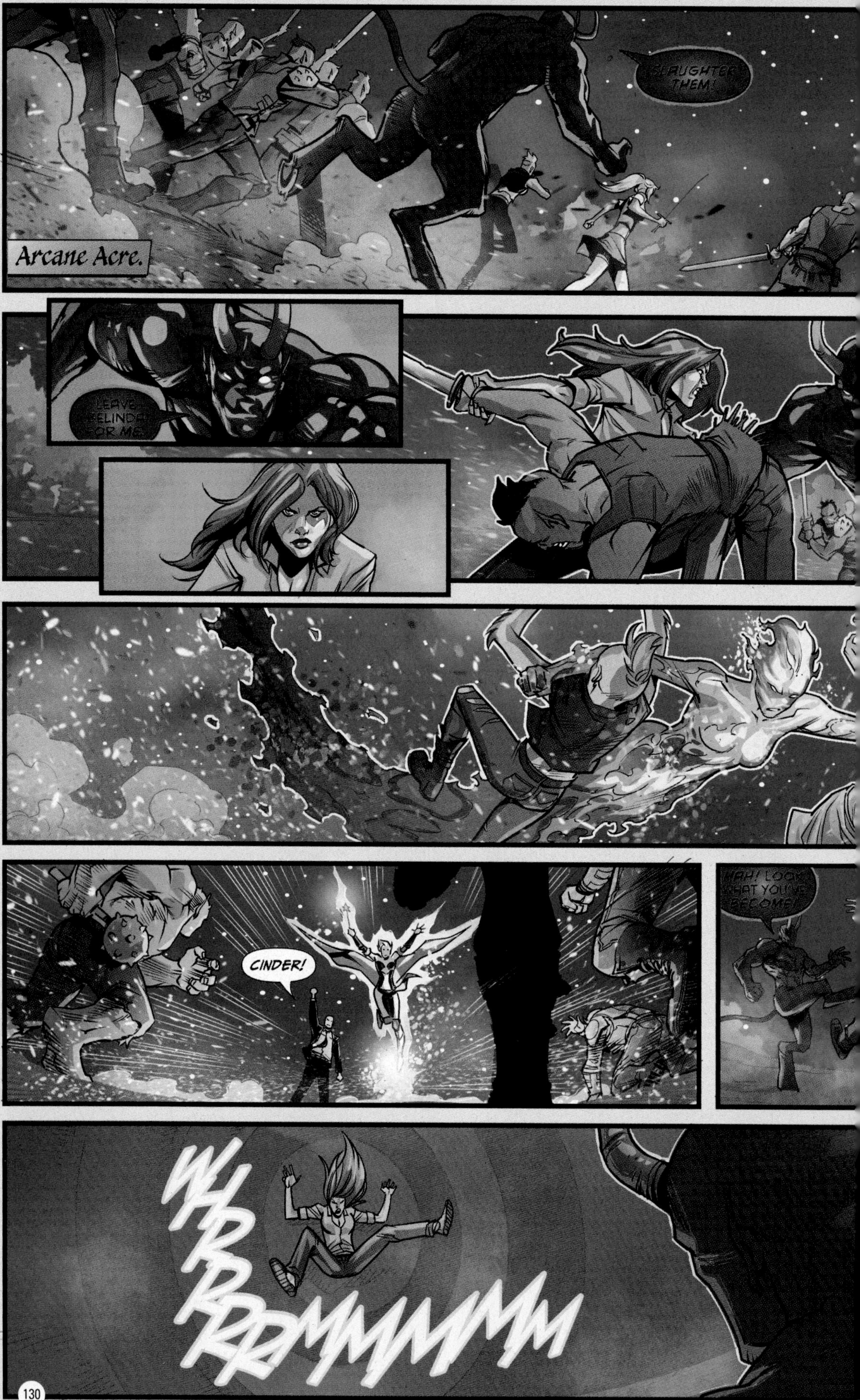
Arcane Acre.
SLAUGHTER THEM!
LEAVE BELINDA FOR ME.
CINDER!
HAH! LOOK WHAT YOU'VE BECOME!
WHRRRMMMMMM

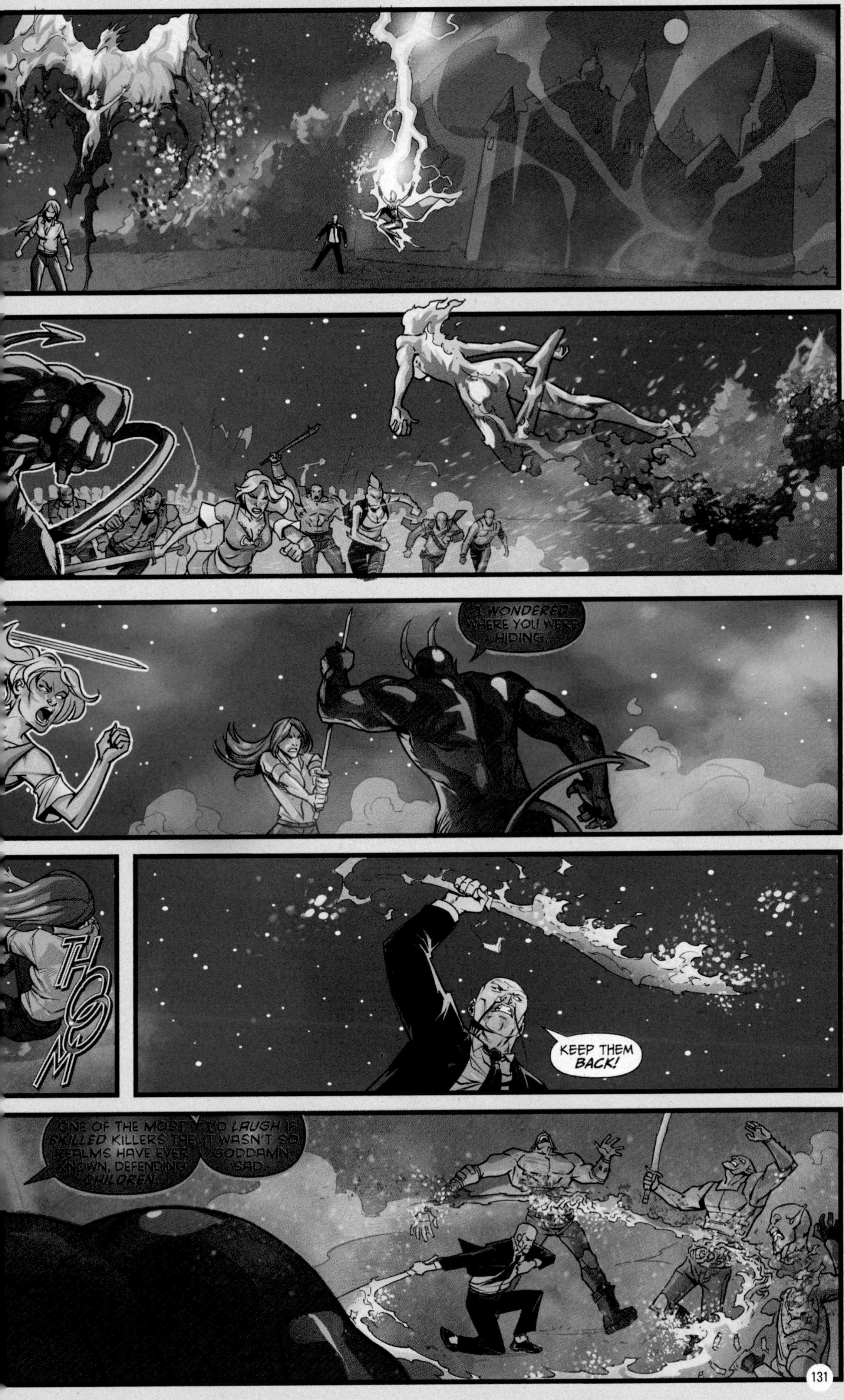
I WONDERED WHERE YOU WERE HIDING.
THOOM
KEEP THEM BACK!
ONE OF THE MOST SKILLED KILLERS THE REALMS HAVE EVER KNOWN, DEFENDING CHILDREN.
I'D LAUGH IF IT WASN'T SO GODDAMN SAD.

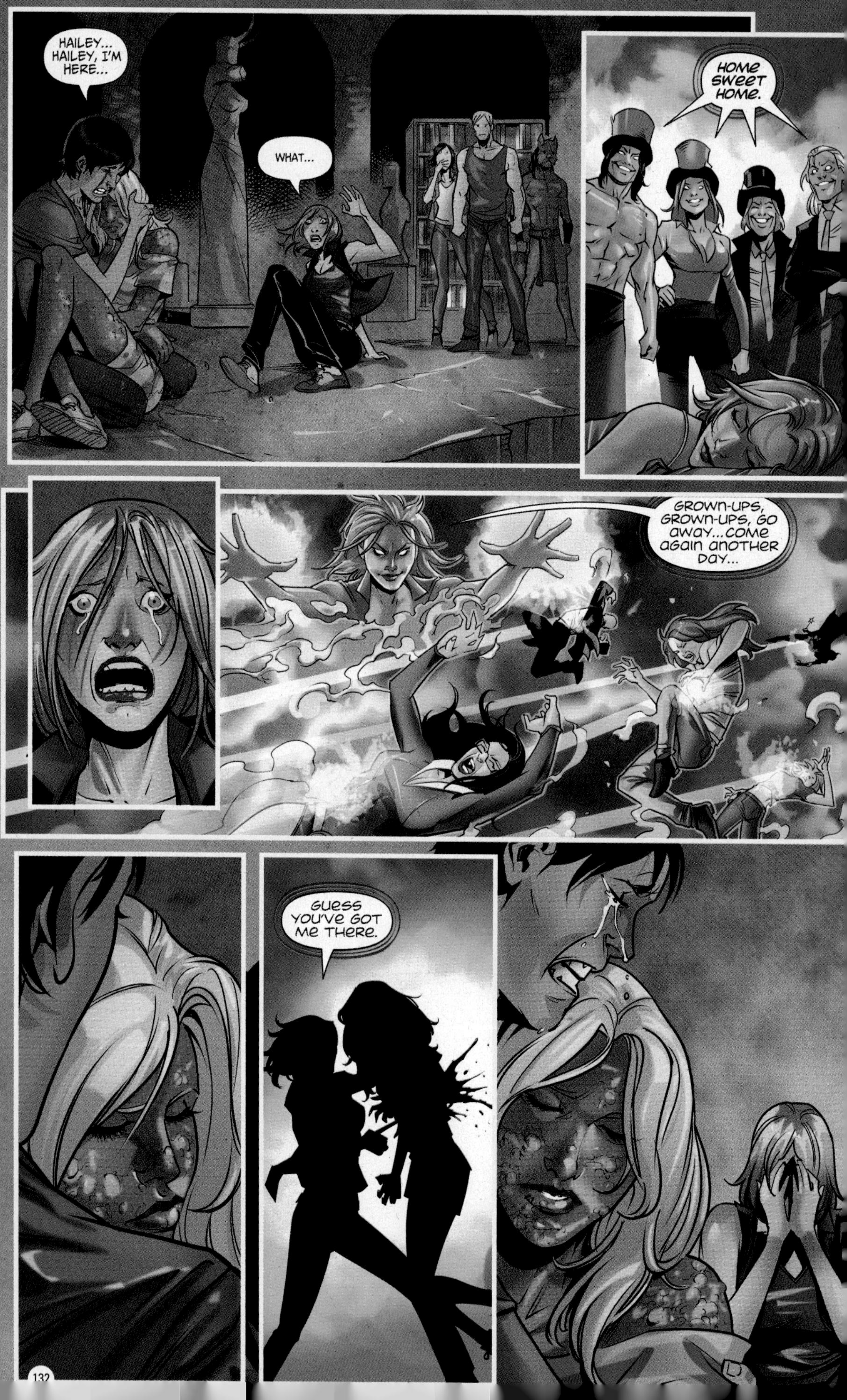

HAILEY... HAILEY, I'M HERE...
WHAT...
HOME SWEET HOME.
GROWN-UPS, GROWN-UPS, GO AWAY...COME AGAIN ANOTHER DAY...
GUESS YOU'VE GOT ME THERE.

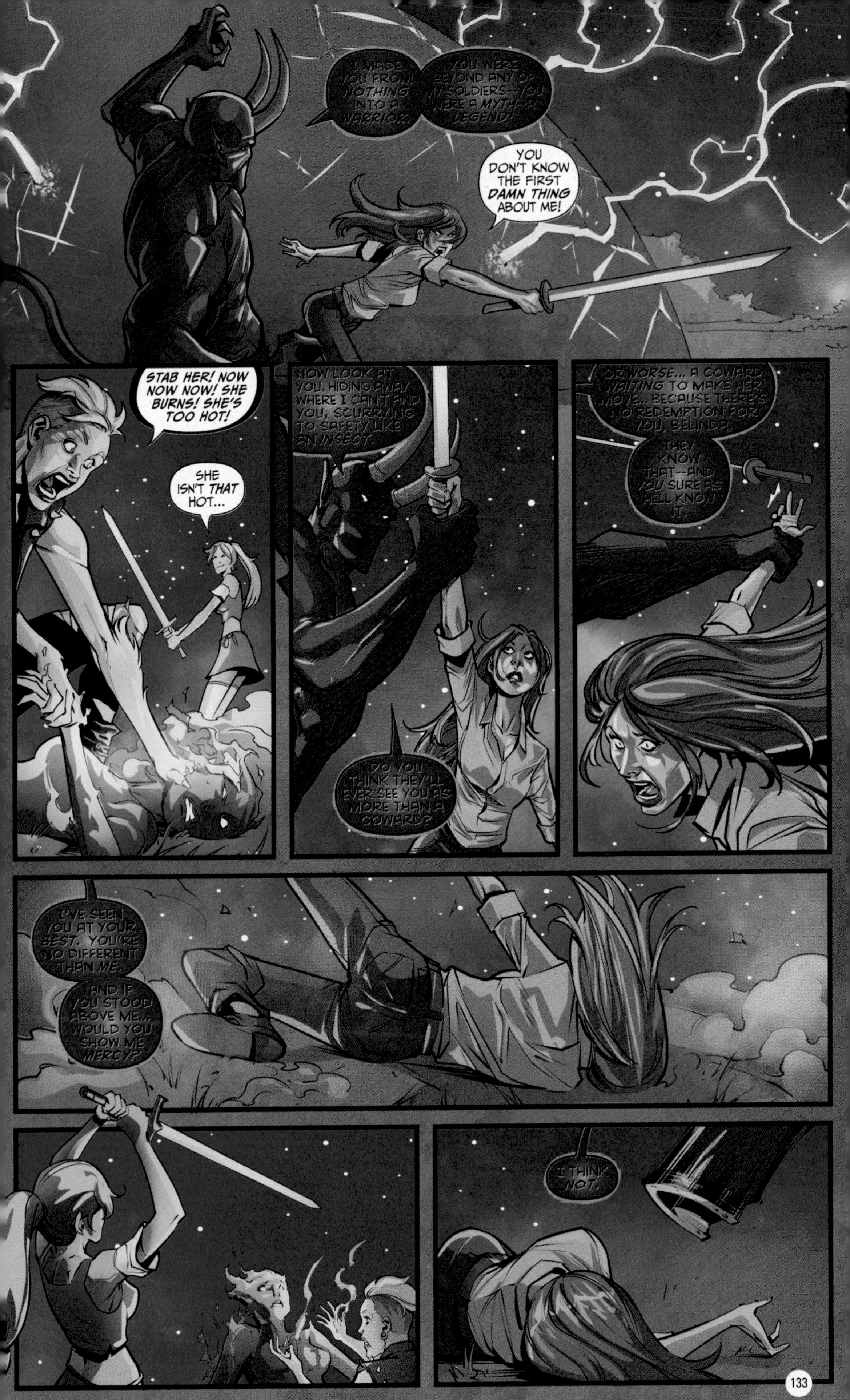

I MADE YOU FROM NOTHING INTO A WARRIOR!
YOU WERE BEYOND ANY OF MY SOLDIERS--YOU WERE A MYTH--A LEGEND!
YOU DON'T KNOW THE FIRST DAMN THING ABOUT ME!
STAB HER! NOW NOW NOW! SHE BURNS! SHE'S TOO HOT!
SHE ISN'T THAT HOT...
NOW LOOK AT YOU, HIDING AWAY WHERE I CAN'T FIND YOU, SCURRYING TO SAFETY LIKE AN INSECT.
DO YOU THINK THEY'LL EVER SEE YOU AS MORE THAN A COWARD?
OR WORSE... A COWARD WAITING TO MAKE HER MOVE... BECAUSE THERE'S NO REDEMPTION FOR YOU, BELINDA.
THEY KNOW THAT--AND YOU SURE AS HELL KNOW IT.
I'VE SEEN YOU AT YOUR BEST. YOU'RE NO DIFFERENT THAN ME.
AND IF YOU STOOD ABOVE ME... WOULD YOU SHOW ME MERCY?
I THINK NOT.

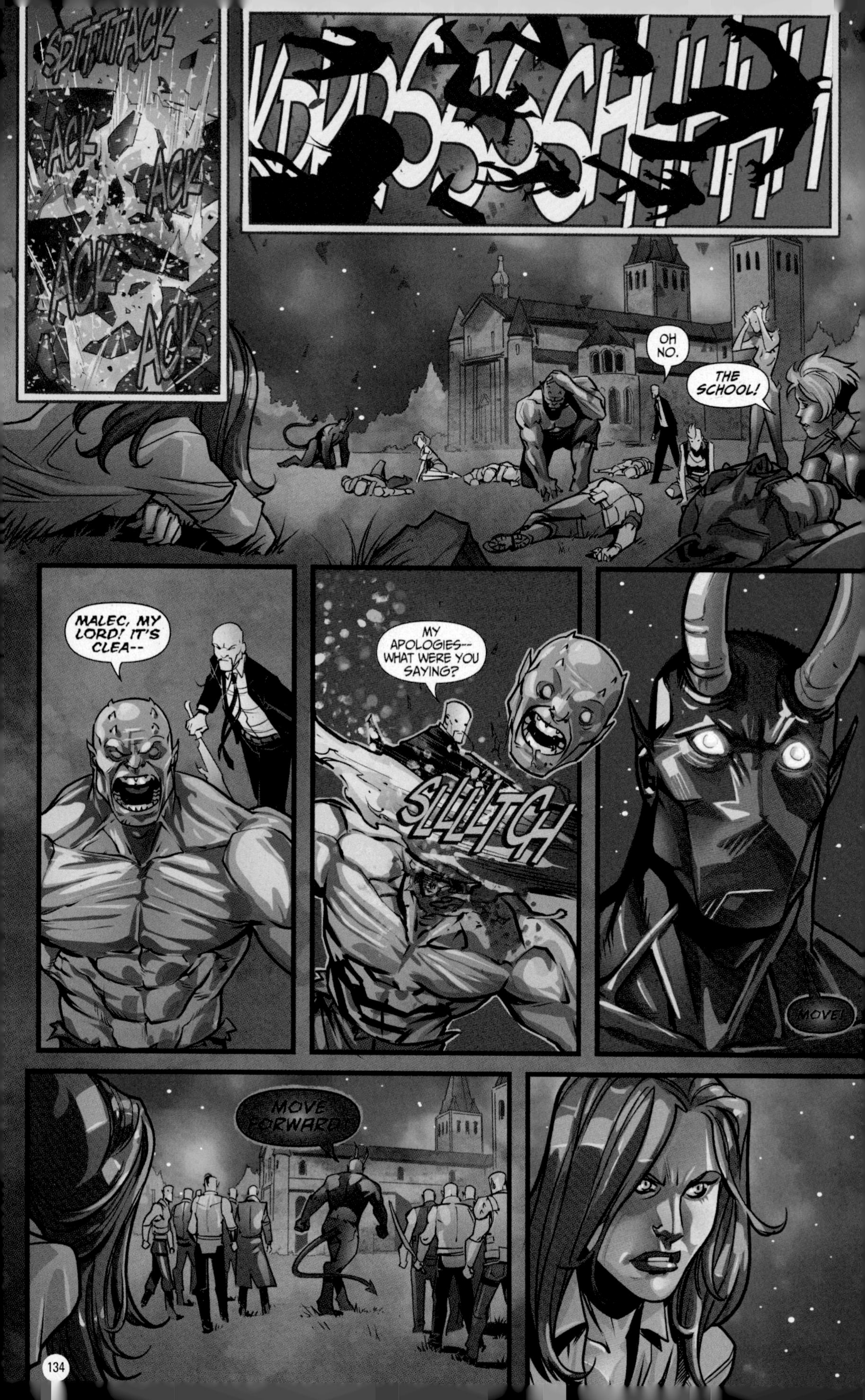
SPTTTTTACK
ACK
ACK
ACK
ACK
KRRSSSCHHH
OH NO.
THE SCHOOL!
MALEC, MY LORD! IT'S CLEA--
MY APOLOGIES--- WHAT WERE YOU SAYING?
SLLLLTCH
MOVE!
MOVE FORWARD!

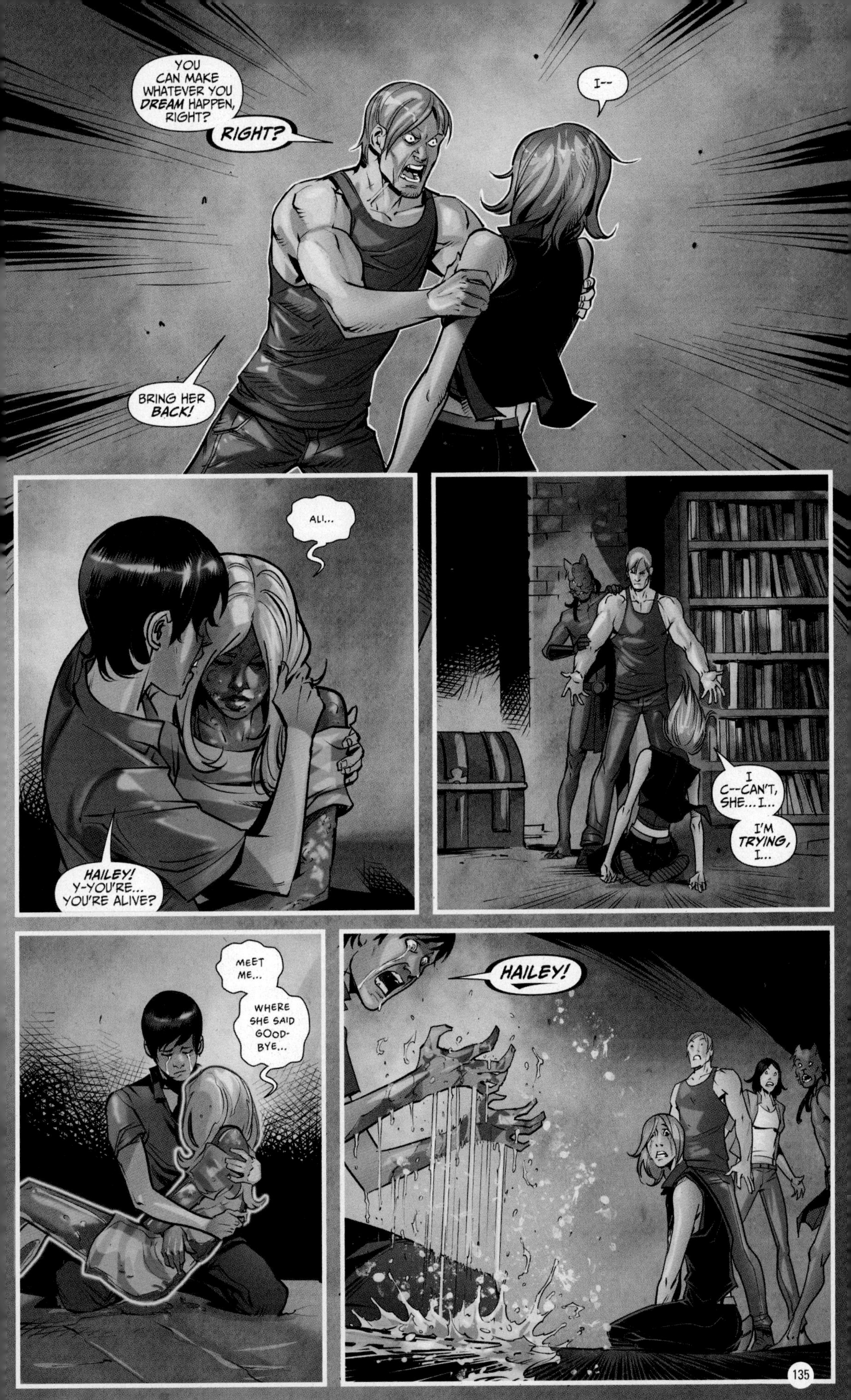
YOU CAN MAKE WHATEVER YOU DREAM HAPPEN, RIGHT?
RIGHT?
I--
BRING HER BACK!
ALI...
HAILEY! Y-YOU'RE... YOU'RE ALIVE?
I C--CAN'T, SHE... I...
I'M TRYING, I...
MEET ME...
WHERE SHE SAID GOOD-BYE...
HAILEY!

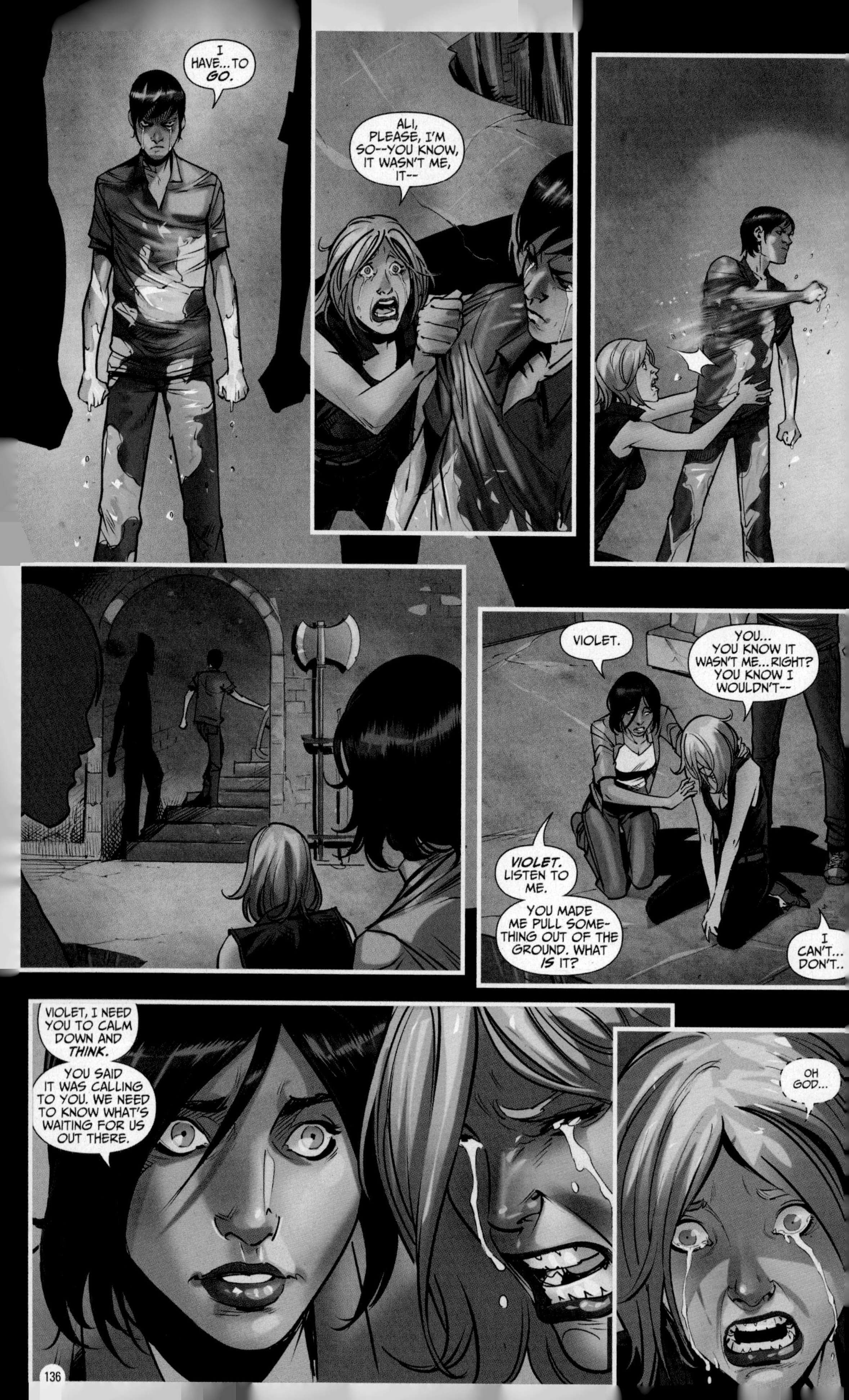
I HAVE...TO GO.
ALI, PLEASE, I'M SO--YOU KNOW, IT WASN'T ME, IT--
VIOLET.
YOU... YOU KNOW IT WASN'T ME...RIGHT? YOU KNOW I WOULDN'T--
VIOLET. LISTEN TO ME.
YOU MADE ME PULL SOME-THING OUT OF THE GROUND. WHAT IS IT?
I CAN'T... DON'T..
VIOLET, I NEED YOU TO CALM DOWN AND THINK.
YOU SAID IT WAS CALLING TO YOU. WE NEED TO KNOW WHAT'S WAITING FOR US OUT THERE.
OH GOD...

SO...UH... WHAT'S THE... YOU KNOW, PLAN?

FIND OUT WHAT'S GOING ON.

AND STOP IT.

NOT TO BE A DICK BUT...IS YOUR SCHOOL ALWAYS LIKE THIS?

AND YOU WONDER WHY I GOT BOOTED.

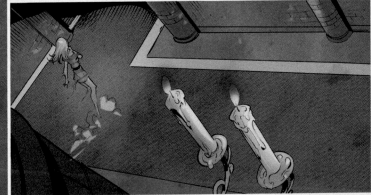

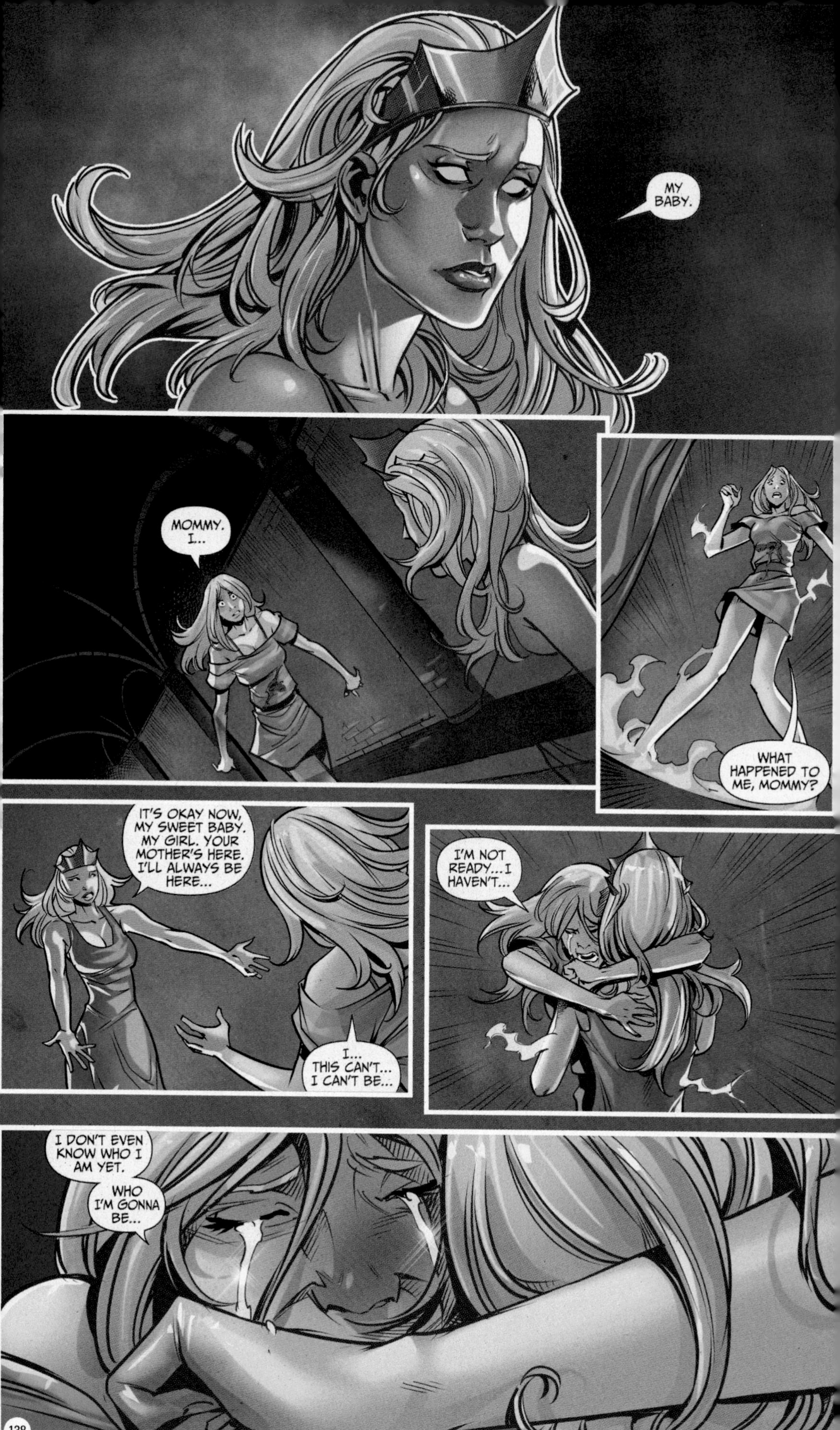
MY BABY.
MOMMY. I...
WHAT HAPPENED TO ME, MOMMY?
IT'S OKAY NOW, MY SWEET BABY. MY GIRL. YOUR MOTHER'S HERE. I'LL ALWAYS BE HERE...
I... THIS CAN'T... I CAN'T BE...
I'M NOT READY...I HAVEN'T...
I DON'T EVEN KNOW WHO I AM YET.
WHO I'M GONNA BE...

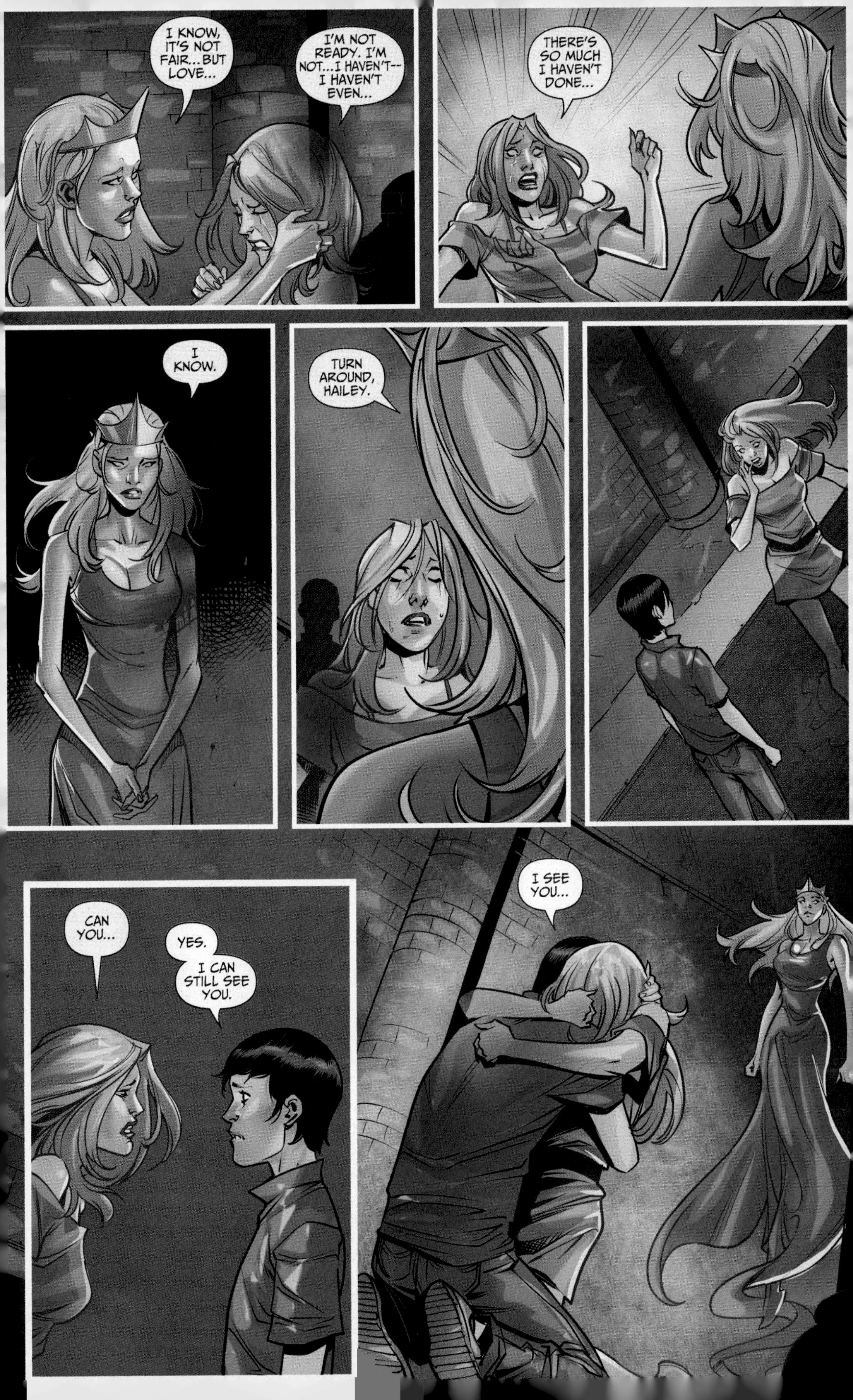
I KNOW, IT'S NOT FAIR...BUT LOVE...
I'M NOT READY. I'M NOT...I HAVEN'T-- I HAVEN'T EVEN...
THERE'S SO MUCH I HAVEN'T DONE...
I KNOW.
TURN AROUND, HAILEY.
CAN YOU...
YES. I CAN STILL SEE YOU.
I SEE YOU...

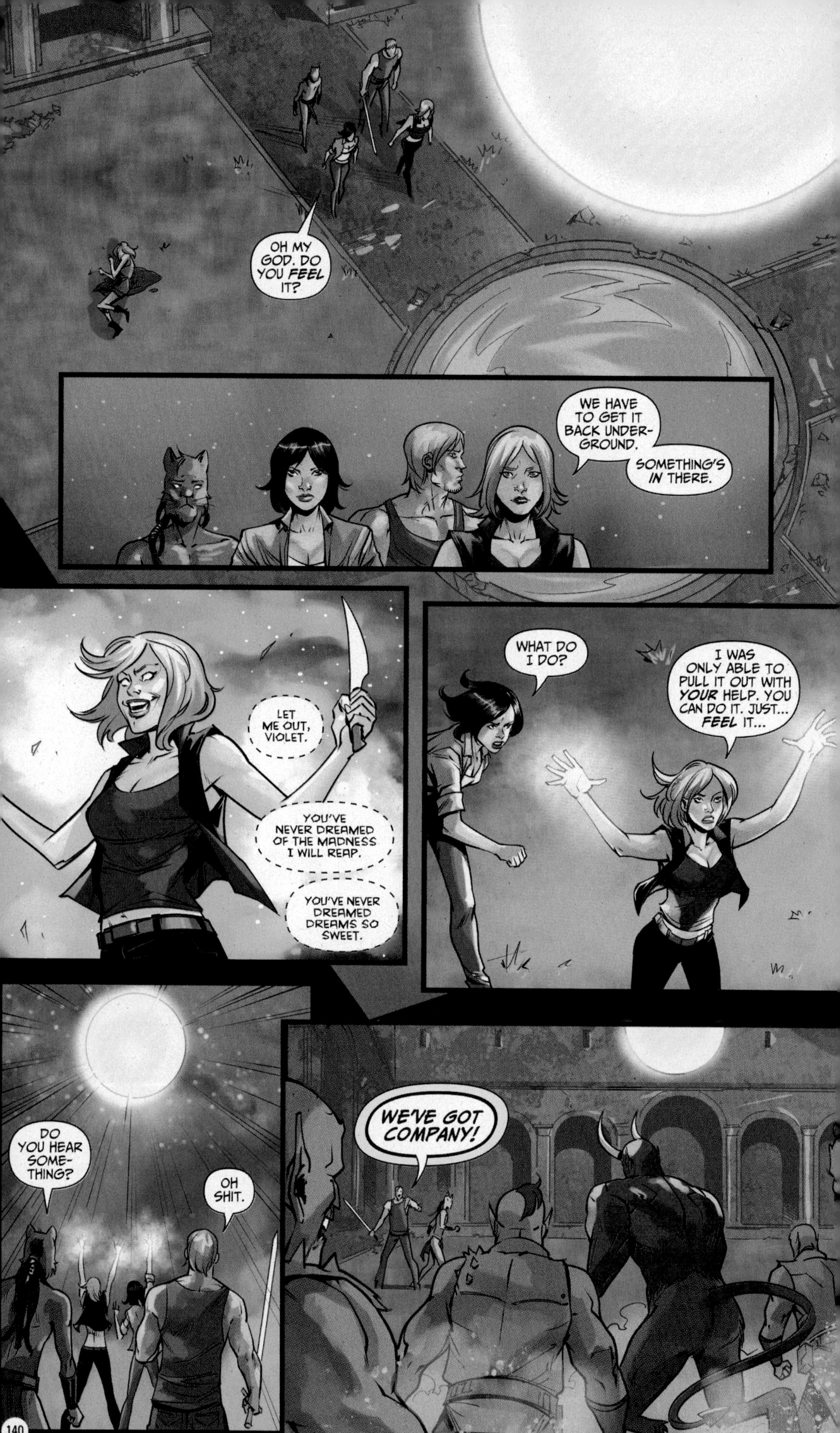
OH MY GOD. DO YOU FEEL IT?
WE HAVE TO GET IT BACK UNDER-GROUND.
SOMETHING'S IN THERE.
LET ME OUT, VIOLET.
YOU'VE NEVER DREAMED OF THE MADNESS I WILL REAP.
YOU'VE NEVER DREAMED DREAMS SO SWEET.
WHAT DO I DO?
I WAS ONLY ABLE TO PULL IT OUT WITH YOUR HELP. YOU CAN DO IT. JUST... FEEL IT...
DO YOU HEAR SOME-THING?
OH SHIT.
WE'VE GOT COMPANY!

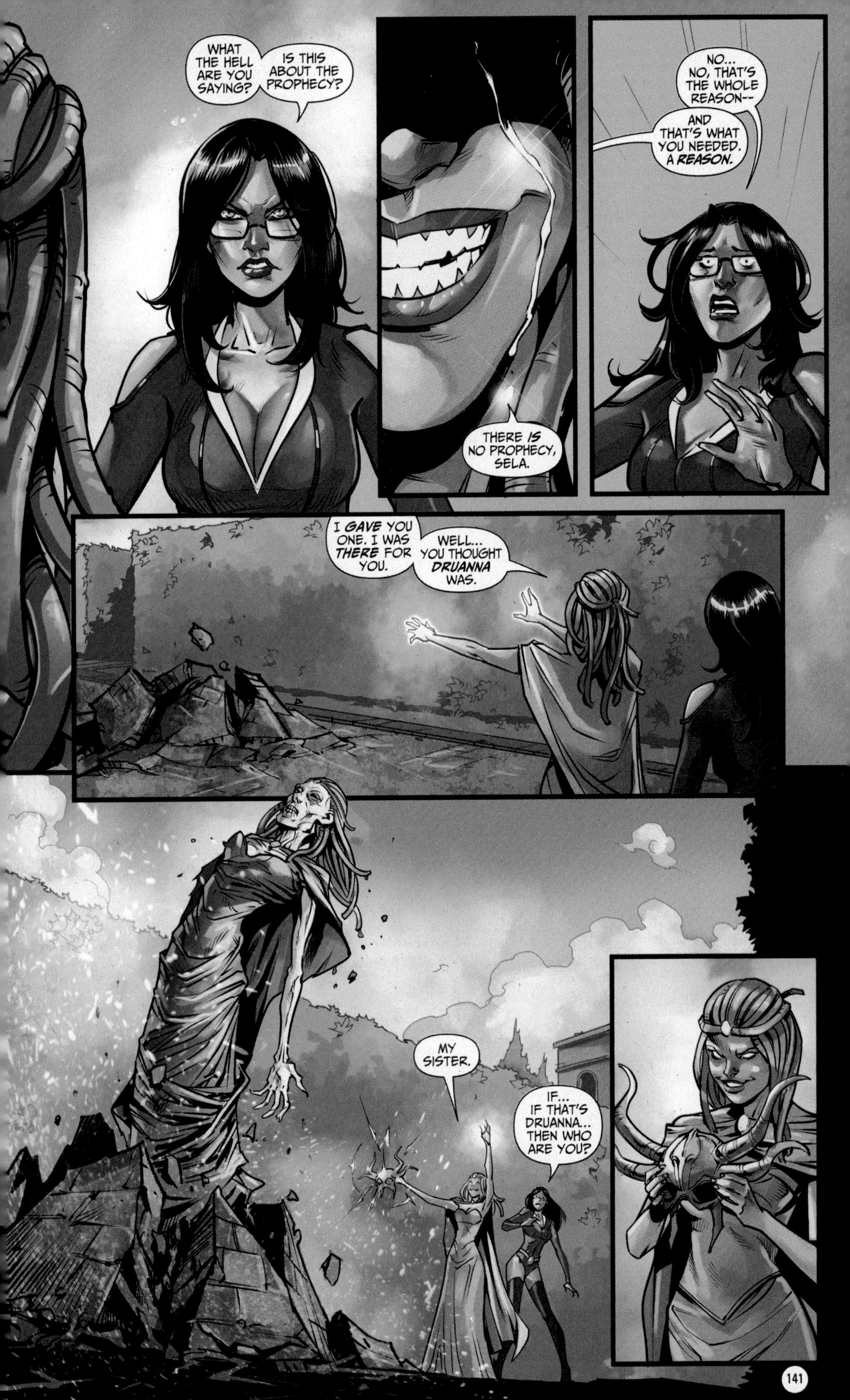

WHAT THE HELL ARE YOU SAYING?
IS THIS ABOUT THE PROPHECY?
THERE *IS* NO PROPHECY, SELA.
NO... NO, THAT'S THE WHOLE REASON--
AND THAT'S WHAT YOU NEEDED. A *REASON.*
I *GAVE* YOU ONE. I WAS *THERE* FOR YOU.
WELL... YOU THOUGHT *DRUANNA* WAS.
MY SISTER.
IF... IF THAT'S DRUANNA... THEN WHO ARE YOU?

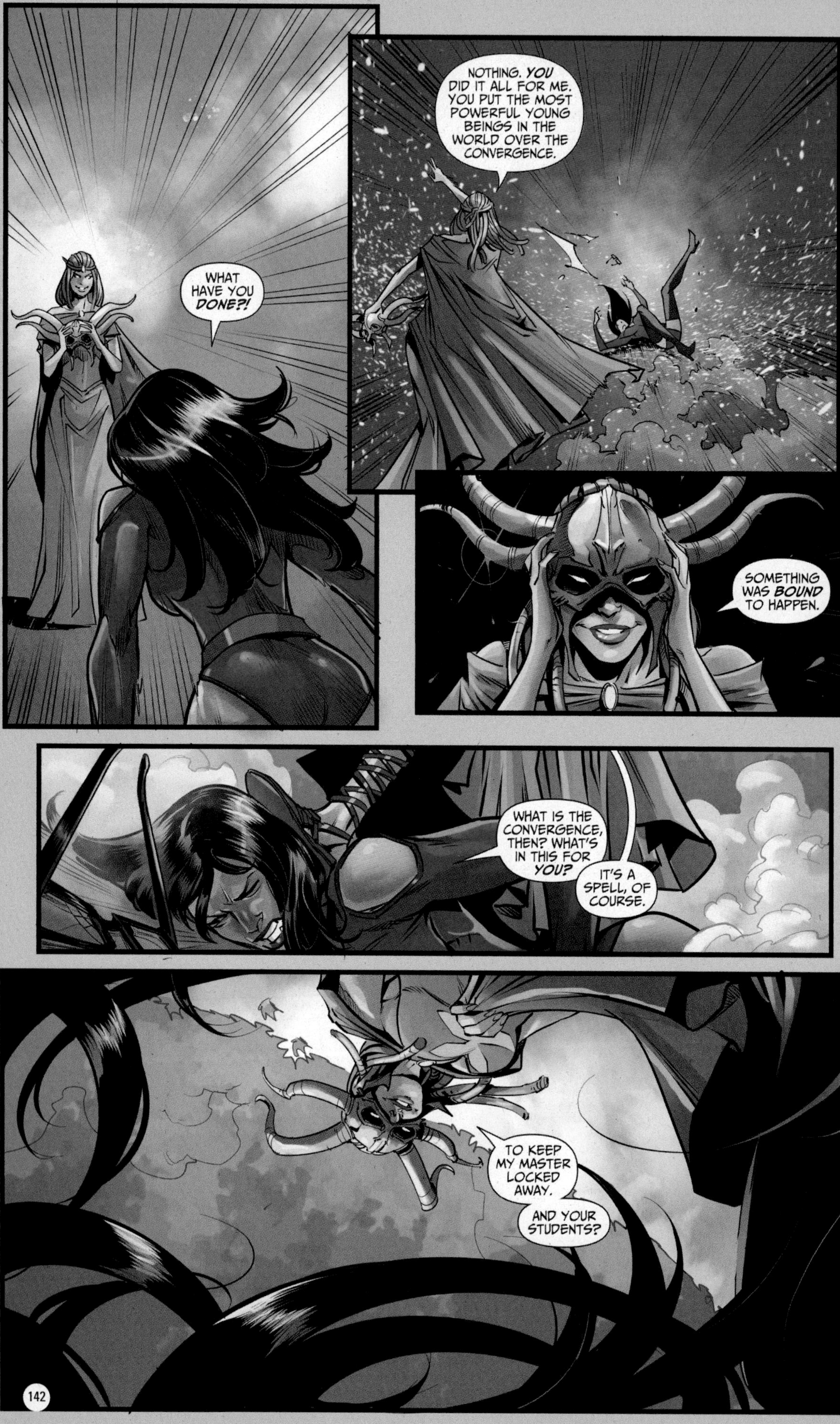
WHAT HAVE YOU DONE?!
NOTHING. YOU DID IT ALL FOR ME. YOU PUT THE MOST POWERFUL YOUNG BEINGS IN THE WORLD OVER THE CONVERGENCE.
SOMETHING WAS BOUND TO HAPPEN.
WHAT IS THE CONVERGENCE, THEN? WHAT'S IN THIS FOR YOU?
IT'S A SPELL, OF COURSE.
TO KEEP MY MASTER LOCKED AWAY.
AND YOUR STUDENTS?

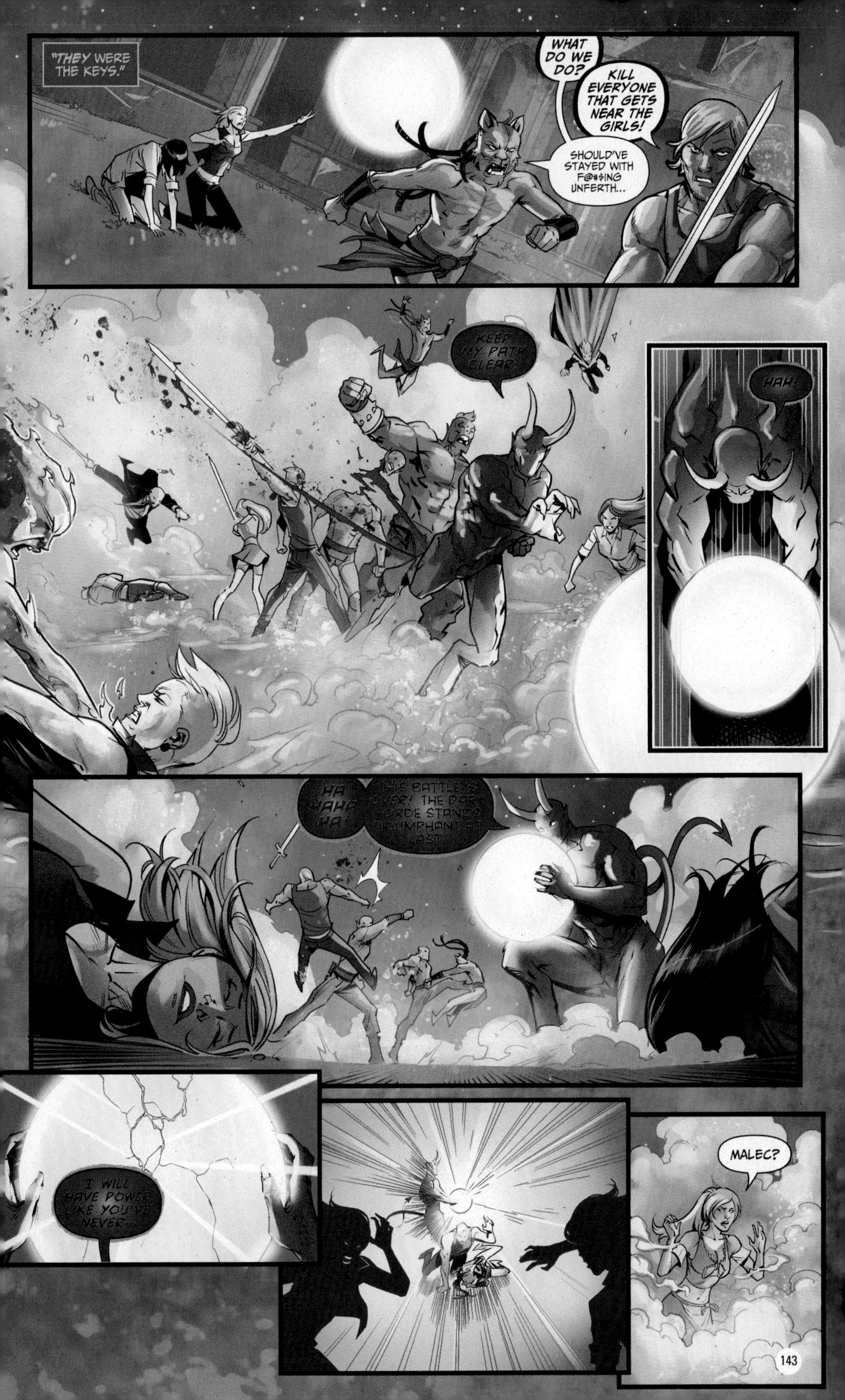
"THEY WERE THE KEYS."
WHAT DO WE DO?
KILL EVERYONE THAT GETS NEAR THE GIRLS!
SHOULD'VE STAYED WITH F@#$ING UNFERTH...
KEEP MY PATH CLEAR!
HAH!
HA HAHA HA!
THIS BATTLE IS OVER! THE DARK HORDE STANDS TRIUMPHANT AT LAST!
I WILL HAVE POWER LIKE YOU'VE NEVER...
MALEC?

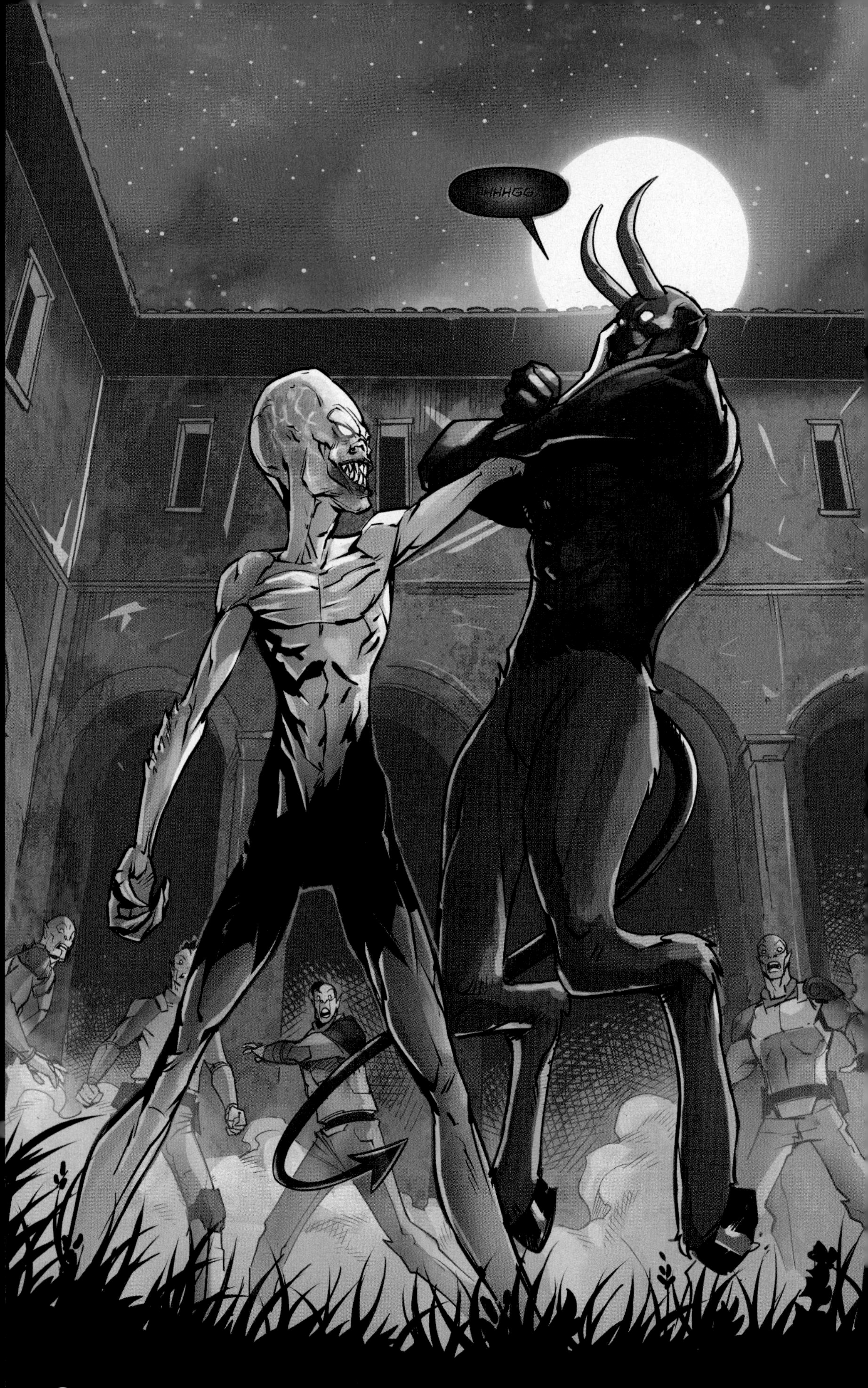
AHHHGG!

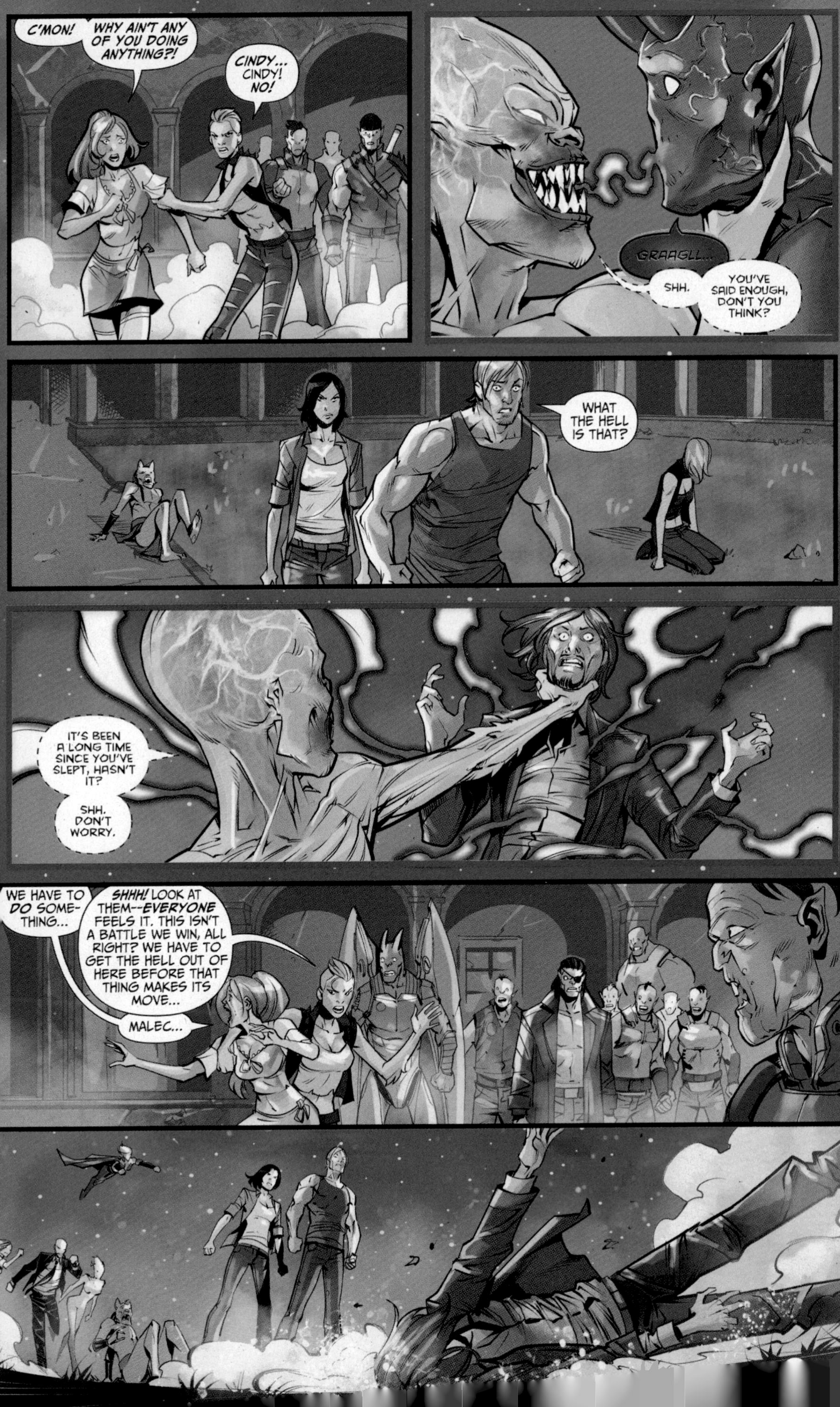
C'MON!
WHY AIN'T ANY OF YOU DOING ANYTHING?!
CINDY... CINDY! NO!
GRAAGLL...
SHH.
YOU'VE SAID ENOUGH, DON'T YOU THINK?
WHAT THE HELL IS THAT?
IT'S BEEN A LONG TIME SINCE YOU'VE SLEPT, HASN'T IT?
SHH. DON'T WORRY.
WE HAVE TO DO SOMETHING...
SHHH! LOOK AT THEM--EVERYONE FEELS IT. THIS ISN'T A BATTLE WE WIN, ALL RIGHT? WE HAVE TO GET THE HELL OUT OF HERE BEFORE THAT THING MAKES ITS MOVE...
MALEC...

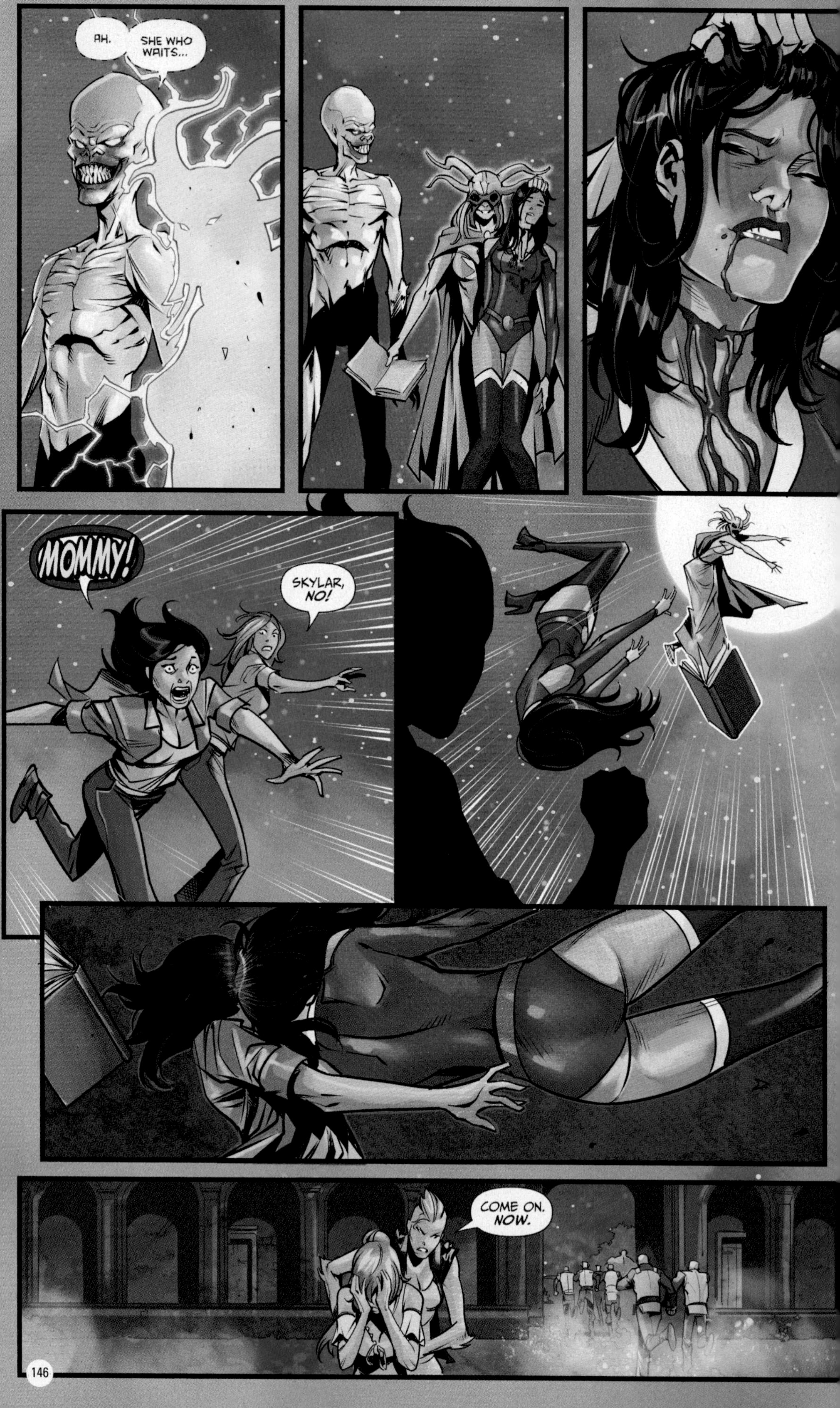
AH.
SHE WHO WAITS...
MOMMY!
SKYLAR, NO!
COME ON. NOW.

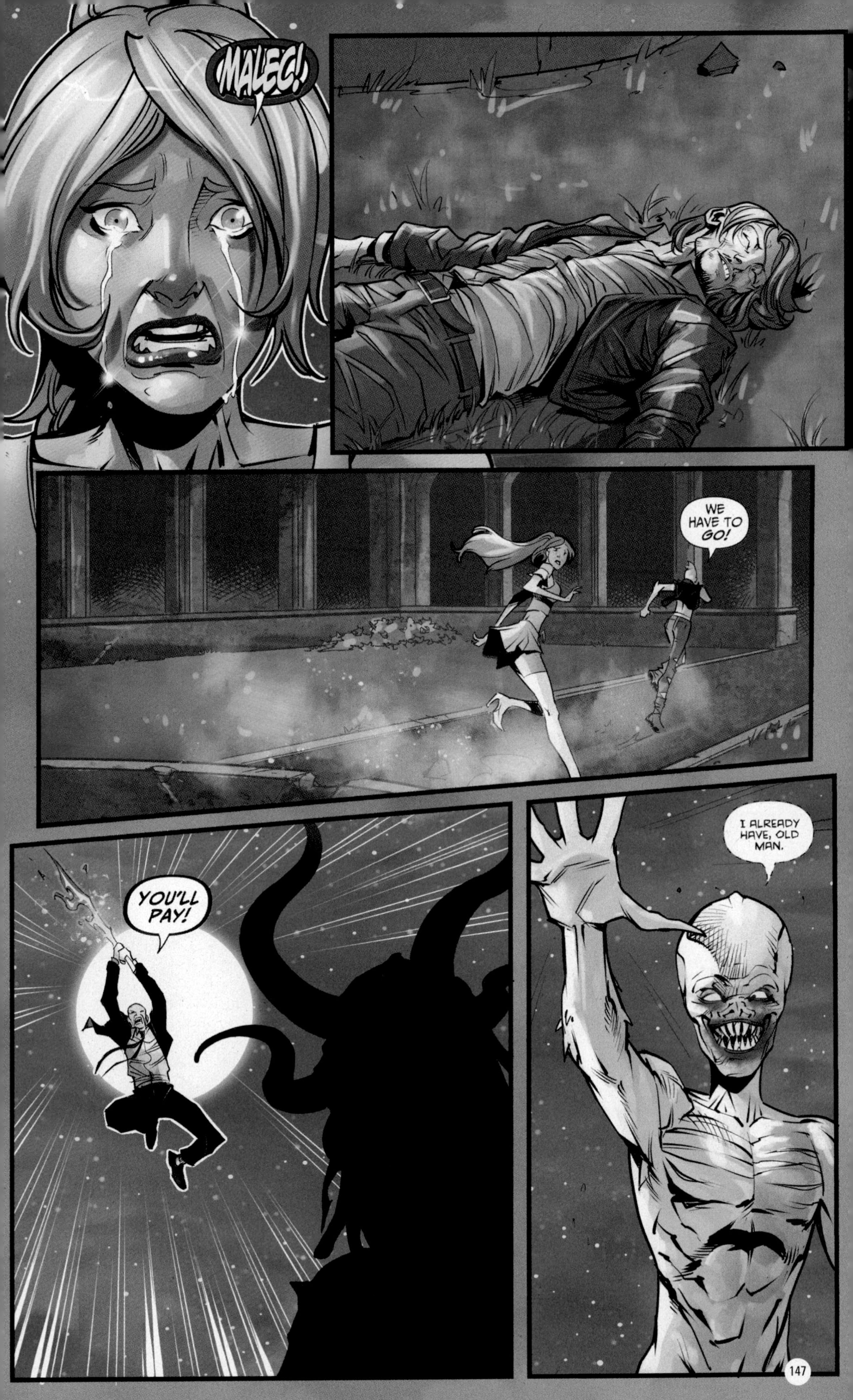
MALEC!
WE HAVE TO GO!
YOU'LL PAY!
I ALREADY HAVE, OLD MAN.

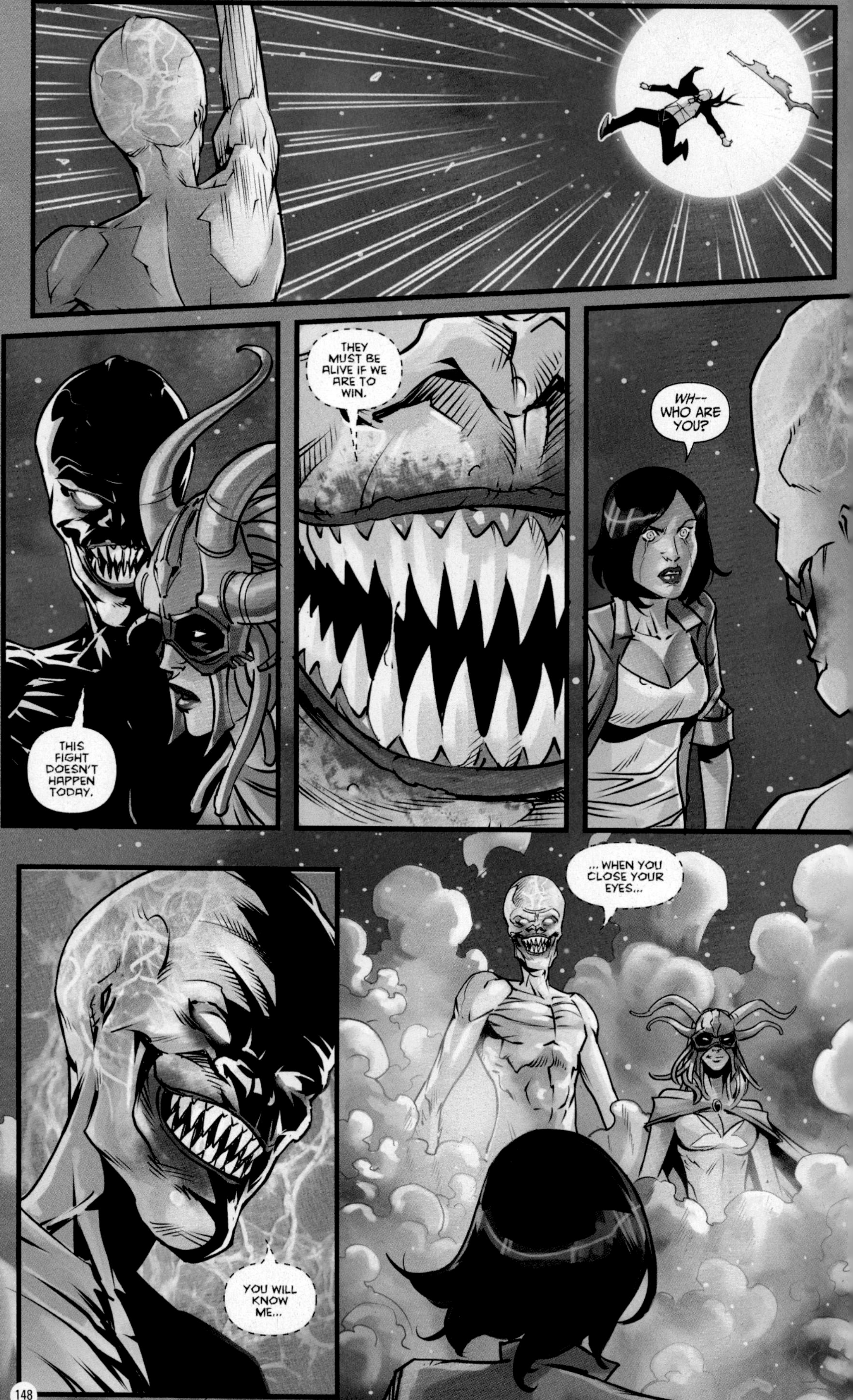
THIS FIGHT DOESN'T HAPPEN TODAY.
THEY MUST BE ALIVE IF WE ARE TO WIN.
WH-- WHO ARE YOU?
YOU WILL KNOW ME...
...WHEN YOU CLOSE YOUR EYES...

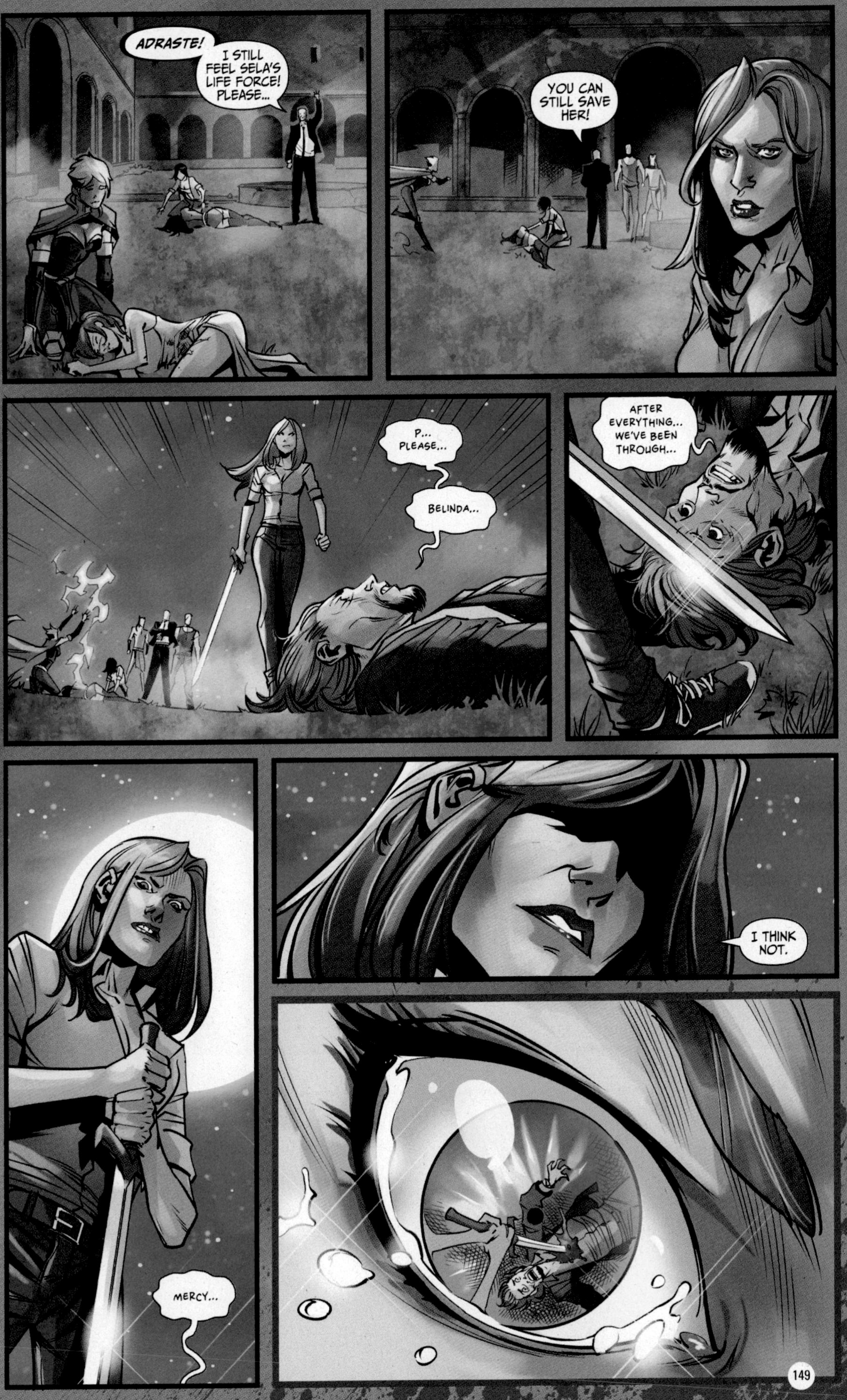
ADRASTE!
I STILL FEEL SELA'S LIFE FORCE! PLEASE...
YOU CAN STILL SAVE HER!
P... PLEASE...
BELINDA...
AFTER EVERYTHING... WE'VE BEEN THROUGH...
I THINK NOT.
MERCY...

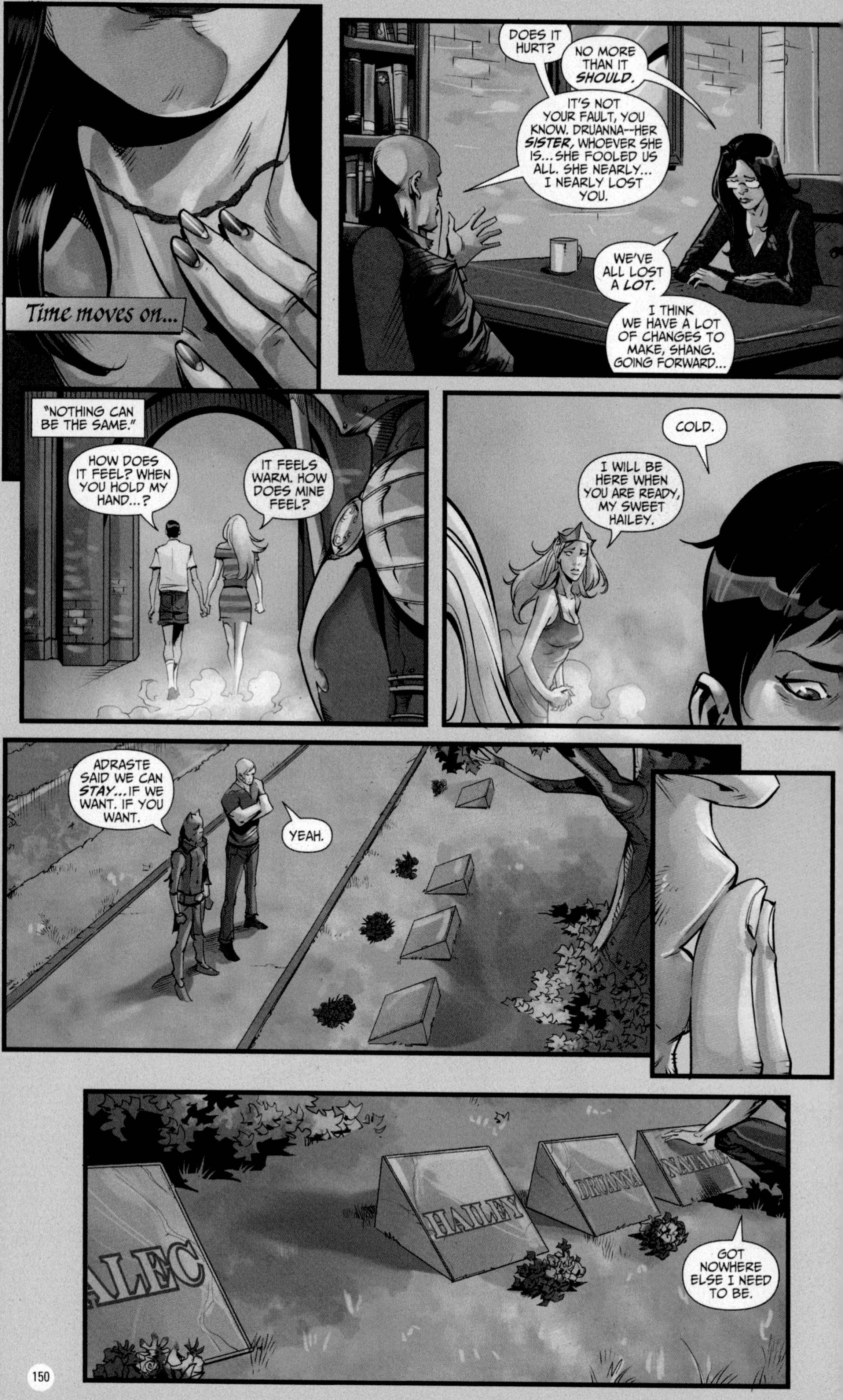
Time moves on...
DOES IT HURT?
NO MORE THAN IT SHOULD.
IT'S NOT YOUR FAULT, YOU KNOW. DRUANNA--HER SISTER, WHOEVER SHE IS... SHE FOOLED US ALL. SHE NEARLY... I NEARLY LOST YOU.
WE'VE ALL LOST A LOT.
I THINK WE HAVE A LOT OF CHANGES TO MAKE, SHANG. GOING FORWARD...
"NOTHING CAN BE THE SAME."
HOW DOES IT FEEL? WHEN YOU HOLD MY HAND...?
IT FEELS WARM. HOW DOES MINE FEEL?
COLD.
I WILL BE HERE WHEN YOU ARE READY, MY SWEET HAILEY.
ADRASTE SAID WE CAN STAY... IF WE WANT. IF YOU WANT.
YEAH.
ALEC
HAILEY
DRUANNA
NATALIE
GOT NOWHERE ELSE I NEED TO BE.

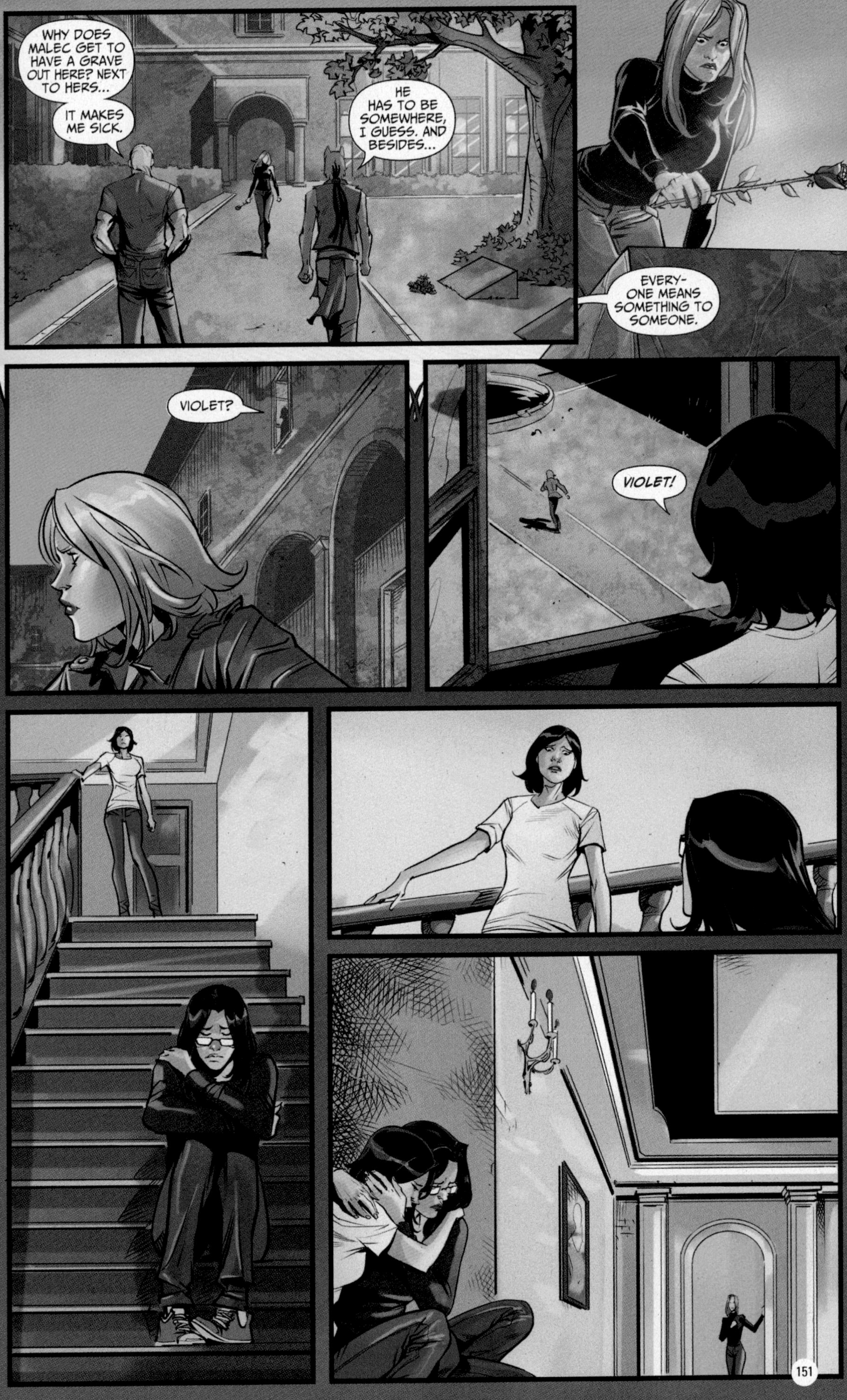
WHY DOES MALEC GET TO HAVE A GRAVE OUT HERE? NEXT TO HERS...
IT MAKES ME SICK.
HE HAS TO BE SOMEWHERE, I GUESS. AND BESIDES...
EVERY-ONE MEANS SOMETHING TO SOMEONE.
VIOLET?
VIOLET!

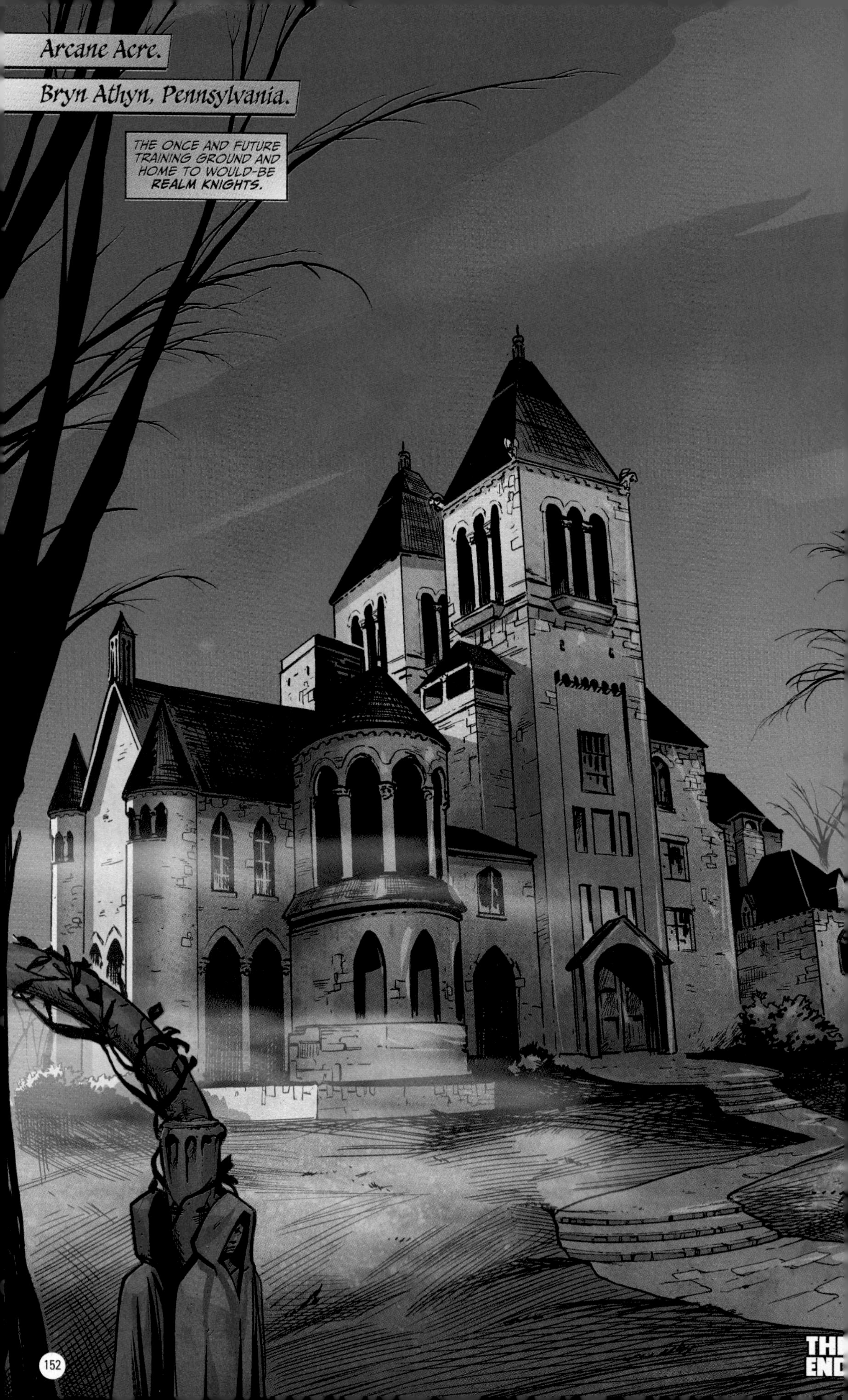
Arcane Acre.
Bryn Athyn, Pennsylvania.
THE ONCE AND FUTURE TRAINING GROUND AND HOME TO WOULD-BE REALM KNIGHTS.
THE END

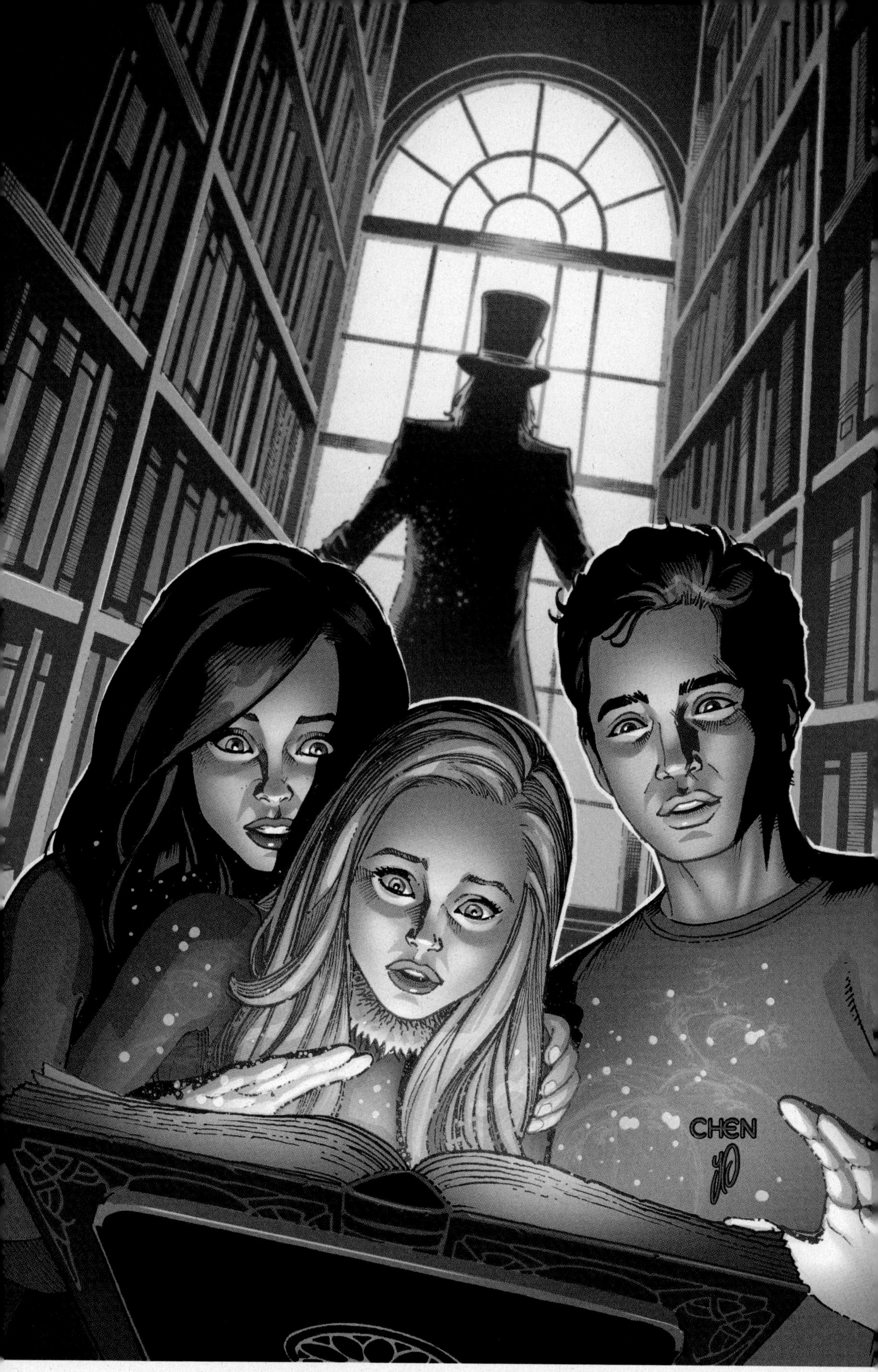
CHEN

GRIMM FAIRY TALES 107 • COVER A
ARTWORK BY SEAN CHEN • COLORS BY YLENIA DI NAPOLI

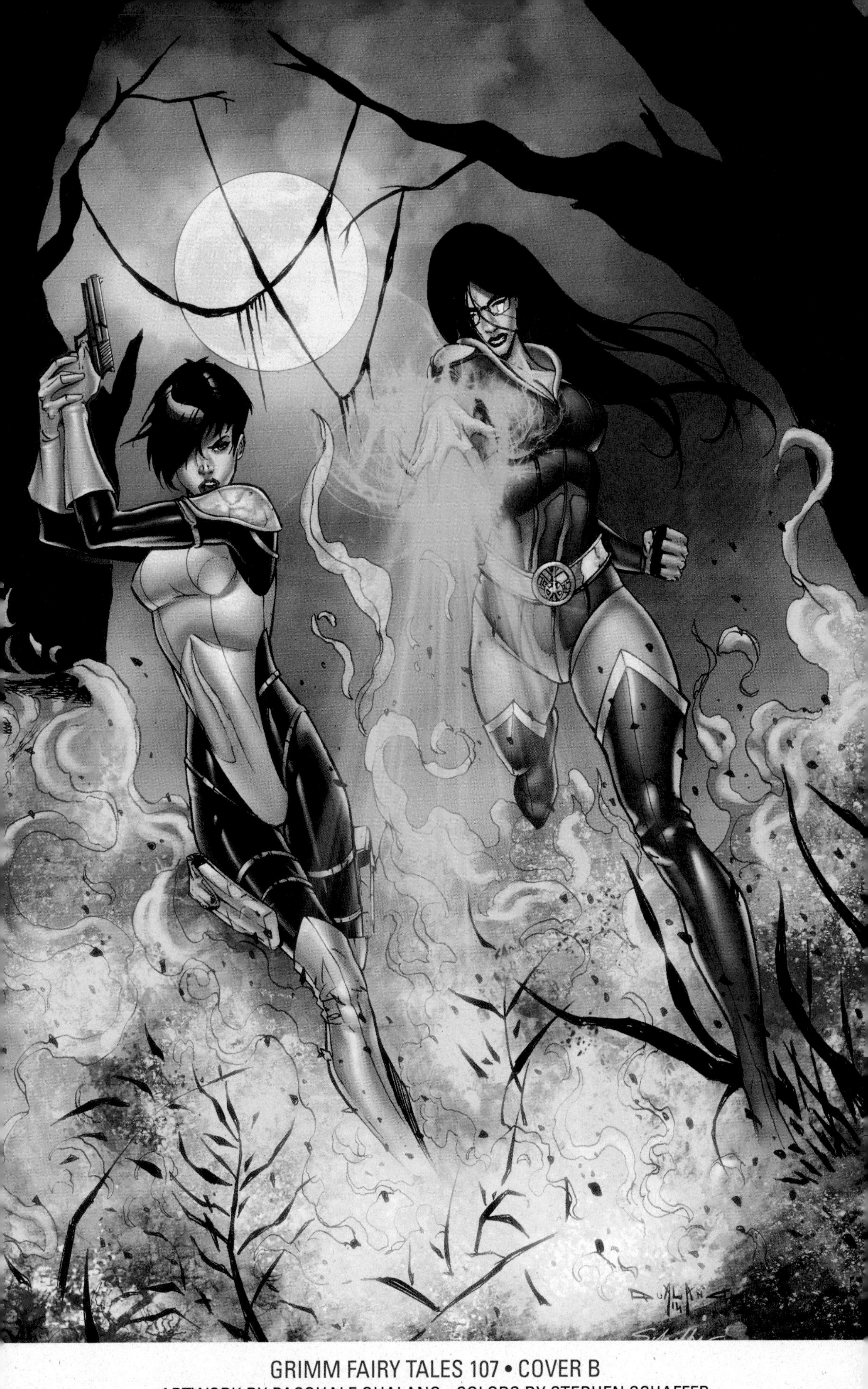

GRIMM FAIRY TALES 107 • COVER B
ARTWORK BY PASQUALE QUALANO • COLORS BY STEPHEN SCHAFFER

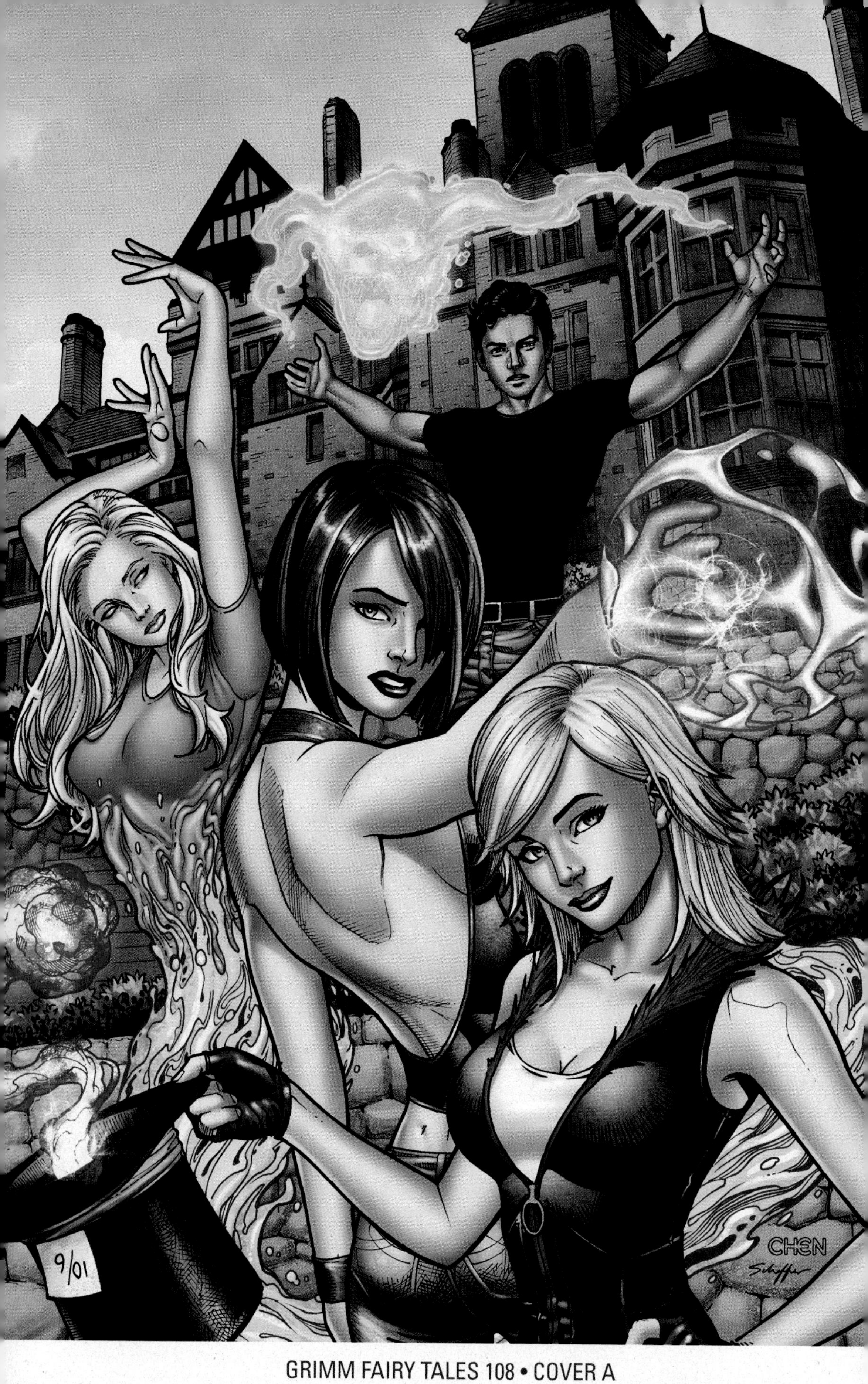
9/01
CHEN
Schaffer

GRIMM FAIRY TALES 108 • COVER A
ARTWORK BY SEAN CHEN • COLORS BY STEPHEN SCHAFFER

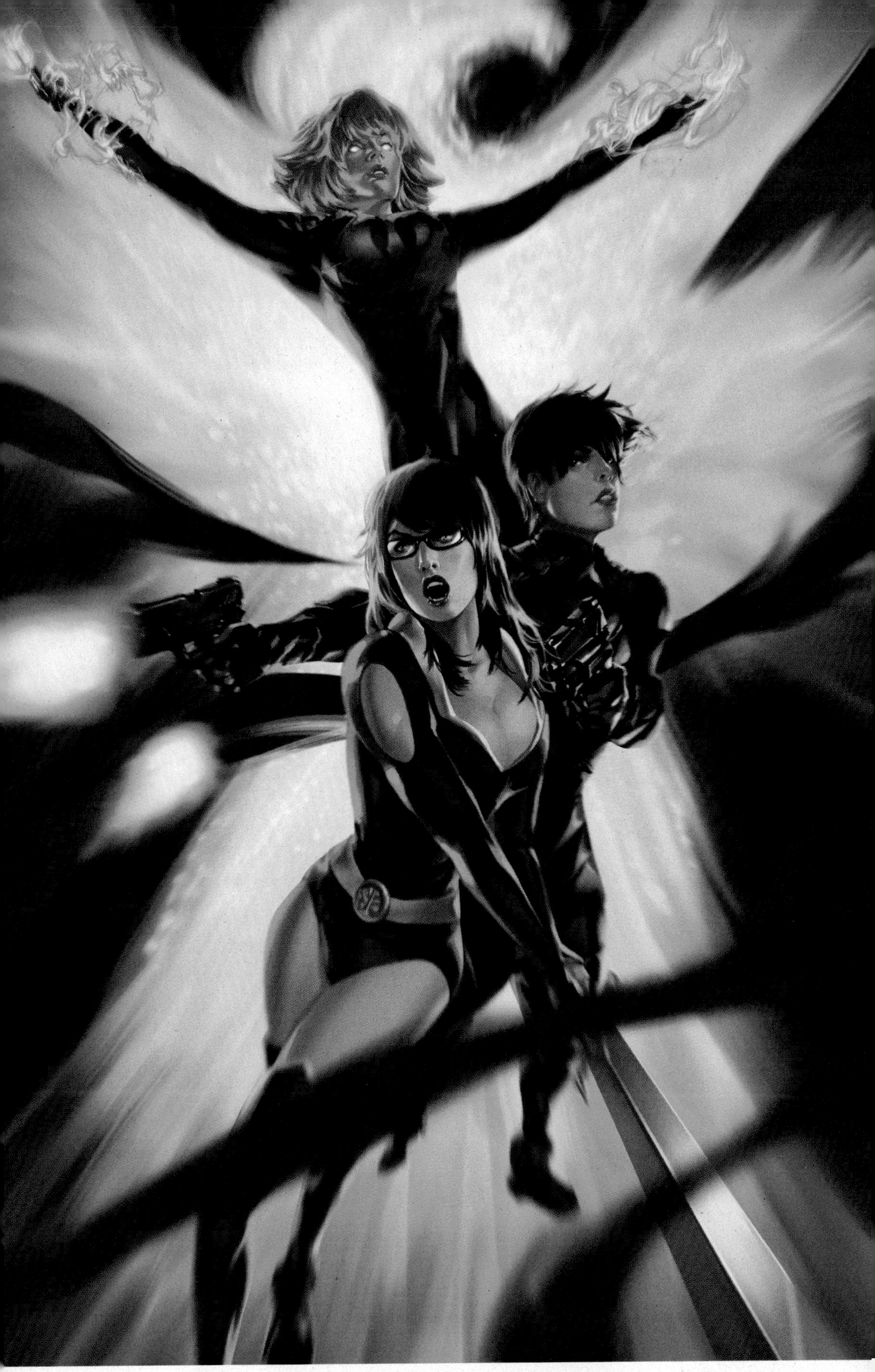

GRIMM FAIRY TALES 108 • COVER B
ARTWORK BY JARREAU WIMBERLY

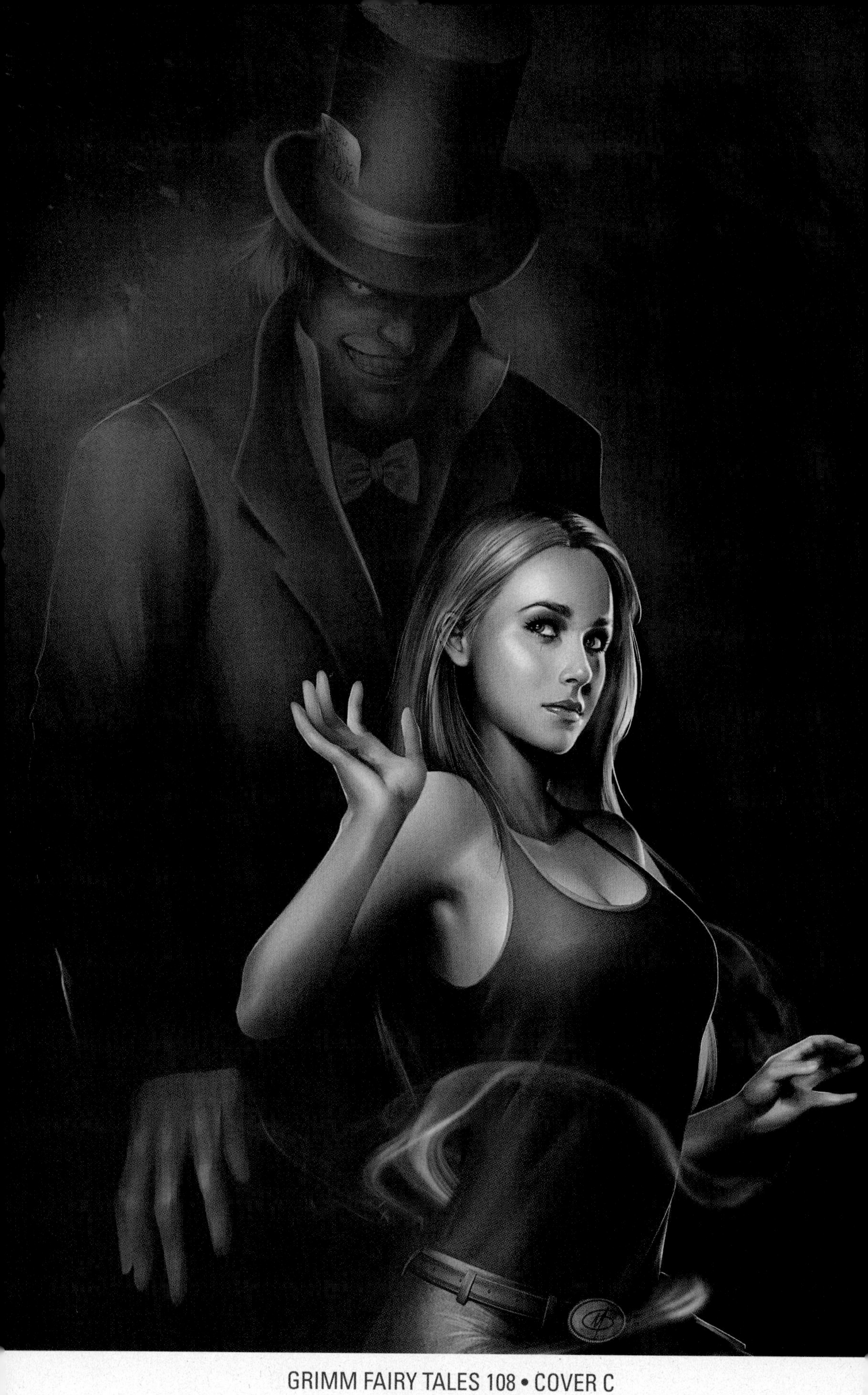

GRIMM FAIRY TALES 108 • COVER C
ARTWORK BY MEGURO

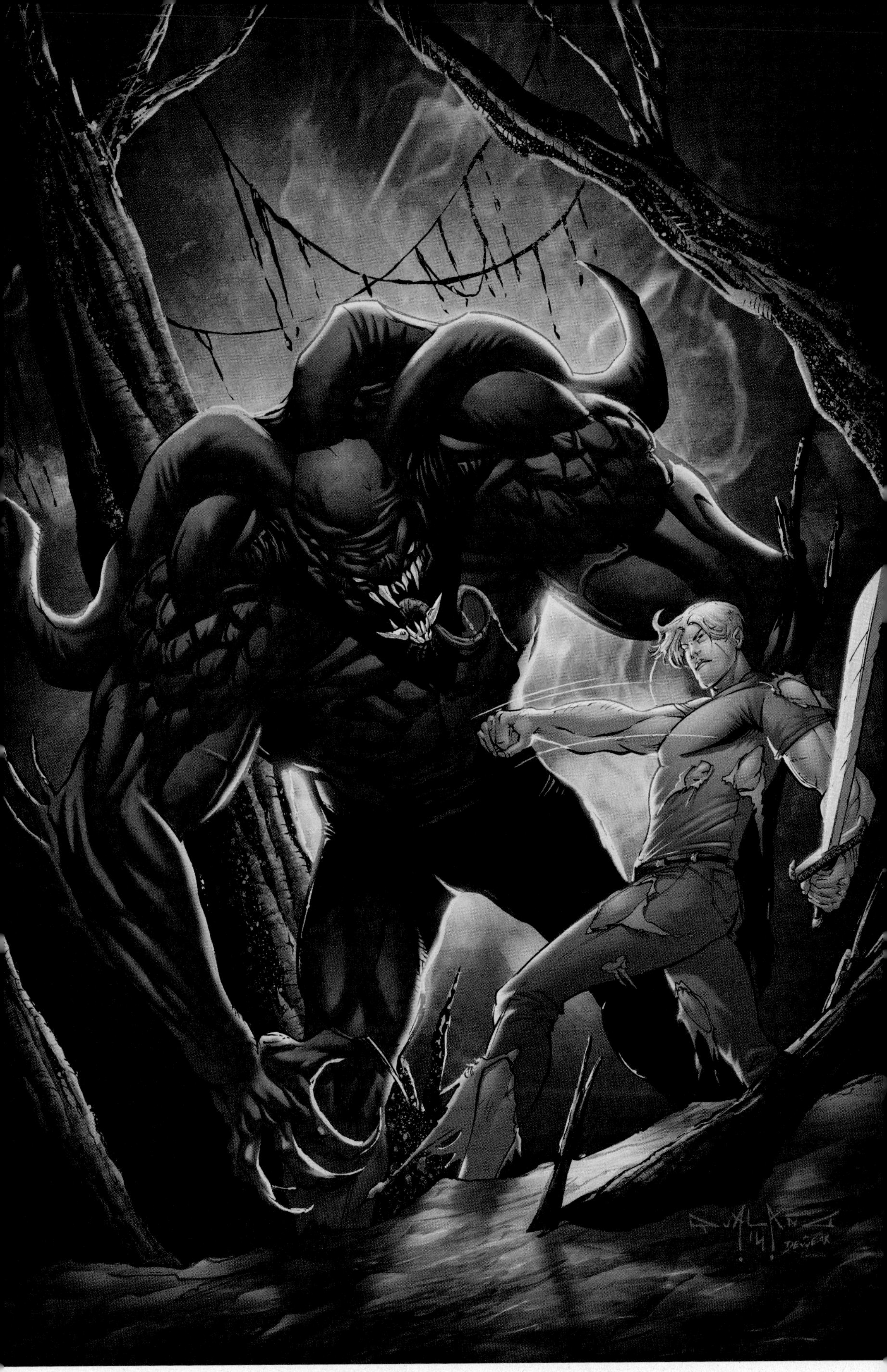

GRIMM FAIRY TALES 109 • COVER A

ARTWORK BY PASQUALE QUALANO • INKS BY DEVGEAR • COLORS BY SEAN ELLERY

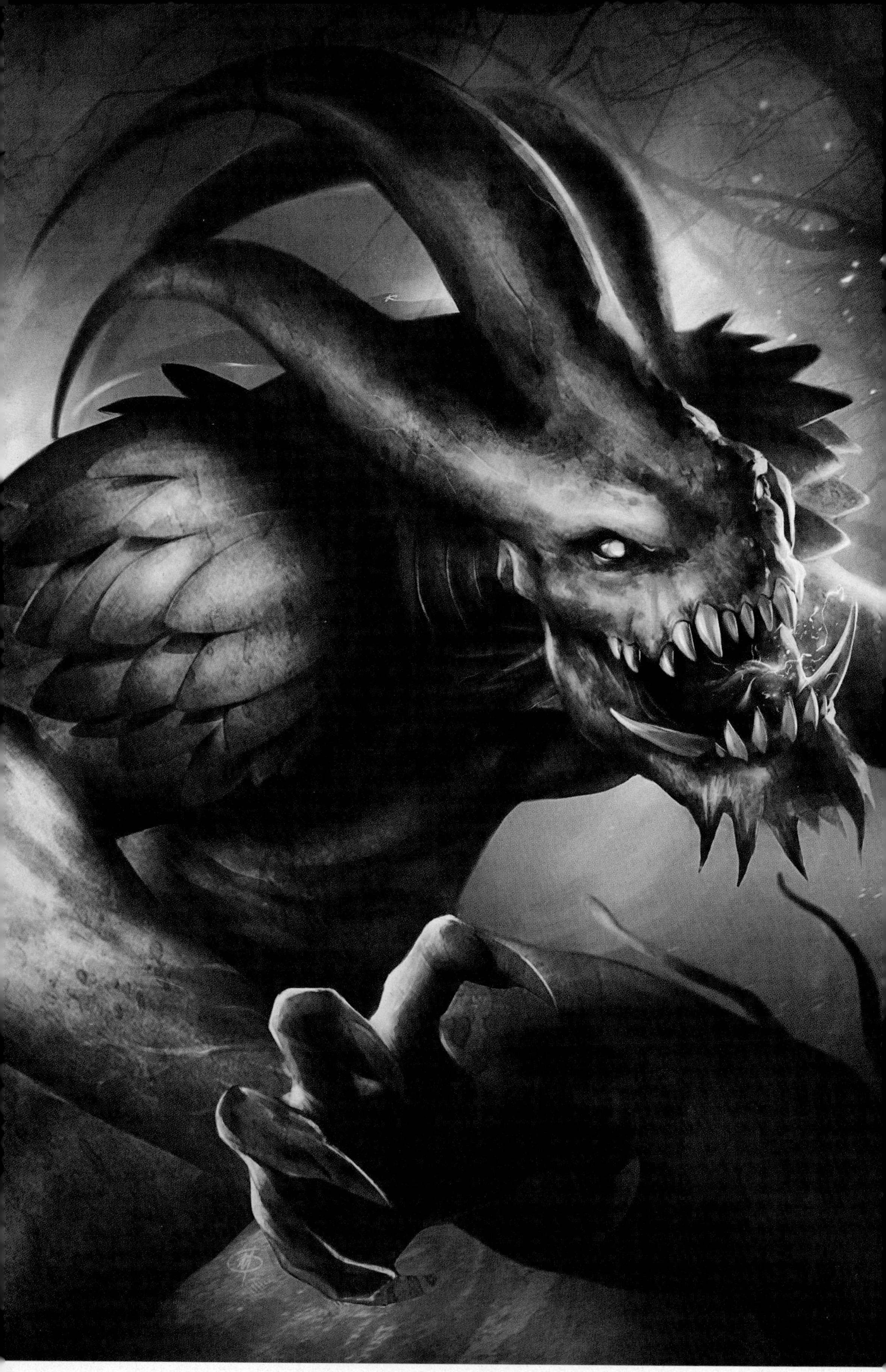

GRIMM FAIRY TALES 109 • COVER B
ARTWORK BY MEGURO

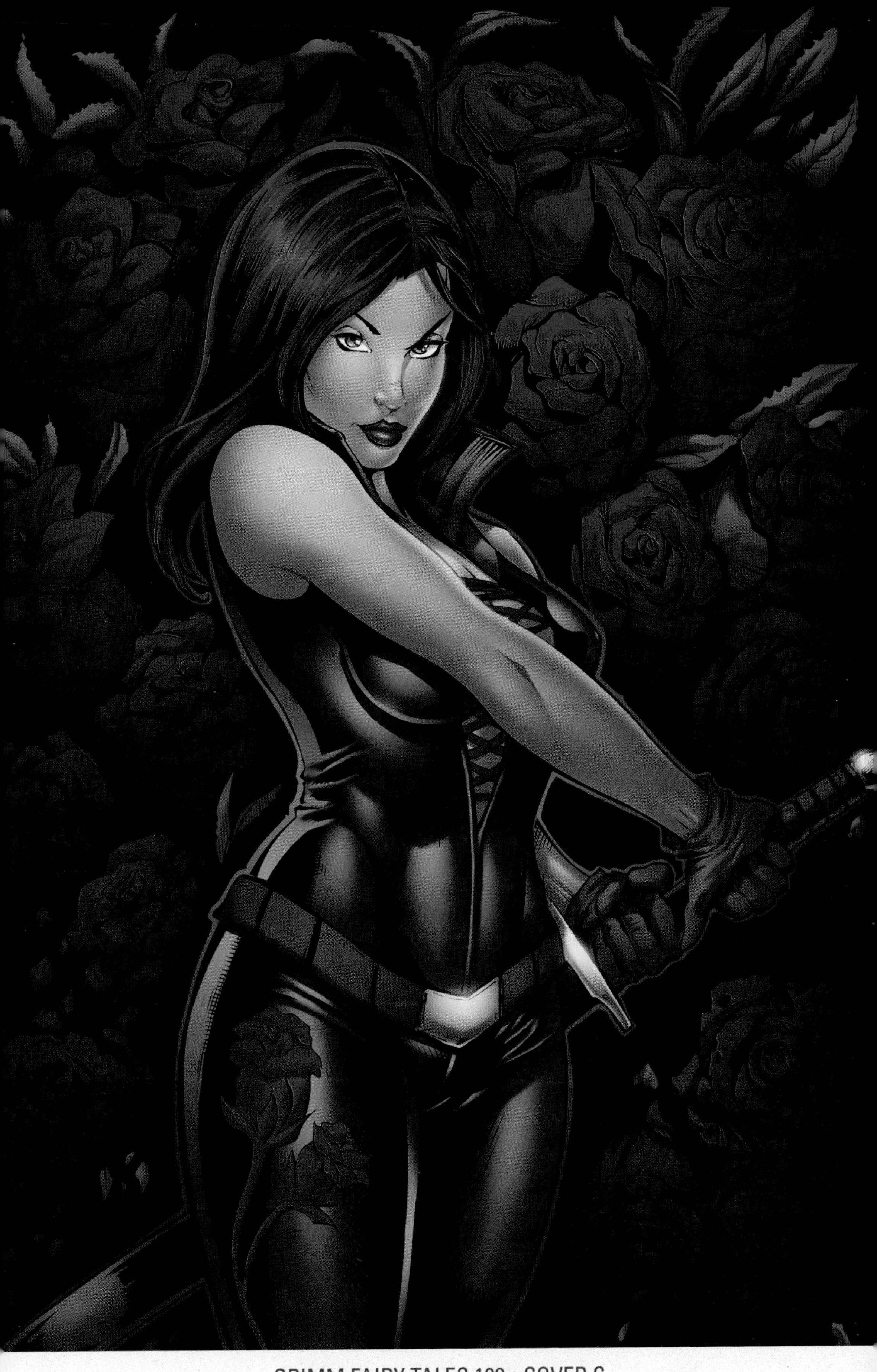

GRIMM FAIRY TALES 109 • COVER C
ARTWORK BY ALEX KOTKIN • INKS BY DEVGEAR • COLORS BY SEAN ELLERY

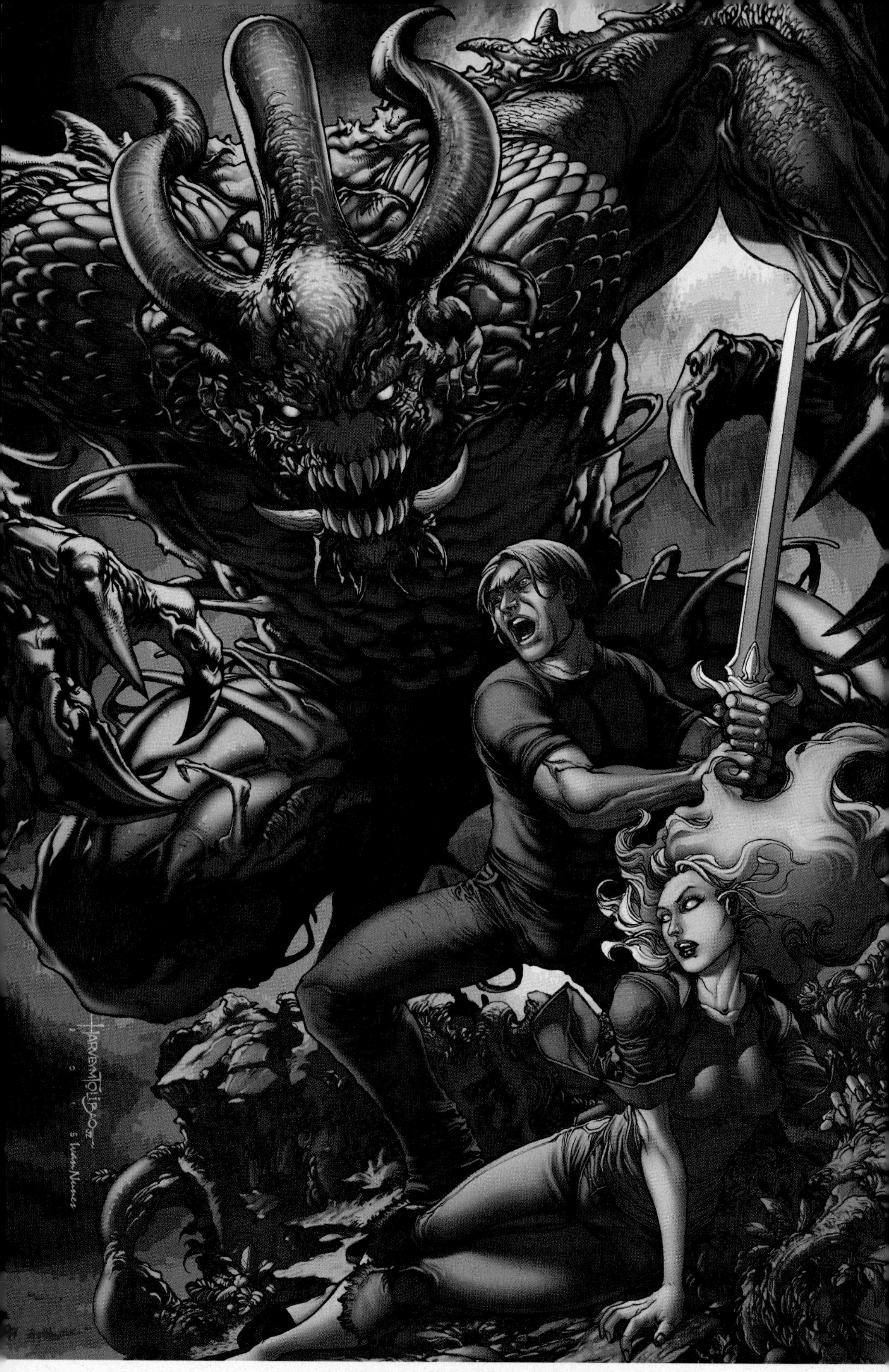

GRIMM FAIRY TALES 110 • COVER A
ARTWORK BY HARVEY TOLIBAO • COLORS BY IVAN NUNES

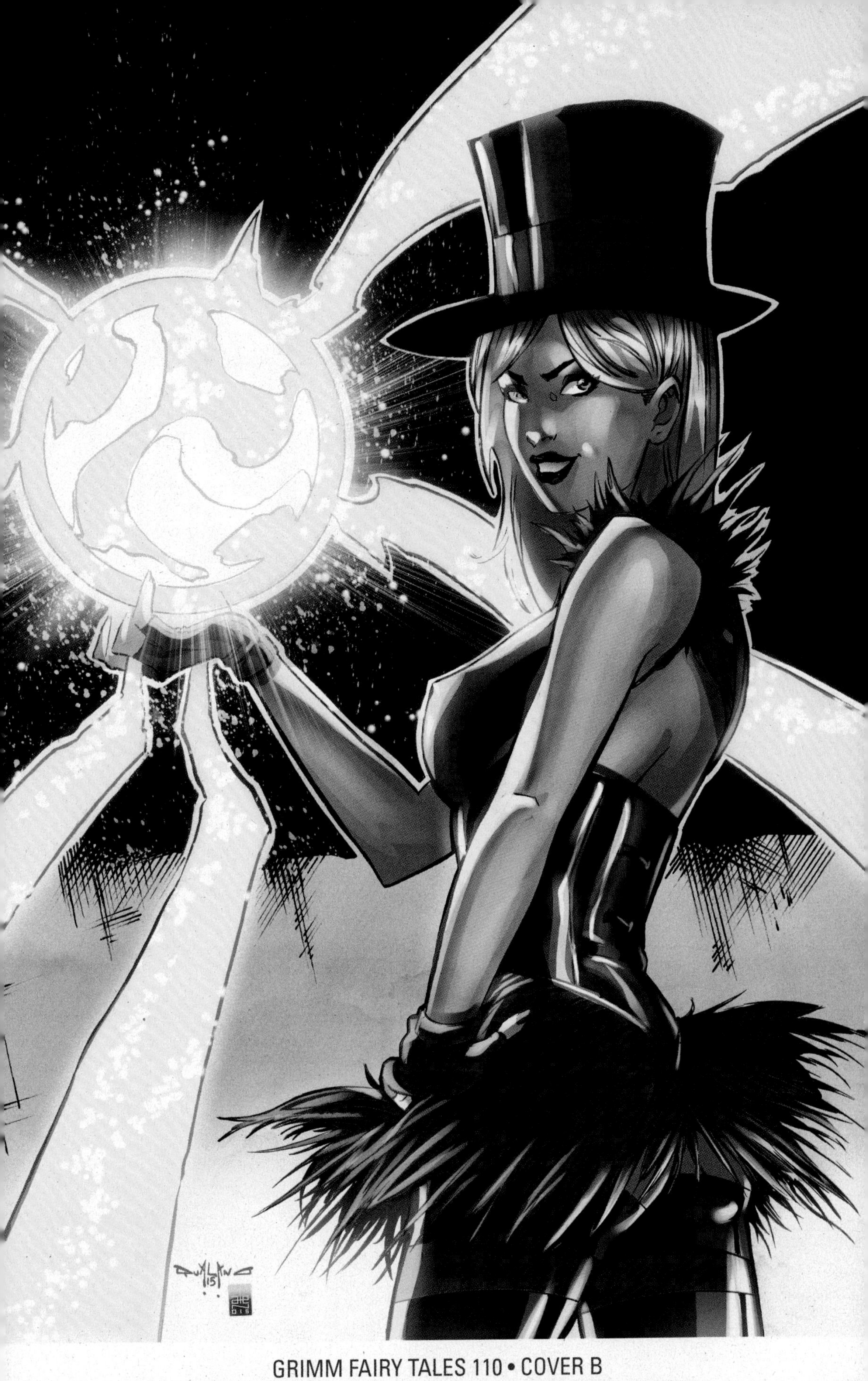

GRIMM FAIRY TALES 110 • COVER B
ARTWORK BY PASQUALE QUALANO • COLORS BY ALESSIA NOCERA

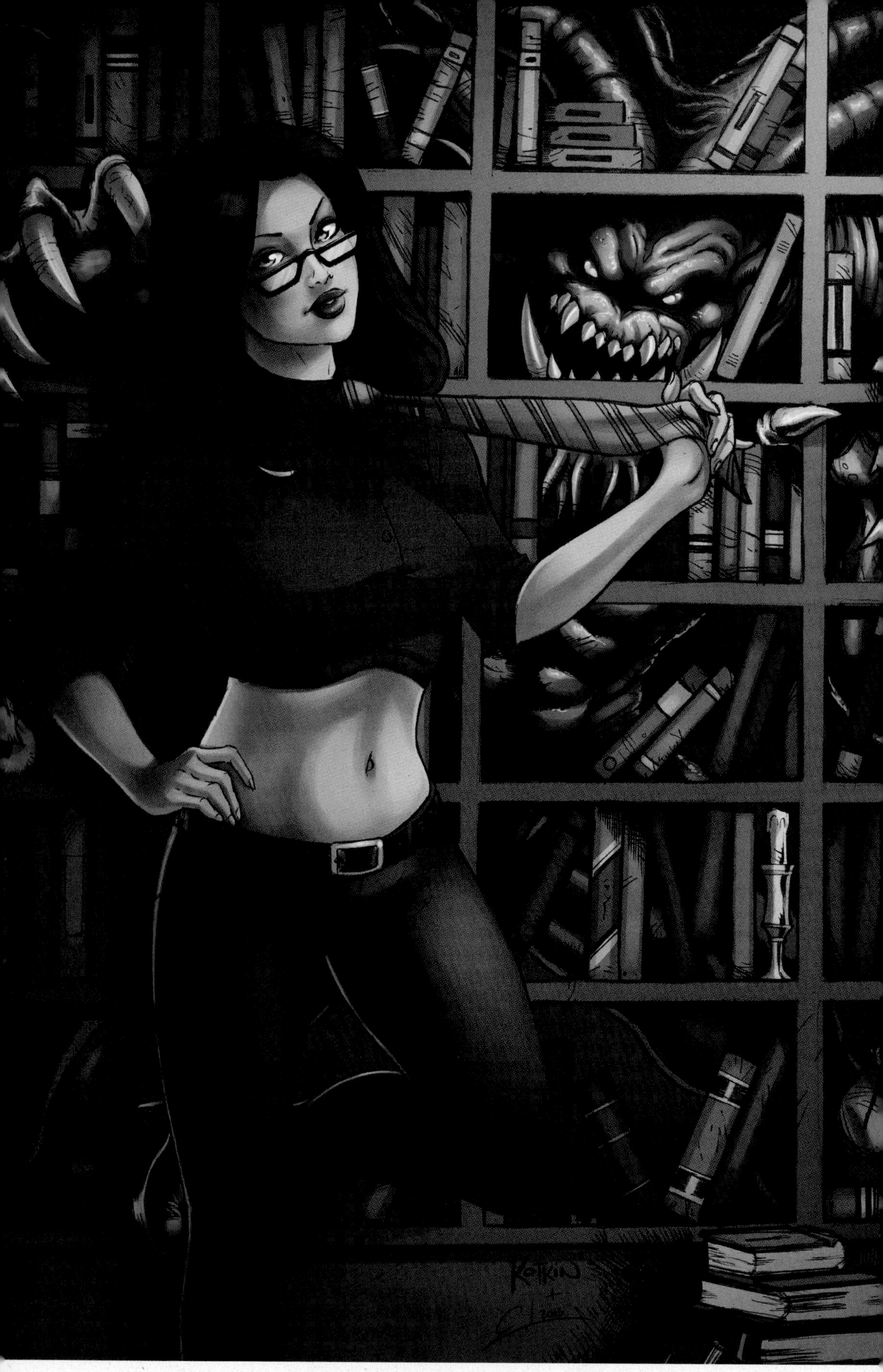
KOTKIN

GRIMM FAIRY TALES 110 • COVER C
ARTWORK BY ALEX KOTKIN • COLORS BY GIORGIA LANZA OF MAD5 FACTORY

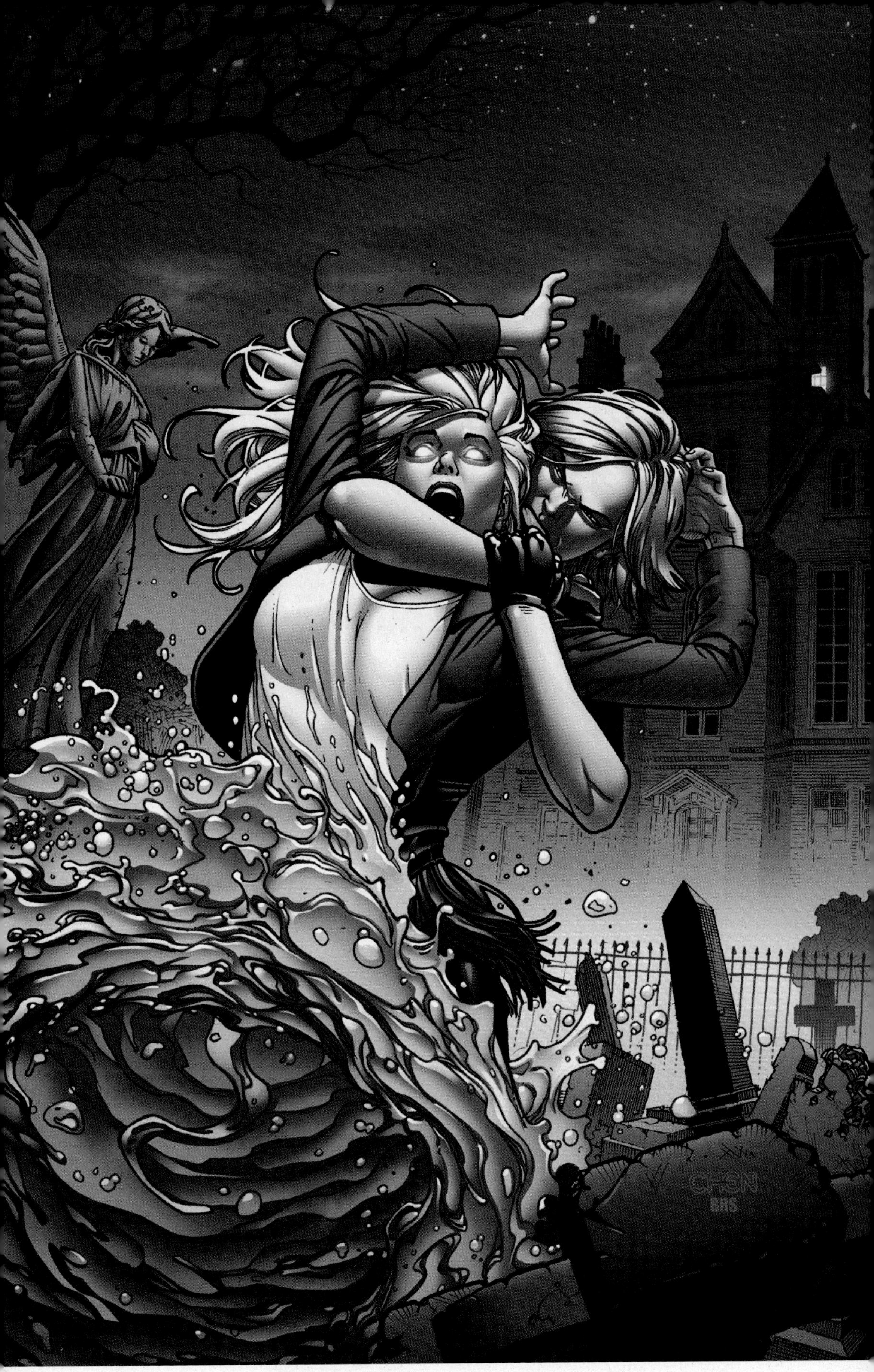
CHEN
BRS

GRIMM FAIRY TALES 111 • COVER A
ARTWORK BY SEAN CHEN • COLORS BY BRETT SMITH

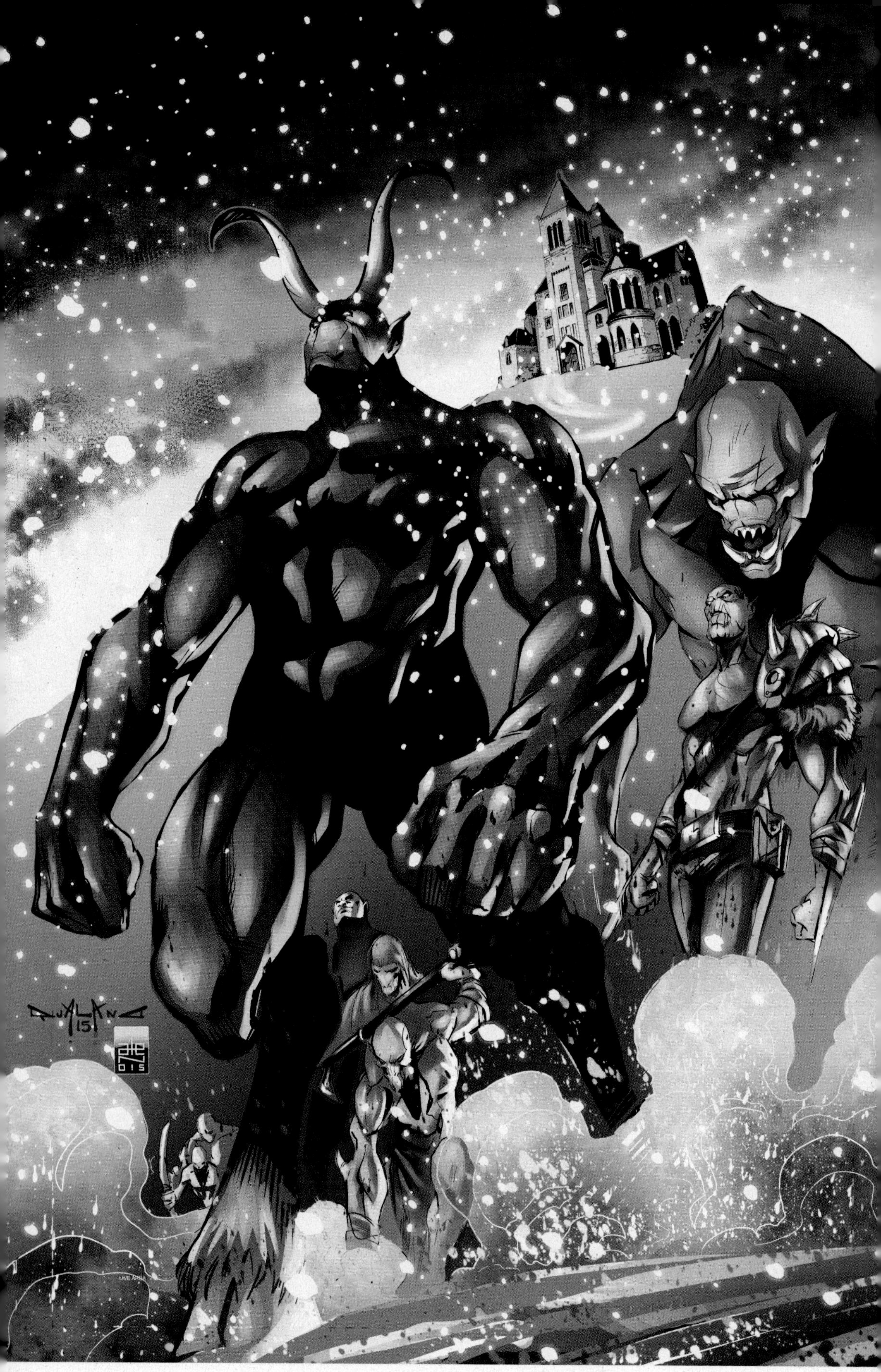
QUALANO 15

GRIMM FAIRY TALES 111 • COVER B
ARTWORK BY PASQUALE QUALANO • COLORS BY ALESSIA NOCERA

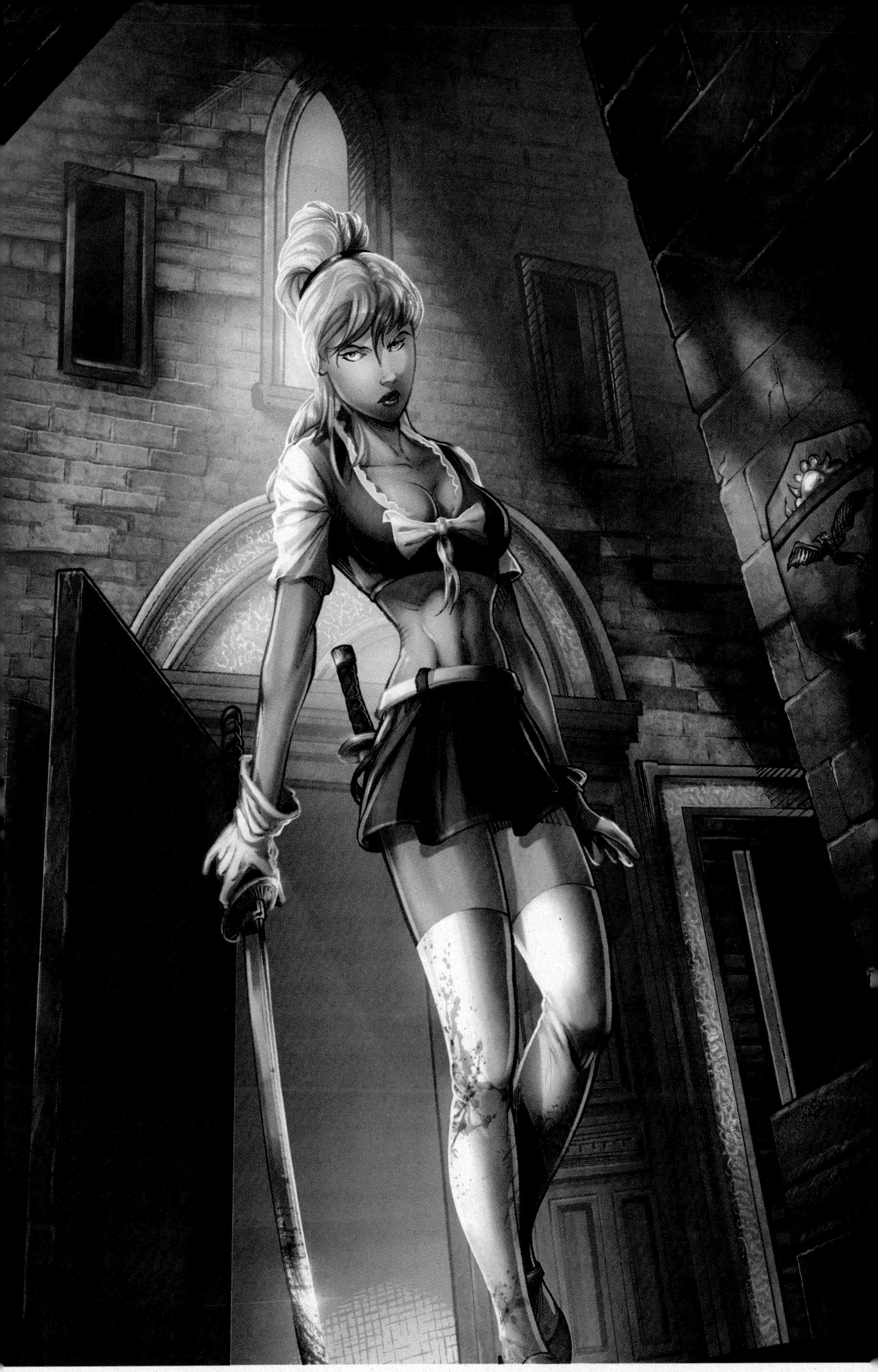

GRIMM FAIRY TALES 111 • COVER C
ARTWORK BY MARAT MYCHAELS • COLORS BY DAVID DELANTY

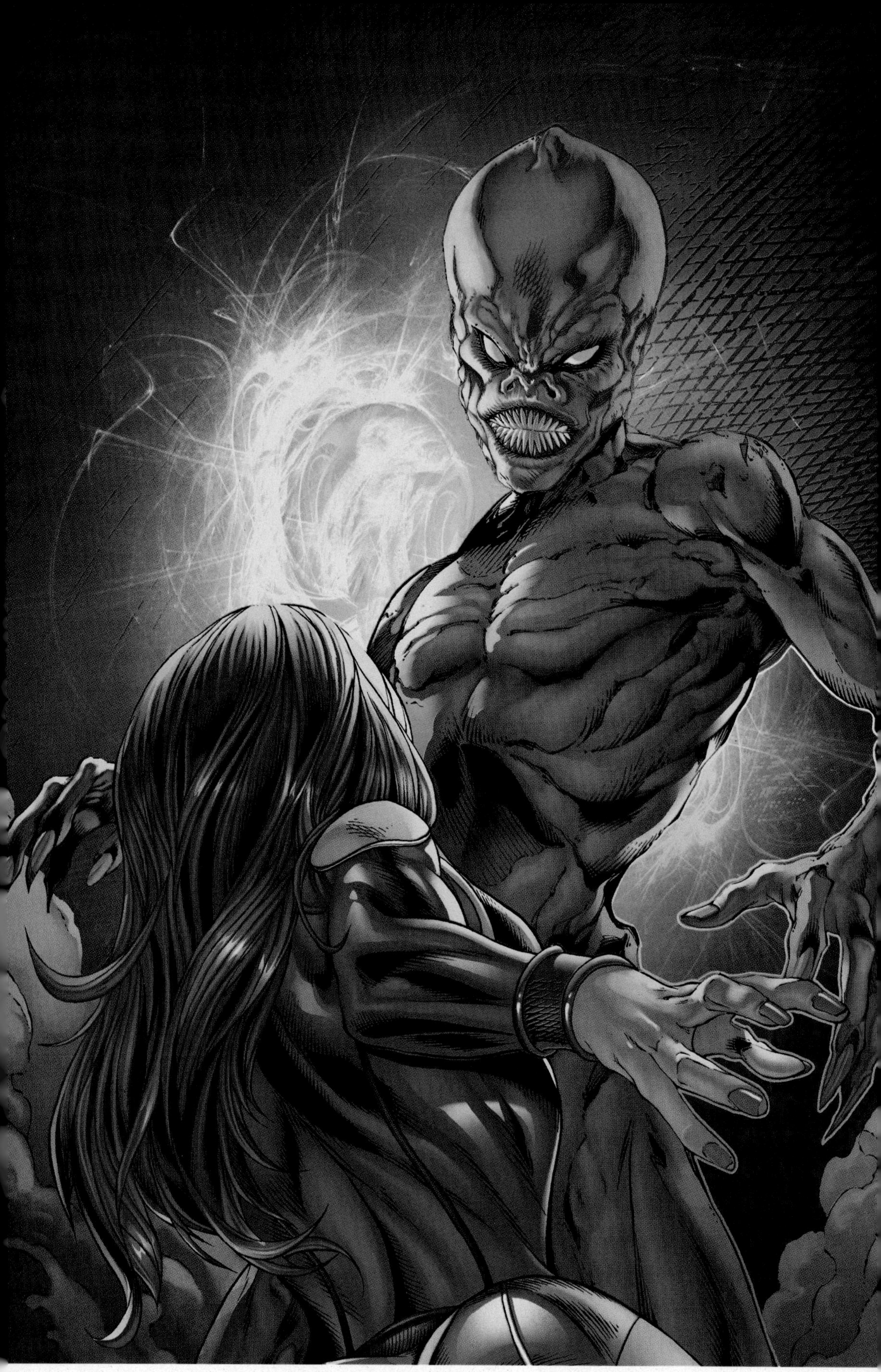

GRIMM FAIRY TALES 112 • COVER A
ARTWORK BY MARAT MYCHAELS • COLORS BY IVAN NUNES

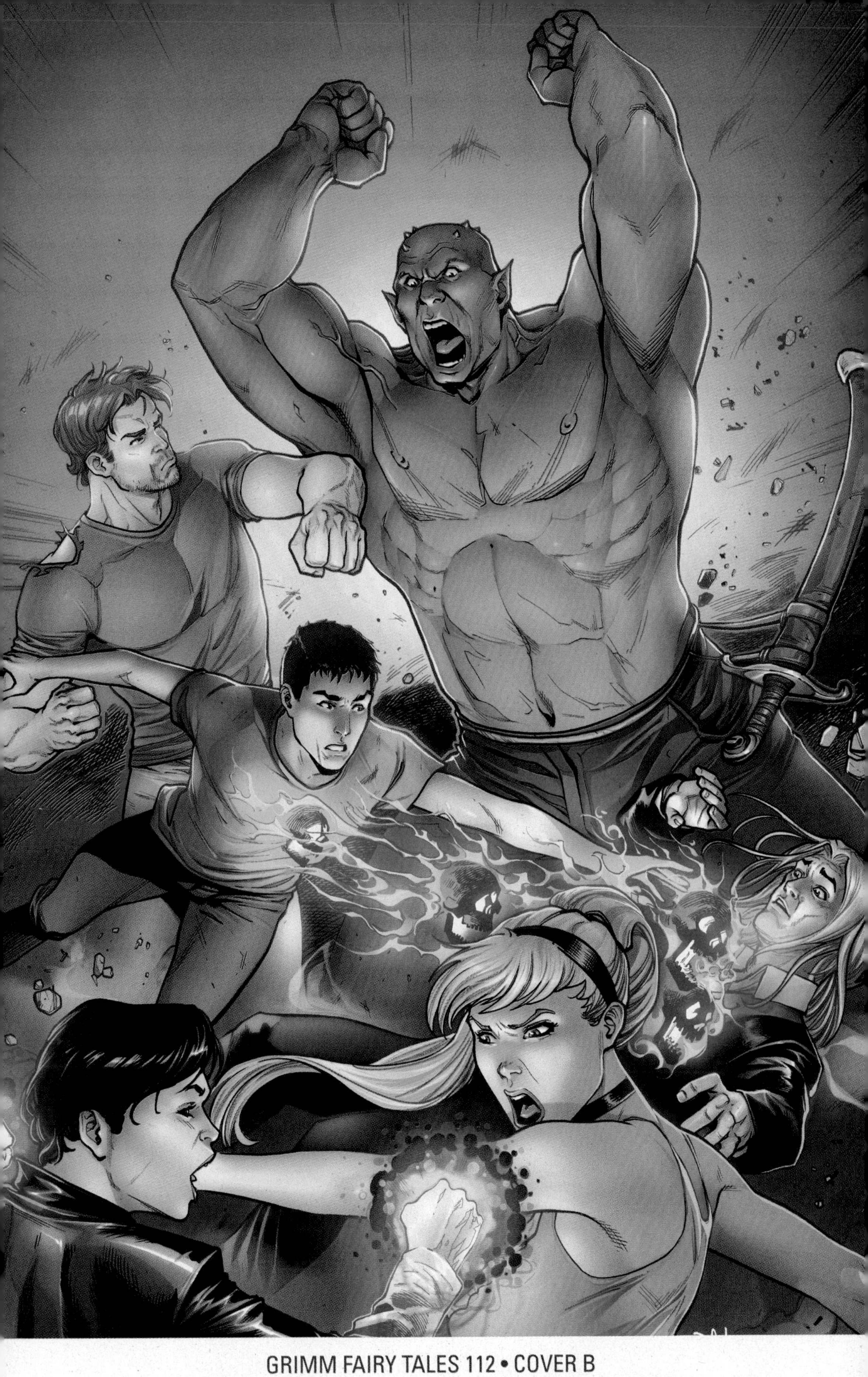

GRIMM FAIRY TALES 112 • COVER B
ARTWORK BY ANDREA MELONI • COLORS BY HEDWIN ZALDIVAR

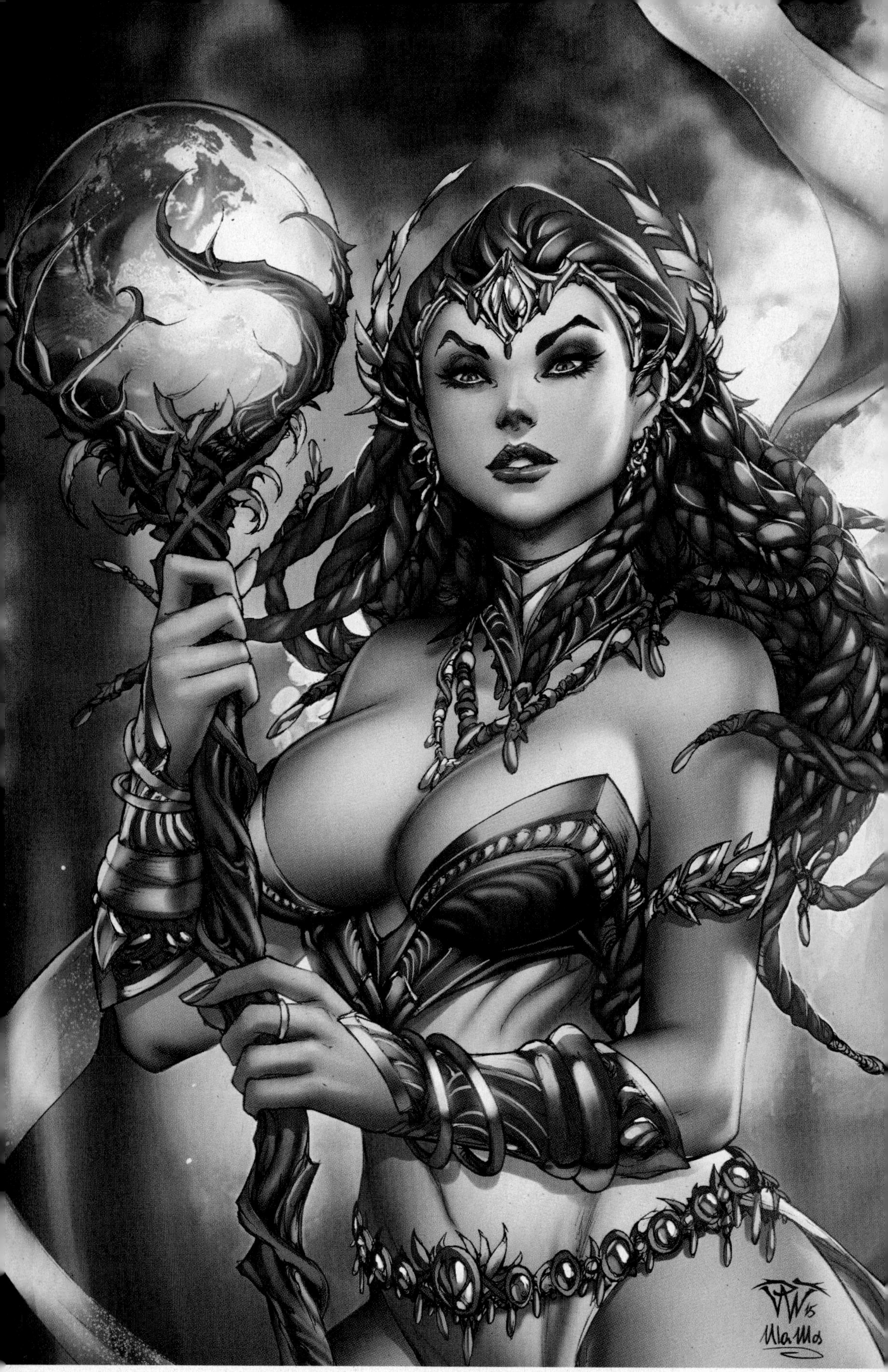

GRIMM FAIRY TALES 112 • COVER C

ARTWORK BY PAOLO PANTALENA • COLORS BY ULA MOS

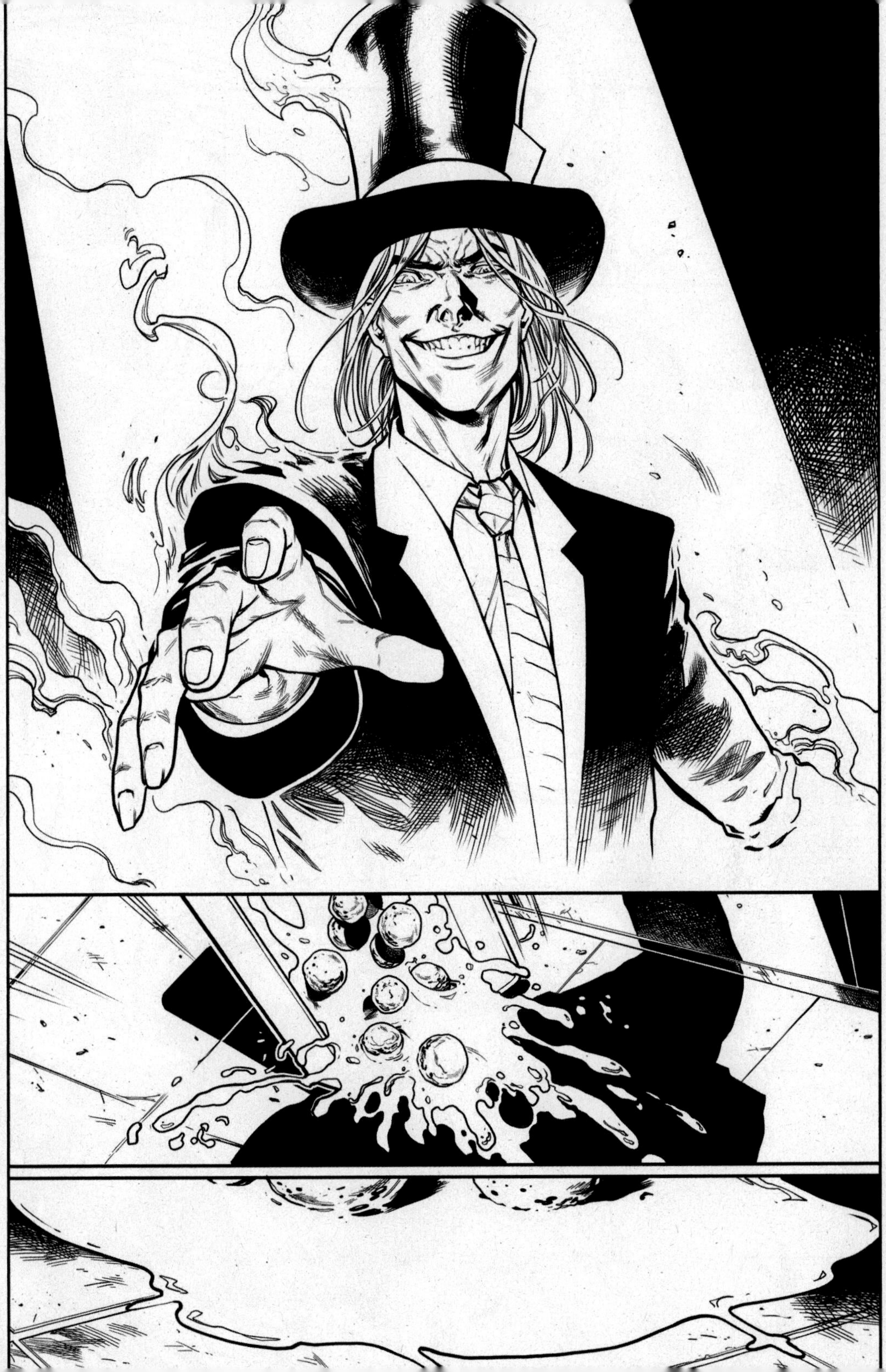

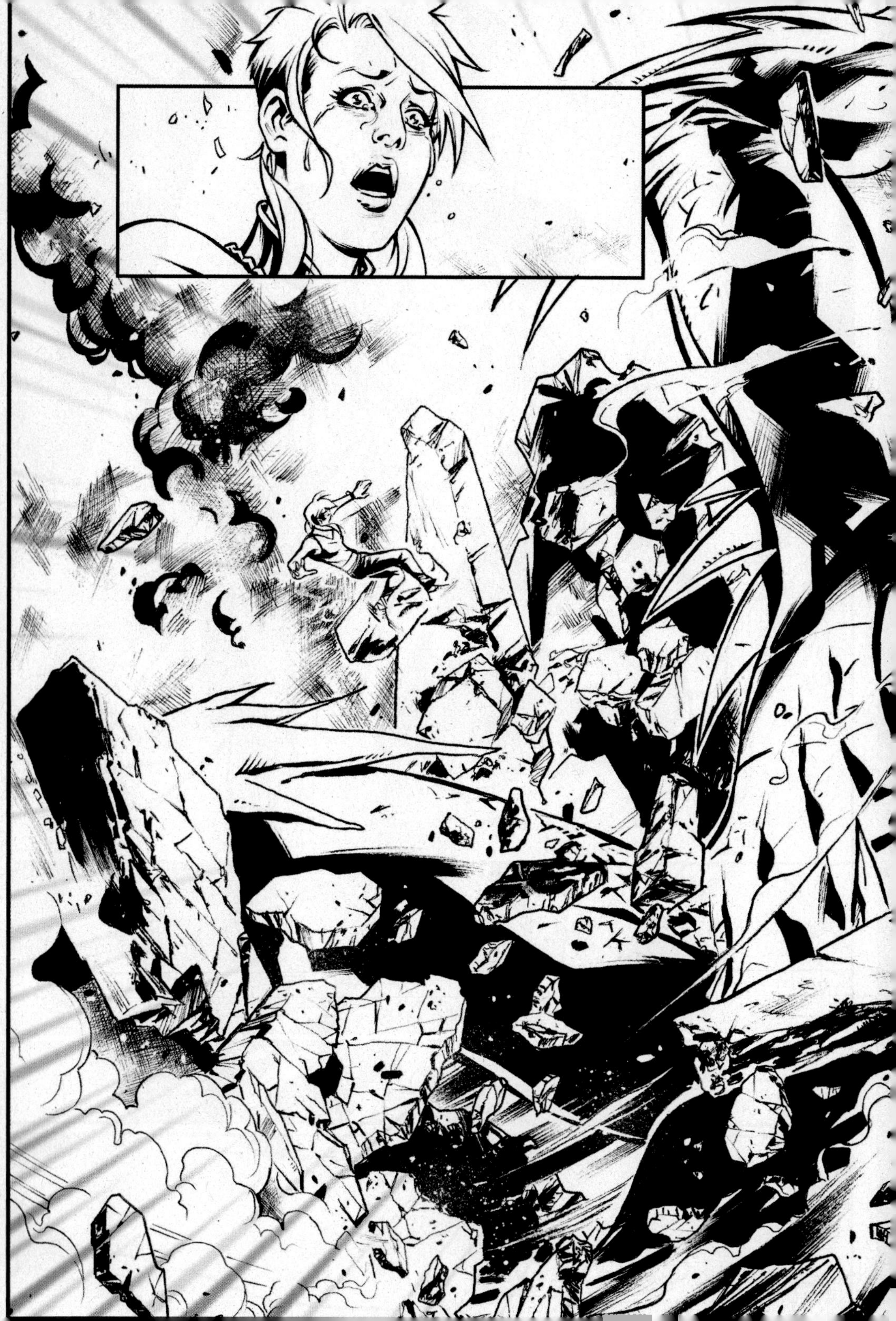

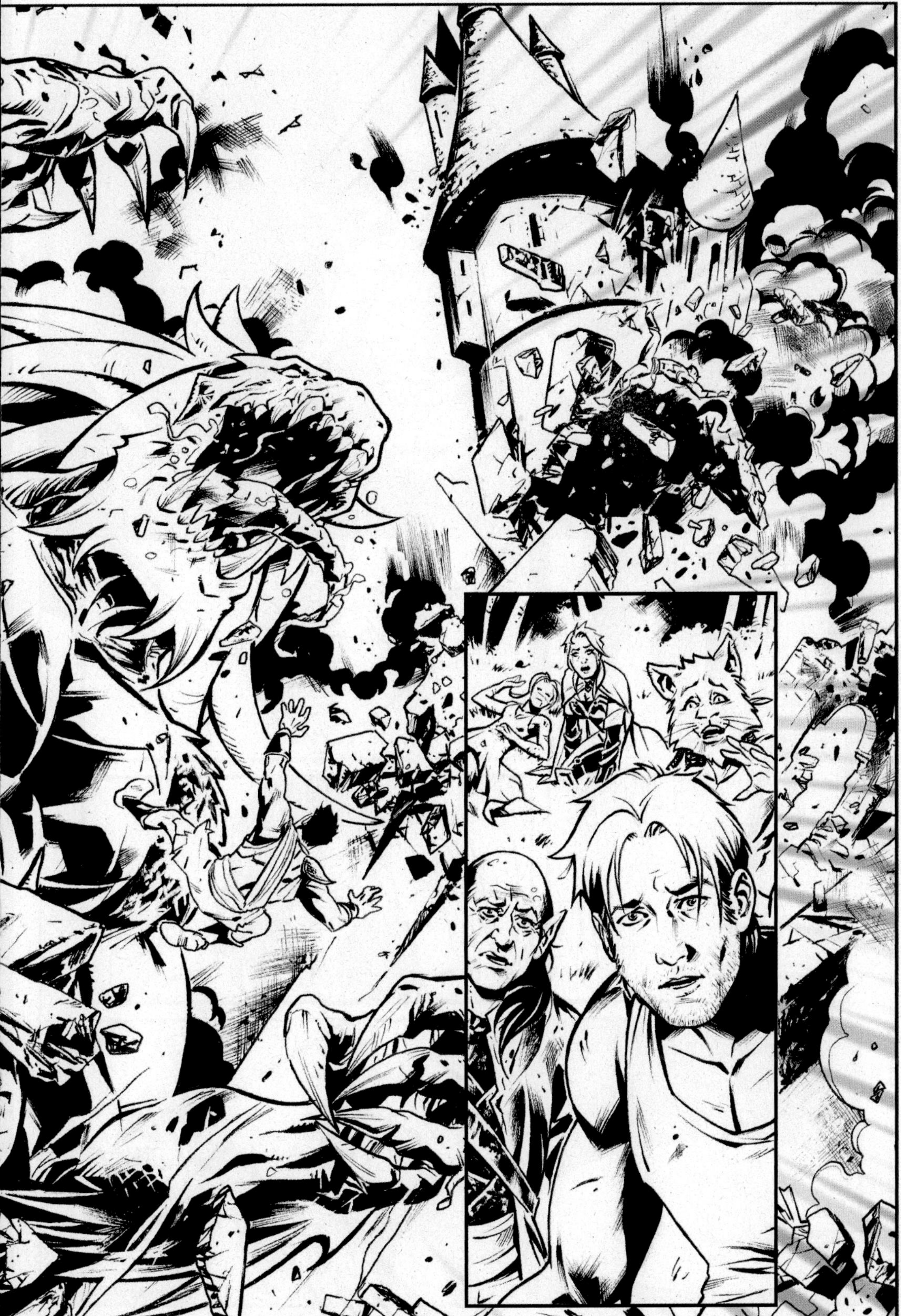

INTERIOR ART BY DAVID LORENZO RIVEIRO

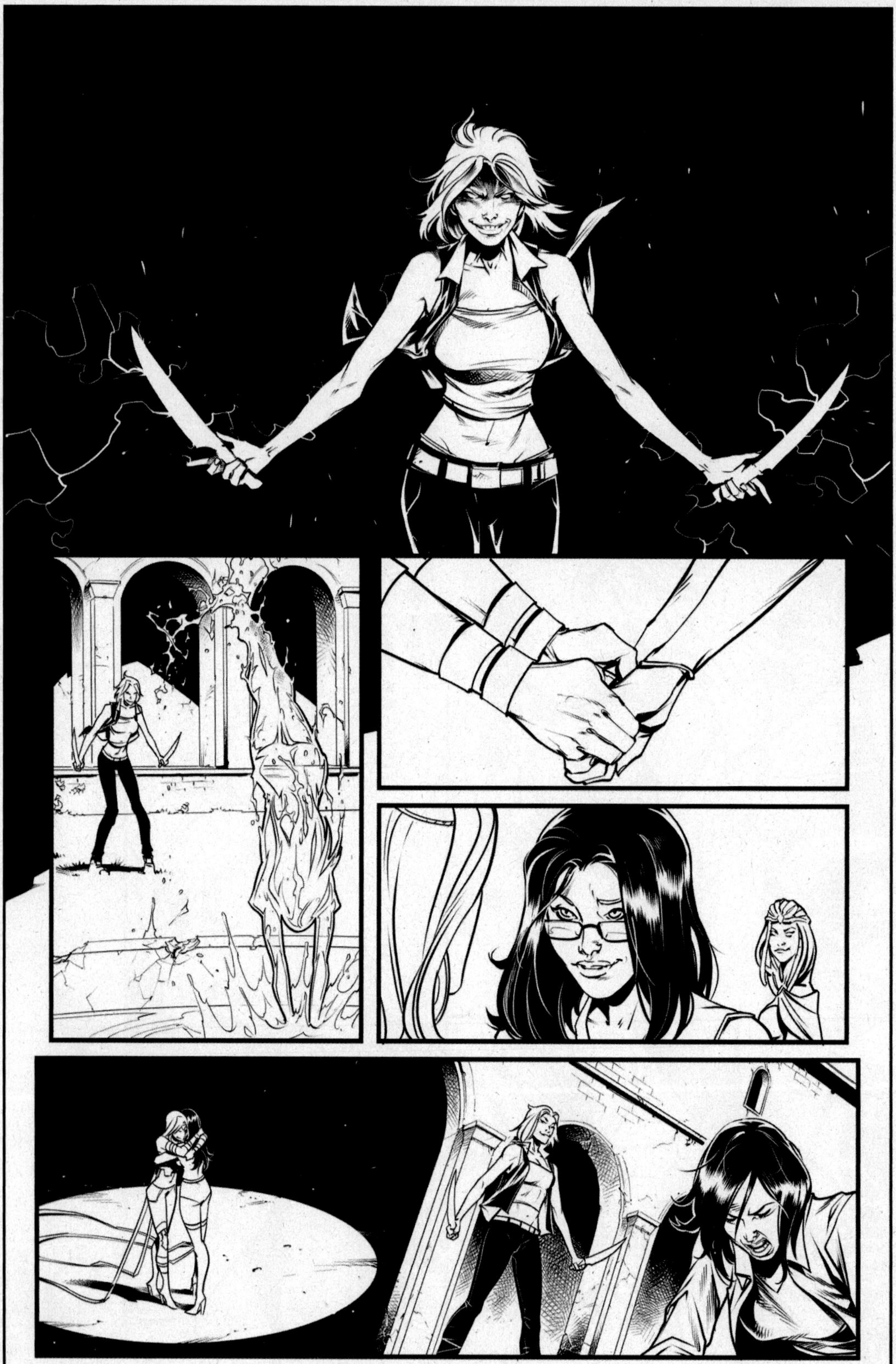

INTERIOR ART BY LUCA CLARETTI

THE ART OF GRIMM FAIRY TALES

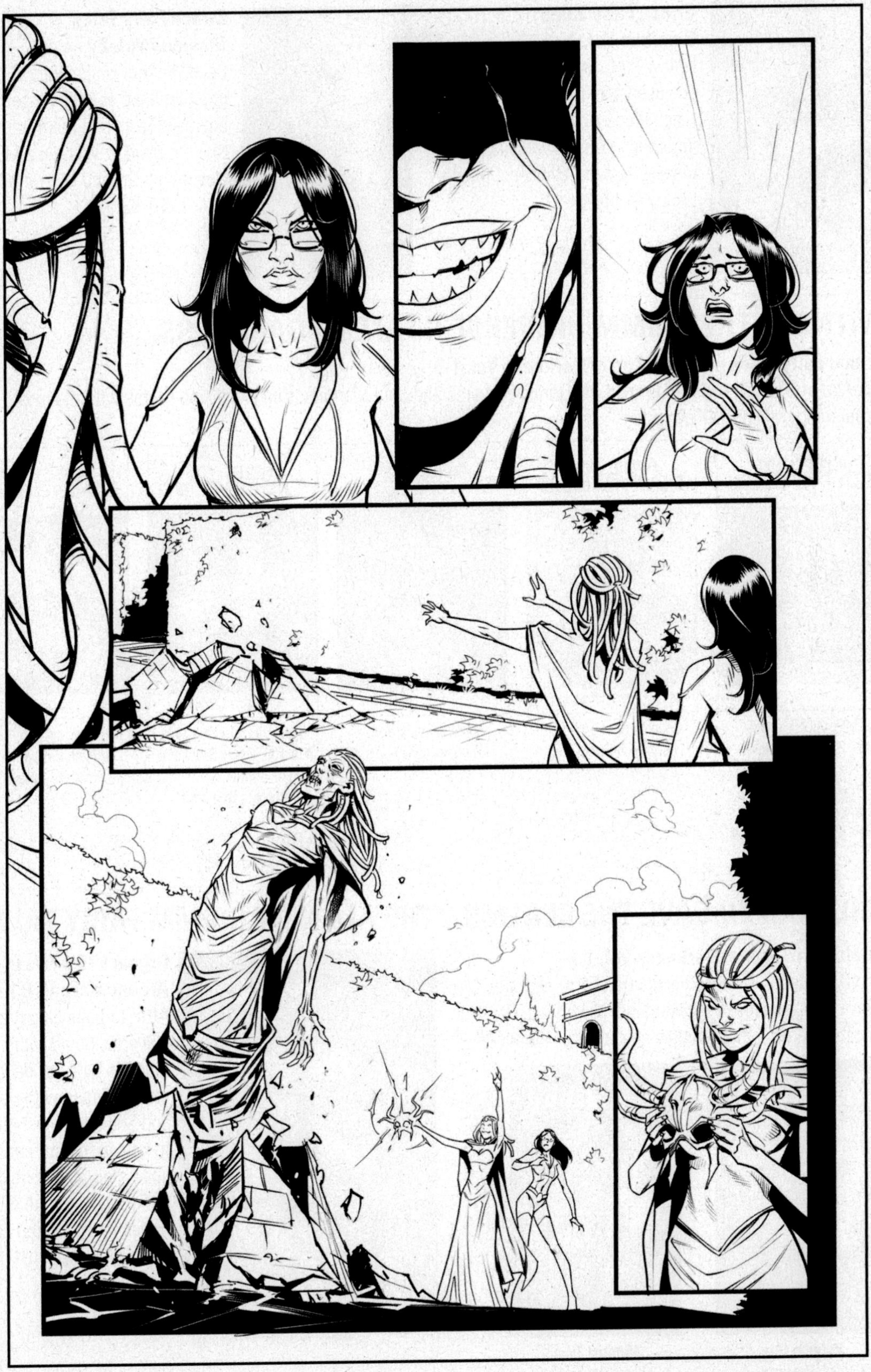

INTERIOR ART BY LUCA CLARETTI

RELIVE THE BEGINNING OF THE GRIMM UNIVERSE.

Grimm Fairy Tales Omnibus Vol. 1
Follow Professor Sela Mathers as she uses fairy tales and fables to teach life lessons to those who find themselves on the cusp of making immoral choices. Collects issues #1-50

Rated M Mature
Diamond: MAR121300
ISBN: 978-1-937068-44-8

Grimm Fairy Tales Omnibus Vol. 2
Sela Mathers is humanit[y] greatest hope at keeping [] between Earth and the f[] that surround it: Wonder[] Neverland, Oz, and Myst [] issues #51-93

Rated M Mature
Diamond ID: AUG141842
ISBN: 978-1-939683-86-1

WITNESS THE GRIMM UNIVERSE'S FALL TO DARKNESS.

Grimm Fairy Tales presents Age of Darkness Vol. 1-5
The Age of Darkness descends upon the Grimm Universe and Sela Mathers is on a collision course with the m[] threatening evil she will ever face.

Collects GFT issues #94-97 & Dark Queen One-shot
Rated M Mature
Diamond: MAY141776
ISBN: 978-1-939683-73-1

Collects Robyn Hood, Inferno, & Dark One One-shots
Rated M Mature
Diamond: JUN141615
ISBN: 978-1-939683-74-8

Collects Godstorm, Wonderland, & Oz One-shots
Rated M Mature
Diamond: JUL141623
ISBN: 978-1-939683-80-9

Collects GFT issues #0, #99-100, Giant-Size 2014, 2014 Annual, & Realm Knights One-shot
Rated M Mature
Diamond: AUG141843
ISBN: 978-1-939683-87-8

Collects Infer[] of Hell, Cind[] White O[]
Rated M M[]
Diamond: M[]
ISBN: 978-1-9[]

THE WAR TO SAVE THE REALMS.

Realm War: Age of Darkness Vol. 1-2
The Dark Queen successfuly merged Earth with the surrounding realms of Wonderland, Neverland, Oz, and Myst to create a frighteningly apocalyptic new world.

Volume One
Collects issues #1-6
Rated M Mature
Diamond: NOV141793

Volume Two
Collects issues #7-12
Rated M Mature
Diamond: SEP151803

THE ALL NEW GRIMM FAIRY T[]

Grimm Fairy Tal[]
Arcane Acre Vo[]
After re-balancin[] universe, Sela M[] reunites with her [] Skye. Teamed wi[] and Shang they s[] to help highborn [] hone their uniqu[] to fight against th[] forces that threat[]

Collects issues #[]
Rated T Teen
Diamond: DEC14184[]
ISBN: 978-1-9422750[]